Angela D. Friederici

Language Comprehension:
A Biological Perspective

Springer

Berlin
Heidelberg
New York
Barcelona
Budapest
Hong Kong
London
Milan
Paris
Santa Clara
Singapore
Tokyo

Angela D. Friederici

Language Comprehension:

A Biological Perspective

With 6 Figures

 Springer

PROF. DR. ANGELA D. FRIEDERICI
Max-Planck-Institute
of Cognitive Neuroscience
Inselstrasse 22-26
D-04103 Leipzig
Germany

ISBN 3-540-64232-3 Springer-Verlag Berlin Heidelberg New York

Library of Congress Cataloging–in–Publication Data

Language comprehension: a biological perspective / Angela D. Friederici (ed).   p. cm.
Includes bibliographical references and index.   ISBN 3-540-64232-3 (hardcover)
1. Neurolinguistics. 2. Psycholinguistics.   I. Friederici, Angela D.   QP399.L35 1998
612.7'8–dc21   98–3122 CIP

© Springer-Verlag Berlin Heidelberg 1998
Printed in Germany

The use of general descriptive names, registered names, trademarks, etc. in this publication does not imply, even in the absence of a specific statement, that such names are exempt from the relevant protective laws and regulations and therefore free for general use.

Product liability: The publisher cannot guarantee the accuracy of any information about dosage and application thereof contained in this book. In every individual case the user must check such information by consulting the relevant literature.

Cover design: design & production GmbH, Heidelberg
Typesetting: Camera ready by the editor
SPIN 10665111 31/3137 5 4 3 2 1 0 - Printed on acid free paper

Authors

Anne Cutler

Max-Planck-Institute for Psycholinguistics
PO Box 1142
47552 Kranenburg
Germany

Johannes Engelkamp

Fachrichtung Psychologie im FB-6 der Universität des Saarlandes
Universitätscampus Bau 1.1
66123 Saarbrücken
Germany

Evelyn C. Ferstl

Max-Planck-Institute of Cognitive Neuroscience
Inselstraße 22
04103 Leipzig
Germany

Caroline Floccia

Department de Psychologie
3, Place de l'Université
1211 Genéve 4
Switzerland

Giovanni Flores d'Arcais

Max-Planck-Institute for Psycholinguistics
PO Box 1142
47552 Kranenburg
Germany

Ulrich H. Frauenfelder

Department de Psychologie
3, Place de l'Université
1211 Genéve 4
Switzerland

Angela D. Friederici

Max-Planck-Institute of Cognitive Neuroscience
Inselstraße 22
04103 Leipzig
Germany

Gerard A.M. Kempen

Graduate Research Institute for Experimental Psychology
Department for Psychology
Leiden University
PO Box 9555
2300 RB Leiden
Netherlands

Leo G.M. Noordman

Department of Linguistics
Tilburg University
5000 LE Tilburg
Netherlands

Ralf Rummer

Fachrichtung Psychologie im FB-6 der Universität des Saarlandes
Universitätscampus Bau 1.1
66123 Saarbrücken
Germany

Herbert Schriefers

Nijmegen Institute for Cognition and Information
PO Box 9104
6500 HE Nijmegen
Netherlands

Wietske Vonk

Max-Planck-Institute for Psycholinguistics
Nijmegen University
PO Box 310
6500 AH Nijmegen
Netherlands

Pienie Zwitserlood

Westfälische Wilhelms-Universität Münster
Psychologisches Institut IV
Fliednerstraße 21
48149 Münster

Preface

Language comprehension and production is a uniquely human capability. We know little about the evolution of language as a human trait, possibly because our direct ancestors lived several million years ago. This fact certainly impedes the desirable advances in the biological basis of any theory of language evolution.

Our knowledge about language as an existing species-specific biological system, however, has advanced dramatically over the last two decades. New experimental techniques have allowed the investigation of language and language use within the methodological framework of the natural sciences. The present book provides an overview of the experimental research in the area of language comprehension in particular.

A biological perspective on language appears to be the common ground for all the contributors. Their research view is based on the conviction that knowledge about the language system can be gained on the basis of empirical research guided by modifiable theories. Each of the contributors reports and discusses the relevant work in hers or his specific field of research. Each of the nine chapters in this book focuses on a different level or aspect of language comprehension thereby covering the level of input processes and word recognition, the level of sentence processing as well as the level of text processing. Aspects of structural representation, and access to this representation are also discussed. One chapter finally attempts to describe the neurobiological basis of the different aspects of the language comprehension process.

When trying to bring together a group of people who were willing to participate in this project, I realized that the first list of people I had contacted as possible contributors read like a list of good friends and close scientific colleagues of Pim Levelt, director of the Max-Planck-Institute for Psycholinguistics in Nijmegen. This was the moment when the idea was born to publish a book on language comprehension 'in honor of Pim Levelt'. Coincidentally, I realized that Pim was about to reach his sixtieth birthday. Upen being informed of this, all contributors agreed to go with an almost impossible deadline in order to meet the time constraints actually set sixty years ago, but remembered almost too late. They did it for you, Pim.

Pim, you know everything one can possibly know about language production. Here we have collected what we know about language comprehension. With this book we would like to thank you, each in her and his own way, for your scientific discussions, guidance, and support throughout the past years.

Angela D. Friederici   Leipzig, January 6, 1998.

Acknowledgments

A book project like this can not evolve without the help of many. In the first place I thank Herbert Schriefers, who supported the idea for this book from the beginning to its final realization.

Technical assistance in shaping the manuscripts and the making up of the index was provided by Katja Kühn and Claudia Misch. The final appearance of the text is due to the aesthetic intuitions and technical knowledge of Andrea Gast-Sandmann. I would like to thank each of them for their ideal cooperation.

Angela D. Friederici

Contents

Chapter 1   1

The Recognition of Spoken Word
Ulrich H. Frauenfelder & Caroline Floccia

Chapter 2   41

Prosodic Structure and Word Recognition
Anne Cutler

Chapter 3   71

Spoken Words in Sentence Contexts
Piennie Zwitserlood

Chapter 4   101

Morphology and Word Recognition
Herbert Schriefers

Chapter 5   133

The Architecture of the Mental Lexicon
Johannes Engelkamp & Ralf Rummer

Chapter 6   177

The Reading of Words and Sentences
Evelyn C. Ferstl & Giovanni Flores d'Arcais

Chapter 7   213

Sentence Parsing
Gerard A.M. Kempen

Chapter 8   229

Discourse Comprehension
Leo G.M. Noordman & Wietske Vonk

Chapter 9   263

The Neurobiology of Language Processing
Angela D. Friederici

Index   303

Chapter 1

The Recognition of Spoken Word[1]

Ulrich H. Frauenfelder
Caroline Floccia

1.1   Introduction

Listening to speech is one of our favorite activities. Our ears and brain are increasingly solicited by speech sounds, as our means of communication - radio, TV, and most recently, the mobile phone - continue to develop. Fortunately, in most instances the processing of our native language is rapid, automatic, and efficient. However, this remarkable and seemingly effortless ability to understand speech from diverse speakers in various situations - ranging from face to face conversations to the filtered speech received in phone transmissions - in fact hides a highly complex cognitive device. As complexity only becomes truly apparent when this device is damaged, as in the case of aphasia, or is presented with a language that it does not master, or is placed in an experimental situation that is particularly difficult or constraining.

At the heart of this language understanding device lies the so-called *lexical processing system* which is in large part responsible for translating a sensory input into a meaningful interpretation. Psycholinguists assume the existence of a *mental lexicon* that contains our lexical knowledge. This lexicon solves the difficult problem of the arbitrary mapping from form (both phonology and orthography) to meaning by storing in long term memory both the form and meaning information associated with individual lexical entries. Given the central role played by the lexical processing system in language understanding, it should come as no great surprise that considerable research energy has been invested over the past 30 years in studying how a listener recognizes and represents words in the mental lexicon.

Three major problem areas can be identified in characterizing this system: the lexical representation problem, the lexical identification problem, and the lexical integration issue. The first is concerned with the nature and internal structure of the basic lexical entry, and the organization of these entries in the mental lexicon. The second deals with the processes by which the intended lexical entry is located in the

[1]   Support for this research was provide by a grant from the Swiss National Fund for Scientific Research (grant 1113-049698.96).

lexicon, and lexical information associated with it is accessed on the basis of bottom-up (sensory) and top-down (contextual) information lastly, the integration issue concerns how the different types of stored lexical information are combined and integrated in constructing a meaningful interpretation of the utterance being heard. It should be obvious that the answers to these questions are highly related. For example, the way in which a word is recognized depends critically upon how it is stored and represented, and vice-versa. In this introduction we will, however, attempt to limit ourselves to the problem of word recognition, touching on issues of lexical representation that are relevant for recognition.

This paper proposes to introduce the reader to some basic concepts and assumptions underlying this research and to examine some of the leading models of word recognition in light of recent experimental findings. The first part sets the stage for the word recognition problem and introduces theoretical notions used to characterize lexical processing. In doing so, it presents some of the major theoretical options available to characterize sublexical and lexical processing.

In the next part, the major models of word recognition are presented together with a comparison of their specific properties and predictions. Then, the basic mechanisms assumed in these models are confronted with the experimental data. The sixth part examines the neglected problem of spoken word recognition in continuous speech. Words rarely occur in isolation in natural communication, but nonetheless, the recognition of isolated words has generally been the focus of laboratory experiments. In the final Section we consider another major challenge: how current models handle the problem of acquisition of the lexicon during infancy.

1.1.1   Word Recognition: The Challenge

The listener's ability to identify correctly and almost instantly a word from amongst the tens of thousands of other words stored in the mental lexicon constitutes one of the most extraordinary feats in language processing. The results of psycholinguistic experiments (Marslen-Wilson, 1985) show that words can be recognized before they are heard completely. The process by which words can be identified is indeed very efficient and rapid.

The rapidity with which the listener can recognize words is all the more astonishing when considering the nature of the input and the content of the lexicon. With respect to the latter, the lexicon contains a large number of often highly similar lexical entries (e.g., *pat* and *bat* differ by only a single distinctive feature) which must be discriminated extremely quickly. Moreover, longer words are frequently made up of shorter words, creating the problem of lexical embedding (e.g., the words *star*, *tar*, *tart*, *are*, *art* can be found in the word *start*). This ambiguity of a phoneme string with respect to its proper lexical interpretation, complicates the spoken word recognition process since a match between the input string and a lexical entry does not guarantee that this entry was actually produced.

The nature of the speech signal, itself, also presents a formidable challenge. Speech is variable: every word takes a different phonetic or phonological shape each time that it is produced. An extremely large number of acoustically different tokens of any word must be recognized depending on the characteristics of the speaker (age, sex and origin) and of the word (segmental make-up and prosodic structure). Moreover, phonological processes triggered by appropriate phonological contexts and speech rate contribute to modifying the word's physical manifestation further. This variability creates the problem of a complex mapping from many diverse phonetic tokens to a single type.

Furthermore, speech is continuous. Indeed, unlike written text, speech has no systematic "spaces" or periods of silence to indicate where one word ends and the next one begins. Such information is critical for aligning the speech input with internally stored lexical entries. This continuous and uninterrupted nature of speech introduces the problem of continuous to discrete mapping, that is, the mapping from a continuous speech input to discrete internally represented units.

1.1.2 Word Recognition: Some Theoretical Notions

A first hurdle in approaching the psycholinguistic research devoted to the lexical processing system involves coming to grips with the terminology used. Unfortunately, terms like lexical identification, lexical access, word recognition, lexical processing, etc. have been used quite inconsistently so that no terminological consensus has yet emerged. In fact, theoretical models make use of the same terms in different ways. This state of affairs is in part attributable to the fact that models have very different conceptions of how word recognition takes place, and, in particular, what the relationship between the two basic operations in word recognition is. For the purposes of this paper we will reserve the term *lexical identification* for the operation which consists in locating the form description or address of the target entry in the mental lexicon. The second operation, *lexical access*, involves gaining access to the different types of information (phonological, orthographic, semantic and syntactic) associated with this entry. Finally, *word recognition* will refer more generally to both processes together.

Most commonly, it is assumed that lexical identification precedes lexical access. This concept of word recognition is analogous to looking up a word in a dictionary. The appropriate lexical entry is located, and only then does its informational content (or definition) become available. An alternative to this *single access* view of word recognition effectively reverses these two processes with lexical access preceding lexical identification. This means that the listener has access to the syntactic and semantic information associated with several different lexical entries before finally identifying the appropriate one. We call this the *multiple access* view.

Most current models view spoken lexical identification as a matching process in which some internal representation(s) of the speech input, the *prelexical input representation*, are matched with internally stored *lexical representations*. Thus, two main processing steps can be distinguished. First, a representation composed of sublexical units[2] is extracted from the acoustic signal. Second, this input representation is matched and aligned with the lexical representations to locate the correct entry in the lexicon. These two processing stages will be examined more closely in the following Sections.

1.2   From Speech to Prelexical Input Representations: Processing and Units

How do listeners process the incoming speech signal? This question is of central interest to both phoneticians and psycholinguists. However, until recently, attempts to answer this question have been hampered by a division of labor between these respective research traditions. Research in phonetics has focused on the acoustic-phonetic analysis of the speech signal and, for the most part, has not dealt with the problem of how this analysis relates to word recognition and sentence processing. In contrast, psycholinguists have generally concentrated on processing at the lexical level or higher and have tended to neglect the complexities of the acoustic-phonetic input and its analysis. One unhappy outcome of this division of labor is that some major problems in speech and word recognition have fallen into the cracks between the interests of these two disciplines. For example, it remains unclear at what level - prelexical, or lexical, or both - the problem of the variability intrinsic to the speech signal is handled by the listener and is to be addressed by the researcher. Similar ambiguities arise in the study of the segmentation of continuous speech input; does the continuous-to-discrete mapping take place at a phonetic, or lexical level, or both?

Fortunately, there is considerable agreement concerning the existence of an input representation that mediates between the mapping of the speech signal onto the mental representations of lexical form. This input representation functions as an interface representation and can be studied from two perspectives. From a phonetic perspective, it is the *representation of the sensory input* from a psycholinguistic perspective, and it represents the *input to the lexical matching process.*. The first function of the input representation is thus to recode internally the relevant information present in the acoustic signal. In this capacity, it is constrained in its form and content by the properties of the speech wave and its analysis. The second function of the input representation is serve in the mapping onto lexical representations. For this mapping process to be effective, the input representation must be discriminative with respect

---

[2]   Sublexical units or representations are simply defined with respect to their size; they must be smaller than the word (phoneme, syllable, etc.). In contrast, prelexical input representations are defined with respect how and when they are computed. Unlike, the lexical phonological representation which becomes available after lexical access, prelexical representations are computed before lexical access and are used for lexical identification. In this chapter, we will use, preferentially, the terms prelexical representation and prelexical processing.

to the set of lexical alternatives and it must be compatible and comparable with the lexical representations. Three related questions that are raised by this hypothesis of a prelexical input representation must be addressed.

1.2.1 Why a Prelexical Input Representation?

The postulation of a prelexical input representation is more than a convenient line of demarcation between psycholinguistics and phonetics. This representation plays a key role in solving the problems described above. A phonetic or phonological representation provides a less variable and more abstract format for representing the information in the input and for accessing the lexicon. This hypothesis is based in part on an economy principle. Instead of trying to match each unique sensory input directly onto a huge number of lexical entries, listeners first recode the variable input into a smaller number of abstract sublexical units like phonemes or syllables. These units, in turn, serve to contact the lexicon. In computing such representations, listeners are assumed to be able to identify words more efficiently with fewer processing resources. Furthermore, the computation of prelexical units can simplify the segmentation process. Either the boundaries of the prelexical units can be used as starting points for a lexical template matching process, or the lexical hypotheses can be restricted to those matching certain prelexical units. Either way, wasteful matching of misaligned lexical candidates can, in principle, be reduced.

Prelexical input representations were proposed in part to eliminate irrelevant acoustic information and to optimize word recognition. However, this hypothesis has some problems as well. The question remains as to how such representations integrate information related to the prosody, or information, about the speaker. An input representation simply made up of concatenated phonological units - like a string of phonemes or syllables is clearly inadequate since it does not allow for the coding of this important information. Indeed, all variations in the speech signal are far from irrelevant. For instance, prosody helps to retrieve word boundaries in the continuous speech signal (Cutler & Norris, 1988; Nakatani & Schaffer, 1978). Phonotactic regularities or allophonic variations also contribute to signal boundaries of words or prosodic structure or to eliminate lexical candidates (Church, 1987; Frazier, 1987). Thus, the input representation is probably quite rich, containing different types of information and having considerable internal structure.

However, not all word recognition models agree with the assumption that such a prelexical input representation is thus constructed. An alternative view holds that no prelexical representation is computed at all, but that the information extracted from the sensory input is mapped directly onto the lexicon. However, even this type of model must identify units of processing. For instance, according to the Marslen-Wilson Cohort II model (see Section 1.4.2), the listener retrieves from the speech input a set of distinctive features that are used to contact the lexical representations (Marslen-Wilson & Warren, 1994).

1.2.2   What Kind of Units?

Although there is considerable agreement that some prelexical representations are computed during word recognition, we have found considerable variety in the types of units that have been proposed. It is useful, before examining the various proposals, to consider some constraints on these units.

Cutler & Norris (1985) have proposed three prerequisite conditions that a candidate unit must meet to serve as a unit of perception. First, it must be distinguishable in the speech signal, and, second, it must be able to characterize, or 'transcribe', completely any stretch of speech corresponding to a given utterance. Finally, these authors argue that the unit must correspond to or be aligned with the lexical units with which they are matched. Although these are reasonable criteria, they do not impose strong enough constraints to uniquely identify a perceptual unit. Moreover, some important trade-offs exist between different dimensions (especially unit size) of the proposed units and properties of the processing. The nature of speech recognition and lexical mapping - including its immediacy, it reliability and its cost - should, in theory, depend upon the size of the unit and the size of the unit inventory. Following are a few examples of such relations.

Immediacy of analyzis: The smaller the unit, the more immediate or faster the mapping onto the lexicon can be. Proponents of the distinctive feature (Lahiri & Marslen-Wilson, 1991) have argued that this unit permits an almost continuous mapping of the signal onto the lexicon. In contrast, larger units, like the syllable, potentially introduce long delays into the mapping process- especially if it is assumed that the lexical mapping takes place only when the end of the unit is reached. For example, this would require a listener to wait for the /f/ before initiating the mapping onto the lexicon of the syllable *smurf.*

Reliability of the analyzis: The smaller the unit, the less information there is in the signal to support the unit's identification. In addition, there is a relation between the unit's size and the amount of variability it shows. For example, the phoneme is subject to more variability than the syllable: there is less coarticulation between adjacent syllables than adjacent phonemes. Klatt (1980) has argued against the segmental unit, pointing out that making segmental decisions can introduce errors of classification that misdirect the lexical access process.

Difficulty of analyzis: The complexity of the speech analysis should, in principle, depend upon the size of the unit inventory- which also varies as a function of the size of the linguistic unit. The inventory size of different linguistic units varies considerably, at least by a factor 100. For instance, a database analysis (Goldman, Content & Frauenfelder, 1996) in French counted 30 phoneme as opposed to 3000 syllable types. The difficulty of recognizing a given unit is a function of the number of other units from which it must be discriminated. This argues for a smaller number of units, assuming that some constant function relates unit discriminability and inventory size. This is probably not the case, however. For example, as the syllables, inventory size increases across languages, so does the diversity of the syllable structures (CV, CVC, etc...). This greater diversity in the syllable structure could again decrease the processing complexity due to the increased discriminability of syllables.

For these reasons as well as others, many different speech units have been proposed to making up prelexical representations. They include: temporally defined spectral templates (Klatt, 1980), distinctive features (Lahiri & Marslen-Wilson, 1991; Marslen-Wilson & Warren, 1994), phonemic segments (Marslen-Wilson & Welsh, 1978; Pisoni & Luce, 1987), demi-syllables (Samuel, 1989), morae (Cutler & Otake, 1994), the syllable (e.g., Mehler, 1981; Segui, Dupoux & Mehler, 1990), and prosodic units (Grosjean & Gee, 1987). We will return below in detail to the experimental studies that have provided support for these different units.

1.2.3 How is the Prelexical Representation Computed and Organized?

There are basically two ways of viewing the organization and computation of the prelexical level of representation. According to the first, listeners try to match previously stored prelexical representations to the incoming sensory input - just as they match the sequence of prelexical representations to previously stored lexical representations (see Levelt & Wheeldon, 1994, for this kind of proposal in word production). According to the second, the listener's task is to extract information from the signal to construct a prelexical representation that is not stored.

These two hypotheses seem to be quite complementary, with arguments favoring each. It is difficult to conceive of a recognition system that does not exploit the regularities of the incoming input (such as the frequency of occurrence of the units) in order to optimize its functioning. This fact favors the hypothesis based upon a set of stored prelexical representations. However, this hypothesis alone cannot explain how we are able to perceive novel but phonotactically plausible syllables (e.g., *mIv*), assuming for a moment that the syllable constitutes a prelexical unit. If prelexical processing consisted solely of matching the incoming input to stored representations, such syllables should not be retrievable at all. Thus, it seems that we also have a prelexical routine to extract phonological representations from input sequences that does not involve matching the incoming input to previously stored representations.

1.3 From Prelexical Representations to the Lexicon: Lexical Identification

In characterizing the problem of lexical identification, models must account for the way in which the input representation is matched and aligned with the lexical representation. We will consider these two operations in turn in the following Sections.

1.3.1 Lexical Matching Mechanisms

One general way of classifying models of word recognition is according to the manner in which they compare or match the input and lexical representations, and, in particular, the number of such comparisons that they permit at the same time. According to *direct activation* models (cf., Marslen-Wilson & Welsh, 1978; Morton, 1969), the input representation is compared simultaneously with all lexical entries. The state of each entry or its *activation level* changes as a function of the quantity and quality of its fit with input representation. By contrast, in *lexical search* models (cf., Bradley & Forster, 1987; Forster, 1976) only one lexical entry is examined at a time. Lexical identification consists of a sequential search through the lists of entries that can be organized according to different principles. Lexical identification times are assumed to depend upon the number of sequential comparisons that must be made before the appropriate entry is encountered.

Essentially all models of spoken word recognition are in the direct activation family, and thus are based upon the activation metaphor in which the goodness of fit between an input representation and a lexical representation is defined in terms of the latter's level of activation. This is probably no coincidence. One explanation for this fact lies in properties of the speech input itself. Speech is produced over time, and hence the listener is generally in a position of having received only partial information about the target word and in the process of receiving more. As a consequence, it is not obvious when, according to a search model, the listener must initiate a lexical search.

Direct activation models diverge, however, in their specification of the nature of the activation flow that produces lexical activation and identification. In some models, only the matching lexical entries are activated via bottom-up activation whereas in others, mismatching lexical entries are also deactivated by means of bottom-up inhibition or by lateral inhibition. In addition, there is disagreement between models upon the maximal amount of mismatch that still produces some lexical activation. In some proposals, activation requires an exact fit, whereas in other more tolerant models, the lexical activation varies: the closer and more complete the fit, the greater the activation of the word.

1.3.2   Lexical Alignment Mechanisms

As we pointed out above, speech is continuous, and word boundaries are not overtly marked in a systematic fashion. Thus, the listener is confronted with the challenge of finding the correct alignment between the input and lexical representation. By alignment we mean that listeners must determine which part of the input representation is to be matched or compared with which part of the lexical representations. The different solutions proposed to handle this alignment problem can be classified in two ways. The first classification (cf., Frauenfelder & Peeters, 1990) depends upon the class of words whose alignment is actually tested. The second depends upon the level of processing and the type of information that is used in making the alignment decisions.

According to the first classification, we can identify one extreme approach, *exhaustive alignment*, which involves testing every alignment by comparing each successive unit of the input with every lexical entry. For example, each newly perceived unit is compared with every part of every word. Since every possible match between the input and lexical representations is tested, an extremely large number of erroneous or partial alignments and matches is obviously produced. Alternative proposals for alignment generate fewer lexical hypotheses. In models assuming *positional alignment,* only those lexical items that are aligned with a specific position in the input are considered for recognition. Both Cole & Jakimik (1980) and Marslen-Wilson & Welsh (1978) have developed models assuming onset alignment. Here, only word onsets generate the lexical hypotheses entering into competition for recognition. The activated lexical hypotheses can also be restricted to only those that match certain salient parts of the input, irrespective of the position of these parts. An example of such *landmark alignment* can be found in a model proposed by Grosjean & Gee (1987). In this model, the stressed syllable with its perceptual saliency constitutes the unit of alignment. Thus, all lexical hypotheses containing this unit in any position become active candidates for recognition. Finally, positional and landmark alignment can be combined as in the Metrical Segmentation Strategy (MSS) advanced by Cutler and Norris (1988). Here, listeners are assumed to segment the speech input whenever they encounter a metrically strong syllable. When such a syllable is detected, a word boundary is postulated immediately before the onset of this syllable and the lexical candidates aligned, or beginning, with this syllable are matched with the input representation.

According to the second classification, alignment is defined in terms of the processing mechanisms and levels at which lexical segmentation decisions are made. A first type of segmentation is prelexical and is based upon the processing of information in the signal, whereas a second is based upon processing at the lexical level. Within the former, diverse types of information (acoustic and prosodic) have been proposed to support segmentation decisions, ranging from allophonic cues (Church, 1987), phonotactic constraints (Frazier, 1987), and rhythmic structure (Cutler & Butterfield, 1992). Lexically-based segmentation can be of different types according to which component of lexical processing is involved. It can depend upon lexical competition between activated competitors as instantiated in the Trace model (McClelland & Elman, 1986). The most activated lexical items inhibit and deactivate, via lateral inhibition, the lexical items with other lexical alignments, or starting points, in the signal. Alternatively, lexically-based segmentation can be based upon the result of lexical access. Here the listener is assumed to access the phonological representation associated with a word before reaching its offset. Once this phonological information becomes available, the listener can predict the offset of the current word and the onset of the following word.

These different proposals for prelexical and lexical segmentation are not mutually exclusive. Segmentation can be the result of the processing of multiple cues at different levels.

1.4   Models of Word Recognition

In this Section, we describe four leading models of word recognition to illustrate some of the different mechanisms of matching and alignment just discussed. These models include two versions of the COHORT model (COHORT I - Marslen-Wilson & Welsh, 1978; and COHORT II - Marslen-Wilson, 1987), TRACE (McClelland & Elman, 1986) and SHORTLIST (Norris, 1994).

1.4.1   The COHORT I Model

The COHORT I model represents one of the first attempts at developing a model specifically for the recognition of spoken words. This model assumes two successive stages of processing. During the first, all words that match the onset (i.e., the initial one or two phonemes) of the target word exactly are activated in a bottom-up fashion. On the basis of this initial contact between a phonemic prelexical representation and the lexicon, a set of competitors or the *word initial cohort* of the target is generated. For example, given the phonemic input, /El/, words sharing this sequence - like *elephant, element,* and *elk* - are assumed to be activated and introduced into the cohort competitor set. This initial activation phase is followed by a second stage of deactivation via bottom-up inhibition during which the cohort members that mismatch later arriving sensory input are eliminated from the cohort. The deactivation of mismatching competitors is assumed to continue until the uniqueness point (UP) is reached, i.e., the moment that the word becomes unique with respect to the other words in the lexicon. A given target word spoken in isolation is assumed to be recognized at its UP, that is, when it is the only word remaining in its cohort. For example, a word like *elephant* heard in isolation, is predicted to be identified at the sound /f/ at which there are no other words in the lexicon sharing its initial part.

For words in continuous speech, lexically-based segmentation is assumed to ensure that only the words that are aligned with word onsets are introduced into the cohort. Listeners exploit the phonological representation that is the product of lexical access to segment the speech stream. By recognizing words efficiently and gaining rapid access to this representation, the listener is assumed to be able to predict the offset of the word being processed before it has been heard completely and then to anticipate the onset of the following word.

By making clear and simple assumptions, this model generates precise predictions about word recognition. Most importantly, it can predict the moment at which any word can be recognized in a given lexicon on the basis of an analysis of its cohort members. The fact that these predictions can be tested and falsified has made this model attractive and influential.

1.4.2 The Cohort II Model

Marslen-Wilson (1987) proposed a new version of his model, Cohort II, to incorporate some psychologically more realistic assumptions. Like its predecessor, this version presupposes that the competitor set is limited to those candidates that are aligned with the onset of the target word. However, the membership of the cohort is enlarged to include words that mismatch the sensory input to some minimal (but still unspecified) degree. The model is more explicit, however, on the issue of prelexical representations (Lahiri & Marslen-Wilson, 1991). It does not include an intermediate level of prelexical representation, but rather maps the distinctive features extracted from the signal directly onto the lexical entries.

In order to express the varying degree of match between the input and different competitors, the model appeals to the notion of level of activation. In particular, cohort members vary in activation level as a function of their fit with the input and of their lexical frequency. Unlike the clear binary status of words in the original cohort model (i.e., words are either in or out of the cohort), the identity and status of cohort members is defined less well in this newer formulation of the model. The model does not specify how the degree of match with the input and how word frequency determine activation, since these factors, and their relative contribution to lexical activation, are difficult to quantify in a verbal model. As a consequence, no precise definition of the competitor set is yet available in this model.

As in the original version, there is no lateral inhibition between lexical candidates, the cohort members exert no direct influence upon the target word or its activation level. However, the decision as to when a particular word is recognized does depend upon the activation level of its competitors. Marslen-Wilson (1990) has suggested that isolated word recognition takes place when the difference in activation between the target word and its most activated competitor has reached a certain criterion. In this way, the most activated cohort members influence the decision phase of the recognition process.

A comparison between the two versions of the Cohort model illustrates a general dilemma confronting efforts to model lexical processing. Cohort I makes clear and testable predictions and therefore has been useful in generating considerable empirical research. However, to do so, it has made several simplifying assumptions. In contrast, Cohort II is a more complex verbal model and fits better with what we know about lexical processing. However, it does not specify the nature of the competitor set and therefore cannot predict the time-course of word recognition. One way of dealing with this trade-off between complexity and testability is to implement models on a computer, as was done for the Trace model.

1.4.3 The Trace Model

Trace is an interactive activation model that has been implemented as a computer program (McClelland & Elman, 1986). It is made up of distinctive feature, phoneme and word units, each representing hypotheses about the sensory input. These three types of units are organized hierarchically. There are bottom-up and top-down facilitatory connections between units on adjacent levels (feature-phoneme, phoneme-word, and word-phoneme) and inhibitory connections between units within levels (feature-feature, phoneme-phoneme, and word-word). Incoming sensory input provides bottom-up excitation of distinctive feature units, which in turn, excite phoneme units. Phoneme units are activated as a function of their match with the activated distinctive features so that several alternative phonemic units are activated for a given input. As the phonemes become excited, they increase the level of activation of words that contain them.

As words receive some activation, they begin to inhibit each other. Thus, unlike both versions of the Cohort model, but like the Shortlist model, TRACE assumes that lexical competitors can exert a direct influence upon the activation level of the target, and vice-versa. The model incorporates a lateral flow of inhibition between units at the same level. By this mechanism the target word inhibits its competitors, but is also inhibited by them. The degree to which one word inhibits another is a function of the former's activation level: the more a word is activated, the more efficiently it can inhibit its competitors. The dynamics of interactive activation and, in particular, of this inhibition between competitors allows TRACE to keep the actual activated competitor set small, and to converge on a single lexical entry despite the mass of lexical candidates that are potentially in contention for recognition.

TRACE generates a potentially large competitor set since it assumes exhaustive alignment. This means that the activated competitor set for a particular stretch of speech is not restricted to those lexical candidates that are aligned with particular points of alignment (i.e., like word onsets as for the COHORT model). Rather the competitor set can include words matching the input but not aligned with word onsets. As a result, all words in the lexicon are in constant potential contention for recognition - continuously increasing or decreasing in activation level - at every processing moment as a function of the incoming signal.

Another aspect in which TRACE deviates from both versions of the COHORT model and SHORTLIST is its assumption of a top-down activation flow from the word to the phoneme level. This top-down feedback is the subject of considerable debate between proponents of autonomous and interactive models of processing (Massaro, 1989; McClelland, 1991).

Finally, time is represented spatially in TRACE. For each *time-slice*, this model constructs a complete network in which all the units at every level are represented. Thus, to recognize an input made up of four phonemes, TRACE constructs at least four (in fact, 4 x 6 slices/phonemes) complete lexical networks and marks the time cycle at which each lexical unit begins. This solution of spatial reduplication is not particularly realistic or efficient.

1.4.4 The SHORTLIST Model

The SHORTLIST model (Norris, 1994) represents an attempt to improve upon some of the shortcomings of TRACE, in particular, its rather implausible architecture. SHORTLIST involves two distinct processing stages. During the first, a restricted set of lexical candidates, the *shortlist*, is established using both bottom-up excitation and bottom-up inhibition. Any word – whatever its alignment – can be included in the activated candidate set as long as it matches the input to some pre-set criterion. Unlike TRACE where all the words are prewired into such a network, the modeler sets an upper limit (e.g., ranging from 3 to 30 words) upon the number of candidates retained. For practical reasons, this shortlist is based upon the match of the input with the phonological form representations of words found in a lexical database. During the second stage, the best fitting words – even those with different alignments – are wired into an interactive activation network similar to that assumed by TRACE. The competition between the lexical items in the shortlist takes place via lateral inhibition, such that the words that best match the input inhibit their competitors most effectively.

More recently, the SHORTLIST model (Norris, McQueen & Cutler, 1995) has been modified in two important respects. First, a mechanism was introduced in the model to exploit prosodic information and more specifically to incorporate the Metrical Segmentation Strategy (MSS) developed for the segmentation of English (Cutler & Norris, 1988). To do so, the new model boosts the level of activation of words which have a strong initial syllable (not containing a reduced vowel), and decreases the activation of words that are not aligned in their onsets with a strong syllable in the input. Second, the model introduced a recomputation routine so as to prevent highly activated competitors from completely inhibiting later arriving matching words. By recomputing the activation of the shortlist after each phoneme is received, the model avoids committing itself completely to the lexical candidates that are activated early, and it allows later matching words to become activated. This mechanism allows the model to account for the activation of words that are embedded non-initially within longer words.

1.5 Experimental Data and Model Fitting

In this Section we confront the models and the mechanisms that they incorporate with some experimental results. We will first consider the mapping from the signal to the input representation and then the mapping of this latter representation onto the lexicon.

1.5.1 Mapping onto Prelexical Input Representation

The experimental search for the existence of a prelexical *level* of processing cannot easily be dissociated from that of a prelexical *unit* of representation. Indeed, showing that listeners rely on a specific unit of speech perception during prelexical processing is a privileged way of demonstrating that there *is* a prelexical level of representation, and of specifying its nature. Thus, most research on prelexical processing has aimed to determine the nature of prelexical units. A wide variety of experimental procedures has been used to generate support for one or another of the perceptual units. For example, the perceptual difficulty as a function of the rate of ear switching (Huggins, 1967), the migration of different-sized units in dichotic presentation (Kolinsky, Morais & Cluytens, 1995), and the effect upon speech perception of backward masks of varying size (Massaro & Oden, 1980) have all been measured to support one unit or another.

We cannot do justice here to the large literature on processing units. Rather we will present some findings with three different experimental approaches: fragment detection, phonological priming, and speech migration. Then we will consider what kinds of experimental evidence can be used to investigate the organization of the prelexical level of processing. Finally, we will discuss how the current models of word recognition can handle these data.

1.5.1.1 Searching for Prelexical Units with Fragment Detection

One heavily exploited technique is the so called fragment detection paradigm (cf., Frauenfelder & Kearns, 1997, for a review) which involves the detection of different phonological targets. One of its original applications (Mehler, Dommergues, Frauenfelder & Segui, 1981) produced evidence for the "syllable effect". Here, subjects are presented with lists of bisyllabic words and must detect prespecified targets. Targets and target-bearing carrier words either shared their first syllable or did not. For instance, subjects were to detect /ba/ or /bal/ in /ba.lance/, or /ba/ and /bal/ in /bal.con/ (where '.' represents the syllable boundary). The /ba/ target matches the first syllable of /ba.lance/, while /bal/ does not, and the reverse is true for the word /bal.con/. Reaction times were found to be significantly faster when targets and carrier words shared the first syllable than when they did not. This result was interpreted as showing that subjects were using the syllable during prelexical processing to access their mental lexicon. According to these authors: "...The subjects' detection response probably precedes lexical access and thus is based on the prelexical code." (p. 304).

Following this seminal study, other experiments were carried out in recent years with the same logic (e.g., Bradley, Sanchez-Casas & Garcia-Albea, 1993; Cutler, Mehler, Norris & Segui, 1986; Mehler, Dommergues, Frauenfelder & Segui, 1981; Zwitserlood, Schriefers, Lahiri & Van Donselaar, 1993). These studies suggest that the nature of the prelexical unit is at least in part determined by the phonological structure of the language - and especially by its rhythmic characteristics. For instance, Spanish is a language usually described as syllable-timed just like French. Spanish listeners showed the same kind of syllabic effects as the French subjects (Bradley et al., 1993; Sebastiàn-Gallés, Dupoux, Segui & Mehler, 1992). Another example is provided by fragment detection studies conducted in Japanese (Cutler &

Otake, 1994). These indicate suggesting that the mora is a processing unit in this language, the mora being a sub-syllabic unit traditionally used to describe Japanese rhythmic characteristics. Moreover, it has been shown that native listeners 'export' their segmentation strategy when processing words from another language. For instance, French listeners who were tested with English words displayed the same kind of syllable effects as they did when tested with French materials (Cutler et al., 1986). Thus, adults have developed a segmentation strategy related to their native language phonology, and they apply it to any incoming speech input. As pointed out by Zwitserlood et al., it seems that "different processing routines are used for different languages, depending on their phonological structure and on the availability of low-level cues in the signal" (p. 269).

Although these results present a relatively coherent picture, they have not led to an accepted solution to the access unit debate. For instance, the case of English is still unresolved. In fragment detection paradigms, English listeners always failed to produce a syllabic effect. One reason for this failure could be that, unlike French or Spanish, English has unclear syllabic boundaries, a phenomenon referred to as ambisyllabicity. This hypothesis was tested by Zwitserlood et al. (1993) in Dutch, a language in which there is ambisyllabicity as well. The authors reported evidence for the syllable effect in Dutch listeners who were presented with Dutch words having clear syllable boundaries (such as *stremsel*), as well as with words having unclear syllabic boundaries (such as *stre[m]ing*). These results suggest that the failure of English listeners to show any syllabic effects cannot be linked to the sole presence of unclear syllabic boundaries in their native language. Furthermore, these findings for English do not tell us what kind of prelexical processing is actually used by this population.

There are other problems - much more difficult to solve - that arise with the fragment detection procedure. First, even in syllable-timed languages, the syllabic effect discovered with this paradigm is not systematically obtained. For instance, Sebastiàn-Gallés et al. (1992) reported that Spanish listeners do not produce such an effect in speeded versions of the task, or in experiments in which the target-bearing syllable is stressed. According to the authors, this was due to the fact that subjects bypass syllabic segmentation under certain conditions. More specifically, the 'acoustic transparency' of the carrier items (for instance, an accented syllable is considered to be more 'transparent' than an unaccented one), makes it possible for subjects to respond on the basis of an acoustic-phonetic representation. If this interpretation is correct, *several* segmentation routines would be accessible to the listeners, complicating the preceding conclusions about the relationship between the rhythmic properties of the language and the prelexical unit.

Second - and this point is related to the preceding one - recent experimental work has been concerned with determining whether the perceptual units that are supported by experiments using the fragment detection tasks are computed prelexically, so as to mediate word recognition, or whether they are the results of post-perceptual processes. The difficulty in establishing the temporal locus of effects observed with on-line techniques is, of course, quite general. Indeed, it is unclear as to whether the fragment detection paradigm taps into perceptual processes (including prelexical processing), or into post-perceptual processes (often called also metaphonological processes) involving intentional and conscious access to speech representations. As pointed out by Kolinsky (in press), variants of this task have not only been used for studying perceptual processes by measuring time to detect targets, but also for exploring metaphonological development by measuring detection accuracy in infants or illiterate adults (Morais, Content, Cary, Mehler & Segui, 1989). It is assumed that the speeded version of the fragment detection paradigm is an on-line task (e.g., Mehler et al., 1981; Cutler, van Ooijen, Norris & Sanchez-Casas, 1996), while the same procedure used as a measure of detection accuracy requires metaphonological judgments. Does the speed of the subject's response determine whether these responses reflect prelexical processing or post-lexical strategies? The results obtained by Sebastiàn-Gallés et al. (1992), discussed above, are consistent with such an explanation: the syllabic effects emerging late for longer RTs (at around 620 ms.) would be due to post-perceptual analyses of the stimuli, while the absence of such an effect with faster reaction times (around 380 ms.) reflects prelexical processing. But this explanation is not satisfying since in the original study by Mehler et al. (1981) with French subjects, syllable effects emerged even for extremely rapid RTs (around 350 ms.). So we still do not know exactly what level of processing is being reflected in the fragment detection task.

Finally, a third point raises some doubts concerning the appropriateness of the fragment detection tasks for the study of prelexical processing. In a recent study, Meunier, Content, Frauenfelder & Kearns (1997) have not replicated the syllable effect originally produced by French listeners when targets were detected in French *non-words*. If syllables are computed prelexically, the syllabic effect should be obtained independently of the lexical status of these items. This fact strongly suggests that the syllabic effect is due to analyses of the speech input at a lexical or post-lexical level. Thus, the prelexical locus of the syllable effect in sequence detection paradigms must be seriously questioned.

In conclusion, numerous studies have searched for the prelexical unit through the fragment detection paradigm. It is not clear now whether this paradigm is adapted to the study of prelexical representations (see Kolinsky, in press, for a comprehensive review of this problem).

1.5.1.2   Prelexical Units and other Tasks: Phonological Priming and Speech Migration

The search for prelexical units has also been conducted with other experimental paradigms such as phonological priming. Basically, priming in the auditory modality consists in presenting subjects with auditory (or visual) primes, followed by an auditory target, on which subjects have to perform some psycholinguistic task (lexical decision, target detection, shadowing, etc.). Primes and targets are to be phonologically (or semantically) related, or not related. The basic idea is that it should be easier to process a prime-related target than an unrelated one, since the target is pre-activated by the prime or since a mechanism involved in the processing of a shared property may still be activated in memory.

Radeau, Morais & Segui (1995) presented French-speaking subjects with phonologically related monosyllabic 3-phoneme word primes and targets, sharing their two initial or their two final phonemes. Moreover, primes and targets were selected according to their relative or absolute lexical frequencies. Subjects had to perform either a lexical decision or a shadowing task on the target. The results showed no priming in the initial overlap condition, while a facilitatory effect was found in the case of final overlap. The authors argue that this priming effect is due to the activation of the prelexical level of processing, for at least three reasons. First, the size of the priming effect did not differ significantly as a function of item lexical frequency, suggesting that this effect depended upon a prelexical processing. Second, this final overlap facilitation effect was modality specific; it was obtained only when both the prime and the target were presented auditorily, but not in another study (Radeau, Morais & Segui, 1994) involving auditory primes and visual targets. Finally, the final overlap facilitation effect did not depend on the lexical status of the primes: the size of this effect was similar when both words and pseudo-words were used as primes (Slowiaczek & Hamburger, 1992). Taken together, these results suggest that the phonological priming paradigm is useful for investigating the prelexical processing.

However, at least two issues need to be addressed. The first concerns explaining why initial (unlike final) phonological overlap does not lead systematically to a priming effect (see the discussion in Radeau et al., 1995; but see also Slowiaczek & Hamburger, 1993, for inhibitory effects in initial overlapping). Second, it is important to determine the actual size of the unit(s) involved in the prelexical processing as reflected by phonological priming. On the basis of the Radeau et al.'s study (1995), it can only be concluded that the priming effect was due to a rime overlap. The results do not tell us whether a syllabic overlap would have led to stronger priming. Recall that the syllable has been proposed as the prelexical unit in French (e.g., Mehler et al., 1981). This question has been addressed recently by Dumay & Radeau (1997) who compared priming effects in rime and final syllable overlap in disyllabic French words. A strong priming effect occurred with syllable overlap, while a smaller effect was found with rime overlapping, there by arguing in favor of the role of the syllable in prelexical processing in French.

Prelexical processing has also been studied by means of a paradigm based on auditory illusions in the presentation of dichotic stimuli (Kolinsky & Morais, 1997; Kolinsky, Morais & Cluytens, 1995). French-speaking subjects had to detect or identify words created by blending 2 dichotic non-word stimuli. For instance, subjects heard the non-word [biton] in one ear and the non-word [cojou] in the other. Word targets were more frequently reported when they were the result of a fusion of syllables than of other units. In this example, the migration of syllables lead frequently to the perception of the two French words [bijou] and [coton]. Moreover, in the identification task, illusory percepts were only obtained for syllable combinations. This paradigm was used with Portuguese and Japanese listeners as well, and produced the same pattern of results as for the fragment detection paradigms. The size of the unit that is more likely to migrate is language-specific. In Japanese, both the mora and the syllable appeared to elicited a high migration rate (Kolinsky & Morais, 1993), while in Portuguese, the initial phoneme of words showed the highest migration rate (Morais, Kolinsky & Nakamura, 1996).

1.5.1.3 Organization of Prelexical Input Representation

In Section 1.2.3, we argued that the representations at the prelexical level could either be pre-stored in memory or extracted from the signal. One way of testing these two hypotheses is to search for a syllable frequency effect. Indeed, according to the first hypothesis, frequency could well determine the internal organization of the prelexical units just as it did for the lexicon. More frequent syllables - if the syllable is the appropriate unit - would be recognized more quickly than less frequent ones. According to the latter hypothesis, there is no particular reason to suppose that syllable frequency plays a role in speech processing and word identification.

Syllable frequency effects in prelexical processing have not been subjected to systematic study until now. However, some auditory lexical decision experiments showed that words made up of high-frequency syllables yielded slower decision times than words made up of low-frequency ones (Dominguez, Cuetos & De Vega, 1992; Zhou & Marslen-Wilson, 1994). These data cannot be related directly to prelexical processing since, in making lexical decisions subjects must process the input to at least the lexical level. To address this issue, we conducted a shadowing experiment (Frauenfelder & Floccia, in preparation) involving monosyllabic words and non-words varying in their syllabic frequency (but controlled for their syllabic complexity). Preliminary results showed no evidence of syllabic frequency, in words or in non-words. According to a first explanation, the null effect is due to the insensitivity of the shadowing task to the variable manipulated. Alternatively, the task involves higher levels than just the prelexical processing. But, in this case, it remains to be explained why non-words did not show a syllabic frequency effect. Finally, another explanation is that the prelexical level of representation is not organized as a set of prestored syllabic representation, but that listeners compute syllabic units directly from the sensory input without relying on any stored representations. More studies manipulating syllable frequency are clearly needed to determine which is the most appropriate explanation.

1.5.1.4   Model Fitting

Can any of the experimental data presented above distinguish between the different models of word recognition? The models described above - with the exception of COHORT II - make the assumption that some intermediate representation is computed or activated before contacting the lexicon. More precisely, COHORT I and SHORTLIST both include some segmental or phonemic representation, while TRACE includes both a distinctive feature and a phoneme level. COHORT II explicitly rejects the idea of a prelexical level of representation, but assumes that distinctive features are extracted from the input and mapped directly onto the lexical entries. The main difference between Lahiri & Marslen-Wilson's (1991) position and that of the others is the following: "Contrary to the segmental hypothesis [that is, the prelexical hypothesis as considered in the current chapter], the system does not wait until segmental labels can be assigned before communicating to the lexicon. Featural cues start to affect lexical choice as soon as they become available in the speech input" (p. 258). Thus in any case, the failure to demonstrate the existence of a speech unit - whatever the speech unit - would be problematic for all those models.

1.5.2   Mapping onto the Lexicon

Having examined the mapping of the signal onto the input representation, we now turn to the next level of processing; that responsible for the mapping of the input representation onto lexical representations. We will compare the assumptions of four models concerning the mechanisms underlying the lexical activation and identification processes, and the resulting membership of the activated competitor set.

The make-up of the activated competitor set for any given model depends upon its assumptions concerning three main factors: the nature of the input units used to contact the lexicon (e.g., phonemes or syllables), the manner in which this representation is aligned with the lexical representation, and the nature of the activation flow (bottom-up, top-down, and lateral). We discussed the first factor in the previous Section and will focus here on activation flow.

These models appeal to different mechanisms to activate the competitors and subsequently to reduce the competitor set. According to the COHORT model, lexical selection is achieved by means of bottom-up activation combined with bottom-up inhibition. When mismatching sensory information is received, it deactivates the inappropriate lexical units. According to TRACE, competitor set reduction is achieved through lateral inhibition, since there is no bottom-up inhibition. This inhibition between lexical competitors allows the stronger candidates, and in particular, the target, to dominate and eliminate the weaker ones. Bottom-up inhibition and lateral inhibition can also be combined as is demonstrated by the SHORTLIST model.

It is crucial to examine the cases in which the mechanisms for activating and reducing the lexical competitor set lead to divergent empirical predictions. By all accounts, the amount of bottom-activation received by any given word unit, target or competitor, depends upon the quality and the quantity of its fit with the sensory input. While all the models assume that cohort competitors - which match and are aligned with the input - are activated, they make divergent predictions concerning the activation (or the non-activation) of mismatching and misaligned competitors. The tolerance of mismatch in the sensory input by the models varies. It can range from extreme intolerance and total lexical deactivation by any mismatch in the sensory input via strong bottom-up inhibition (like in COHORT I) to relative tolerance and partial activation despite some mismatch. Another critical difference between the two selection mechanisms is that for models with lateral inhibition, the competitors have a direct influence upon target activation and vice-versa. Consequently, the quality of the fit of the input (not only with target, but with its competitors), the number of competitors, and their frequency all affect the level of relative activation of the words in the competitor set. For models without lateral inhibition, none of these factors, except the fit with the target, influences word recognition.

1.5.2.1 Experimental Evidence for Competitor Activation

There is, at present, considerable evidence for the multiple activation of lexical candidates. However, it is impossible to treat the different types of competitors in a homogeneous fashion as well as make generalizations about their behavior. In fact, given the variability in the predictions and the experimental results, it is necessary to examine the specific types of competitors individually as we do in this Section.

Activation of Matching and Aligned or Cohort Competitors

Clear experimental evidence is now available that cohort competitors are activated during processing. One important study (Zwitserlood, 1989) used the cross-modal semantic priming procedure (Swinney, 1979; Tabossi, 1997). This procedure involves presenting subjects with a spoken sentence or a list of isolated spoken words (or non-words). During, or just after, this auditory presentation, subjects receive a visually presented word. Upon receiving this word, they are required to make a lexical decision. In the critical condition, the visual word is related in some fashion (e.g., semantically or phonologically) to the auditorily presented word or to one of its competitors. The lexical decision latencies in these conditions are compared with the RTs obtained in matched unrelated control conditions. Any RT advantage in the related over the unrelated conditions is taken as evidence for the semantic activation of the auditorily presented word or its competitor. This study showed that the meanings of a target word and its cohort competitors were activated as long as the presented sensory information did not distinguish between them. Thus, given the partial spoken input [kæpt], the meanings of both *captain* and *captive* were activated. This finding is consistent with all four models presented here.

It is also of interest to consider what support the psycholinguistic literature provides for the notion of uniqueness point since this notion is based upon cohort competitors. The relation between the location of the UP and the moment at which words are recognized has been investigated with different experimental procedures. Experiments with the gating task (Grosjean, 1980; Tyler & Wessels, 1983) have shown that the amount of information required for word identification corresponded closely to the uniqueness point defined using phonetic descriptions found in a lexical database. An effect of the location of the UP upon subjects' word recognition performance has also been demonstrated with other experimental tasks. Marslen-Wilson (1984) collected the response latencies of subjects to detect phoneme targets located in different positions in words and found a high correlation (r = 0.96 for trisyllabic carrier words) between these RTs and the distance separating the target phoneme from the UP of the word. Using the same task, Frauenfelder, Segui & Dijkstra (1990) found significant differences in the detection times to phonemes in matched words and non-words only when the targets were located after the UP, thus suggesting that the UP defined the moment at which lexically-based phonological information becomes available. Lastly, experimental research using the shadowing (Radeau & Morais, 1990) and gender decision (Radeau, Mousty & Bertelson, 1989) tasks also produced results that are at least in part explained by the UP variable. Here subjects responded more quickly to the stimuli with early UPs than to those with late UPs. However, the UP did not explain all of the variance in the RTs. For instance, in the gender study, the temporal distance between early and late UPs did not translate directly into RT differences. Taken together, these experimental findings suggest that the cohort competitors were activated and relevant in the definition of the time-course of word recognition in human listeners, but appear not to be the only conditioning factor.

Activation and Deactivation Mismatching Competitors

It is useful - especially for isolated word recognition studies - to distinguish mismatching sensory information that is located at item-onset from that arriving later in the speech sequence. In the first case, we must ask whether mismatching competitors are activated at all, and if so, in which conditions. In the second case, we must determine what happens to the matching, and hence, activated competitors once mismatching information does arrive. We will consider each of these cases in turn.

Onset Mismatch

The results concerning the activation of initially mismatching lexical candidates are not yet completely clear. A first cross-modal semantic priming study (Marslen-Wilson & Zwitserlood, 1989) produced results in Dutch suggesting that only matching lexical candidates are activated. These authors showed that a spoken word or non-word prime that mismatched the target word in its initial phoneme by several distinctive features did not activate the meaning of the latter word (e.g., neither the rhyming word *mat* nor the rhyming non-word *dat* activated the semantic associate *dog* of the source word *cat*). This finding indicates that words differing by several distinctive features in their first phoneme do not belong to one another's cohort. In a follow-up study (Marslen-Wilson, Moss & van Halen, 1996) using the same technique, found some activation of mismatching competitors was obtained in certain conditions. More specifically, when the priming non-word was phonologically close to the source word and had no other rhyming competitors, significant priming was obtained, but, importantly, less than when the source word was the prime. A second experiment produced conflicting results with no priming for either close rhyming words or non-words. However, Connine, Blasko and Titone (1993) also used the cross-modal priming technique and manipulated the phonological distance between a priming non-word and the target word. The results showed priming by non-words that were created from words by making small phonological changes in their onsets. When this phonological distance was increased, no activation was obtained.

We can draw two main conclusions from these studies. First, lexical candidates appear to be activated, but only when they mismatch the sensory input initially by a small phonological distance. Second, the lexical status of the sensory input - word or non-word - determines if there is activation of mismatching competitors. Evidence for activation of lexical competitors was restricted to cases where the input was a non-word. These results appear to be more consistent with the predictions of the TRACE and SHORTLIST models than those of COHORT I which allows no activation of mismatching lexical competitors. In principle, the former two predict competitor activation, especially for non-word inputs. Indeed, for these inputs, no exact matching lexical candidate exists that would strongly inhibit any mismatching words.

A word of caution is in order here concerning the predictions of these latter two models. First, it has been shown that although TRACE allows some competitors with initial mismatches to be activated, these words are generally not actually recognized (Frauenfelder & Peeters, in press). Hence, when presented with the inputs like *shigarette*, it does not systematically recognized the word *cigarette*. Second, although, in spirit, phonological distance determines lexical activation in the SHORTLIST, the current implementations of the model do not yet include this property since they are based upon phonemes and do not take into account phonological distance.

Non-Initial Mismatch

Now what happens when the mismatch comes later in the input, and several lexical competitors have already been partially activated by matching information? Zwitserlood (1989) conducted some relevant experiments that showed that activated candidates were immediately deactivated when mismatching information was received. When longer auditory primes were presented that included some mismatching sensory information (e.g., the [I] in [kæptI]), the semantic associate of the then mismatching competitor (e.g., *captain*) was no longer primed, and this competitor was assumed to be deactivated. Unfortunately, it was impossible in this study to determine whether it was the mismatching input that eliminated this competitor in a bottom-up fashion, or whether the matching competitor (e.g., *captive*) had received sufficient activation from the additional phoneme input to strongly inhibit this mismatching competitor. This confound was avoided in a phoneme monitoring study (Frauenfelder, Content & Scholten, in prep.) in which phonemic mismatches were introduced non-initially. This mismatching information (/n/) preceded the phoneme target (/r/) in the non-word (*vocabunaire*). The monitoring latencies did not differ from those in a control non-word condition in which no lexical activation is expected (*satobunaire*), but were much slower than those in the original word (*vocabulaire*). This pattern of results suggests that the mismatching phoneme immediately deactivated the lexical candidate. These results are consistent with SHORTLIST which assumes bottom-up inhibition, but inconsistent with TRACE which only includes lateral inhibition. .

Activation of Misaligned (embedded) Competitors
Another class of potential competitors that must also be considered are those words that are embedded somewhere in longer words. For example, during the processing of the word *party*, the embedded words *par* and *tea* could potentially be activated since they both match the input. It is important, in particular for models assuming lateral inhibition, to distinguish between both the position of the embedded word (initial and non-initial) and the lexical status of the embedding item (word or non-word). In TRACE, initially-embedded words are activated in both longer word and non-word strings, whereas non-initially embedded words are activated only in non-words (Frauenfelder & Peeters, 1990).

Initially Embedded Words
In a phoneme monitoring study, Frauenfelder & Henstra (1988) tested for the activation of embedded words by comparing the detection latencies to phoneme targets (e.g., for target /p/) in matched monosyllabic words (e.g., *mop*) and non-words (e.g., *nop*) in three conditions: baseline (e.g., *mop* vs. *nop*), initially embedded (e.g., *mopel* vs. *nopel*), and finally embedded (e.g., *temop* vs. *tenop*). Since the acoustic properties of these targets and their local environment varied minimally across the pairs being compared, the faster RTs obtained from targets in embedded words than in embedded non-words can be interpreted in terms of the lexical activation in the former condition. Such an advantage was found for both initially and finally embedded words, suggesting that these embedded words are activated during the processing of the longer non-word string. These results are consistent with both TRACE and SHORTLIST.

Non-Initially Embedded Words

Shillcock (1990) examined whether words, embedded non-initially in longer words, are activated, again with the cross-modal semantic priming task. He obtained significant priming of a word (e.g., *rib*) by the second syllable (e.g., *bone*) of a bisyllabic target word (e.g., *trombone*). This suggests that the embedded word is activated during the processing of the longer carrier word, a result that is consistent with the predictions of the SHORTLIST model but not of the TRACE model. This finding was not replicated by Gow and Gordon (1995) who obtained no cross-modal priming of non-initial embedded words (e.g., *lips*) when presented with longer carrier words (e.g., *tulips*). It is, at present, not understood why these two studies produced contradictory results.

On the basis of these rather limited studies on the activation of embedded words, it appears that such words are activated in both initial and noninitial position in word and non-word carrier sequences. The TRACE model, it should be recalled, predicts effects of the lexical status of the carrier sequence upon embedded word activation. When the carrier sequence is a non-word, and when no matching lexical candidates are aligned to the left of this target, the embedded word will be activated. However, in the case of word carriers, non-initial targets suffer too much lateral inhibition from the carrier word to be activated. These predictions differ from those made by SHORTLIST which, because of its reset mechanism, allows the activation of non-initially embedded words in longer words.

1.5.2.2   Experimental Evidence for Lexical Competition

In the preceding Section, we examined the experimental literature concerned with the activation of lexical candidates. We will pursue here the question of what effect these activated lexical candidates have upon target word recognition. There are relatively fewer studies of lexical competition since it is more difficult to demonstrate the effects of competition than the effects of activation.

Effects of Lexical Competition

Some evidence for competition comes from priming studies by Goldinger, Luce and Pisoni (1989) and Goldinger, Luce, Pisoni and Marcario (1992) which indicate that the recognition of a word is slower when it is preceded by a phonologically similar word than by a dissimilar word. This inhibition is most likely attributable to competition between the prime and target. More direct evidence for competition effects has been provided in a word spotting experiment (McQueen, Norris & Cutler, 1994). Here, the recognition of a non-initial embedded word (e.g., *mess*) was delayed by its overlapping competitor (e.g., *domestic*). Subjects had to detect these non-initial embedded words in the initial fragment of words (e.g., *domes*) or in control non-word fragments (e.g., *nemes*). The longer spotting latencies for the words embedded in word fragments suggest not only that words with different alignments (carrier and embedded words) are activated simultaneously, but also that the longer carrier word competes with and inhibits the embedded word.

Effects of Number of Competitors

The effects of competitor set size upon word recognition have also been studied. Marslen-Wilson (1984) showed that subjects' latencies to decide that a speech string was a non-word did not depend upon the number of cohort members just prior to the non-word segment; constant RTs were found independent of cohort size. Conflicting findings were obtained by Jakimik (1979) who obtained evidence for cohort size effects. Slower mispronunciation detection latencies were obtained for non-words derived from words with a large competitor set (e.g., *complain*) than those with a small set (e.g., *shampoo*). Unfortunately, the stimuli with large cohorts were mostly prefixed words, introducing the additional confounding factor of morphological complexity.

A series of experimental studies (Goldinger, Luce & Pisoni, 1989; Luce, 1986; Luce, Pisoni & Goldinger, 1990) examined the role of the number of competitors with another competitor definition, the *N-count* definition. Here, words with a mismatch in any single phonemic position are competitors. Larger competitor sets produced longer auditory lexical decision and word naming times, and also more incorrect perceptual identification. The inhibitory influence of the competitors is consistent with the predictions made by the authors' Neighborhood Activation model (Luce et al., 1990). To compare these results with the predictions of other models fairly, the effect of cohort and n-count competitors must be teased apart more systematically.

More recently, a word spotting experiment (Norris et al., 1995) manipulated the number of words consistent with the onset of the second syllable of a bisyllabic non-word. Subjects were required to spot an initially embedded word (e.g., *mask* in *maskuk*) that overlapped with these competitors (which started with *sk*). The results showed that spotting latencies were slower when there were more overlapping competitors. Using a cross-modal repetition priming procedure, Vroomen and de Gelder (1995) obtained convergent results. Subjects made slower lexical decisions to visually presented targets (e.g., *melk*) when primed by a spoken sequence (e.g., *melka:m*) with many overlapping competitors than by sequence with few competitors (e.g., *melkom*).

Let us consider how these findings relate to the predictions of the different models. These results provide further evidence in support of the TRACE and SHORTLIST models which both predict effects of competitor set size, but run counter to the predictions of the COHORT model. There is, however, one additional complicating factor in drawing the negative conclusion about the Cohort model. COHORT II, while excluding competitor inhibition during lexical selection, nonetheless, includes certain competitors in the computation of its decision rule. The decision rule establishes the principles for determining when the winning (or perceived) lexical entry is identified. By taking the activation level of the most activated competitor into consideration, this model reintroduces effects of competitors.

1.6   And what about Continuous Speech: A Remaining Challenge?

For the years to come, an important challenge for psycholinguistic research in spoken word recognition - as well as for engineering ventures in automatic speech recognition - will be to deal with the problem of recognizing words in spontaneous continuous speech. Indeed, until now, most spoken word recognition research has been carried out with single words, often produced in citation form, or less frequently, with read continuous speech. It goes without saying that the use of such speech in experiments constitutes a major simplification of the recognition problem in several ways. The properties of speech that were alluded to above, such as its variable and continuous nature, are not as acutely present for the stimuli used in laboratory experiments. Words found in continuous speech tend to be more variable than those produced in isolation or read, in part because phonemes are more often elided, assimilated or distorted in spontaneous than in read speech (e.g., Brown, 1977; Labov, 1972, Milroy, 1980). As far as prosodic characteristics are concerned, in spontaneous speech, the rate is slower (e.g., Johns-Lewis, 1986), pauses are more frequent and longer (e.g., Levin, Schaffer & Snow, 1982), and prosodic units are shorter (Crystal & Davy, 1969). In addition, experiments with isolated words obviously circumvent the problem of segmenting continuous speech. As compared to the linguistic stimuli used in the laboratory, more extraneous noise also accompanies spontaneous speech signals and affects its quality. Finally, at a higher level, continuous spontaneous speech obviously differs from words pronounced in isolation since syntactic, semantic, and pragmatic information is available in the latter but not in the former speech mode.

1.6.1   Research on Spoken Word Recognition in Continuous Speech

Using simplified stimuli and idealized experimental conditions is of course a reasonable and defensible scientific strategy. It is clearly important to control the experimental materials carefully so as to eliminate as many parasitic variables as possible. This is quite difficult with spontaneous speech and natural listening conditions. Moreover, it is widely believed that the results obtained in such artificial experiments generalize to the processing of natural continuous speech since the same basic mechanisms are assumed to be operating. This hypothesis, however, has not been tested adequately, since it remains to be determined how the processing mechanisms vary as a function of input.

Only a few studies have compared the processing of spontaneous continuous speech with that of read speech directly using the same or similar experimental procedures. One such study (Metha & Cutler, 1988) underscores the necessity of more such systematic comparisons. In this phoneme detection experiment in English, the authors found that detection latencies depended on the position of syllabic stress within the word; listeners were faster if the word started with a strong syllable than with a weak one. This difference was greater in continuous spontaneous speech than in continuous read speech, presumably because listeners make a greater use of prosodic information in spontaneous speech, or because prosodic information is more salient in this speech mode. In studies involving the gating of continuous speech (Bard, Shillcock & Altmann, 1988; Grosjean, 1985), subjects were found to be unable to recognize words immediately as they were presented, but often needed to hear the following words. This finding points to a much less immediate lexical analysis than that suggested by gating results with isolated words. Globally, these differences in results as a function of the nature of the input demonstrate the urgent need for more systematic comparisons.

1.6.2 Questions Raised by the Differences in Input

The differences that can be observed in both the input characteristics and the listeners' processing mechanisms for continuous spontaneous speech and read speech (isolated or continuous) also raise some serious questions about the validity of the current models of spoken word recognition. Indeed, these models have been elaborated primarily to account for human recognition performance with laboratory stimuli only. In trying to adapt these models to the processing of continuous spontaneous speech, we must ask whether their structure has to change fundamentally, or whether additional modules are required?

If, following the latter strategy, additional modules are incorporated into current models, they will have to take into account several sources of information available in the continuous speech stream, such as prosody, distributional regularities in the language (such as phonotactic constraints, phoneme and syllable frequencies), and morphology. Moreover, the role of higher level contextual information such as syntax and semantics should be considered more seriously.

More experimental data are needed to determine what kind of architectural modifications are required to adapt the current models to spontaneous continuous speech. These data should provide systematic comparisons of listeners' performances in two situations: word recognition from isolated or continuous read speech and from spontaneous continuous speech. But experimentally speaking, this kind of comparison is problematic with respect to the choice of stimuli and tasks. Perhaps brain imaging techniques will provide a useful tool for comparing word recognition in different speech modes.

1.7 Acquisition of Speech and Word Recognition: Another Challenge

According to one major psycholinguistic constraint on theory construction, the processing mechanisms postulated in adults should be tied to acquisition mechanisms in infants. In the case of speech and lexical processing, this constraint has been taken quite seriously. In constructing an adult-like word recognition device, infants have to solve the non-trivial problem of discovering the words of their native language without prior knowledge of these words. To learn the words, it would be useful for them to first acquire the phonemes of their native language. However, the reverse would also be important, that is, first acquiring words to learn the phonemes. This is known as a bootstrapping problem: what do infants learn first, phonemes or words? To complicate matters, isolated words are very infrequent in the maternal input (Aslin, 1993). Since infants do not possess the syntactic or pragmatic knowledge that adults exploit to segment continuous speech, the bootstrapping problem is even more acute in this situation. Infants have to find other sources of information to extract words from the continuous speech signal.

In this Section, we will present experimental data that shows the kind of information infants exploit to acquire a phonological representation of the words of their native language and to extract words from the continuous speech signal. We will then consider how the contemporary models of adult word recognition could integrate the conclusions drawn from these data.

1.7.1   Acquisition of Phonological Representations

Before the end of their first year of life, infants have acquired the phoneme inventory of their native language. Already around the age of 6 months infants perceive the prototypical vowels of their language differently than those of another language (Kuhl, Williams, Lacerda, Stevens & Lindblom, 1992). The internal structure of phonetic categories has been adapted to the native language. Language-specific consonants are acquired somewhat later at around 10-12 months when infants have lost their universal sensitivity to consonant phonetic categories (Werker & Tees, 1984). We can now ask whether infants must initially acquire a certain number of words for this learning to take place. At the age of 6 months, when infants show perceptual sensitivity to the native language vowels, it is rather unlikely that they would have acquired a first lexicon. Indeed, studies exploring the nature of the first lexical representations at around 11 months reveal that even at this age, infants' phonetic representation of words is still poorly specified (Hallé & Boysson-Bardies, 1996). This evidence shows that infants do not seem to possess a well-specified phonetic representation of their first lexical entries although they appear to have acquired the phoneme inventory of their native language. If this is the case, what kind of units do they actually use to represent these first words?

Recent data suggests that new-borns may use some kind of a 'universal' representational unit to process the incoming speech input (at least in isolated words): the syllable, or at least, a unit organized around a vocalic node (Bijeljac-Babic, Bertoncini & Mehler, 1993; Bertoncini, Floccia, Nazzi & Mehler, 1995; van Ooijen, Bertoncini, Sansavini & Mehler, in press). It is hypothesized that further exposure to the native language leads the infant to tune this 'universal' perceptual unit to a language-specific representation. This latter representation is based upon the rhythmic unit specific to the native language (or at least, specific to several broad classes of natural languages). For instance, infants exposed to syllable-timed languages such as Spanish or French would increase their perceptual sensitivity to the syllable, while Japanese-learning infants would focus on syllabic and subsyllabic units such as the mora. Further data are needed to determine when this sensitivity to language-specific units is acquired. The experimental data suggest that at birth infants already possess the perceptual capacity to represent (short) speech inputs in terms of linguistic units. It is this representation which might help them to both memorize and recognize lexical items.

1.7.2   Information Sources for Word Retrieval by Infants

As we just suggested above, infants face the particularly complex problem of extracting word from continuous speech since, unlike adults, they have no a priori knowledge of the possible words in the language. However, there are four sources of information available in natural languages that infants could exploit to discover words in the speech signal.

Distributional regularities. Generally, a phoneme string is more frequent in the speech input when it belongs to a word than when it does not. For instance, the string [eybi] that belongs to a word (*baby*) is more frequent than the string [tbey] that does not, but it can appear in two adjacent words (*sweet baby*). Brent & Cartwright (1996) have developed an algorithm that uses these distributional regularities to locate the boundaries of 40% of words in a corpus. Can infants make use of these regularities? Using the visual orienting conditioning paradigm, Goodsitt, Morgan & Kuhl (1993) showed that 7-month-old infants were able to make use of this information to recognize syllables in multisyllabic strings.

Phonotactic constraints. These constraints refer to the fact that certain phoneme combinations are forbidden within words. For instance, no English words contain the string [skb], although this string can be found between two words, as in *ask baby*. Some studies (Friederici & Wessels, 1993; Jusczyk, Friederici, Wessels, Svenkerud & Jusczyk, 1993) have explored whether, and at what age, infants were aware of these constraints. These authors presented 9-month-old American and Dutch infants with lists of English and Dutch words, differing only by their phonotactic properties. American infants preferred to listen to the English list rather than to the Dutch one, while the opposite was found for the Dutch infants. This indicates that by 9 months of age infants seem to have learned some of the phonotactic constraints of their native language which could help them to locate word boundaries in the continuous speech signal.

Typical word form. It is thought that the typical phonological form of words may be language-specific. For instance, a large proportion of English content words start with a stressed syllable (Cutler & Carter, 1987). Jusczyk, Cutler & Redanz (1993) have shown that 9-month-old American infants prefer to listen to a list of English words starting with a stressed syllable, such as *beaver*, rather than to words starting with an unstressed one, such as *abeam*. Thus at around 9 months of age English-learning infants can exploit this typical word form regularity to segment the speech stream into words.

Prosodic cues correlating to word boundaries. A subset of word boundaries, those corresponding to major prosodic group boundaries, can be derived from prosodic cues, especially by variations in rhythm and intonation. Using the non-nutritive sucking paradigm, Christophe, Dupoux, Bertoncini & Mehler (1994) have shown that new-borns' sensitivity to those prosodic markers correlated with word boundaries, suggesting that infants could use them to segment the continuous speech stream.

In summary, all four sources of information described above could be exploited by infants during language acquisition to discover words in the speech signal. Some do not require previous knowledge of words (distributional regularities and prosodic cues), whilst others can in principle be computed using only a small number of lexical items (phonotactic constraints and typical word form). Each of these sources of information alone is probably not sufficient to segments words and develop a lexicon, but taken together they could allow infants to discover enough words to bootstrap the process of lexicon acquisition.

1.7.3   Lexicon Acquisition and Adult Word Recognition Models

One important hypothesis holds that adults and infants possess language processing devices that share some basic architecture. From this perspective, we are led to seek the features that are common to adult word recognition models and to the mechanisms allowing the acquisition of the lexicon during infancy.

As we just saw, data on infant speech perception suggest that from birth infants rely on an 'universal' syllable-like unit to represent the incoming speech signal (at least in short speech stimuli). This representation could be related to the prelexical unit used in the process of lexical identification in adults. Indeed, linguistic representational units used by infants to represent speech inputs may well be similar to these used by adults. However, as we saw in Section 1.5.1 the adults' prelexical unit appears to differ according to the rhythmic properties of their native language (for example: the syllable in French and Spanish, the mora in Japanese). Thus, an important research objective will be to determine how and when the primary speech perception unit evolves from a universal representation into a language-specific one.

Concerning infants' use of distributional regularities to discover word boundaries in continuous speech, the relation of such mechanisms to adult processing may be slightly different. As we saw, adults can rely on their lexical, syntactic and semantic knowledge to identify words in sentences. Therefore, it is possible that they require less lower level information, such as that used by infants, to perform this task. However, recent studies have shown that adult listeners are sensitive to the phonotactic constraints in their native language (McQueen & Cox, 1995) and to the prosodic cues correlating to word boundaries (Banel & Bacri, 1994). What remains to be determined is whether and how these cues are used in on-line lexical processing. Finally, there seem to be no studies yet exploring whether the descriptions of the lexical activation and competition processes that fit with adult word recognition data are also appropriate for infants. If one agrees that infant and adult language processing devices share a common global architecture, then lexical access during language acquisition should be based on the same principles of lexical activation and competition, at least once a certain number of words have been acquired.

1.8 Conclusion

In this chapter, we have presented the reader with an overview of recent work on spoken word recognition. In so doing, we have identified some of the major theoretical options that psycholinguists have taken in developing word recognition models, and we have reviewed a selection of the experimental data available to constrain this modeling effort. We have identified an emerging consensus according to which listeners first compute an input representation, then activate a set of lexical candidates, and finally select the appropriate lexical entry from amongst this set. Although the findings supporting these general conclusions are quite conclusive, insufficient data exist at present to specify completely the more detailed processing mechanisms and representations. In fact, differentiating between the models remains extremely difficult for both methodological and theoretical reasons.

Many methodological challenges confront our efforts to test models of word recognition. Numerous independent variables (e.g., stimulus quality, word frequency, word length, word form class, uniqueness point, etc.) have been demonstrated to play a role in word identification and hence, must be controlled or manipulated experimentally. In contrast to independent variables, dependent variables are scarce. There are unfortunately far too few ways of collecting data that accurately reflect lexical processing. The use of on-line experimental techniques has provided psycholinguists with increased power to resolve the temporal properties of word recognition necessary. The first enthusiastic reaction to these techniques has given way to caution. The possibility that each task - or even worse, that as was suggested for fragment detection, even the same task - taps into different phases of lexical processing is receiving increasing attention. Indeed, individual tasks are now coming under closer scrutiny, and psycholinguists have begun to make more systematic comparisons to identify their relative strengths and weaknesses. We can expect that brain imaging techniques will make further contributions in this area by providing convergent data.

In addition to these methodological difficulties associated with devising experimental tests of these models, there are also theoretical problems with the models themselves. Although word recognition models have become increasingly well-specified in terms of the dimensions described above, in many instances they are still not worked out in sufficient enough detail to make clear predictions. For example, most current models cannot predict either the simultaneous effect upon word recognition performance of several independent variables, or the differences in these effects as a function of the experimental task.

There appear to be two complementary ways of dealing with this complexity. One potential solution is to restrict the experimental focus to certain aspects of models (like the dimensions outlined above) rather than to test full-blown models. This would translate, for example, into experimental attempts at determining whether or not there is inhibition between lexical candidates. Resolving issues like this would contribute to our understanding of word recognition by constraining the choices of models along these different dimensions. A more ambitious approach involves developing and implementing computational models which express the theoretical assumptions about several dimensions more directly. Such models should be able to make quantitative predictions that can be tested experimentally.

Clearly, these approaches are both worth pursuing and should be taken to make further progress in the two challenging areas just described. The first involves moving from the artificial stimuli used in laboratory experiments to continuous speech in more natural experimental situations. The second requires researchers to link two relatively distinct research areas, that of the adult listener and the child who is beginning to construct its lexical processing system. Research in both these areas will be confronted with the same problems of complexity and inaccessibility of the mental processes underlying language understanding. But it is precisely this challenge that makes psycholinguistic problems so exciting!

References

Aslin, R.N. (1993). Segmentation of fluent speech into words: Learning and the role of maternal input. In B. de Boysson-Bardies, S. de Schonen, P. Jusczyk, P. MacNeilage & J. Morton (eds.), Developmental Neurocognition: Speech and Face Processing in the First Year of Life. Dordrecht: Klüwer.

Banel, M.H. & Bacri, N. (1994). On the metrical patterns and lexical parsing in French. *Speech Communication, 15*, 115-126.

Bard, E.G., Shillcock, R.C. & Altmann, G.T.M. (1988). The recognition of words after their acoustic offsets: Effect of subsequent context. *Perception and Psychophysics, 44*, 395-408.

Bertoncini, J., Floccia, C., Nazzi, T. & Mehler, J. (1995). Morae and syllables: Rhythmical basis of speech representations in neonates. *Language and Speech, 38*, 311-329.

Bijeljac-Babic, R., Bertoncini, J. & Mehler, J. (1993). How do four-day-old infants categorize multisyllabic utterances? *Developmental Psychology, 29*, 711-721.

Bradley, D.C. & Forster, K.I. (1987). A reader's view of listening. *Cognition, 25*, 103-134.

Bradley D.C., Sànchez-Casas R.M. & Garcìa-Albea J.E. (1993). The status of the syllable in the perception of Spanish and English. *Language and Cognitive Processes, 8*, 197-233.

Brent, M.R. & Cartwright, T.A. (1996). Distributional regularity and phonotactic constraints are useful for segmentation. *Cognition, 61*, 93-125.

Brown, G. (1977). *Listening to spoken English*. London: Longman.

Christophe, A., Dupoux, E., Bertoncini, J. & Mehler, J. (1994). Do infants perceive word boundaries ? An empirical study of the bootstrapping of lexical acquisition. *Journal of the Acoustical Society of America, 95*, 1570-1580.

Church, K. (1987). Phonological parsing and lexical retrieval. *Cognition, 25(1-2)*, 53-69.

Cole, R.A. & Jakimik, J. (1980). A model of speech perception. In R.A. Cole (ed.), *Perception and production of fluent speech* . Hillsdale, NJ: Lawrence Erlbaum.

Connine, C.M., Blasko, D.M. & Titone, D.A. (1993). Do the beginning of words have a special status in auditory word recognition? *Journal of Memory and Language, 32,* 193–210.

Crystal, D. & Davy, D. (1969). *Investigating English style.* London: Longman.

Cutler, A. & Butterfield, S. (1992). Rhythmic cues to speech segmentation: Evidence from juncture misperception. *Journal of Memory and Language, 31,* 218-236.

Cutler, A. & Carter, D.M. (1987). The predominance of strong initial syllables in English vocabulary. *Computer Speech and Language, 2,* 133-142.

Cutler, A., van Ooijen, B., Norris, D. & Sanchez-Casas, R. (1996). Speeded detection of vowels: A cross-linguistic study. *Perception & Psychophysics , 58,* 807-822.

Cutler A., Mehler J., Norris D. & Segui J. (1986). The syllable's differing role in the segmentation of French and English. *Journal of Memory and Language, 25,* 385-400.

Cutler, A. & Norris, D.G. (1985). Juncture detection. *Linguistics, 23,* 689-706.

Cutler, A. & Norris, D.G. (1988). The role of strong syllables in segmentation for lexical access. *Journal of Experimental Psychology: Human Perception and Performance, 14,* 113–121.

Cutler, A. & Otake, T. (1994). Mora of phoneme? Further evidence for language-specific listening. *Journal of Memory and Language, 33,* 824-844.

Dominguez, A., Cuetos, F. & De Vega, M. (1992). Differential effects of syllabic frequency: Dependence of the type of task and stimulus characteristics. *Estudios de Psicologia, 50,* 5-31.

Dumay, N. & Radeau, M. (1997). Rime and syllabic effects in phonological priming between French spoken words. Poster presented at *the 5th European Conference on Speech Communication and Technology*, Rhodes, Greece, 22-25 September.

Forster, K.I. (1976). Accessing the mental lexicon. In R.J. Wales & E. Walker (eds.), *New Approaches to Language Mechanisms.* Amsterdam: North Holland.

Frauenfelder, U.H. (1996). Computational models of spoken word recognition. In A. Dijkstra & K. de Smedt (eds.), *Computational psycholinguistics: Symbolic and subsymbolic models of language processing.* London: Harvester Press.

Frauenfelder, U.H., Content, A. & Scholten, M. (in preparation). Activation and deactivation of lexical candidates in spoken word recognition.

Frauenfelder, U.H. & Floccia, C. (in preparation). Syllable frequency effects in shadowing.

Frauenfelder, U.H. & Henstra, J. (1988). Activation and deactivation of phonological representations. *Proceedings of the 4th International Phonology Congress, Krems, Austria.*

Frauenfelder, U.H. & Kearns, R. (1997). Sequence detection. In F. Grosjean & U.H. Frauenfelder (eds.), *A guide to spoken word recognition paradigms.* East Sussex, UK: Psychology Press

Frauenfelder, U.H. & Peeters, G. (1990). On lexical segmentation in TRACE: An exercise in simulation. In G.T.M. Altmann (ed.), *Cognitive models of speech processing: Psycholinguistic and computational perspectives.* Cambridge, MA: MIT Press.

Frauenfelder, U.H. & Peeters, G. (in press). Simulating the time-course of spoken word recognition: An analysis of lexical competition in TRACE.

Frauenfelder, U.H., Seguí, J. & Dijkstra, T. (1990). Lexical effects in phonemic processing: Facilitatory or inhibitory? *Journal of Experimental Psychology: Human Perception and Performance, 16,* 77–91.

Frazier, L. (1987). Structure in auditory word recognition. *Cognition, 25(1-2),* 157-187.

Friederici, A.D. & Wessels, J.M.I. (1993). Phonotactic knowledge of word boundaries and its use in infant speech perception. *Perception and Psychophysics, 54,* 287-295.

Goldinger, S.D., Luce, P.A. & Pisoni, D.B. (1989). Priming lexical neighbors of spoken words: Effects of competition and inhibition. *Journal of Memory and Language, 28,* 501-518.

Goldinger, S.D., Luce, P.A., Pisoni, D.B. & Marcario, J.K. (1992). Form-based priming in spoken word recognition: The roles of competition and bias. *Journal of Experimental Psychology: Learning, Memory and Cognition, 18,* 1211-1238.

Goldman, J.P., Content, A. & Frauenfelder, U.H. (1996). Comparaison des structures syllabiques en français et en anglais. *Actes des XXIe Journées d'Etude sur la Parole, Avignon, 10-14 juin 1996,* 119-122.

Goodsitt, J.V., Morgan, J.L. & Kuhl, P.K. (1993). Perceptual strategies in prelingual speech segmentation. *Journal of Child Language, 20,* 229-252.

Gow, D.W. & Gordon, P.C. (1995). Lexical and prelexical influences on word segmentation: Evidence from priming. *Journal of Experimental Psychology: Human Perception and Performance, 21,* 344-359.

Grosjean, F. (1980). Spoken word recognition processes and the gating paradigm. *Perception and Psychophysics, 28*, 267-283.

Grosjean, F. (1985). The recognition of words after their acoustic offset: Evidence and implications. *Perception and Psychophysics, 38*, 299-310.

Grosjean, F. & Gee, J.P. (1987). Prosodic structure and spoken word recognition. *Cognition, 25*, 135-155.

Hallé, P. & de Boysson-Bardies, B. (1996). The format of representation of recognized words in infants' early receptive lexicon. *Infant Behavior and Development, 19*, 463-481.

Huggins, A.W.F. (1967). Distortion of the temporal pattern of speech by syllable tied alternation. *Language and Speech, 10*, 133-140.

Jakimik, J. (1979). *The interaction of sound and knowledge in word recognition from fluent speech.* Unpublished doctoral dissertation, CMU.

Johns-Lewis, C. (1986). Prosodic differentiation of discourse modes. In C. Johns-Lewis (ed.), *Intonation and Discourse* . London: Croom Helm.

Jusczyk, P.W., Cutler, A. & Redanz, N.J. (1993). Infants' preference for the predominant stress patterns of English words. *Child Development, 64*, 675-687.

Jusczyk, P.W., Friederici, A., Wessels, J., Svenkerud, V. & Jusczyk, A.M. (1993). Infant's sensitivity to the sound patterns of native language words. *Journal of Memory and Language, 32*, 402-420.

Klatt, D.H. (1980). Speech perception: A model of acoustic-phonetic analysis and lexical access. In Cole, R.A. (ed.), *Perception and Production of Fluent Speech* . Hillsdale, NJ: Lawrence Erlbaum.

Kolinsky, R. (in press). Spoken word recognition: A stage-processing approach to language differences. *European Journal of Cognitive Psychology.*

Kolinsky, R. & Morais, J. (1993). Intermediate representations in spoken word recognition: A cross-linguistic study of word illusions. *Proceedings of the 1993 Eurospeech Conference* (pp. 731-734), Berlin, Germany.

Kolinsky, R. & Morais, J. (1997). Migrations in speech recognition. In F. Grosjean & U.H. Frauenfelder (eds.), *A guide to spoken word recognition paradigms.* East Sussex, UK: Psychology Press.

Kolinsky, R., Morais, J. & Cluytens, M. (1995). Intermediate representations in spoken word recognition: Evidence from word illusions. *Journal of Memory and Language, 34*, 19-40.

Kuhl, P.K., Williams, K.A., Lacerda, F., Stevens K.N. & Lindblom, B. (1992). Linguistic experience alters phonetic perception in infants by 6 months of age. *Science, 255*, 606-608.

Labov, W. (1972). *Sociolinguistic Patterns*. Philadelphia, PA: University of Pennsylvania Press.

Lahiri, A. & Marslen-Wilson, W.D. (1991). The mental representation of lexical form: A phonological approach to the recognition lexicon. *Cognition, 38*, 245-294.

Levelt, W.J.M. & Wheeldon, L. (1994). Do speakers have access to a mental syllabary? *Cognition, 50*, 239-269.

Levin, H., Schaffer, C.A. & Snow, C. (1982). The prosodic and paralinguistic features of reading and telling stories. *Language and Speech, 25*, 43-54.

Luce, P.A. (1986). Neighborhoods of words in the mental lexicon. *Research on speech perception technical report No. 6*, Indiana University, Bloomington.

Luce, P.A., Pisoni, D.B. & Goldinger, S.D. (1990). Similarity neighborhoods of spoken words. In G.T.M. Altmann (ed.), *Cognitive models of speech processing: Psycholinguistic and computational perspectives* . Cambridge, MA: MIT Press.

Marslen-Wilson, W.D. (1984). Function and process in spoken word recognition. In H. Bouma & D.G. Bouwhuis (eds.), *Attention and Performance X: Control of Language Processes*, Hillsdale, NJ: Lawrence Erlbaum.

Marslen-Wilson, W.D. (1985). Speech shadowing and speech comprehension. *Speech Communication, 4*, 55-73

Marslen-Wilson, W.D. (1987). Functional parallelism in spoken word-recognition. *Cognition, 25*, 71-102.

Marslen-Wilson, W.D. (1990). Activation, competition and frequency in lexical access. In G.T.M. Altmann (ed.), *Cognitive models of speech processing: Psycholinguistic and computational perspectives* . Cambridge, MA: MIT Press.

Marslen-Wilson, W.D., Moss, H.E. & van Halen, S. (1996). Perceptual distance and competition in lexical access. *Journal of Experimental Psychology: Human Perception and Performance, 22, 6*, 1376-1392..

Marslen-Wilson, W.D. & Warren, P. (1994). Levels of perceptual representation and process in lexical access: Words, phonemes and features. *Psychological Review, 101*, 653-675.

Marslen-Wilson, W.D. & Welsh, A. (1978). Processing interactions and lexical access during word recognition in continuous speech. *Cognitive Psychology, 10*, 29-63.

Marslen-Wilson, W. D. & Zwitserlood, P. (1989). Accessing spoken words: The importance of word onsets. *Journal of Experimental Psychology: Human Perception and Performance, 15, 3*, 576–585.

Massaro, D.W. (1989). Testing between the TRACE model and the fuzzy logical model of speech perception. *Cognitive Psychology, 21*, 398-421.

Massaro, D.W. & Oden, G.C. (1980). Speech perception: A framework for research and theory. In N.J. Lass (ed.), *Speech and Language: Advances in Basic Research and Practice*. New York: Academic Press.

McClelland, J.L (1991). Stochastic interactive processes and the effects of context upon perception. *Cognitive Psychology, 23*, 1-44.

McClelland, J.L. & Elman, J.L. (1986). The TRACE model of speech perception. *Cognitive Psychology, 18*, 1-86.

McQueen, J.M., Cutler, A., Briscoe, T. & Norris, D. (1995). Models of continuous speech recognition and the contents of the vocabulary. *Language and Cognitive Processes, 10*, 309-331.

McQueen, J.M. & Cox, E. (1995). The use of phonotactic constraints in the segmentation of Dutch. In J.M. Pardo et al. (eds.), Proceedings of Eurospeech '95, Madrid: ESCA.

McQueen, J.M., Norris, D. & Cutler, A. (1994). Competition in spoken word recognition: Spotting words in other words. *Journal of Experimental Psychology: Learning, Memory and Cognition, 20*, 621-638.

Mehler, J. (1981). The role of syllables in speech processing. Infant and adult data. *Philosophical Transactions of the Royal Society London, B 295*, 333-352.

Mehler J., Dommergues J.Y., Frauenfelder U. & Segui J. (1981). The syllable's role in speech segmentation. *Journal of Verbal Learning and Verbal Behavior, 20*, 298-305.

Metha, G & Cutler, A, (1988). Detection of target phonemes in speech and read speech. *Language & Speech, 31, 2*,135-156.

Meunier, C., Content, A., Frauenfelder, U. & Kearns R. (1997). The locus of the syllable effect: Prelexical or lexical? *Proceedings of the 5th European Conference on Speech Communication and Technology*, Rhodes, Greece, 22-25 September.

Milroy, L. (1980). *Language and Social Networks*. Oxford: Blackwell.

Morais J., Content A., Cary L., Mehler J. & Segui J. (1989). Syllabic segmentation and literacy. *Language and Cognitive Processes, 4*, 57-67.

Morais, J., Kolinsky, R. & Nakamura, M. (1996). The psychological reality of speech units in Japanese. In T. Otake & A. Cutler (eds.), *Phonological Structure and Language Processing: Cross-Linguistic Studies*. Berlin: Mouton de Gruyter.

Morton, J. (1969). Interaction of information in word recognition. *Psychological Review, 76*, 165-178.

Nakatani, L.H. & Schaffer, J.A. (1978). Hearing "words" without words: Prosodic cues for word perception. *Journal of the Acoustical Society of America, 63,* 234-245.

Norris, D. (1994). SHORTLIST: A connectionist model of continuous speech recognition. *Cognition, 52,* 189-234.

Norris, D., McQueen, J.M. & Cutler, A. (1995). Competition and segmentation in spoken word recognition. *Journal of Experimental Psychology: Learning, Memory and Cognition, 21,* 1209-1228.

Pisoni, D.B. & Luce, P.A. (1987). Acoustic-phonetic representations in word recognition. *Cognition, 25,* 21-52.

Radeau, M. & Morais, J. (1990). The uniqueness point effect in the shadowing of spoken words. *Speech Communication, 9,* 155–164.

Radeau, M., Morais, J. & Segui, J. (1994). The effect of overlap position in phonological priming between spoken words. *Proceedings of 1994 International Conference on Spoken Language Processing, vol. 3,* pp. 1419-1422. Yokohama, Japan: The Acoustical Society of Japan.

Radeau, M., Morais, J. & Segui., J. (1995). Phonological priming between monosyllabic spoken words. *Journal of Experimental Psychology: Human Perception and Performance, 21,* 1297-1311.

Radeau, M., Mousty, P. & Bertelson, P. (1989). The effect of the uniqueness point in spoken word recognition. *Psychological Research, 51,* 123–128.

Samuel, A. G. (1989). Insights from a failure of selective adaptation: Syllable-initial and syllable-final consonants are different. *Perception and Psychophysics, 45,* 485-493.

Sebastiàn-Gallés N., Dupoux E., Segui J. & Mehler J. (1992). Contrasting syllabic effects in Catalan and Spanish. *Journal of Memory and Language, 31,* 18-32.

Segui, J., Dupoux, E. & Mehler, J. (1990). The role of the syllable in speech segmentation, phoneme identification and lexical access. In G.T.M. Altmann (ed.), *Cognitive Models of Speech Processing: Psycholinguistic and Computational Perspectives.* Cambridge, MA: MIT Press.

Shillcock, R. (1990). Lexical hypotheses in continuous speech. In G.T.M. Altmann (ed.), *Cognitive Models of Speech Processing: Psycholinguistic and Computational Perspectives.* Cambridge, MA: MIT Press.

Slowiaczek, L.M. & Hamburger, M.B. (1992). Prelexical facilitation and lexical interference in auditory word recognition. *Journal of Experimental Psychology: Learning, Memory and Cognition, 18,* 1239-1250.

Slowiaczek, L.M. & Hamburger, M.B. (1993). Phonological priming in spoken word recognition is not strategic. Paper presented at *the 34th annual meeting of the Psychonomic Society*, Washington, DC.

Swinney, D.A. (1979). Lexical access during sentence comprehension: (Re)consideration of context effects. *Journal of Verbal Learning and Verbal Behavior, 18*, 645–660.

Tabossi, P. (1997). Cross-modal priming. In F. Grosjean & U.H. Frauenfelder (eds.), *A guide to spoken word recognition paradigms*. East Sussex, UK: Psychology Press.

Tyler, L.K. & Wessels, J. (1983). Quantifying contextual contributions to word-recognition processes. *Perception and Psychophysics, 34*, 409-420.

van Ooijen, B., Bertoncini, J., Sansavini, A. & Mehler, J. (in press). Do weak syllables count for newborns? *Journal of the Acoustical Society of America*.

Vroomen, J. & de Gelder, B. (1995). Metrical segmentation and lexical inhibition in spoken word recognition. *Journal of Experimental Psychology: Human Perception and Performance, 21*, 98-108.

Werker, J.F. & Tees, R.C. (1984). Cross-language speech perception: Evidence for perceptual reorganization during the first year of life. *Infant Behavior and Development, 7*, 49-63.

Zhou, X. & Marslen-Wilson, W. (1994). Words, morphemes and syllables in the Chinese mental lexicon. Special Issue: Morphological Structure, Lexical Representations and Lexical Access. *Language and Cognitive Processes, 9(3)*, 393-422.

Zwitserlood, P. (1989). The locus of the effects of sentential-semantic context in spoken-word processing. *Cognition, 32*, 25-64.

Zwitserlood P., Schriefers H., Lahiri A. & van Donselaar W. (1993). The role of syllables in the perception of spoken Dutch. *Journal of Experimental Psychology: Learning, Memory and Cognition, 19*, 260-271.

Chapter 2

Prosodic Structure and Word Recognition

Anne Cutler

2.1 Introduction

Prosodic structure is a dimension which belongs to spoken language. Although a good writer may aim for, say, rhythmic effects in prose, these rely upon the reader's ability to 'hear' them 'in the mind's ear', i.e. mentally to convert the written prose to a spoken form. As this chapter will outline, listeners make extensive and varied use of prosodic information in recognizing spoken utterances. However, because prosody is a property of spoken language, and because there has (purely for reasons of empirical tractability) been much less psycholinguistic research on spoken than on written language, the study of prosody's role in recognition is relatively underdeveloped. A recent comprehensive literature review in this area, covering the role of prosody in the comprehension of syntactic and discourse structure as well as in the recognition of spoken words (Cutler, Dahan & van Donselaar, 1997), lists some three hundred references, but this is a tiny amount compared with, for instance, the literature on visual word recognition, even that based on just one laboratory task (lexical decision). Moreover, as Cutler et al. conclude, the literature is very unbalanced: some topics have been repeatedly examined, in studies differing only in minor details, while other topics have been ignored completely. This is also true of research in different languages; as in all areas of psycholinguistics, most research has been conducted in English, but among other languages some have received considerable research attention, some none at all. Particularly relevant here is the comparison between German and Dutch: the prosodic structure of these two languages is very similar, and has been comprehensively described for both languages in the phonetic literature, but although the psycholinguistic literature now contains a quite substantial number of experimental studies of the processing of Dutch prosody, there have been remarkably few comparable studies in German.

The present chapter concentrates on how prosodic structure can contribute to the recognition of words in spoken utterances. By prosodic structure is meant (as is generally assumed in phonetics and psycholinguistics) the linguistic structure expressed in the suprasegmental properties of utterances. Note that there are other definitions of prosody in active use in neighboring disciplines; thus to engineers and other applied speech researchers, the term refers to suprasegmental properties themselves - the pitch, tempo, loudness and timing patterns of speech; to phonologists, it means the abstract organization determining the grouping and relative salience of phonological units; to students of poetry it describes the norms of verse metrics. Although these definitions are all related (to an extent that researchers can sometimes unwittingly talk at cross purposes when they fail to realize that colleagues may be operating with a different definition), they carry different implications for what falls within the realm of research on prosody. The scope of this chapter will be restricted to the processing of linguistic structure (and only those elements of linguistic structure directly relevant to word identification) which is conveyed by the suprasegmental structure of an utterance.

All the evidence to be surveyed comes from experimental studies of language processing in psycholinguistic laboratories. The usual issues of experimental control of course arise; thus where some linguistically relevant structure is in fact realized via multiple sources of information in the signal, it is sometimes necessary to conduct separate studies to tease out the individual contributions, and to take into consideration parallel evidence which may itself be either non-linguistic or not directly concerned with suprasegmentals. For instance, as later Sections will make clear, the processing of lexical stress in English (which has both segmental and suprasegmental correlates in the form of words) cannot be understood without consideration of evidence on segmental processing, the processing of rhythm, and the acoustic distribution of suprasegmental features. Similar situations arise with other topics in the area; at bottom, this is due to the very nature of prosodic information, namely that it is not in some way overlaid upon the signal, but is an intrinsic determinant of every aspect of the spoken form.

Prosody's role in recognizing words in spoken utterances is, similarly, multifaceted. On the one hand, there are several ways in which prosodic structure at the sentence level indirectly but importantly facilitates word recognition. On the other hand, prosodic information at the word level can also be directly involved in lexical processing. These two topics provide the major divisions to follow.

2.2 Sentence Prosody

At the sentence level, prosodic structure comprises an overall utterance rhythm, the various ways in which words are grouped together, and the patterns of relative prominence of the sentence constituents. Listeners can directly and indirectly derive information about syntactic relationships and discourse structure from the sentence prosody (Cutler et al., 1997); but they can also draw upon sentence prosody in the process of recognizing words. Prominence patterns, for example, can render individual words easier or harder to recognize; rhythmic structure can provide a framework within which the boundaries between individual words can be ascertained; and where a higher-level boundary is encoded in the prosodic structure it will also correspond to a word boundary.

Rhythm and Grouping

Most spoken utterances are more or less continuous - obstruent consonants may cause brief discontinuities in the signal, but boundaries between phonetic segments and lexical elements do not. Nonetheless, listeners must effectively impose discontinuity on the signal, by identifying the individual words of which the utterance is composed. Listeners cannot (usually) know in advance what speakers will say; they can only understand what is said by recognizing the words of which utterances are made up, and to do that they have to work out which portions of the speech input belong to which words. The continuity of the speech signal complicates matters by affording no explicit cues to aid this segmentation process.

Syntactic phrase boundaries, however, often have correlates in the prosodic structure, and listeners can extract boundary information from this structure, as is shown by studies in which listeners are presented with utterances from which segmental information has been removed (e.g., by filtering or spectrally manipulating the speech); judgments of the boundary locations in such input are quite accurate (Collier & Hart, 1975; de Rooij, 1976; de Pijper & Sandeman, 1994). Listeners can base such judgments most efficiently on pitch movements (e.g., Streeter, 1978; Beach, 1991; Wightman, Shattuck-Hufnagel, Ostendorf & Price, 1992) or on durational information (e.g., Lehiste, Olive & Streeter, 1976; Nooteboom, Brokx & de Rooij, 1978; Scott, 1982). Where listeners use such cues to postulate the presence of a syntactic boundary, they are by implication postulating the presence of a word boundary as well. Although the derivation of word-boundary cues from syntactic- boundary perception has not been explicitly addressed in experiments on word recognition, some indirect evidence summarized below does suggest that it is a real option for listeners.

Apart from this option of eliciting word-boundary information via the computation of syntactic boundaries, however, listeners can - and do - also derive word-boundary information by exploiting their knowledge of the rhythmic structure of their native language. Rhythm is a fundamental property of language (and much other human behavior), but it is not the same in every language; and thus the way rhythm relates to word boundaries differs across languages. In English, for example, rhythm is stress-based. It is easy to tell this by considering the forms of English poetry - they are all defined by the number and location of stress beats (hexameter, trochee, etc.). Stress beats in English verse can only fall on strong syllables - syllables containing a full (unreduced) vowel. Thus *JACK and JILL went UP the HILL* has beats on *Jack, Jill, up, hill. Went* is also a possible beat location - *JACK and JILL, they WENT upHILL* could be spoken with the same rhythm. But *and* and *the* would normally be spoken as weak syllables, with reduced vowels, therefore they cannot bear stress beats - *JACKson AND Jill WENT inLAND*, or *JACK and JILL climbed THE big HILL* are deeply unpleasant to the English ear.

There is abundant experimental evidence that English listeners make use of this stress-based rhythm to derive word-boundary information, namely by segmenting speech at the onset of strong syllables (i.e. those syllables with full vowels that can potentially be stressed). For example, when English-speakers make slips of the ear which involve misperception of word boundaries, they tend most often to insert boundaries before strong syllables (e.g., hearing *by loose analogy* as *by Luce and Allergy*) or delete boundaries before weak syllables (e.g., hearing *how big is it?* as *how bigoted?*; Cutler & Butterfield, 1992). Similarly, English listeners find word-spotting - detecting a real word embedded in a spoken nonsense sequence - hard if the word is spread over two strong syllables (e.g., *mint* in [m ntef]), but it is easier for them to detect a word spread over a strong and a following weak syllable (e.g., *mint* in [m nt f]; Cutler & Norris, 1988). Cutler and Norris argued that this difference arises because listeners divide [m ntef] at the onset of its second strong syllable, so that to detect the embedded word they must recombine speech material across a segmentation point; [m nt f], in contrast, offers no obstacles to embedded- word detection, as it is simply not divided, because the second syllable is weak.

Why should English listeners exploit stress rhythm in this way? Statistical studies of the English vocabulary and of distributional patterns in spontaneous speech (Cutler & Carter, 1987) have shown that a strategy of segmenting English at strong syllable onsets is in fact an extremely useful way of locating word onsets - most lexical words (nouns, verbs, adjectives) do indeed being with strong syllables. Distributional patterns in the Dutch vocabulary are similar to those of English - indeed, even more Dutch words than English words have a full vowel in the first syllable (van Heuven & Hagman, 1988; Schreuder & Baayen, 1994). Experiments modelled on those both of Cutler and Norris (1988) and Cutler and Butterfield (1992) have produced similar results in Dutch (Vroomen, van Zon & de Gelder, 1996). Thus the exploitation of stress rhythm seems to be a strategy which listeners use because it offers an efficient (partial) solution to the problem raised by the difficulty of location word boundaries in continuous speech. (German, like Dutch, has a very high proportion of words with full vowel in the first syllable [J. Bölte, personal communication], but relevant experimental evidence has not as yet been collected.)

Such a solution is, however, not open to speakers of languages without stress rhythm. French, for example, does not exhibit the type of contrast between strong and weak syllables observed in the Germanic languages. Experimental studies of the processing of spoken French suggest that listeners can draw on a process of segmentation of the input into syllable-sized units; thus in the words *palace* and *palmier* (which begin with the same three phonemes) the first two phonemes function as the initial unit in *pa-lace*, the first three in *pal-mier*. A wide variety of experimental tasks, involving prelexical processing, lexical processing, and representation of words in memory, produce results showing how important this procedure is in the recognition of French (Mehler, Dommergues, Frauenfelder & Segui, 1981; Segui, Frauenfelder & Mehler, 1981; Cutler, Mehler, Norris & Segui, 1986; Dupoux & Mehler, 1990; Kolinsky, Morais & Cluytens, 1995; Pallier, Sebastián-Gallés, Felguera, Christophe & Mehler, 1993; Peretz, Lussier & Béland, 1996).

Although the use of stress-based rhythm in English and the use of syllabic segmentation in French might seem to be quite different solutions to the segmentation problem in continuous speech, they can also be viewed as similar: like stress in English, the syllable in French is the basis of rhythmic structure. This symmetry prompted the hypothesis (see, e.g., Cutler, Mehler, Norris & Segui, 1992) that listeners might in fact adopt a universally applicable solution to the segmentation problem, in that to solve it they exploit whatever rhythmic structure happens to characterize their language. This implies that if a language has a rhythmic structure based on some phonological construct other than stress or the syllable, it should be possible to find evidence for exploitation of such rhythmic structure in speech segmentation. Japanese is such a language; its rhythm is described in terms of a sub-syllabic unit, the mora (e.g., the word *tanshi* has three morae: *ta-n-shi*). Otake, Hatano, Cutler and Mehler (1993), Cutler and Otake (1994), and Otake, Hatano and Yoneyama (1996) conducted studies of prelexical processing by Japanese listeners, and indeed found consistent evidence favoring mora-based segmentation.

It is not the rhythmic structure of the input itself which produces the appropriate segmentation procedure; if this were so, then any listener could listen to any language and effectively 'hear' the word boundaries. Experience tells us that this certainly does not happen. Instead, it appears that listeners have developed segmentation procedures on the basis of experience with their native language, and that they do not command the appropriate procedures for other languages. Thus English listeners show no evidence of syllabic segmentation with French input (Cutler et al., 1986), and neither do Japanese listeners (Otake et al., 1996); English listeners likewise show no evidence of mora-based segmentation of Japanese input (Otake et al., 1993; Cutler & Otake, 1994), and nor do French listeners (Otake et al., 1993) or Dutch listeners (Kakehi, Kato & Kashino, 1996). Moreover, listeners may apply their native language-specific procedures to foreign language input, even in cases where the procedures may not operate efficiently at all. Thus French listeners apply syllabic segmentation to English words such as *palace* and *palpitate* where English listeners do not (Cutler et al., 1986); likewise, they apply syllabic segmentation to Japanese input (e.g., preferring to segment *tanshi* as *tan-shi*; Otake et al., 1993); and Japanese listeners apply moraic segmentation where possible to English input (e.g., showing facilitated processing of the syllable-final nasal in words like *incur*, where English listeners do not; Cutler & Otake, 1994) and to French and Spanish input (e.g., responding equally rapidly to a consonant-vowel target such as *pa-* in an open and in a closed syllable; Otake et al., 1996).

Finally, it should be pointed out that the exploitation of different levels of linguistic structure in segmentation is not determined by the simple availability of these types of structure in a language. Every concept which has proved relevant in describing these cross-linguistic differences in segmentation - stress, syllable, mora - is a phonological construct which can in principle be applied to any language. It is the role of the relevant units in the rhythm of the language via which the units attain a role in segmentation. And even though the concept stress, for instance, is dependent on the concept syllable (stressed/unstressed are properties of syllables, not of parts of syllables), this does not accord the syllable the same role in a stress-rhythm language as it has in a syllable-rhythm language. Cutler et al. (1986) failure to find syllabic segmentation by English listeners has been replicated many times (Bradley, Sánchez-Casas & García-Albea, 1993; Cutler, Norris & Williams, 1987; Kearns, 1994). In German, a study by Höhle and Schriefers (1995) found response patterns consistent with syllabic segmentation only for finally-stressed words with open initial syllables (i.e. *ku-* was detected more rapidly that *kul-* in *Kulanz*). In Dutch, Zwitserlood, Schriefers, Lahiri and van Donselaar (1993) found evidence of syllabic segmentation, but a comparable study by Vroomen and de Gelder (1994) found no such effects. Cutler (1997) presented Dutch listeners with the easily-syllabified French materials of Mehler et al. (1981); like the English listeners tested by Cutler et al. (1986), they did not show the response pattern shown by French listeners, although like Höhle and Schriefers' German subjects, they did respond faster to the syllabic targets in words with an open initial syllable (i.e. *pa-* was detected more rapidly than *pal-* in *palace*). Note that in the citation pronunciation of French words, accent falls on the final syllable, so that in both these cases the result is consistent with segmentation at the onset of a stressed syllable, the default segmentation in stress-rhythm languages.

Note that the stress rhythm of English, Dutch or German is not itself determined by word-boundary location; stress in these languages can occur at differing positions in the word. But in some languages stress is fixed, i.e. it must always fall at the same word-internal position. Fixed-stress languages include, for example, Finnish, in which the first syllable of every word is stressed, or Polish, in which stress always falls on the penultimate syllable. It might be imagined that fixed stress could provide an excellent cue to word-boundary location; but in fact, rather paradoxically, it is possible that fewer explicit acoustic correlates of stress may be available for listeners' use in fixed-stress languages than in free-stress languages. This is because the explicit realization of stress may be unnecessary when its location is fully predictable. Suomi, McQueen and Cutler (1997) carried out a segmentation experiment in Finnish, using the same word-spotting task as in the experiment by Cutler and Norris (1988) described above; the focus of their study was in fact not stress but vowel harmony (which in Finnish requires that two vowels in the same word must be drawn from compatible classes). The listeners in Suomi et al.'s study heard bisyllabic words (e.g., *palo*) with preceding or following CV contexts (*kupalo*, *paloku*); all of the resulting trisyllabic nonsense items were spoken with the unmarked prosodic pattern for trisyllabic words, traditionally described as stress on the initial syllable. The principal result of Suomi et al.'s study was that vowel harmony functioned as a segmentation cue: words preceded by disharmonious contexts (syllables containing a vowel from a class incompatible with the vowels of the word) were detected more rapidly than words preceded by harmonious contexts. Stress was relevant for the interpretation of a control experiment, however, in which the words were excised from their contexts and presented to listeners in a lexical decision task; for the words from which preceding contexts had been removed, this resulted in loss of the syllable which had nominally been stressed, and these words might therefore have been expected to be prosodically abnormal compared to those from following contexts. Listeners' responses showed no effect attributable to abnormality of this kind, however; if anything, words like *palo* from *kupalo* were recognized slightly faster than words like *palo* from *paloku*. Suomi et al. suggested that the so-called initial stress of Finnish is actually a gradual drop in fundamental frequency and amplitude across the word, and that what is important for its correct realization is simply the relationship between consecutive syllables; this relationship would be unaffected by removal of preceding or following syllables.

French is another language with a consistent prosodic pattern which could provide information about some word boundaries. French does not have English-like stress, but accent falls on the final syllable of rhythmic groups, and the right boundary of a rhythmic group is always also the right boundary of a word. French listeners appear to be able to use this regularity to speed detection of a target syllable located at a rhythmic group boundary in comparison to the same syllable at another location (Dahan, 1996); the rhythmic structure thus indirectly facilitates lexical processing..

Prosodic structure, in the form of language rhythm, thus helps listeners in a number of ways to perform lexical segmentation efficiently. The characteristic rhythm of a language is undoubtedly real; it plays a role not only in lexical segmentation and other forms of processing, but most obviously in preferred poetic metres. However, it does not provide direct signals of word boundary location, but rather assists segmentation indirectly, establishing a framework within which listeners can hypothesize probable word boundary locations, or allowing lexical segmentation to proceed by inference from segmentation into higher-level constituents.

Early investigations of speech rhythm often assumed that rhythm should be directly encoded as regularity of timing of units in the speech signal; this line of research ended in rejection of the direct-encoding assumption by phonetic researchers (see Cutler, 1991, for a review). The possibility that rhythmic regularity existed and could be exploited by listeners was also addressed in psycholinguistic studies. Thus

Shields, McHugh and Martin (1974) presented listeners in a phoneme-detection study with nonsense words embedded in real sentences, and found that listeners detected the initial phoneme of the nonsense word more rapidly when the first (target-bearing) syllable was stressed rather than unstressed. However, the effect disappeared when the nonsense word was embedded in a string of other nonsense words, suggesting that the facilitation was not due simply to acoustic advantage. The authors concluded that the timing of speech events is predictable from temporal redundancy in the signal, and listeners can use the temporal structure to predict upcoming stresses.

Other studies supported this predictive view, by showing that disrupting the temporal structure impairs performance on many perceptual tasks. Martin (1979), for example, found that either lengthening or shortening a single vowel could cause a perceptible momentary alteration in the tempo of a spoken sentence, and increase listeners' phoneme-detection response times. Meltzer, Martin, Mills, Imhoff and Zohar (1976) found that phoneme targets which were slightly displaced from their position in normal speech (by deleting a short portion of the signal immediately prior to the target phoneme) were detected more slowly. Buxton (1983) found that when the word which preceded a target-bearing word in phoneme-detection was replaced by a different word, the replacement increased detection time to a greater extent if the two words differed in number of syllables. All these results were consistent with the proposal that listeners process a regular rhythm, using it to make predictions about temporal patterns; when manipulations of the speech signal cause these predictions to be proven wrong, recognition is momentarily disrupted.

Later results, however, called this interpretation into question. Mens and Povel (1986) conducted (in Dutch) an experiment modelled on that of Buxton (1983) in English, in which temporal modification was again achieved by replacing the pretarget word by one with a different number of syllables (e.g., *kat* - cat - was replaced by *kandidaat* - candidate). Mens and Povel failed to replicate the effects of predictability observed in the earlier studies. Pitt and Samuel (1990) similarly only weakly replicated Shields et al.'s (1974) result, in a phoneme-detection study using acoustically controlled target-bearing words embedded in natural sentence context. They found that predictability was only possible when the word was embedded in a rhythmically highly regular word list. Pitt and Samuel speculated that natural sentence contexts may in fact offer little opportunity for exercising prediction with respect to the location of stressed syllables.

A similar conclusion was also reached by Mehta and Cutler (1988), who found differences in the pattern of effects observed with spontaneously spoken versus read materials in a phoneme-detection experiment. One difference was that in read materials, but not in spontaneously spoken materials, targets occurring later in a sentence were detected faster than targets occurring earlier in a sentence; since the two sets of materials were identical in content (the former being read, by the original speaker, from a transcript of the spontaneous conversation), Mehta and Cutler concluded that the effect in the read speech reflected not semantic predictability but temporal regularity. Together these results however suggest very little role for rhythmic regularity. To achieve real predictability which listeners can exploit at the word-by-word level, there must be sustained regularity, as Pitt and Samuel showed, and this appears not to occur at all in spontaneous speech; in read speech, it can come into play in longer sentences, in which the latter part of the sentences become easier to process than the earlier parts.

Using a word-monitoring task (in which listeners respond when they detect a specified target word), Tyler and Warren (1987) explored the effects of disrupting the temporal structure of meaningless (but syntactically acceptable) sentences as a function of the effects of this disruption on prosodic grouping; longer detection latencies were observed when phonological phrasing was disrupted, suggesting that grouping effects as realized in the prosodic structure play a stronger role than simple temporal predictability arising from regularity of rhythm. Rhythmic structure is used in lexical segmentation, but indirectly, in that it guides hypotheses about word-boundary location; however, rhythmic structure usually does not guide speech processing by allowing advance prediction of the speech structure itself.

However, there is one way in which the timing of speech events can be of assistance in word boundary perception - though this occurs not at the level of sentence prosody, but at the segmental level. Segmental timing varies with position in the word, and listeners can make use of this variation in segmentation. Thus Quené (1992, 1993) investigated minimal junctural pairs such as *naam op - na mop* in Dutch; he found that the lengthened duration of a consonant (especially sonorant consonants such as [m]) in word-final position was especially helpful to listeners. Overall syllable duration (but principally: duration of the vowel) formed a reliable cue in other studies: thus Nakatani and Schaffer (1978) found that relative syllable duration allowed listeners to distinguish English adjective-noun sequences such as *noisy dog* and *bold design* when these were presented as reiterant speech (in which a natural utterance is mimicked in a series of repetitions of a single syllable such as *ma*), and Rietveld (1980) reported similar results for French ambiguous strings (e.g., *le couplet complet - le couple est complet*). Such ambiguous strings may, of course, not often occur in natural speech; nevertheless temporarily ambiguous sequences do occur. Embedded words provide a case in point (thus *Stau* is embedded in *Staub*, which in turn is embedded in *Staupe*); listener sensitivity to segmental duration helps to avoid temporary ambiguity resulting from such embedding. Christophe, Dupoux, Bertoncini and Mehler (1994) showed that newborn infants can discriminate between bisyllabic sequences such as *mati* taken from within a word (*mathematicien*) versus across two words (*panorama typique*); relative syllable duration differed significantly across the two types of bisyllable. It is clear that human listeners do have finely tuned temporal-discrimination capacities, and these assist in segmentation just as sentence-level rhythm and grouping does.

Prominence

Words which bear sentence accent are processed more rapidly than words which do not. Thus targets on accented words are detected more rapidly than targets on unaccented word in phoneme detection (Cutler & Foss, 1977; Mehta & Cutler, 1988); verification of heard words is faster if the words were accented than if they were not (van Donselaar & Lentz, 1994); and mispronunciations are registered more rapidly in accented than in unaccented words (Cole, Jakimik & Cooper, 1978; Cole & Jakimik, 1980). Accented words have heightened acoustic clarity (increased spectral definition: Koopmans-van Beinum & van Bergem, 1989; and increased duration: Klatt, 1976, van Santen & Olive, 1990; Eefting, 1991; Dahan & Bernard, 1996), and this certainly could help to make them easier to process.

Nonetheless, the processing advantage of accented words is not solely due to acoustic factors. This is shown by Cutler's (1976) finding that the preceding prosodic contour leading up to an accented word in itself produces speeded processing. Cutler recorded sentences in two prosodic versions, one in which the word bearing the phoneme target was contrastively accented, and one in which contrastive accent fell elsewhere; for example, with the target phoneme /d/: *She managed to remove the DIRT from the rug, but not the berry stains; She managed to remove the dirt from the RUG, but not from their clothes.* The target-bearing word itself (i.e. in this case, the word *dirt*) was then edited out of each version and replaced by acoustically identical copies of the same word taken from a third recording of the same sentence, in which no contrastive accents had been applied. This resulted in two versions of each experimental sentence, with acoustically identical target-bearing words but with different prosodic contours on the words preceding the target: in one case the prosody was consistent with sentence accent occurring at the location of the target, in the other case it was consistent with accent falling elsewhere. Cutler found that subjects nevertheless responded significantly faster to the target in the 'accented' position than to the target in the 'unaccented' position. Since there were no acoustic differences between the target words themselves that could account for this result, and the only difference in the preceding context lay in the prosody, listeners must have been using this preceding prosodic information to predict where accent would occur.

A later study by Cutler and Darwin (1981) showed that this predicted accent effect was unaffected by the removal of pitch variation, i.e. the presentation of the sentences in a monotonized form; and it was also not affected by manipulation of the duration of closure for the target stop consonant. Thus the effect does not appear to be dependent on any particular prosodic dimension. When speech hybridization techniques were used to interchange timing patterns between the two versions of an utterance, however, so that 'impossible' utterances resulted (e.g., an utterance in which the F0 contour suggested that accent would fall on the target-bearing word while the durational patterns of the preceding words suggested that it would fall elsewhere), the predicted accent effect disappeared (Cutler, 1987), suggesting that consistency among the separate prosodic dimensions is important for listeners to be able to exploit them efficiently.

The effects of predictability which are robustly observed in these accent studies contrast with the fragile predictability effects observed when rhythmic regularity was at issue. Interestingly, in the experiments of Shields et al. (1974) and Meltzer et al. (1976), the target-bearing nonsense words seem to have been carrying the main information of the clause in which they occurred, so that the speaker would presumably have assigned them sentence accent. It is possible, therefore, that these authors unwittingly manipulated sentence accent as well as rhythmic structure, and that the effects that they observed were due to the former rather than the latter factor. The difference between the results of Buxton (1983) and Mens and Povel (1986) could have a similar root. Buxton's target-bearing words were nouns, and the rhythmic manipulation was carried out on an immediately preceding adjective; nouns are more likely to bear sentence accent than adjectives, so that it is likely that the manipulation in Buxton's study disrupted the prosodic structure immediately preceding an accented word. Mens and Povel, on the other hand, manipulated nouns and (in a minority of cases) verbs, and the following target-bearing word was in nearly all cases a preposition or adverb; their manipulation therefore most likely involved an accented word, while the target occurred in post-nuclear position in both the intact and the cross-spliced sentences.

Certainly the accent prediction effects do not appear to be based on any relation of sentence accent to the temporal structure of an utterance. Instead, it has been argued that listeners direct attention to accented words because these are semantically focussed, and hence convey information that is particularly important for apprehension of the speaker's message. Semantic focussing by itself leads to faster responses in phoneme detection in just the same way that prosodic accentuation does; Cutler and Fodor (1979) demonstrated this in a study in which semantic focus was manipulated by means of a question preceding the sentence in which the target occurred. Once located, focussed words receive more detailed semantic processing: Multiple meanings of homophones are activated if the words are in focus, but not necessarily if the words are not in focus (Blutner & Sommer, 1988), and recall of the surface form of a word is more likely if the word was in focus in a heard sentence than if it was not (Birch & Garnsey, 1995). Thus listeners may actively search for accented words because these provide the semantically most central portion of a speaker's message. Sedivy, Tanenhaus, Spivey-Knowlton, Eberhard and Carlson (1995) demonstrated just how rapidly accent can be processed, in a study in which they tracked the eye movements of listeners who were required to select one of four items in a display. When the display set consisted of, for instance, a large red square, a large blue circle, a small red square and a small yellow triangle, and the listeners heard *touch the LARGE red square*, they were able to select the correct item on hearing the contrastively accented word *large*. Apparently the contrastive accent allowed them to choose the one member of the set of large items which contrasted, by being large, with some other item.

The relation of accentuation to semantic structure is also underlined by a number of studies which show that listeners prefer, or find it easier to process, sentences in which accent falls on information which is new, i.e. has not previously occurred in the discourse (Bock & Mazzella, 1983; Terken & Nooteboom, 1987; Birch & Clifton, 1995). Syntactic disambiguation can also be effected by accent placement; Read, Kraak and Boves (1980) found that in the ambiguous Dutch sentence *wie zoent de vrouw?* accent on the verb led listeners to prefer the interpretation, in which the woman is the subject and the object of the action is questioned. However, their explanation of this result drew on the relationship of accent to information structure: the accent on the verb effectively deaccented the following noun (*vrouw*), implying that it should be taken as existing topic of the discourse, which in turn implies that it is the grammatical subject of the sentence, and the question word is therefore the grammatical object.

The relative prominence of words which is conveyed by sentence prosody is thus exploited by listeners to derive information about the semantic relations within utterances; words which are accented effectively receive favored processing.

2.3 Word Prosody

Words may be uniquely distinguished from one another by differences in segmental structure (e.g., *Bein* from *mein*, *Bahn*, and *Beil*); but in many languages they may also be distinguished solely by suprasegmental means: *übersetzen* from *übersetzen*, in German (a stress language), *ame* with HL pitch accent (meaning *rain*) from *ame* with LH pitch accent (meaning *candy*) in Japanese, [si] with high level tone 1 (meaning *poem*), from [si] with high rising tone 2 (meaning *history*), from [si] with low level tone 6 (meaning *time*) in Cantonese. Thus word recognition in spoken-language understanding involves the processing of prosodic structure which may contribute to or even solely determine word identity.

The process of lexical access in spoken-word recognition is described in detail in this volume in the chapter by Frauenfelder. Current models of word recognition assume that multiple lexical candidates are activated by incoming speech input, and compete among one another for recognition. Both matching and mismatching information in the signal may contribute to a candidate word's fate: information in the signal which matches the stored lexical representation can increase the corresponding word's activation, while activation can be decreased by incoming information which fails to match what is stored. No current model of spoken-word recognition, whether computationally implemented or not, has as yet addressed specifically the role of prosodic information in this process. However, there is a large amount of relevant experimental evidence available, which can shed light on such questions as whether prosodic information constrains the initial stages of lexical activation, or whether it plays a subordinate role by only coming into play in order to allow selection among alternative candidate words.

Lexical Tone

In lexical tone languages, words may be distinguished by the pitch height or contour of syllables, as in the Cantonese example given above. Thus only the single suprasegmental dimension of fundamental frequency (F0) is involved in signalling tone. This F0 information can be highly informative even in the absence of segmental information; thus Ching (1985, 1988) found that identification scores for lip-read Cantonese words improved greatly when F0 information was provided, in the form of pulses synchronized with the talker's pitch (there was however very little improvement when F0 information was provided for lip-read English words). Lexical priming studies in Cantonese suggest that the role of a syllable's tone in word recognition is analogous to the role of the vowel (Chen & Cutler, 1997; Cutler & Chen, 1995); in an auditory lexical decision task, overlap between a prime word and the target word in tone or in vowel exercise analogous effects.

Although it might seem that a contrast realized in F0 should be perceptually simple to process (it resumbles, for instance, the contrast between two musical notes), listeners without experience with a tone language find tone discrimination difficult. Burnham, Francis, Webster, Luksaneeyanawin, Attapaiboon, Lacerda and Keller (1996) compared same-different discrimination of Thai tones and musical transformations of the same tones, by speakers of Thai, Cantonese and English; Thai and Cantonese listeners could discriminate the speech and musical tones equally well, but English listeners discriminated the musical tones significantly better than the speech tones. Lee, Vakoch and Wurm (1996) also found that English listeners had difficulty making same-different judgments on Cantonese or Mandarin tone pairs; speakers of the two tone languages always performed better than the English listeners (although they also performed better with the tone contrasts of their own language than with those of the other language).

Fox and Unkefer (1985) conducted one of the first psycholinguistic investigations of tone in word recognition, in a categorization experiment using a continuum varying from one tone of Mandarin to another. The crossover point at which listeners in their experiment switched from reporting one tone to reporting the other shifted as a function of whether the CV syllable upon which the tone was realized formed a real word when combined only with one tone or only with the other tone (in comparison to control conditions in which both tones, or neither tone, formed a real word in combination with the CV). This lexical effect appeared only with native-speaker listeners; English listeners showed no such shift, and on the control continua the two subject groups did not differ. Because the categorization task is not an 'on-line' task (i.e. it does not tap directly into the process of word recognition), however, Fox and Unkefer's finding does not shed light on the issue of whether tone plays a role in initial activation of word candidates or only in selection between them.

However, tonal information may constrain word recognition less surely than segmental information. In a study by Tsang and Hoosain (1979), Cantonese subjects heard sentences presented at a fast rate and had to choose between two transcriptions of what they had heard; the transcriptions differed only in one character, representing a single difference of one syllable's vowel, tone, or vowel+tone. Accuracy was significantly greater for vowel differences than for tone differences, and vowel+tone differences were no more accurately distinguished than vowel differences alone. Repp and Lin (1990) asked Mandarin listeners to categorize nonword CV syllables according to consonant, vowel, or tone; categorization of tone was slower than categorization of vowel or consonant. Taft and Chen (1992) found that homophone judgments for written characters in both Mandarin and Cantonese were made less rapidly when the pronunciation of the two characters differed only in tone, as opposed to in vowel. Cutler and Chen (1997) similarly found that Cantonese listeners were significantly more likely erroneously to accept a nonword as a real word in auditory lexical decision when the nonword differed from a real word only in tone; and in a same-different judgment task, these listeners were slower and less accurate in their responses when two syllables differed only in tone, compared to when a segmental difference was present. In both tasks, an error was most probable when the correct tone of the real word and the erroneous tone on the nonword began similarly, in other words when the tone distinction was perceptually hard to make. Similar effects appear in the perception of Thai tones, in this case by non-native listeners: Burnham, Kirkwood, Luksaneeyanawin and Pansottee (1992) found that the order of difficulty of tone pairs presented in a same-different judgment task to English-speaking listeners was determined by the starting pitch of the tones.

Although tone contrasts are realized in F0, they are realized upon vowels, and therefore they are processed together with the vowel information. Yet vowels themselves can be identified very early; in a consonant-vowel sequence the transition from the consonant into the vowel is enough for listeners to achieve vowel identification (Strange, 1989). The evidence reviewed above suggests that tones can often not be identified so quickly - in speeded response tasks, subjects sometimes issue a response before the tonal information has effectively been processed. Thus although tone information is crucial for distinguishing between words in languages such as Cantonese, it may be the case that segmental information constrains initial lexical activation more strongly than tone information does.

Lexical Pitch Accent
Words in Japanese have patterns of pitch accent - high or low pitch levels associated with each mora of a polysyllabic word. Thus the word *Tokyo*, for example, has four

morae: *to-o-kyo-o*, of which the first has low pitch accent and the following three high, giving the word as a whole the pattern LHHH. Like lexical tone, pitch accent contrasts are realized via F0 variation. There are quite a number of pairs of short Japanese words which differ only in accent pattern (such as *ame*) but very few such pairs of long words. Only a limited number of possible patterns exist. Japanese listeners find cross-spliced words with a correct segmental sequence but an impossible accent pattern (one which does not occur in the language) hard to process (Otake, Yoneyama, Cutler & van der Lugt, 1996).

Some recent experiments have suggested that Japanese listeners can make use of pitch accent information in early stages of word recognition, i.e. in the initial activation of word candidates. Cutler and Otake (1996) presented Japanese listeners with single syllables edited out of bisyllabic words differing in accent pattern, and asked them to judge, for each syllable, in which of two words it had originally been spoken. Thus the listeners might hear *ka* and be asked to choose between *baka* HL and *gaka* LH, or between *kage* HL and *kagi* LH; in other words, the listeners had to judge whether the syllable had H or L accent, since the syllable occurred in the same position in the two choice words, and the phonetic context adjacent to the *ka* was matched. The listeners performed this task with high accuracy, and their scores were significantly more accurate for initial (80% correct) than for final syllables (68%). This might suggest that pitch accent information is realized most clearly early in the word, where it would be of most use for listeners in on-line spoken-word recognition.

In a subsequent repetition priming study, Cutler and Otake (submitted) found that minimal pitch accent pairs such as *ame* HL and *ame* LH did not facilitate one another's recognition. Presentation of one member of the pair, in other words, apparently did not activate the other member, suggesting that a mismatch in pitch accent can rule out a candidate lexical item. In a gating study, the same authors presented listeners with successively larger fragments of words such as *nimotsu* HLL or *nimono* LHH - i.e. pairs of words with initial syllables (here, *nimo-*) having the same segmental structure but opposite pitch accent values. Listeners' incorrect guesses from about the end of the first vowel (*ni-*) overwhelmingly tended to be words with the same accent pattern as the actually spoken word. These results strongly suggest that Japanese pitch accent is exploited by listeners in word activation.

However, like lexical tone, pitch accent is realized via F0, and thus can only be reliably identified once a substantial part of the segment carrying it has been heard. In the gating study, the vowel in the first syllable constituted this necessary carrier segment. Walsh Dickey (1996) conducted a same-different judgment experiment in which Japanese listeners heard pairs of bisyllabic words or nonwords which were either the same, or differed either in pitch accent or in segmental structure. Just as Cutler and Chen (1997) observed for lexical tone, Walsh Dickey found that 'different' judgments were significantly slower for pairs varying in pitch accent than for pairs which varied segmentally. Moreover, this was true irrespective of the position of the segmental difference; thus even a difference in a word-final vowel (at which time the pitch accent pattern of the whole bisyllable should be beyond doubt) led to significantly faster responses than the pitch accent difference.

Lexical Stress

Most experimental studies of word prosody have concerned lexical stress; and most of the research has been carried out in English. However, as this Section will outline, the role of lexical stress in word recognition may not be the same in English and in other stress languages.

In English, pairs of unrelated words differing only in stress pattern are rare; thus although stress oppositions between words of differing form class derived from the same stem *(import, contest)* are common, there are very few such pairs which are lexically clearly distinct (such as *forearm*, or *insight/incite*). Although stress could in principle provide minimal distinctions between words, in practice it rarely does so.

The rarity of minimal stress pairs is also true of German, Dutch and other languages with stress. However, the realization of stress in English differs somewhat even from other closely related languages. Unstressed syllables in English nearly always contain reduced vowels, and most full vowels bear either primary or secondary stress. This correlation is not nearly as strong in the other Germanic languages. The English word *cobra* for example has a reduced vowel - the vowel schwa - in the second syllable, where the equivalent German and Dutch words have the full vowel [a]; likewise, the English word *cigar* has schwa in the first syllable, while German *Zigarre* and Dutch *sigaar* have the full vowel [i]. Unstressed full vowels occur much more often in German and Dutch than they do in English.

The result of this crosslinguistic difference is that in English there are fewer pairs of words which can be distinguished suprasegmentally before they can be distinguished segmentally. Consider the words *alibi* and *alinea* (which exist both in German and in Dutch); both begin *ali-*, but in one the first syllable is stressed, in the other the second syllable. Such pairs practically do not exist in English; the initially-stressed word will almost certainly have schwa in the second syllable (this is true for instance of the word *alibi*, which does exist in English). Consequently, the earliest mismatching information which will become available to rule out a lexical candidate in English word recognition will virtually always be segmental information; the processing of suprasegmental information may make little useful contribution to constraining word activation. (In fact, statistical analyzes by Altmann and Carter [1989] established that the information value conveyed by phonetic segments in English is highest for vowels in stressed syllables.)

English listeners indeed find the distinction between full and reduced vowels more crucial than the distinction between stress levels; cross-splicing vowels with different stress patterns produces unacceptable results only if vowel quality is changed

(Fear, Cutler & Butterfield, 1995). In Fear et al.'s study, listeners heard tokens of words such as *audience*, which has primary stress on the initial vowel, and *audition*, which is one of the rare English words with an unstressed but unreduced initial vowel; when the initial vowels of these words had been exchanged, listeners rated the resulting tokens as insignificantly different from the original, unspliced, tokens. In a study of the recognition of words under noise-masking, Slowiaczek (1990) found that if vowel quality is not altered, mis-stressing has no significant effect on word identification. Changing vowel quality, on the other hand, does disrupt word recognition: thus Bond and Small (1983) found that mis-stressed words with vowel changes were not restored to correct stress in shadowing (indicating that subjects perceived the mis-stressed form and may not at all have accessed the intended word); and Bond (1981) found that the segmental distortion which could most adversely affect word recognition was changing full vowels to reduced and vice versa. A mis-stressing experiment by Cutler and Clifton (1984) similarly found a much stronger inhibitory effect of shifting stress in words with a reduced vowel (*wallet, saloon*) - since this necessarily involved a change in vowel quality - than in words with two full vowels (*nutmeg, canteen*). Puns which involve a stress shift do not work (Lagerquist, 1980). Finally, a 'migration' experiment (in which phantom word recognitions are induced by combination of material presented separately to the two ears) by Mattys and Samuel (1997) demonstrated that mispronunciation in a stressed syllable inhibited construction of the phantom percept.

Knowing the stress pattern in advance does not facilitate word recognition in English: neither visual nor auditory lexical decision is speeded by prior specification of stress pattern (Cutler & Clifton, 1984). There are certain canonical correlations between stress pattern and word class in English (e.g., initial stress for bisyllabic nouns, final stress for bisyllabic verbs), and listeners know and can use this patterning in making 'off-line' decisions, i.e. responses that are not made under time pressure. Thus in studies by Kelly and colleagues (Cassidy & Kelly, 1991; Kelly, 1988, 1992; Kelly & Bock, 1988), subjects who were asked to use bisyllabic nonwords in a sentence as if they were words treated initially-stressed nonwords as nouns and finally-stressed nonwords as verbs; similarly, when asked to use a verb as a nonce-noun subject chose a verb with initial stress, while for a noun acting as a nonce-verb they chose a noun with final stress. However, this patterning again does not speed word recognition: whether or not a bisyllabic word conforms to the canonical pattern does not affect how rapidly its grammatical category is judged - *cigar* is perceived as a noun just as rapidly as *apple*, and *borrow* is perceived as a verb as rapidly as *arrive* (Cutler & Clifton, 1984).

In another off-line study, Connine, Clifton and Cutler (1987) asked listeners to categorise an ambiguous consonant (varying along a continuum between [d] and [t]) in either *DIgress-TIgress* (in which *tigress* is a real word) or *diGRESS-tiGRESS* (in which *digress* is a real word). Listeners' responses showed effects of stress-determined lexical status, in that /t/ was reported more often for the *DIgress-TIgress* continuum, but /d/ more often for the *diGRESS-tiGRESS* continuum. The listeners clearly could use the stress information in the signal, and in their stored representations of these words, to resolve the phonetic ambiguity. However, as with the correlation of stress pattern and word class, this off-line result can not shed light on the role of stress in on-line word activation.

If what matters for word recognition is primarily segmental identity, then the few minimal stress pairs in English, such as *forearm*, should be effectively homophones, just like all the many other English homophones (*match, count* etc.). Indeed, Cutler (1986) showed that this is so. In a cross-modal priming experiment (in which listeners hear a sentence and at some point during the sentence perform a visual lexical decision), Cutler found that both stress patterns, *FOREarm* and *foreARM*, facilitated recognition of words related to *each* of them (e.g., *elbow, prepare*). L. Slowiaczek (personal communication) similarly found priming for associates related to both phrase-stress and compound-stress readings of sequences such as *green house*. Thus English listeners apparently do not distinguish between two word forms distinguished only suprasegmentally in the process of achieving initial access to the lexicon; stress plays no role in on-line word activation.

As foreshadowed earlier, however, this state of affairs may hold for English only. The only other stress language for which a substantial body of experimental evidence exists is Dutch, but in Dutch, at least, the evidence now suggests a different picture. Van Heuven & Hagman (1988) analyzed a 70,000 word Dutch corpus to ascertain the contribution of stress to specifying word identity; they found that words could on average be identified after 80% of their phonemes (counting from word onset) had been considered; when stress information was included, however, a forward search was successful on average given only 66% of the phonemes. Off-line experiments in Dutch have demonstrated effects of stress on word identification. For instance, van Heuven (1988) and Jongenburger (1996) found that listeners could correctly select between two Dutch words with a segmentally identical but stress-differentiated initial syllable (e.g., *ORgel* and *orKEST*, or a minimal pair such as *SERvisch-serVIES*) when presented with only the first syllable. In a gating experiment, mis-stressing harms recognition, with mis-stressing of finally-stressed words (*PIloot* instead of *piLOOT*) more harmful than mis-stressing of initially-stressed words (*viRUS* instead of *VIrus*; van Heuven, 1985; van Leyden & van Heuven, 1996; Koster & Cutler, 1997). Interestingly, another gating experiment by Jongenburger and van Heuven (1995a; see also Jongenburger, 1996), using minimal stress pairs (e.g., *VOORnaam-voorNAAM*) presented in a sentence context, found that listeners' word guesses only displayed correct stress judgments for the initial syllable of the target word once the whole of that initial syllable and part of the following vowel were available; this suggests that at least for minimal stress pairs, suprasegmental information may not exercise strong constraints on word activation.

Consistent with this, a cross-modal priming study in Dutch, planned as a direct replication of Cutler's (1986) experiment, failed to find any significant priming at all from initially-stressed members of stress pairs (*VOORnaam*), and inconsistent results for finally-stressed tokens (*voorNAAM*; Jongenburger & van Heuven, 1995b; Jongenburger, 1996).

Nonetheless, more recent results, using a larger population of words than is provided by the small set of minimal stress pairs, suggest that mis-stressing a Dutch word can prevent lexical activation. In word-spotting, embedded words are detected less rapidly when they occur within a string which itself could be continued to form a longer word; thus English *mess* is detected less rapidly in *doMES* than in *neMES*, presumably because *doMES* could be continued to form the word *domestic*, while *neMES* cannot be continued to form a longer real word (McQueen, Norris & Cutler, 1994). This finding replicates in Dutch: *zee* (sea) is harder to spot in *muzee* (which can be continued to form *museum*) than in *luzee*. However, if *muzee* is stressed not on the second syllable like *museum*, but on the initial syllable instead, i.e. listeners hear *MUzee* and *LUzee*, then there is no longer a significant difference between these in detection time for *zee* (Donselaar, Koster & Cutler, in preparation). This suggests that there was in this case no competition from *museum* because it simply was not activated by input lacking the correct stress pattern. Further, the fragment *aLI-* will prime *aLInea* but not *Alibi*, and the fragment *Ali-* will prime *Alibi* but not *aLInea* (Donselaar, Koster & Cutler, in preparation); this result was also observed with similar fragments of Spanish words (e.g., the first two syllables of *ARtico* or *arTIculo*) presented to Spanish listeners (Soto, Sebastián-Gallés & Cutler, in preparation).

These last experiments in Dutch have not been attempted in English; can we in fact be sure that the same pattern of results would not after all show up in English with these new experimental methods? In fact, both experiments simply could not be replicated in English. The competition experiment (*zee* in *muzee*) requires words beginning with two strong syllables and containing a single embedded word; English does not contain sufficient numbers of such words. The fragment priming experiment (*ali-* in *alibi* and *alinea*) likewise requires pairs of words beginning with two strong syllables; but equivalent words in English (such as *alibi*) contain a reduced vowel in one of the relevant syllables. The fact that such experiments are impossible in English is of course itself informative: it means that opportunities for listeners to use stress in the early stages of word recognition rarely occur in English, and words can virtually always be distinguished by segmental analysis without recourse to stress.

What then, can we conclude about the role of stress in word recognition? Indirectly, it of course plays a role due to the fact that stressed syllables are more acoustically reliable than unstressed syllables. Thus stressed syllables are more readily identified than unstressed syllables when cut out of their original context (Lieberman, 1963), and distortions of the speech signal are more likely to be detected in stressed than in unstressed syllables (Cole et al., 1978; Cole & Jakimik, 1980; Browman, 1978; Bond & Garnes, 1980). In spontaneous speech, detection of word-initial target phonemes is also faster on lexically stressed than unstressed syllables (Mehta & Cutler, 1988); acoustic differences between stressed and unstressed syllables are relatively large in spontaneous speech, and such differences do not arise with laboratory-read materials. Stressed syllables are also recognized earlier than unstressed syllables in gated words, in spontaneously spoken but not in read materials (McAllister, 1991).

This does not imply that contrasts between stressed and unstressed syllables are salient to all listeners. Speakers of French, a language which does not distinguish words by stress, have great difficulty processing stress contrasts in nonsense materials, e.g., deciding whether a token *bopeLO* should be matched with an earlier token of *bopeLO* or *boPElo* (Dupoux, Pallier, Sebastián & Mehler, 1997). The same contrasts are easy for speakers of Spanish, a language which does distinguish words via stress. In fact, it should be noted that this entire Section has dealt with free-stress languages. There is as yet no direct evidence concerning the role of stress (e.g., the effects of mis-stressing) in fixed-stress languages, where contrasts between stressed and unstressed syllables exist but do not serve to distinguish one word from another. Indirect evidence is available from the word-spotting findings of Suomi, McQueen and Cutler (1997) in Finnish described above - the words excised from preceding monosyllabic contexts could be considered at least not to have their canonical stress, but no deleterious effects of this on word recognition were observed. Nevertheless there is room for new evidence from languages such as Finnish or Polish.

For free-stress languages, however, the evidence now suggests that stress may have a role in the initial activation of lexical entries in those languages where it contributes significant information to word identification; English is not one of these. Unfortunately, therefore, the language in which most psycholinguistic research (on any topic) is conducted turns out to be unrepresentative in the role its word prosody plays in word recognition.

2.4   Conclusion

The focus of the present chapter has been the process of recognizing spoken words and the ways in which prosodic structure directly influences that aspect of listening. There are of course much more general indirect influences which could have been considered. For instance, prosody plays a role in general intelligibility; just as sentences with acceptable syntax are understood more easily than sentences with abnormal syntax, sentences with plausible semantics are understood more easily than sentences with implausible semantics, and sentences with accurate phonetic realization are understood more easily than sentences with distorted phonetic structure, so are sentences with intact prosodic structure understood more easily than sentences in which the prosodic structure has been in some way disrupted. This has been demonstrated in many languages (including German), and it is clear that word recognition would be one of the components of language processing affected by such manipulations. However, such general considerations fell outside the scope of this chapter.

The specific contributions of prosodic structure to word recognition, it has been argued, come on the one hand from sentence-level prosody - in which rhythm and grouping play a role in the discovery of word boundaries, and prominence can facilitate lexical processing - and on the other hand from the prosodic structure of words themselves, which, where it is suitably informative, is exploited to distinguish between candidate words. In all these research areas experimental evidence concerning the German language hardly exists, although evidence is indeed available from closely related languages. The review motivates the general conclusion that prosodic structure - like, one assumes, every other level of linguistic structure - is exploited by listeners in the process of word recognition to the extent that it can provide relevant and non-redundant information.

Acknowledgments
The overview given in this chapter overlaps to a considerable extent with the word-recognition Sections of the literature review compiled by Cutler, Dahan and van Donselaar (1997). I am very grateful to my co-authors Delphine Dahan and Wilma van Donselaar for joining me in that laborious but eventually rewarding project; the present chapter owes much to their advice and insights. I am also grateful to the publisher and editors of *Language and Speech* for permission to exploit further in this context the work done for the previous paper. Further thanks are due to Jens Bölte for assistance in tracking down studies of word recognition in German.

References

Altmann, G.T.M. & Carter, D.M. (1989). Lexical stress and lexical discriminability: Stressed syllables are more informative, but why? *Computer Speech and Language, 3*, 265-275.

Beach, C.M. (1991). The interpretation of prosodic patterns at points of syntactic structure ambiguity: Evidence for cue trading relations. *Journal of Memory and Language, 30*, 644-663.

Birch, S. & Clifton, C.E. (1995). Focus, accent and argument structure: Effects on language comprehension. *Language and Speech, 38*, 365-391.

Birch, S.L. & Garnsey, S.M. (1995). The effect of focus on memory for words in sentences. *Journal of Memory and Language, 34*, 232-267.

Blutner, R. & Sommer, R. (1988). Sentence processing and lexical access: The influence of the focus-identifying task. *Journal of Memory and Language, 27*, 359-367.

Bock, J.K. & Mazzella, J.R. (1983). Intonational marking of given and new information: Some consequences for comprehension. *Memory and Cognition, 11*, 64-76.

Bond, Z.S. (1981). Listening to elliptic speech: Pay attention to stressed vowels. *Journal of Phonetics, 9*, 89-96.

Bond, Z.S. & Garnes, S. (1980). Misperceptions of fluent speech. In R. Cole (ed.), *Perception and Production of Fluent Speech*. Hillsdale, NJ: Erlbaum.

Bond, Z.S. & Small, L.H. (1983). Voicing, vowel and stress mispronunciations in continuous speech. *Perception & Psychophysics, 34*, 470-474.

Bradley, D.C., Sánchez-Casas, R.M. & García-Albea, J.E. (1993). The status of the syllable in the perception of Spanish and English. *Language and Cognitive Processes, 8*, 197-234.

Browman, C.P. (1978). Tip of the tongue and slip of the ear: Implications for language processing. *UCLA Working Papers in Phonetics, 42*.

Burnham, D., Francis, E., Webster, D., Luksaneeyanawin, S., Attapaiboon, C., Lacerda, F. & Keller, P. (1996). Perception of lexical tone across languages: Evidence for a linguistic mode of processing. *Proceedings of the Fourth International Conference on Spoken Language Processing* (pp. 2514-2516). Philadelphia.

Burnham, D., Kirkwood, K., Luksaneeyanawin, S. & Pansottee, S. (1992). Perception of Central Thai tones and segments by Thai and Australian adults. Pan-Asiatic Linguistics: *Proceedings of the Third International Symposium of Language and Linguistics* (pp. 546-560). Bangkok: Chulalongkorn University Press.

Buxton, H. (1983). Temporal predictability in the perception of English speech. In A. Cutler & D.R. Ladd (eds.), *Prosody: Models and Measurements* . Heidelberg: Springer-Verlag.

Cassidy, K.W. & Kelly, M.H. (1991). Phonological information for grammatical category assignments. *Journal of Memory and Language, 30,* 348-369.

Chen, H.-C. & Cutler, A. (1997). Auditory priming in spoken and printed word recognition. In H.-C. Chen (ed.), *The Cognitive Processing of Chinese and Related Asian Languages.* Hong Kong: Chinese University Press.

Ching, Y.C. (1985). Lipreading Cantonese with voice pitch. Paper presented to the 109th meeting, Acoustical Society of America, Austin *(Abstract Journal of the Acoustical Society of America, 77, Supplement 1,* 39-40).

Ching, Y.C. (1988). Voice pitch information for the deaf. *Proceedings of the First Asian-Pacific Regional Conference on Deafness* (pp. 340-343). Hong Kong.

Christophe, A., Dupoux, E., Bertoncini, J. & Mehler, J. (1994). Do infants perceive word boundaries? An empirical study of the bootstrapping of lexical acquisition. *Journal of the Acoustical Society of America, 95,* 1570-1580.

Cole, R.A. & Jakimik, J. (1980). How are syllables used to recognize words? *Journal of the Acoustical Society of America, 67,* 965-970.

Cole, R.A., Jakimik, J. & Cooper, W.E. (1978). Perceptibility of phonetic features in fluent speech. *Journal of the Acoustical Society of America, 64,* 44-56.

Collier, R. & Hart, J. (1975). The role of intonation in speech perception. In A. Cohen & S.G. Nooteboom (eds.), *Structure and Process in Speech Perception* . Heidelberg: Springer-Verlag.

Connine, C.M., Clifton, C.E. & Cutler, A. (1987). Lexical stress effects on phonetic categorization. *Phonetica, 44,* 133-146.

Cutler, A. (1976). Phoneme-monitoring reaction time as a function of preceding intonation contour. *Perception and Psychophysics, 20,* 55-60.

Cutler, A. (1986). *Forbear* is a homophone: Lexical prosody does not constrain lexical access. *Language and Speech, 29,* 201-220.

Cutler, A. (1987). Components of prosodic effects in speech recognition. *Proceedings of the Eleventh International Congress of Phonetic Sciences* (pp. 84-87). Tallinn, Estonia.

Cutler, A. (1991). Linguistic rhythm and speech segmentation. In J. Sundberg, L. Nord & R. Carlson (eds.), *Music, Language, Speech and Brain* . London: Macmillan.

Cutler, A. (1997). The syllable's role in the segmentation of stress languages. *Language and Cognitive Processes, 12,* 839-845.

Cutler, A. & Butterfield, S. (1992). Rhythmic cues to speech segmentation: Evidence from juncture misperception. *Journal of Memory and Language, 31,* 218-236.

Cutler, A. & Carter, D.M. (1987). The predominance of strong initial syllables in the English vocabulary. *Computer Speech & Language, 2,* 133-142.

Cutler, A. & Chen, H.-C. (1995). Phonological similarity effects in Cantonese word recognition. *Proceedings of the Thirteenth International Congress of Phonetic Sciences* (pp. 106-109). Stockholm.

Cutler, A. & Chen, H.-C. (1997). Lexical tone in Cantonese spoken-word processing. *Perception & Psychophysics, 59,* 165-179.

Cutler, A. & Clifton, C.E. (1984). The use of prosodic information in word recognition. In H. Bouma & D.G. Bouwhuis (eds.), *Attention and Performance X: Control of Language Processes* . Hillsdale, N.J.: Erlbaum.

Cutler, A., Dahan, D. & van Donselaar, W. (1997). Prosody in the comprehension of spoken language: A literature review. *Language and Speech, 40,* 141-201.

Cutler, A. & Darwin, C.J. (1981). Phoneme-monitoring reaction time and preceding prosody: Effects of stop closure duration and of fundamental frequency. *Perception & Psychophysics, 29,* 217-224.

Cutler, A. & Fodor, J.A. (1979). Semantic focus and sentence comprehension. *Cognition, 7,* 49-59.

Cutler, A. & Foss, D.J. (1977). On the role of sentence stress in sentence processing. *Language and Speech, 20,* 1-10.

Cutler, A., Mehler, J., Norris, D.G. & Segui, J. (1986). The syllable's differing role in the segmentation of French and English. *Journal of Memory and Language, 25,* 385-400.

Cutler, A., Mehler, J., Norris, D.G. & Segui, J. (1992). The monolingual nature of speech segmentation by bilinguals. *Cognitive Psychology, 24,* 381-410.

Cutler, A. & Norris, D.G. (1988). The role of strong syllables in segmentation for lexical access. *Journal of Experimental Psychology: Human Perception and Performance, 14,* 113-121.

Cutler, A., Norris, D.G. & Williams, J.N. (1987). A note on the role of phonological expectations in speech segmentation. *Journal of Memory and Language, 26,* 480-487.

Cutler, A. & Otake, T. (1994). Mora or phoneme? Further evidence for language-specific listening. *Journal of Memory and Language, 33,* 824-844.

Cutler, A. & Otake, T. (1996). The processing of word prosody in Japanese. *Proceedings of the Sixth Australian International Conference on Speech Science and Technology* (pp. 599-604). Adelaide.

Cutler, A. & Otake, T. (submitted). Pitch accent in spoken-word recognition in Japanese.

Dahan, D. (1996). The role of rhythmic groups in the segmentation of continuous French speech. *Proceedings of the Fourth International Conference on Spoken Language Processing* (pp. 1185-1188). Philadelphia.

Dahan, D. & Bernard, J.M. (1996). Interspeaker variability in emphatic accent production in French. *Language and Speech, 39,* 341-374.

van Donselaar, W., Koster, M. & Cutler, A. (in preparation). *Voornaam* is not a homophone: Lexical prosody and lexical access in Dutch.

van Donselaar, W. & Lentz, J. (1994). The function of sentence accents and given/new information in speech processing: Different strategies for normal-hearing and hearing-impaired listeners? *Language and Speech, 37,* 375-391.

Dupoux, E. & Mehler, J. (1990). Monitoring the lexicon with normal and compressed speech: Frequency effects and the prelexical code. *Journal of Memory and Language, 29,* 316-335.

Dupoux, E., Pallier, C., Sebastián-Gallés, N. & Mehler, J. (1997). A destressing deafness in French? *Journal of Memory and Language, 36,* 406-421.

Eefting, W. (1991). The effect of 'information value' and 'accentuation' on the duration of Dutch words, syllables and segments. *Journal of the Acoustical Society of America, 89,* 412- 424.

Fear, B.D., Cutler, A. & Butterfield, S. (1995). The strong/weak syllable distinction in English. *Journal of the Acoustical Society of America, 97,* 1893-1904.

Fox, R.A. & Unkefer, J. (1985). The effect of lexical status on the perception of tone. *Journal of Chinese Linguistics, 13,* 69-90.

van Heuven, V.J. (1985). Perception of stress pattern and word recognition: Recognition of Dutch words with incorrect stress position. *Journal of the Acoustical Society of America*, 78, 21.

van Heuven, V.J. (1988). Effects of stress and accent on the human recognition of word fragments in spoken context: Gating and shadowing. *Proceedings of Speech '88, 7th FASE symposium* (pp. 811-818). Edinburgh.

van Heuven, V.J. & Hagman, P.J. (1988). Lexical statistics and spoken word recognition in Dutch. In P. Coopmans & A. Hulk (eds.), *Linguistics in the Netherlands 1988*. Dordrecht: Foris.

Höhle, B. & Schriefers, H. (1995). Ambisyllabizität im Deutschen: Psycholinguistische Evidenz. *Akten des 29. Linguistischen Kolloquiums*. Tübingen: Niemeyer.

Jongenburger, W. (1996). *The role of lexical stress during spoken-word processing*. Ph.D. thesis, Leiden.

Jongenburger, W. & van Heuven, V.J. (1995a). The role of linguistic stress in the time course of word recognition in stress-accent languages, *Proceedings of the Fourth European Conference on Speech Communication and Technology* (pp. 1695-1698). Madrid.

Jongenburger, W. & van Heuven, V.J. (1995b). The role of lexical stress in the recognition of spoken words: Prelexical or postlexical?, *Proceedings of the Thirteenth International Congress of Phonetic Sciences* (pp. 368-371). Stockholm.

Kakehi, K., Kato, K. & Kashino, M. (1996). Phoneme/syllable perception and the temporal structure of speech. In T. Otake & A. Cutler (eds.), *Phonological Structure and Language Processing: Cross-Linguistic Studies*. Berlin: Mouton de Gruyter.

Kearns, R.K. (1994). *Prelexical speech processing in mono- & bilinguals*. PhD thesis, University of Cambridge.

Kelly, M.H. (1988). Phonological biases in grammatical category shifts. *Journal of Memory and Language*, 27, 343-358.

Kelly, M.H. (1992). Using sound to solve syntactic problems: The role of phonology in grammatical category assignments. *Psychological Review*, 99, 349-364.

Kelly, M.H. & Bock, J.K. (1988). Stress in time. *Journal of Experimental Psychology: Human Perception and Performance*, 14, 389-403.

Klatt, D.H. (1976). Linguistic uses of segmental duration in English: Acoustic and perceptual evidence. *Journal of the Acoustical Society of America*, 59, 1208-1221.

Kolinsky, R., Morais, J. & Cluytens, M. (1995). Intermediate representations in spoken word recognition: Evidence from word illusions. *Journal of Memory and Language*, 34, 19-40.

Koopmans-van Beinum, F.J. & van Bergem, D.R. (1989). The role of 'given' and 'new' in the production and perception of vowel contrasts in read text and in spontaneous speech. *Proceedings of the European Conference on Speech Communication and Technology* (pp. 113-116). Edinburgh.

Koster, M. & Cutler, A. (1997). Segmental and suprasegmental contributions to spoken-word recognition in Dutch. *Proceedings of the Fifth European Conference on Speech Communication and Technology* (pp. 2167-2170). Rhodes.

Lagerquist, L.M. (1980). Linguistic evidence from paranomasia. *Papers from the Seventh Regional Meeting of the Chicago Linguistic Society*, 185-191.

Lee, Y.-S., Vakoch, D.A. & Wurm, L.H. (1996). Tone perception in Cantonese and Mandarin: A cross-linguistic comparison. *Journal of Psycholinguistic Research*, 25, 527-542.

Lehiste, I., Olive, J.P. & Streeter, L. (1976). Role of duration in disambiguating syntactically ambiguous sentences. *Journal of the Acoustical Society of America*, 60, 1199-1202.

van Leyden, K. & van Heuven, V.J. (1996). Lexical stress and spoken word recognition: Dutch vs. English. In C. Cremers & M. den Dikken (eds.), *Linguistics in the Netherlands 1996* . Amsterdam: John Benjamins.

Lieberman, P. (1963). Some effects of semantic and grammatical context on the production and perception of speech. *Language and Speech, 6,* 172-187.

Martin, J.G. (1979). Rhythmic and segmental perception are not independent. *Journal of the Acoustical Society of America, 65,* 1286-1297.

Mattys, S.L. & Samuel, A.G. (1997). How lexical stress affects speech segmentation and interactivity: Evidence from the migration paradigm. *Journal of Memory and Language, 36,* 87-116.

McAllister, J. (1991). The processing of lexically stressed syllables in read and spontaneous speech. *Language and Speech, 34,* 1-26.

McQueen, J.M., Norris, D.G. & Cutler, A. (1994). Competition in spoken word recognition: Spotting words in other words. *Journal of Experimental Psychology: Learning, Memory and Cognition, 20,* 621-638.

Mehler, J., Dommergues, J.-Y., Frauenfelder, U. & Segui, J. (1981). The syllable's role in speech segmentation. *Journal of Verbal Learning and Verbal Behavior, 20,* 298-305.

Mehta, G. & Cutler, A. (1988). Detection of target phonemes in spontaneous and read speech. *Language and Speech, 31,* 135-156.

Meltzer, R.H., Martin, J.G., Mills, C.B., Imhoff, D.L. & Zohar, D. (1976). Reaction time to temporally displaced phoneme targets in continuous speech. *Journal of Experimental Psychology: Human Perception and Performance, 2,* 277-290.

Mens, L. & Povel, D. (1986). Evidence against a predictive role for rhythm in speech perception. *The Quarterly Journal of Experimental Psychology, 38A,* 177-192.

Nakatani, L.H. & Schaffer, J.A. (1978). Hearing "words" without words: Prosodic cues for word perception. *Journal of the Acoustical Society of America, 63,* 234-245.

Nooteboom, S.G., Brokx, J.P.L. & de Rooij, J.J. (1978). Contributions of prosody to speech perception. In W.J.M. Levelt & G.B. Flores d'Arcais (eds.), *Studies in the perception of language* . Chichester: John Wiley & Sons.

Otake, T., Hatano, G., Cutler, A. & Mehler, J. (1993). Mora or syllable? Speech segmentation in Japanese. *Journal of Memory and Language, 32,* 358-378.

Otake, T., Hatano, G. & Yoneyama, K. (1996). Speech segmentation by Japanese listeners. In T. Otake & A. Cutler (eds.), *Phonological Structure and Language Processing: Cross-Linguistic Studies* . Berlin: Mouton de Gruyter.

Otake, T., Yoneyama, K., Cutler, A. & van der Lugt, A. (1996). The representation of Japanese moraic nasals. *Journal of the Acoustical Society of America, 100,* 3831-3842.

Pallier, C., Sebastián-Gallés, N., Felguera, T., Christophe, A., & Mehler, J. (1993). Attentional allocation within the syllabic structure of spoken words. Journal of *Memory and Language, 32,* 373-389.

Peretz, I., Lussier, I. & Béland, R. (1996). The roles of phonological and ortho- graphic code in word stem completion. In T. Otake & A. Cutler (eds.), *Phonologi- cal Structure and Language Processing: Cross-Linguistic Studies* . Berlin: Mou- ton de Gruyter.

de Pijper, J.R. & Sanderman, A.A. (1994). On the perceptual strength of prosodic boundaries and its relation to suprasegmental cues. *Journal of the Acoustical So- ciety of America, 96,* 2037-2047.

Pitt, M.A. & Samuel, A.G. (1990). The use of rhythm in attending to speech. *Journal of Experimental Psychology: Human Perception and Performance, 16,* 564-573.

Quené, H. (1992). Durational cues for word segmentation in Dutch. *Journal of Pho- netics, 20,* 331-350.

Quené, H. (1993). Segment durations and accent as cues to word segmentation in Dutch. *Journal of the Acoustical Society of America, 94,* 2027-2035.

Read, C. Kraak, A. & Boves, L. (1980). The interpretation of ambiguous who-ques- tions in Dutch: The effect of intonation. In W. Zonneveld & F. Weerman (eds.), *Linguistics in the Netherlands 1977 - 1979* . Dordrecht: Foris.

Repp, B.H. & Lin, H.-B. (1990). Integration of segmental and tonal information in speech perception. *Journal of Phonetics, 18,* 481-495.

Rietveld, A.C.M. (1980). Word boundaries in the French language. *Language and Speech, 23,* 289-296.

de Rooij, J.J. (1976). Perception of prosodic boundaries. *IPO Annual Progress Report, 11,* 20-24.

van Santen, J.P.H. & Olive, J.P. (1990). The analysis of contextual effects on segmental duration. *Computer Speech & Language, 4,* 359-390.

Schreuder, R. & Baayen, R. H. (1994). Prefix stripping re-revisited. *Journal of Memory and Language, 33,* 357-375.

Scott, D.R. (1982). Duration as a cue to the perception of a phrase boundary. *Journal of the Acoustical Society of America, 71,* 996-1007.

Sedivy, J., Tanenhaus, M., Spivey-Knowlton, M., Eberhard, K. & Carlson, G. (1995). Using intonationally-marked presuppositional information in on-line language processing: Evidence from eye movements to a visual model. *Proceedings of the Seventeenth Annual Conference of the Cognitive Science Society* (pp. 375-380). Hillsdale, NJ: Erlbaum.

Segui, J., Frauenfelder, U.H. & Mehler, J. (1981). Phoneme monitoring, syllable monitoring and lexical access. *British Journal of Psychology, 72,* 471-477.

Shields, J.L., McHugh, A. & Martin, J.G. (1974). Reaction time to phoneme targets as a function of rhythmic cues in continuous speech. *Journal of Experimental Psychology, 102,* 250-255.

Slowiazcek, L.M. (1990). Effects of lexical stress in auditory word recognition. *Language and Speech, 33,* 47-68.

Soto, S., Sebastián-Gallés, N. & Cutler, A. (forthcoming). Stress and word recognition in Spanish.

Strange, W. (1989). Dynamic specification of coarticulated vowels spoken in sentence context. *Journal of the Acoustical Society of America, 85,* 2135-2153.

Streeter, L.A. (1978). Acoustic determinants of phrase boundary location. *Journal of the Acoustical Society of America, 64,* 1582-1592.

Suomi, K., McQueen, J.M. & Cutler, A. (1997). Vowel harmony and speech segmentation in Finnish. *Journal of Memory and Language, 36,* 422-444.

Taft, M. & Chen, H.-C. (1992). Judging homophony in Chinese: The influence of tones. In H.-C. Chen & O.J.L. Tzeng (eds.), *Language processing in Chinese* . Amsterdam: Elsevier.

Taft, M. & Hambly, G. (1985). The influence of orthography on phonological representations in the lexicon. *Journal of Memory and Language, 24,* 320-335.

Terken, J. & Nooteboom, S.G. (1987). Opposite effects of accentuation and deaccentuation on verification latencies for given and new information. *Language and Cognitive Processes, 2,* 145-163.

Tsang, K.K. & Hoosain, R. (1979). Segmental phonemes and tonal phonemes in comprehension of Cantonese. *Psychologia, 22,* 222-224.

Tyler, L.K. & Warren, P. (1987). Local and global structure in spoken language comprehension. *Journal of Memory and Language, 26,* 638-657.

van Donselaar, W., Koster, M. & Cutler, A. (forthcoming) Lexical stress and lexical activation in Dutch.

Vroomen, J. & de Gelder, B. (1994). Speech segmentation in Dutch: No role for the syllable. *Proceedings of the Third International Conference on Spoken Language Processing,* Yokohama: Vol. 3, 1135-1138.

Vroomen, J., van Zon, M. & de Gelder, B. (1996). Cues to speech segmentation: Evidence from juncture misperceptions and word spotting. *Memory and Cognition, 24,* 744-755.

Walsh Dickey, L. (1996) Limiting-domains in lexical access: Processing of lexical prosody. In M. Dickey & S. Tunstall (eds.), *University of Massachusetts Occasional Papers in Linguistics 19: Linguistics in the Laboratory* .

Wightman, C.W., Shattuck-Hufnagel, S., Ostendorf, M. & Price, P.J. (1992). Segmental durations in the vicinity of prosodic phrase boundaries. *Journal of the Acoustical Society of America, 91,* 1707-1717.

Zwitserlood, P., Schriefers, H., Lahiri, A. & van Donselaar, W. (1993). The role of syllables in the perception of spoken Dutch. *Journal of Experimental Psychology: Learning, Memory and Cognition, 19,* 260-271.

Chapter 3

Spoken Words in Sentence Contexts

Pienie Zwitserlood

3.1 Introduction

Listeners sometimes have the impression that they know exactly which word a speaker is going to say next. However real such observations are, they are the exception rather than the rule. More than forty years of research has shown that recognizing spoken words is not a guessing game. Normally, word recognition is an extremely fast and efficient process that rarely reaches conscious awareness. Fluent speech is uttered at a rate of two to three words per second, and an adult language user has a mental lexicon in which the knowledge of about 30 000 to 50 000 words is stored (Aitchison, 1994). This implies that a listener has about one third of a second to select one word from this huge mental data base.

Because the goal of listening to language is to understand the message a speaker wishes to convey, it does not suffice to identify words. Critically, the listener needs to gain access to syntactic and meaning aspects of these words. Word recognition thus serves as an interface between the speech input and the construction of a structural and interpretative representation of the speaker's utterance. Various sources of knowledge about words become available during lexical processing: phonological, prosodic, morphological, semantic and syntactic. Whereas the phonological and prosodic make-up of words is crucial for the mapping of the products of sublexical processing (e.g., features, phonemes, syllables) onto lexical representations, their semantic and syntactic attributes serve as building blocks for the interpretative processes operating on units larger than words (e.g., phrases, sentences).

An important issue in psycholinguistic research concerns the ways in which sublexical, lexical and sentence (or phrase) level processes are interconnected. This issue is indeed a multi-faceted one; it has been translated into a number of separate research questions. The next two paragraphs outline which questions are focused upon in this chapter. Let us first consider sublexical perception. Processing of the speech signal - the identification of phonemes, for example - could be aided by information about words and their contextual fit. Such effects, often discussed under the heading of *lexical context*, are briefly discussed in this chapter (Connine, 1990;

Massaro, 1994; Tanenhaus & Lucas, 1987, for reviews). The next logical step is to consider the interplay between word recognition and processing at phrasal or sentential levels. One question to ask is whether and when semantic attributes of words influence the construction of the syntactic form of the utterance. This line of research falls within the domain of syntactic parsing, and is not reviewed here.

The focus is on a similar issue, but with a different directionality: the potential influences of sentential information on the actual business of recognizing words. The question is whether, how and when lexical processing is influenced by the semantic and syntactic context in which a word is embedded. What is normally measured in experiments in this field are responses to words, as a function of structural and semantic properties of the sentences in which they occur. Common to each research area mentioned so far is the concern with the interplay between what are considered to be distinct domains of processing: sublexical, lexical, sentence or phrase level. Thus, it does not come as a surprise that research has been strongly influenced by the debate on the modularity of subcomponents of language processing (Fodor, 1983; Tanenhaus, Dell & Carlson, 1987). Exempt from this discussion may be priming by single-word contexts, which could originate within one level of processing or representation (Tanenhaus & Lucas 1987; Frauenfelder & Tyler, 1987; Schwanenflugel, 1991; Tabossi, 1991, but see O'Seaghdha, 1989; Ratcliff & McKoon, 1988). For instance, semantic priming - the finding that a word is responded to faster when preceded by a semantically or associatively related word (Meyer & Schvaneveldt, 1971) - can be explained as an effect within one module.

But this does not hold for effects of sentence contexts which do not contain words strongly related to the word under measurement. The label *semantic context* will be reserved to refer to this type of semantic information, involving the meaning of the utterance as a whole. Studies in this domain constitute the bulk of this chapter. Evidence for the effectiveness of *syntactic context*, originating from the structural requirements of the sentence in which a word is embedded, is also included. Notably, such studies are rare, particularly in the spoken domain. One reason might be that it is not easy to constrain words by means of syntactic structure. Whereas a word can be made more or less predictable by the semantic content of a preceding sentence, syntactic constraints - at least in the languages investigated - can merely narrow down the lexical space to, say, nouns only. Research on syntactic context thus often resorts to the manipulation of syntactic violations. Two distinct types of background information should serve to facilitate the discussion and interpretation of the available evidence. One concerns the tools of word recognition research. A classification of paradigms and tasks will be presented below. First, however, some words on the functions of spoken word recognition and the ways in which these are implemented in different models are necessary (see also Frauenfelder, this volume).

3.2 Functions and Models of Spoken Word Recognition

The functional architecture of word recognition includes three basic functions: access, selection, and integration (Marslen-Wilson, 1987; Tyler, 1990; Zwitserlood, 1989a, 1994). Lexical access concerns the relationship between the sensory input and the mental lexicon. Before the lexical system is involved, perceptual parsing processes, operating on the speech input, extract information relevant for the lexical system. Although it is unclear as to what the exact nature of the parsing process or its products is (Cutler & McQueen, 1995; Frazier, 1987; Pisoni & Luce, 1987), it is often assumed that units of some form (features, phonemes, syllables) serve as input to the lexicon. Lexical access involves the mapping of this information onto phonological descriptions (or word forms) stored in the mental lexicon, resulting in the activation of these word forms and, at some point, of their syntactic and semantic properties.

After initial lexical access, information from ongoing perceptual parsing continues to map onto the activated forms. Selection involves the singling out, from the subset of activated elements, of the one that best matches the input available to the system. Successful selection is synonymous with word recognition. Integration, finally, concerns the binding of syntactic and semantic information associated with word forms into a semantic and syntactic representation of the whole utterance. Initial access to lexical information necessarily precedes selection. Whether selection precedes integration is an empirical issue. Integration clearly cannot be accomplished before semantic and syntactic specifications of lexical element(s) are available. The earliest point at which this information could be available is upon lexical access. So, in principle, the processes of selection and integration could run in parallel.

Most theories agree on these basic functions of the word recognition system, but diverge with respect to the relationships between the processes involved. Depending on their stance on the modularity or interactivity of subcomponents of language understanding, models of word recognition disagree on what the possible loci for the effects of syntactic and sentential semantic context might be. Although it has become increasingly difficult to distinguish between them, the most prominent models will be briefly characterized, because they have inspired so much of the work on effects of sentence contexts (see Massaro, 1994; Frauenfelder, this volume, for overviews of word recognition models).

Modular models of word recognition (Bradley & Forster, 1987; Forster, 1979, 1981, 1989; Seidenberg, 1985; Tanenhaus, Carlson & Seidenberg, 1985) claim that both lexical access and selection, and thus word recognition, are modular processes. The only information that influences lexical access and selection is information contained in speech input, and in the lexical system itself. In Forster's model, sensory information serves to access a frequency-ordered list of word forms. These word forms are searched serially, and selection occurs as soon as a match is found between the sensory input and one word form. The selected word form subsequently contacts its semantic and syntactic information, which is then output to processes operating at the level of the sentence. Contextual information does not affect selection, and thus word recognition. When words are recognized more easily or more rapidly in appropriate sentence contexts, this can only be due to a more easy integration of the semantic and syntactic specifications of the recognized word into higher-level sentence representations.

In the COHORT model (Marslen-Wilson, 1984), lexical access involves the parallel activation of all word forms that are compatible with some stretch of word-initial sensory input. The activation of multiple word forms is an obligatory and autonomous process, unaffected by contextual variables. Selection, for words heard in isolation, is defined as the reduction of the initially activated set until one remains. This reduction is solely due to the (in)compatibility of word forms with information in the speech signal. Important for the understanding of how contextual constraints work in the model is the availability of semantic (and syntactic) information for all activated word forms. In earlier versions of the model (Marslen-Wilson & Welsh, 1978; Marslen-Wilson & Tyler, 1980), contextual information served to remove contextually inappropriate words from the activated set. This is not the case in more recent versions (Marslen-Wilson, 1987, 1989). Instead, the syntactic and semantic specifications of multiple elements are assessed in parallel by the process responsible for integration. The binding of the specifications of the word that best fits the context can be seen as some form of selection - although Marslen-Wilson reserves the term selection for words heard in isolation.

Both preceding models contrast with fully interactive models, which allow all different sources of information - sensory, lexical, syntactic, semantic, and pragmatic - to interact with each other during word processing. Most prominent representatives of this class are models in the connectionist tradition (McClelland & Rumelhart, 1981; McClelland & Elman, 1986; Rumelhart & McClelland, 1982). In TRACE (Elman, 1989; see also Frauenfelder, 1996), developed for spoken word recognition, word elements (nodes) become activated via excitatory connections with both lower (feature and phoneme) and higher levels of representation. Although a contextual level is not implemented in the model, predictions are straightforward. Contextual information can at any point in time affect the activation level of word nodes (and also of phoneme or feature nodes), thereby influencing the likelihood that a contextually appropriate word will be selected. Selection is defined in terms of winning the competition between activated and mutually inhibiting word nodes.

Clearly, the models in their strict descriptions make different claims with respect to the potential locus of context effects during word processing. They have been empirically put to test in recent years; the evidence is summarized below. The scales tip to the disadvantage of a strict modularity of the complete lexical system, but, as the development of some models show, there is a remedy to everything. Any modular approach can be saved if one assumes that each module can have multiple outputs, which serve as input to the next module. For example, the process responsible for computing sentence meaning selects the best fitting word from a set that is provided by the lexical system (Marslen-Wilson, 1987; Norris, 1986). With such architecture, the distinction between modular and interactive models becomes moot. It is not surprising that research on words in context has moved away from verifying or invalidating models.

3.3 Experimental Approaches to Spoken Word Recognition

As is true for cognitive operations in general, the process of spoken language understanding is not directly observable. The researcher interested in the ways in which speech is perceived and processed must therefore resort to experimental methods, under the assumption that the surface products of these methods reflect underlying cognitive operations. Experiments produce observable results, but not all experimental techniques are equal. By now, there is ample evidence that words are recognized faster or more easily when embedded in a meaningful sentence context. In the spoken domain, effects of context on word recognition have been demonstrated with techniques such as speech shadowing, mispronunciation detection, phoneme monitoring, word monitoring, gating, or crossmodal priming. A crucial question is, what data obtained with each technique reflect (cf., Grosjean & Frauenfelder, 1997; Tyler, 1990).

Experimental methods can be characterized in many ways, one of which is the division into global and local tasks (see Levelt, 1978; Cutler & Norris, 1979, for similar distinctions). Examples of global tasks are the cloze test, sentence verification, paraphrasing, and judgments about the grammaticality or the semantic acceptability of a sentence. With a global task, the net outcome of a plethora of processes is measured. Global tasks can be timed; that is, the time it takes a participant to respond can be registered. Timed or not timed, however, it is difficult, if not impossible, to assess the individual contribution of each process to the obtained result.

This might be different with timed, local tasks. The assumption underlying local measures is that responses are intimately linked with, and tightly lime-locked to, processing at the level which is of interest to the experimenter. Timed local measures are supposed to tap into underlying cognitive processes while these are operating in real-time. Examples of timed local tasks are naming, lexical decision, phoneme monitoring, word monitoring, and mispronunciation detection. Local techniques can be divided further into direct and indirect tasks. This distinction refers to the relationship between the task and the level of processing or representation the researcher wishes to investigate. If this is the lexical level, lexical decision and word monitoring are direct tasks, since responses require information pertaining to words. Phoneme monitoring is indirect, because participants are focused on the speech input rather than on words.

But even with local and timed measures, it is extremely difficult to decide which of the subprocesses that might operate in parallel during language understanding are responsible for obtained effects. Accepting that finding answers to these questions is already extremely problematic, what about strategic task effects? It is by no means easy to ascertain to what extent the participants' behavior unequivocally reflects the cognitive operations and representations one is interested in, and in how far their responses are attributable to strategies particular to the requirements of the task. A distinction is made here between process and strategy, which is not equivalent to definitions used elsewhere (see Fodor, 1983; Friederici, 1987). Strategies are defined as operations induced by the particular task at hand. The existence of such task-induced strategies in normal listening situations, outside the laboratory, is highly questionable. They are considered not to be part of the normal language processing system. Strategies combine various sources of knowledge - linguistic and non-linguistic - to solve specific task demands, in particular when the listener is confronted with incomplete or ambiguous input. Processes, on the other hand, are part and parcel of the repertoire of normal language understanding, independent of whether their operation is monitored or not. Certain tasks seem more susceptible to strategic operations than others. Lexical decision, for example, is considered to be more strategy-prone than naming (Balota & Chumbley, 1984; Seidenberg, Waters, Sanders & Langer, 1984). Indirect tasks can sometimes minimize strategic processing at the level of interest to the researcher, because participants generate their responses at a different level. In general, it is important to compare and weigh data from more than one task, to decide to what extent experimentally observed phenomena reflect underlying processes or task-induced strategies (cf., Grosjean & Frauenfelder, 1997).

One promising way to avoid most of the artefacts due to tasks and strategies is the measurement of brain potentials during language understanding. Given their high temporal resolution, event related potentials (ERPs) are particularly suited, and their registration does not require tasks other than the natural ones of listening or reading. ERPs are non-intrusive, closely time-locked to stimulus events, and provide a continuous measure, compared to the discreteness of reaction time responses (cf., Friederici, this volume; Garnsey, 1993; Osterhout & Holcomb, 1995; Van Petten & Kutas, 1991). In the course of the last decade, an increasing number of ERP studies on language processing has become available. Unfortunately for the focus of this chapter - context effects in spoken word recognition - most of the work has used visual stimulus presentation. The data with spoken words and sentences are discussed under a separate heading.

3.4 Evidence for Effects of Sentential Context on the Recognition of Spoken Words

The above distinctions and caveats serve as a background against which the available evidence for the contributions of sentential context to the processes of spoken word recognition is evaluated. The remainder of this chapter is by no means an exhaustive overview of more than forty years of research on context effects. A few crucial studies are mentioned that are representative of particular research paradigms. Results are evaluated with respect to their potential locus within the functional model of word recognition. Two issues are crucial with respect to the localization of context effects. The first concerns the nature of contextual constraint represented by the materials: can effects truly be attributed to crosstalk between different processing domains, or can they be explained by connections between elements within a given level of lexical representation? Equally important is an assessment of what is measured by the particular experimental method at hand. As argued above, an interpretation of contextual effects in terms of their functional locus crucially depends on the paradigm and/or task used. Whereas some paradigms only provide very global evidence for context effects, others allow for an interpretation of results in terms of particular processing stages. To facilitate an interpretation of effects in terms of their functional locus, the presentation of the available evidence is structured according to paradigms and tasks.

Manipulating the Speech Signal

Almost one hundred years ago, Bagley showed that the identification of words with missing consonants was enhanced by the presence of a sentence context (Bagley, 1900-1901). About 50 years later, essentially the same phenomenon was investigated with a different technique: the identification of speech against a background of noise. In a study by Miller, Heise and Lichten (1951), participants identified words presented in noise more accurately when embedded in a grammatical sentence than when words were scrambled or presented in isolation. Miller and Isard (1963) showed that performance was even better when semantic information was present. The identification-in-noise technique is rarely used nowadays in experiments on word recognition in sentential contexts. An exception is a recent study by Deutsch and Bentin (1994) on syntactic context effects in Hebrew. The identification of words in noise was measured as a function of their syntactic agreement (in number and/or gender) to the preceding context. Positive effects of congruency as well as negative effects of incongruency were observed. Deutsch and Bentin interpret their results at the level of the integration of words with the syntactic specifications of the context.

A number of paradigms share the manipulation of the sensory input with the identification-in-noise technique. The question underlying these paradigms is whether semantic context directly influences perception of speech sounds. Warren (1970, 1976) first reported the phoneme restoration effect: the finding that participants repair a word with a missing sound. When a stretch of speech - corresponding to a phoneme - in a contextually predictable word was replaced by a cough or a buzz, participants consistently restored the utterance. They reported hearing a cough or a buzz in an otherwise completely intact utterance and insisted that they had indeed heard the missing phoneme. Moreover, they had great difficulties in locating the exact position of the extraneous sound.

Although these results are illustrative for the contribution of sentence context to the identification of incomplete or noisy signals, they do not tell us which stage of processing is involved. Context could either directly influence the perception of the speech input, or be of relevance at later stages. Samuel (1981a, 1981b, 1996) conducted a series of experiments on the phoneme restoration phenomenon, using a signal-detection approach to distinguish between genuine perceptual effects (d') and post-perceptual bias (Beta).[1] Words embedded in more or less constraining sentences had one sound either completely replaced with, or superimposed by, noise. If the restoration effect were purely perceptual, Samuel argued, then the words with sounds completely replaced should sound like those with noise added. Post-perceptual bias (Beta) was measured in terms of the proportion of words reported to be intact, that is, with noise added. There was no evidence on the d' measure that sentential contexts affected the actual processing of the sensory input. However, the Beta values showed a large bias in constraining contexts towards reporting predictable words as intact. Thus, the effects of semantic information have to be located after perceptual processing of the input, either at access, selection or integration stages of word recognition.

Instead of using noise to obliterate the speech input, a host of studies have manipulated the signal to create ambiguous inputs at the phoneme and word level (Bond & Garnes, 1980; Connine, 1987; Connine, Blasko & Wang, 1994; Garnes & Bond, 1976; Miller, Green & Schermer, 1984). In such experiments, participants heard sentences such as *check the time and the ...* and *paint the fence and the ...*, followed by either *gate* or *date*, or by one of a number of stimuli drawn from the acoustic continuum ranging from *gate* to *date*. The results from such experiments can be exemplified by data from Connine (1987). In her experiment, two types of data were gathered: identification responses for the first phoneme (e.g., /g/ or /d/) and reaction times to make the response. The percentage contextually appropriate of responses was high in the ambiguous boundary region, where the stimulus is neither /gate/ nor /date/, a result obtained in most studies. Interestingly, reaction times to contextually appropriate and inappropriate responses were statistically identical. A reaction time advantage for contextually appropriate responses was obtained only towards the endpoints of the continua. Given

---

[1]   Whereas d' represents a measure for the true perceptual discriminability of the noise-added and noise-replaced signals, the Beta measure reflects a subjective response criterion, also labeled 'bias', which can change as a function of context (cf., Green & Swets, 1966).

the identical response times for ambiguous stimuli in congruent and incongruent contexts, Connine argues that the high percentage of contextually appropriate identifications do not reflect a perceptual effect. These data, together with Samuel's (1981), show that information from sentence contexts does not meddle with the perception of speech sounds - as is, in principle, possible in fully interactive models such as TRACE. What is not clear is whether the observed contextual bias effects reflect processes of lexical access, selection or integration.

Monitoring the Input

In this Section, I will discuss some experimental techniques which have proven to be very influential in research on spoken-word recognition: speech shadowing, monitoring for deviations, and monitoring for linguistic units. All these paradigms require participants to monitor the incoming speech, but the task demands differ. With shadowing, participants have to continuously respond, by repeating verbatim the auditorily presented message. With the other tasks, participants monitor the utterance for the presence of a specified target. This can be a word, a syllable, a phoneme, or a mispronunciation. A response is required only when the prespecified target is encountered.

Shadowing. To shadow a spoken message is to repeat it aloud as it is heard, staying as close behind the speaker as possible. The technique, introduced by Cherry (1953), was used by Marslen-Wilson (1973, 1985) to study spoken word recognition in context. Marslen-Wilson observed that some participants, so called close shadowers, could repeat back fluent speech at latencies of about 200 ms, that is, after having heard the first syllable of a word. What is important is the depth of processing in shadowing. In principle, shadowing could be no more than the echoic repetition of the incoming speech, reflecting perceptual processing at a shallow level. If, however, the shadower's performance is influenced by contextual information, then it follows that shadowing involves deeper levels of processing. Marslen-Wilson's analysis of errors made while shadowing showed that close shadowers used syntactic and semantic information when repeating back the sentences heard. Also, shadowing latencies increased from normal to semantically anomalous sentences. Marslen-Wilson and Welsh (1978) investigated under which conditions shadowers either repair mispronounced words, or repeat them verbatim. More fluent restorations, that is, repairing the mispronunciation without hesitation, occurred in contextually constrained than in unconstrained words.

Marslen-Wilson and Welsh interpret fluent restorations as evidence that contextual information directly affects sensory processing. Of course, there are alternative explanations. One possibility is that shadowers use context strategically, to predict which words are coming. One would then expect shadowers to produce contextually predictable words that are not present in the input, but such errors are rare. An alternative locus for the effect is the production side. What is measured is the output of the shadower's speech production system. The fact that words are restored does not necessarily imply that the mispronunciation has gone undetected. In fact, speakers can notice imminent phonological errors in their own (covert) speech and intercept them (Baars, Motley & Mackay, 1975). Thus, repairs and fast shadowing latencies do not necessarily imply that context affects perceptual accuracy at the sensory level. An interpretation in terms of postlexical integration is rather unlikely, because shadowers start repeating what they hear well before the end of a word. It is, however, still entirely possible that contextual information influences initial lexical access or selection.

Mispronunciation detection. Closely related to shadowing is monitoring for deviations. Since Cole (1973) introduced listening for mispronunciations as a measure to study speech processing, a fair amount of studies on the effects of context has been reported with this paradigm (Cole & Jakimik, 1978, 1980; Jakimik, 1980; Cole & Perfetti, 1980; Ottevanger, 1986; Walley & Metsala, 1990). With mispronunciation detection, listeners are presented with spoken sentences containing words, of which a single speech segment has been changed to produce a pseudoword: e.g., *globe.* mispronounced as *glose*. Participants have to react, by pressing a button, as soon as they detect the mispronunciation. Detection time is measured from the onset of the altered segment. Detection rates are generally very high, between 85 and 100 percent, depending on the acoustic/phonetic distance between input and original word, and on the position of the mispronunciation in the stimulus. The assumption behind the paradigm is that the time it takes to detect that a word has been mispronounced is directly related to the time it takes to recognize the word. Perceiving the mispronunciation, in this view, is a natural consequence of recognising the original word.

Evidence obtained with this paradigm is easily summarized. Mispronunciations are detected faster when mispronounced words are constrained by the preceding context. To determine the nature and locus of the obtained context effects it is important to consider what the task actually reflects. Cole and Jakimik (1978) admit that listeners have other means to detect mispronunciations than through the recognition of the intended word. They can use a non-word route instead. The listener can decide that a mispronunciation must have occurred as soon as it becomes clear that the input does not constitute a word. If this is what participants do, not much can be inferred about word recognition in context. Moreover, a closer look at the sentence materials shows that most sentences contain words that are strongly associated to the mispronounced word. Thus, effects can easily be attributed to intralexical priming and are not very revealing for potential interactions of lexical and sentence processing.

Cole and Perfetti (1980), and Samuel (1986) note an interesting paradox between shadowing mispronounced materials and monitoring for mispronunciations. Shadowers fluently restore mispronunciations, whereas others, monitoring for mispronunciations on exactly the same material, detect these almost without failure.

With the shadowing task, fluent restorations of mispronounced words are taken to be an index for the effectiveness of higher-level constraints. But since, as far as shadowing accuracy is concerned, each restoration constitutes an error, the participants' performance is actually worse in these cases. If, as Marslen-Wilson and Welsh (1978) state, shadowing performance reflects interactions of contextual constraint with sensory perception, then not only is the participants' performance worse, but also - per implicationem - their actual percept of the sensory input. With mispronunciation detection, however, context facilitates a response to a predictable, be it mispronounced, word. Contrary to what the shadowing results seem to indicate, the word is clearly perceived as being mispronounced. This paradox again demonstrates how difficult it is to decide what exactly is measured with these paradigms. Context aids performance in both tasks, but the observable response pattern is quite different. The question remains how the evidence bears on perceptual, lexical and sentence processing in more natural circumstances.

Monitoring for words. Participants engaged in word monitoring listen to sentences for the occurrence of a target word specified in advance. They press a button as soon as the target is detected. Word targets can be specified in a number of ways. A frequently used variant is identical monitoring: participants know exactly which word target they have to listen for (e.g., *cat*). In rhyme monitoring, information is given on what (part of) the word will sound like, by presenting in advance a word which rhymes with the target (e. g., *hat*). The target word can also be specified semantically, as in category monitoring, where the semantic category to which the target belongs is given (e. g., *animal*). Response latencies to detect the target in the sentence are always measured from its acoustic onset.

All three variants of word monitoring were used in a much cited study by Marslen-Wilson and Tyler (1980) on effects of contextual constraint on word recognition. There were three types of context. Targets were embedded in normal sentences, in syntactically correct but otherwise meaningless sentences, or in utterances with words in random order. Monitoring times were always fastest in normal prose. Also, an advantage was obtained of syntactic prose over random word order, indicating that syntactic information enhanced monitoring performance even in the absence of semantic information.

Marslen-Wilson and Tyler's study has been criticized for aspects of their materials and lack of statistical interactions (Cowart, 1982; but see Marslen-Wilson & Tyler, 1983). Interestingly, Marslen-Wilson and Tyler claimed that effects of sentential context were positive and facilitatory. It is unclear what the basis for this claim is. The finding that words are responded to faster in normal than in semantically deviating sentences does not necessarily mean that normal sentences speed up responses. Response times, in particular with identical monitoring, were extremely short, in fact shorter than the mean length of target words. This fact seems to speak against a locus of context effects at a stage at which selection of the spoken word has been accomplished on the basis of sensory information alone. But extremely fast responses with identical monitoring, relative to mean word durations, have more than one explanation. Participants are clearly tuned to the critical word in identical monitoring. They are in fact actively looking for it, scanning the input for an indication of its occurrence. In particular in the absence of catch trials, a partial match between target and speech might suffice. Participants might respond on the basis of, say, the first one or two phonemes of the spoken word. If they do, responses are not very informative as to the locus of effects of sentential constraint in normal word recognition.

In later years, the paradigm has been used more as a diagnostic to differentiate between groups of listeners, or type of constraint. Friederici (1983) compared monitoring performance of patients with Broca and Wernicke aphasia as a function of semantic and syntactic constraints in the materials. Positive effects of semantic context were found for both groups, but they differed in syntactic conditions. Marslen-Wilson, Brown and Tyler (1988) used the paradigm to compare effects of semantic and syntactic violations (e.g., monitoring latencies to *guitar* in *They ate the guitar* vs. *They slept the guitar*). They observed slower responses for syntactic anomalies than for semantic anomalies. They conclude that a failure to integrate words into a syntactic representation is of a different nature than problems with semantic integration. Thus, the interpretation of locus of context effects in word monitoring has changed quite a bit in the course of two decades.

Phoneme monitoring. In phoneme monitoring, participants monitor for the occurrence of a prespecified sound in the sentence they are listening to. In an early experiment, Morton and Long (1976) measured latencies to detect the same word-initial segment (e.g., /b/) in contextually predictable and unpredictable words (e.g., *the sparrow sat on the branch/bed*). Responses to targets embedded in contextually predictable words were much faster than to the same targets in unpredictable words. These results were replicated by Foss and Blank (1980), using the exact same materials. Foss and Gernsbacher (1983) discovered a serious flaw in those materials, in that certain perceptual characteristics of the words used were almost perfectly confounded with contextual predictability.

There are, however, a number of studies in which the word that contained the target was kept constant, and context was varied. Except for a few studies (Dell & Newman, 1980; Eimas & Nygaard, 1992), the contextual predictability of a critical word was assessed through monitoring responses to the initial phoneme of the word directly following it. With monitoring times to the initial phoneme to the critical word itself, it is uncertain whether responses are made on the basis of lexical or sublexical levels of representation (see Cutler & Norris, 1979; Cutler, Mehler, Norris & Segui, 1987). When responses are made to the first phoneme of the next word, this does not apply. With this variant, positive effects of semantic predictability were obtained (Blank & Foss, 1978; Cairns, Cowart & Jablon, 1981; Foss, Cirilo & Blank, 1979).

Two comments are in order with respect to these results. First, all studies used contexts containing words that were strongly related to the critical word. The same argument made earlier can be repeated here: effects obtained with semantically associated words do not tell us much about interactions between lexical and sentence levels. Second, with responses to the next word, the critical word has already been fully processed. Facilitation indeed can be taken to mean that this processing was enhanced by contextual information, but there is no way of knowing where context exactly had its effect: before, during, or after the processing of the critical word. Comparing effects on the critical word itself with those on the next word, Foss and Ross (1983) argue that the locus of contextual facilitation is most likely at the integration stage.

Gating: A Production Task for Language Comprehension

In the gating paradigm, words are presented in a piecemeal fashion. Participants typically hear successive presentations of fragments (or gates) of target words. The fragment is incremented by a constant amount at each presentation. The first fragment consists of, for example, the first 50 ms of the word, the second of the first 100 ms, and so on, until the whole word is presented. After each fragment, participants have to produce (write down or speak aloud) the word they think is being presented. They usually also have to indicate how confident they are about their response. The task provides information as to how much sensory information suffices to produce, and ipso facto, to recognize the presented word. Since its introduction to the realm of context effects in spoken word recognition by Grosjean (1980), the paradigm has boomed for some years (Bard, Shillcock & Altmann, 1988; Cotton & Grosjean, 1984; Grosjean, 1985; McAllister, 1988; Salasoo & Pisoni, 1985; Tyler & Marslen-Wilson, 1986; Tyler & Wessels, 1983, 1985; Zwitserlood, 1989b).

In most studies, word fragments of increasing length are embedded in sentence contexts that are more or less constraining for the target word. Contextual constraints are either semantic or syntactic in nature. What is typically found is that semantically constraining contexts, relative to neutral ones, substantially reduce the amount of sensory input that is necessary to produce the correct word (Grosjean, 1980; Salasoo & Pisoni, 1985; Tyler & Wessels, 1983; Zwitserlood, 1989b). This holds even when semantic constraints, as established in cloze tests, are minimal (e.g., *Suddenly they walked into a..*). Moreover, the set of elicited responses is smaller in constraining than in neutral contexts (Grosjean, 1980; but see Tyler, 1984). A positive syntactic context (e.g., *Hij begon te..*, he started to..), supposed to narrow down responses to verbs, only had a marginal effect (Tyler & Wessels, 1983).

Thus, there are clear effects of semantic context with the gating paradigm. The interpretation of gating data, in terms of the locus of effects during word recognition, is not an easy enterprise. Some (Grosjean, 1980; Salasoo & Pisoni, 1985) argue that contextual constraints operate as early as lexical access, in narrowing down the set of words which is considered for recognition. Tyler (1984), who found no differences in initial size of the set of responses as a function of context, instead proposes an early and fast selection process. Upon lexical access, all word forms compatible with the sensory input are activated, independent of their contextual fit. Context rapidly serves to narrow down these alternatives. One of the problems with the gating task is that subjects often have ample time (5 to 6 seconds) to exploit the information contained in the sentence context (but see Tyler & Wessels, 1985, for a timed version). Timed or not, context might be particularly relevant when listeners are forced to concentrate on a fragment of a word and have to come up with a possible completion. Task performance in gating would certainly benefit from the conscious and strategic use of contextual information. If listeners use such strategies, the results might not reflect normal word processing so much.

Crossmodal Paradigms

The reader familiar with the literature on context effects in the visual domain might wonder whether the two tasks which have been so extensively used there have their equivalent in the spoken domain. Meant here are *lexical decision* and *naming*. In lexical decision, participants have to decide whether a target is an existing word of their language. In the visual domain, positive and negative effects of sentence contexts on lexical decision latencies have been demonstrated, by Shubert and Eimas (1977), Fischler and Bloom (1979) and Kleiman (1980) amongst others. With naming, the target word has to be read out loud (Stanovich & West, 1981; Forster, 1981; Norris, 1987). With visual presentation, it is relatively easy to ensure that participants react to the critical word embedded in a sentence. Targets can be visually set off from the context. This is far more difficult with auditory presentation. How does the participant know which word to react to? It is not surprising that auditory lexical decision and naming have hardly been used to study context effects.

An exception is a study on Serbo-Croatian by Katz, Boyce, Goldstein, and Lukatela (1987), who used minimal syntactic contexts. They presented inflected real and pseudoword adjectives before noun targets. Participants knew they always had to react to the second of two stimuli. The inflections on the (pseudo-) adjectives were either congruent or incongruent with those of the targets. Clear congruency effects were obtained, both for real and pseudoword adjectives. The authors concluded that effects of inflectional congruency are integrative, that is, located after at least the stem of the inflected noun has been recognized.

A much used variant, in which tasks such as lexical decision and naming can be applied to spoken word recognition, is to present target words visually. This research strategy has been labeled *crossmodal*. The crossmodal presentation format has been used to study a whole range of phenomena: word priming (Warren, 1976), the resolution of anaphora (Tyler & Marslen-Wilson, 1982), the resolution of structural ambiguities (Tyler & Marslen-Wilson, 1977), and syntactic violations (Friederici & Kilborn,

1989). In these studies, a critical word which formed the continuation of the spoken sentence was presented visually, as a target for lexical decision or naming.

First and foremost, the crossmodal presentation format has been used to study the influence of semantic context on semantic ambiguity. The methodology of these experiments differs from the above crossmodal studies in that the relationship between the visual stimulus and the sentence is less direct. In ambiguity studies, the visual target word is not a continuation of the spoken sentence. Instead, visual target words are semantically related to one of the senses of an ambiguous word embedded in the spoken sentence (e.g., *river* and *money* associated with *bank*). This version of the crossmodal paradigm thus uses the established effect of semantic priming to trace the processes of access to word senses and sense selection (Conrad, 1974). Therefore, the paradigm is known as *crossmodal semantic priming*. It is impossible to review the complete ambiguity literature here (see Simpson, 1984, 1994, for excellent overviews). Rather, focusing on the effects of sentential context, a few representative studies will be discussed.

The most frequently studied issue is whether all senses of an ambiguous word are accessed during word recognition. Effects of context on the availability of multiple word senses constitute a critical test of the view that lexical processing is autonomous. Results from crossmodal studies on semantic ambiguities of the *bank* type, quite stimulated by work of Swinney and his colleagues (Swinney & Hakes, 1976; Swinney, Onifer, Prather & Hirshkowitz, 1978; Swinney, 1979) are not easily summarized. Many studies demonstrated activation of both meanings of ambiguous words, even in contexts biasing towards one of the senses (Conrad, 1974; Lucas, 1987; Moss & Marslen-Wilson, 1993; Onifer & Swinney, 1981; Seidenberg, Tanenhaus, Leiman & Bienkowski, 1982; Swinney, 1979). But others have found evidence for contextually driven selective activation of only one sense (Glucksberg, Kreuz & Rho, 1986; Tabossi, 1988; Tabossi, Colombo & Job, 1987; Tabossi & Zardon, 1993). Much depends on the relative dominance of one sense over the other, and on whether ambiguous words and targets are associatively or semantically related.

A second, related issue addressed in crossmodal priming studies concerns the influence of syntactic context on the disambiguation of homonyms, whose members belong to different word classes and have different meanings (e.g., *a watch* vs. *to watch*). When manipulating syntactic constraints (*They all rose* vs. *She bought a rose*; target *flower*), all studies showed consistent facilitation, independent of context, with naming and lexical decision (Seidenberg, Tanenhaus, Leiman & Bienkowski, 1982; Tanenhaus & Donnenwerth-Nolan, 1984; Tanenhaus, Leiman & Seidenberg, 1979). The data thus provide evidence for context-independent multiple activation of the meaning of words from different syntactic categories.

When considering the locus of context effects with ambiguous words, it is worth noting that with one exception (Tabossi & Zardon, 1993), the full ambiguous word was heard in all studies before the targets related to either of its senses were presented. Thus, one particular word form has been fully recognized when the targets are presented (e.g., *bank*, and not *band* was heard). So, these studies are not concerned with the recognition of word forms, but with context effects on sense selection. Whatever the truth on context-dependent or independent activation of multiple senses, it is intriguing that studies which demonstrated context-independent multiple access, nevertheless showed effects of context. Specifically, many studies show more facilitation for contextually appropriate senses than for inappropriate ones, even when both are facilitated, relative to a control condition. The evidence is pervasive, although only few authors acknowledge the existence of such effects. Oden and Spira (1983) explicitly discussed that their evidence for multiple access was modulated by context, and Simpson (1984, 1994) notes the general existence of similar effects throughout the literature. It is important to take these phenomena into consideration if one wishes to understand how and when contextual information modulates processing at the level of sense selection.

Close to home, a different approach to ambiguity was taken by Zwitserlood (1989a). In a crossmodal priming study in Dutch, visual targets were presented at the end of spoken sentences that contained perceptual ambiguities. This was accomplished by presenting perceptually ambiguous fragments of words, such as / kaep/, which could be the first part of *captain* or *capital*. Spoken sentences contained semantic information - but no associated words - that biased towards one of the possible continuations of the spoken word fragment (e.g., *In dampened spirits the men stood around the grave. They mourned the loss of their cap..*). The visual targets were either related to the word which fitted the context (*ship*, related to captain) or to the inappropriate word (*town*, related to capital). Neutral contexts were also included (*The next word is cap..*), and sentences with different word fragments served as baseline (*The next word is pos..*). Facilitation was found for both targets, even in constraining contexts. Thus, the data provide evidence for multiple access. The ambiguous word fragment served to activate more than one word, in fact, the meaning of more than one word, since the targets were semantically related to the possible continuations (cf., Zwitserlood & Schriefers, 1995). Crucially, lexical access was unaffected by contextual constraints. There was equal facilitation for contextually appropriate and inappropriate words. Other conditions, with longer but still ambiguous word fragments, showed that contextual constraints operate at the level of selection and integration.

The crossmodal priming paradigm has the advantage of being an indirect technique. Participants' conscious efforts and strategies to perform well on the task apply to the visual targets, not to the spoken ambiguous words or fragments that the researcher is most interested in. Results obtained with crossmodal semantic priming show that the paradigm is sensitive to differential levels of (sense) activation, and - even in cases of multiple access - to effects of context on this activation. Even when context serves to discard one of the senses of an ambiguity, it is important to keep in mind that this is always after the complete ambiguous word has been heard (or very briefly before, as in Tabossi & Zardon, 1993). Looking much earlier, with perceptual ambiguities, Zwitserlood (1989a) showed that effects of sentential semantic context come into play after lexical access, during the selection of word forms and the integration of their semantic specifications. So, there are apparent differences between selecting different word forms and different senses of one and the same word form (cf., Zwitserlood, 1989b).

Event-Related Potentials and Effects of Context

As stated before, there is yet little evidence on sentence context effects in the spoken domain with brain potentials (see Friederici, this volume). There are by now a number of studies in the visual domain on semantic priming (with word pairs such as *doctor - nurse*) and semantic (in)congruency (H*e ate bread with cheese/socks*). Common to both are clear differences in the N400 component as a function of semantic relatedness and congruency (Kutas & Van Petten, 1994; Van Petten, 1993, for overviews). Context-dependent vs. independent access to word senses of ambiguous words was also investigated with visual presentation (Van Petten & Kutas, 1987), with evidence interpreted in favor of context-dependent access (but see Osterhout & Holcomb, 1995, for a different interpretation). The semantic congruency effect for words in sentences, first shown by Kutas and Hilliard (1980) with visual presentation, was replicated in the auditory domain (Friederici, Pfeifer & Hahne, 1993; Holcomb & Neville; 1991; McCallum, Farmer & Pocock, 1984). Holcomb and Neville observed that the N400 components for contextually appropriate and inappropriate words started to diverge well before the complete spoken word had been heard. Such data are fully compatible with an early selection interpretation of the effects of semantic context.

With respect to syntactic context, most ERP research has resorted to syntactic violations. ERPs on violations in connected speech (e.g., The broker hoped to sell the stock *was..*, violation in italics; from Osterhout & Holcomb, 1993) showed a positive-going component, as opposed to the negative N400 found for semantic incongruency. The peak of this component was around 600 ms after stimulus onset, hence the P600. Except for a somewhat earlier onset, this P600 was very similar to the one found in experiments with visual presentation (Osterhout & Holcomb, 1992). Hagoort, Brown and Groothusen (1993) found similar results for Dutch, with agreement and phrase structure violations, and the same holds for syntactic category violations in German, both with visually and auditorily presented sentences (Friederici, Hahne & Mecklinger 1996). Although there is a continuing debate as to the exact status of this late positive component, it seems to be elicited both by syntactic violations and by processes of syntactic reanalysis (cf., Friederici, 1997; Friederici & Mecklinger, 1996).

3.5   Conclusions

After forty years of intensive empirical work on spoken word processing, there is no doubt whatsoever that information contained in sentence contexts influences word recognition. Still, the state of the art in the context domain is not easily summarised, even when only those experiments are taken into consideration that are free from criticism against material and methodology. A fruitful way to evaluate the data is to assess what they contribute to the question of the locus of context effects in speech perception and word recognition. What can be inferred from the data about the level of processing at which contextual information operates? Four processing domains or levels were distinguished, without taking an a priori stance on their autonomy, their seriality, or on the flow of information within the word recognition system and beyond. These levels include perceptual processing, lexical access, selection, and semantic and syntactic integration.

Some researchers have claimed that their data convincingly show that sentential context directly influences the perception and encoding of speech sounds. In hindsight, the evidence is not as convincing as it seemed. It has never been demonstrated that the actual percept of, say, a speech sound had changed as a function of contextual information. Data from paradigms such as gating and word monitoring were taken as evidence that context influences the amount of sensory information needed for word recognition. But even this evidence has to be digested with caution. It is undoubtedly true that listeners are prepared to make a response on the basis of less sensory evidence. Different interpretations have been put forward as to what this means for speech processing or word recognition. Most convincing is the positive evidence that sentential information does not meddle with speech perception. The data by Samuel (1981) on phoneme restoration still constitute a hall-mark in this respect.

If contextual information does not interact with speech perception, might it then serve to narrow down the number of word forms that become active during lexical access? This issue is not easy to decide. Many researchers state that contextual information interacts with the lexical system at some point after lexical access, but it is more a matter of belief than of evidence. Even though the data are some ten years old, the only evidence that lexical access is not influenced by sentential semantic information comes from my own experiments (Zwitserlood, 1989a). These same data show that the most likely locus for the effects of context on word processing is during a combined phase of selection and integration. If they fit the semantic specifications of the ongoing analysis at a sentential semantic level, words - or more accurately, their semantic properties - are selected before enough sensory information has been heard to uniquely distinguish them from other words in the language. Data from studies with event-related potentials (Holcomb & Neville, 1991) fit this picture very nicely.

As stated before, some models have been adapted to fit the available evidence. Some have not. Models in psycholinguistics serve valuable purposes, as they certainly have in the domain of spoken word recognition. But they can also lead astray, if there is too much belief in them. Currently, the focus is not as much on testing models as on finding out more about what exactly happens at a specific point in time during spoken language understanding, and about the neural processes underlying language comprehension.

Acknowledgments

Parts of my dissertation have found their way into this chapter. In rethinking context effects in spoken word recognition, I had fond remembrances of extensive discussions with my friend and colleague Colin Brown on these issues. I am also grateful to Dirk Vorberg, for his forbearance.

References

Aitchison, J. (1994). Words in the mind: An introduction to the mental lexicon (2nd. ed.). Oxford: Blackwell.

Baars, B.J., Motley, M.T. & MacKay, D. (1975). Output editing for lexical status from artificially elicited slips of the tongue. *Journal of Verbal Learning and Verbal Behavior, 14,* 382-391.

Bagley, W.C. (1990). The apperception of the spoken sentence: A study in the psychology of language. *American Journal of Psychology, 12,* 80-120.

Balota, D.A. & Chumbley, J.I. (1984). Are lexical decisions a good measure of lexical access? The role of word frequency in the neglected decision stage. *Journal of Experimental Psychology: Human Perception and Performance, 10,* 340-357.

Bard, E.G., Shillcock, R.C. & Altmann, G.T.M. (1988). The recognition of words after their acoustic offsets in spontaneous speech: Effects of subsequent context. *Perception and Psychophysics, 44,* 395-408.

Blank, M.A. & Foss, D.J. (1978). Semantic facilitation and lexical access during sentence processing. *Memory and Cognition, 6,* 644-652.

Bond, Z.S. & Garnes, S. (1980). Misperceptions of fluent speech. In R.A. Cole (Ed.), *Perception and production of fluent speech.* Hillsdale, NJ: Erlbaum.

Bradley, D.C. & Forster, K.I. (1987). A reader's view of listening. *Cognition, 25,* 103-134.

Cairns, H.S., Cowart, W. & Jablon, A.D. (1981). Effects of prior context upon the integration of lexical information during sentence processing. *Journal of Verbal Learning and Verbal Behavior, 20,* 445-453.

Cherry, E.C. (1953). Some experiments on the recognition of speech, with one and with two ears. *Journal of the Acoustic Society of America, 25,* 975-979.

Cole, R.A. (1973). Listening for mispronunciations: A measure of what we hear during speech. *Perception and Psychophysics, 13,* 153-156.

Cole, R.A. & Jakimik, J. (1978). Understanding speech: How words are heard. In G. Underwood (ed.), *Strategies of information processing.* London: Academic Press.

Cole, R.A. & Jakimik, J. (1980). A model of speech perception. In R.A. Cole (ed.), *Perception and production of fluent speech.* Hillsdale, NJ: Erlbaum.

Cole, R.A. & Perfetti, C.A. (1980). Listening for mispronunciations in a children s story: The use of context by children and adults. *Journal of Verbal Learning and Verbal Behavior, 19,* 297-315.

Connine, C.M. (1990). Effects of sentence context and lexical knowledge in speech processing. In G.T.M. Altmann (ed.), *Cognitive models of speech processing.* Cambridge, MA: MIT Press.

Connine, C.M. (1987). Constraints on interactive processes in auditory word recognition: The role of sentence context. *Journal of Memory and Language, 26,* 527-538.

Connine, C.M., Blasko, D.G. & Wang, J. (1994). Vertical similarity in spoken word recognition: Multiple lexical activation, individual differences, and the role of sentence context. *Perception and Psychophysics, 56(6),* 624-636.

Conrad, C. (1974). Context effects in sentence comprehension: A study of the subjective lexicon. *Memory and Cognition, 2,* 130-138.

Cotton, S. & Grosjean, F. (1984). The gating paradigm: Successive or individual presentations? *Perception and Psychophysics, 35,* 41-48.

Cowart, W. (1982). Autonomy and interaction in the language processing system: A reply to Marslen-Wilson and Tyler. *Cognition, 12,* 109-117.

Cutler, A. & McQueen, J.M. (1995). The recognition of lexical units in speech. In B. de Gelder and J. Morais (eds.), *Speech and reading: A comparative approach.* Hove, UK: Taylor & Francis.

Cutler, A., Mehler, J., Norris, D. & Segui, J. (1987). Phoneme identification and the lexicon. *Cognitive Psychology, 19,* 141-177.

Cutler, A. & Norris, D. (1979). Monitoring sentence comprehension. In W.E. Cooper & E.C.T. Walker (eds.), *Sentence processing: Psycholinguistic studies presented to Merril Garrett.* Hillsdale, NJ: Erlbaum.

Dell, G.S. & Newman, J.E. (1980). Detecting phonemes in fluent speech. *Journal of Verbal Learning and Verbal Behavior, 19,* 608-623.

Deutsch, A. & Bentin, S. (1994). Attention mechanisms mediate the syntactic priming effect in auditory word identification. *Journal of Experimental Psychology: Learning, Memory and Cognition, 20(3),* 595-607.

Eimas, P.D. & Nygaard, L.C. (1992). Contextual coherence and attention in phoneme monitoring. *Journal of Memory and Language, 31,* 375-395.

Elman, J.L. (1989). Connectionist approaches to acoustic/phonetic processing. In W.D. Marslen-Wilson (ed.), *Lexical representation and process.* Cambridge, MA: MIT Press.

Fischler, I. & Bloom, P.A. (1979). Automatic and attentional processes in the effects of sentence contexts on word recognition. *Journal of Verbal Learning and Verbal Behavior, 18,* 1-20.

Fodor, J.A. (1983). *The modularity of mind.* Cambridge, MA: MIT Press.

Forster, K.I. (1976). Accessing the mental lexicon. In R.J. Wales & E. Walker (eds.), *New approaches to language mechanisms.* Amsterdam: North Holland.

Forster, K.I. (1979). Levels of processing and the structure of the language processor. In W.E. Cooper & E.Walker (eds.), *Sentence processing: Psycholinguistic studies presented to Merril Garrett.* Hillsdale, NJ: Erlbaum.

Forster, K.I. (1981). Priming and the effects of sentence and lexical contexts on naming time: Evidence for autonomous lexical processing. *Quarterly Journal of Experimental Psychology, 33A,* 465-495.

Forster, K.I. (1989). Basic issues in lexical processing. In W.D. Marslen-Wilson (ed.), *Lexical representation and process.* Cambridge, MA: MIT Press.

Foss, D.J. & Blank, M.A. (1980). Identifying the speech codes. *Cognitive Psychology, 12,* 1- 31.

Foss, D.J., Cirilo, R.K. & Blank, M.A. (1979). Semantic facilitation and lexical access during sentence processing: An investigation of individual differences. *Memory and Cognition, 7,* 346-353.

Foss, D.J. & Gernsbacher, M.A. (1983). Cracking the dual code: Toward a unitary model of phoneme identification. *Journal of Verbal Learning and Verbal Behavior, 22,* 609-632.

Foss, D.J. & Ross, J.R. (1983). Great expectations: Context effects during sentence processing. In G.B. Flores d'Arcais & R.J. Jarvella (eds.), *The process of language understanding.* Chichester: Wiley.

Frauenfelder, U.H. (1996). Computational models of spoken word recognition. In T. Dijkstra & K. de Smedt (eds.), *Computational psycholinguistics.* London: Taylor & Francis.

Frauenfelder, U.H. & Tyler, L.K. (1987). The process of spoken word recognition: An introduction. *Cognition, 25,* 1-20.

Frazier, L. (1987). Structure in auditory word recognition. *Cognition, 25,* 157-187.

Friederici, A.D. (1983). Aphasic perception of words in sentential context: Some real-time processing evidence. *Neuropsychologia, 21(4)*, 351-358.

Friederici, A.D. (1987). *Kognitive Strukturen des Sprachverstehens*. Berlin: Springer.

Friederici, A.D. (1997). Neurophysiological aspects of language processing. *Clinical Neuroscience, 4(2)*, 64-72.

Friederici, A.D., Hahne, A. & Mecklinger, A. (1996). Temporal structure of syntactic parsing: Early and late event-related potentials. *Journal of experimental Psychology: Learning, Memory and Cognition, 22(5)*, 1-31.

Friederici, A.D. & Kilborn, K. (1989). Temporal constraints on language processing: Syntactic priming in Broca's aphasia. *Journal of Cognitive Neuroscience, 1(3)*, 262-272.

Friederici, A.D. & Mecklinger, A. (1996). Syntactic parsing as revealed by event-related potentials: First-pass and second-pass parsing. *Journal of Psycholinguistic Research, 25(1)*, 157-176.

Friederici, A.D., Pfeifer, E. & Hahne, A. (1993). Event-related potentials during natural speech processing: Effects of semantic, morphological and syntactic violations. *Cognitive Brain Research, 1(3)*, 183-192.

Garnes, S. & Bond, Z.S. (1976). The relationship between semantic expectations and acoustic information. *Phonologica, 3*, 285-293.

Garnsey, S.M. (1993). Event-related potentials in the study of language: An introduction. *Language and Cognitive Processes, 8(4)*, 337-356.

Glucksberg, S., Kreuz, R.J. & Rho, S.H. (1986). Context can constrain lexical access: Implications for models of language comprehension. *Journal of Experimental Psychology: Learning, Memory and Cognition, 12*, 323-335.

Green, D.M. & Swets, J.A. (1966). *Signal detection theory and psychophysics*. New York: John Wiley.

Grosjean, F. (1980). Spoken word recognition processes and the gating paradigm. *Perception & Psychophysics, 28*, 267-283.

Grosjean, F. (1985). The recognition of words after their acoustic offset: Evidence and implications. *Perception and Psychophysics, 38*, 299-310.

Grosjean, F. & Frauenfelder, U.H. (1997). *A guide to spoken word recognition paradigms*. Hove, UK: Psychology Press.

Hagoort, P., Brown, C. & Groothusen, J. (1993). The syntactic positive shift (SPS) as an ERP measure of syntactic processing. *Language and Cognitive Processes, 8(4)*, 439-483.

Holcomb, P.J. & Neville, H.J. (1991). Natural speech processing: An analysis using event-related brain potentials. *Psychobiology, 19,* 286-300.

Jakimik, J.A. (1980). The interaction of sound and knowledge in word recognition from fluent speech. *Unpublished doctoral dissertation,* Carnegie-Mellon University.

Katz, L., Boyce, S., Goldstein, L. & Lukatela, G. (1987). Grammatical information effects in auditory word recognition. *Cognition, 25(3),* 235-263.

Kleiman, G.W. (1980). Sentence frame contexts and lexical decision: Sentence-acceptability and word-relatedness effects. *Memory and Cognition, 8,* 336-344.

Kutas, M. & Hilliard, S. (1980). Reading senseless sentences: Brain potentials reflect semantic incongruity. *Science, 207,* 203-205.

Kutas, M. & Van Petten, C. (1994). Psycholinguistics electrified: Event-related brain potential investigations. In M. A. Gernsbacher (ed.), *Handbook of psycholinguistics.* San Diego: Academic Press.

Levelt, W.J.M. (1978). A survey of studies in sentence perception: 1970-1976. In W.J.M. Levelt & G.B. Flores d'Arcais (eds.), *Studies in the perception of language.* Chichester: Wiley.

Lucas, M.M. (1987). Frequency effects on the processing of ambiguous words in sentence context. *Language and Speech, 30,* 25-46.

Marslen-Wilson, W.D. (1973). Speech shadowing and speech perception. *Unpublished doctoral dissertation,* Department of Psychology, MIT.

Marslen-Wilson, W.D. (1984). Function and process in spoken word recognition. In H. Bouma & D.G. Bouwhuis (eds.), *Attention and Performance X: Control of language processes.* Hillsdale, NJ: Erlbaum.

Marslen-Wilson, W.D. (1985). Speech shadowing and speech comprehension. *Speech Communication, 4,* 55-73.

Marslen-Wilson, W.D. (1987). Functional parallelism in spoken word recognition. *Cognition, 25,* 71-102.

Marslen-Wilson, W.D. (1989). Access and integration: Projecting sound onto meaning. In W.D. Marslen-Wilson (ed.), *Lexical representation and process.* Cambridge, MA: MIT Press.

Marslen-Wilson, W.D., Brown, C.M. & Tyler, L.K. (1988). Lexical representations in spoken language comprehension. *Language and Cognitive Processes, 3(1),* 1-16.

Marslen-Wilson, W.D. & Tyler, L.K. (1980). The temporal structure of spoken language understanding. *Cognition, 8,* 1-71.

Marslen-Wilson, W.D. & Tyler, L.K. (1983). Reply to Cowart. *Cognition, 15,* 227-235.

Marslen-Wilson, W.D. & Welsh, A. (1978). Processing interactions and lexical access during word recognition in continuos speech. *Cognitive Psychology, 10,* 29-63.

Massaro, D.W. (1994). Psycholinguistic aspects of speech perception: Implications for research and theory. In M.A. Gernsbacher (ed.), *Handbook of psycholinguistics.* San Diego, CA: Academic Press.

McAllister, J.M. (1988). The use of context in auditory word recognition. *Perception and Psychophysics, 44,* 94-97.

McCallum, W.C., Farmer, S.F. & Pocock, P.K. (1984). The effects of physical and semantic incongruities on auditory event-related potentials. *Electroencephalography and clinical Neurophysiology, 59,* 447-488.

McClelland, J.L. & Elman, J.L. (1986). The TRACE model of speech perception. *Cognitive Psychology, 18,* 1-86.

McClelland, J.L. & Rumelhart, D.E. (1981). An interactive activation model of context effects in letter perception: Part 1. An account of basic findings. *Psychological Review, 88,* 375-407.

Meyer, D.M. & Schvaneveldt, R.W. (1971). Facilitation in recognizing pairs of words: Evidence of a dependence between retrieval operations. *Journal of Experimental Psychology, 90,* 227-234.

Miller, G.A. & Isard, S. (1963). Some perceptual consequences of linguistic rules. *Journal of Verbal Learning and Verbal Behavior, 2,* 217-218.

Miller, J.L., Green, K. & Schermer, T.M. (1984). A distinction between the effects of sentential speaking rate and semantic congruency on word identification. *Perception and Psychophysics, 36(4),* 329-337.

Miller, G.A., Heise, G.A. & Lichten, W. (1951). The intelligibility of speech as a function of the context and of the test materials. *Journal of Experimental Psychology, 41,* 329-335.

Morton, J. & Long, J. (1976). Effects of word transitional probability on phoneme identification. *Journal of Verbal Learning and Verbal Behavior, 15,* 43-51.

Moss, H.E. & Marslen-Wilson, W.D. (1993). Access to word meanings during spoken language comprehension: Effects of sentential semantic context. *Journal of Experimental Psychology: Learning, Memory and Cognition, 19(6),* 1254-1276.

Norris, D. (1986). Word recognition: Context effects without priming. *Cognition, 22,* 93-136.

Norris, D. (1987). Strategic control of sentence context in a naming task. *Quarterly Journal of Experimental Psychology, 39A,* 253-275.

Oden, G.C. & Spira, J.L. (1983). Influence of context on the activation and selection of ambiguous word senses. *Quarterly Journal of Experimental Psychology, 35A,* 51-64.

Onifer, W. & Swinney, D.A. (1981). Accessing lexical ambiguities during sentence comprehension: Effects of frequency of meaning and contextual bias. *Memory & Cognition, 9,* 225-236.

O'Seaghdha, P.G. (1989). The dependence of lexical relatedness effects on syntactic correctness. *Journal of Experimental Psychology: Learning, Memory and Cognition, 15,* 73-87.

Osterhout, L. & Holcomb, P. (1992). Event-related brain potentials elicited by syntactic anomaly. *Journal of Memory and Language, 31,* 785-806.

Osterhout, L. & Holcomb, P. (1993). Event-related brain potentials and syntactic anomaly: Evidence of anomaly detection during the perception of continuous speech. *Language and Cognitive Processes, 8,* 413-438.

Osterhout, L. & Holcomb, P. (1995). ERPs and language comprehension. In M.D. Rugg & M.G.H. Coles (eds.), *Electrophysiology of the mind.* New York: Oxford University Press.

Ottevanger, I.B. (1986). Speech processing at the level of word recognition and the influence of sentence context. *Doctoral dissertation,* University of Utrecht.

Pisoni, D.B. & Luce, P.A. (1987). Acoustic-phonetic representations in word recognition. *Cognition, 25,* 21-52.

Ratcliff, R. & McKoon, G. (1988). A retrieval theory of priming in memory. *Psychological Review, 95,* 385-408.

Rumelhart, D.E. & McClelland, J.L. (1982). An interactive activation model of context effects in letter perception: Part 2. The contextual enhancement effect and some tests of the model. *Psychological Review, 89,* 60-94.

Salasoo, A. & Pisoni, D.B. (1985). Interaction of knowledge sources in spoken word identification. *Journal of Memory and Language, 24,* 210-231.

Samuel, A.G. (1981a). Phonemic restoration: Insights from a new methodology. *Journal of Experimental Psychology: General, 110,* 474-494.

Samuel., A.G. (1981b). The role of bottom-up confirmation in the phonemic restoration illusion. *Journal of Experimental Psychology: Human Perception and Performance, 7,* 1124- 1131.

Samuel, A.G. (1986). The role of the lexicon in speech perception. In E.C. Schwab & H.C. Nusbaum (eds.), *Pattern recognition by humans and machines: Speech perception, Vol.1.* New York: Academic Press.

Samuel, A.G. (1996). Does lexical information influence the perceptual restoration of phonemes? *Journal of Experimental Psychology: General, 125(1),* 28-51.

Schwanenflugel, P.J. (1991). Contextual constraint and lexical processing. In G.B. Simpson (ed.), *Understanding word and sentence.* Amsterdam: North-Holland.

Seidenberg, M.S. (1985). The time course of information activation and utilization in visual word recognition. In D. Besner, T.G. Waller & G.E. MacKinnon (eds.), *Reading research: Advances in theory and practice. Vol.5,* New York: Academic Press.

Seidenberg, M.S., Tanenhaus, M.K., Leiman, J.M. & Bienkowski, M. (1982). Automatic access of the meanings of ambiguous words in contexts: Some limitations of knowledge-based processing. *Cognitive Psychology, 14,* 489-537.

Seidenberg, M.S., Waters, G.S., Sanders, M. & Langer, P. (1984). Pre- and postlexical loci of contextual effects on word recognition. *Memory & Cognition, 12,* 315-328.

Shubert, R.E. & Eimas, P.D. (1977). Effects of context on the classification of words and nonwords. *Journal of Experimental Psychology: Human Perception and Performance, 3,* 27-36.

Simpson, G.B. (1984). Lexical ambiguity and its role in model of word recognition. *Psychological Bulletin, 96,* 316-340.

Simpson, G.B. (1994). Context and the processing of ambiguous words. In M.A. Gernsbacher (ed.), *Handbook of psycholinguistics.* San Diego, CA: Academic Press.

Stanovich, K.E. & West, R.F. (1981). The effects of sentence context on ongoing word recognition: Test of a two-process theory. *Journal of Experimental Psychology: Human Perception and Performance, 7,* 658-672.

Swinney, D.A. (1979). Lexical access during sentence comprehension: (Re)consideration of context effects. *Journal of Verbal Learning and Verbal Behavior, 18,* 645-659.

Swinney, D.A. & Hakes, D.T. (1976). Effects of prior context upon lexical access during sentence comprehension. *Journal of Verbal Learning and Verbal Behavior, 15,* 681- 689.

Swinney, D., Onifer, W., Prather, P. & Hirshkowitz, M. (1978). Semantic facilitation across sensory modalities in the processing of individual words and sentences. *Memory & Cognition, 7,* 165-195.

Tabossi, P. (1988). Accessing lexical ambiguity in different types of sentential context. *Journal of Memory and Language, 27,* 324-340.

Tabossi, P. (1991). Understanding words in context. In G.B. Simpson (ed.), *Understanding word and sentence.* Amsterdam: North-Holland.

Tabossi, P., Colombo, L. & Job, R. (1987). Accessing lexical ambiguity: Effects of context and dominance. *Psychological Research, 49,* 161-167.

Tabossi, P. & Zardon, F. (1993). Processing ambiguous words in context. *Journal of Memory and Language, 32,* 359-372.

Tanenhaus, M.K., Dell, G.S. & Carlson, G. (1987). Context effects in lexical processing: A connectionist approach to modularity. In J.L. Garfield (ed.), *Modularity in knowledge representation and natural language understanding.* Cambridge, MA: MIT Press.

Tanenhaus, M.K. & Donnenwerth-Nolan, S. (1984). Syntactic context and lexical access. *Quarterly Journal of Experimental Psychology, 36A,* 649-661.

Tanenhaus, M.K., Carlson, G.N. & Seidenberg, M.S. (1985). Do listeners compute linguistic representations? In D.R. Dowty, L. Kartunnen & A.M. Zwicky (eds.), *Natural language parsing: Psycholinguistic, theoretical and computational perspectives.* Cambridge: Cambridge University Press.

Tanenhaus, M.K., Leiman, J.M. & Seidenberg, M.S. (1979). Evidence for multiple stages in the processing of ambiguous words in syntactic contexts. *Journal of Verbal Learning and Verbal Behavior, 18,* 427-440.

Tanenhaus, M.K. & Lucas, M.M. (1987). Context effects in lexical processing. *Cognition, 25,* 213-234.

Tyler, L.K. (1984). The structure of the initial cohort: Evidence from gating. *Perception & Psychophysics, 36,* 417-427.

Tyler, L.K. (1990). The relationship between sentential context and sensory input: Comments on Connine's and Samuel's chapters. In G.T.M. Altmann (ed.), *Cognitive models of speech processing.* Cambridge, MA: MIT Press.

Tyler, L.K. & Marslen-Wilson, W.D. (1977). The on-line effect of semantic context on syntactic processing. *Journal of Verbal Learning and Verbal Behavior, 16,* 683-692.

Tyler, L.K. & Marslen-Wilson, W.D. (1982). Processing utterances in discourse contexts: On-line resolution of anaphors. *Journal of Semantics, 1,* 297-314.

Tyler, L.K. & Marslen-Wilson, W.D. (1986). The effects of context on the recognition of polymorphemic words. *Journal of Memory and Language, 25,* 49-71.

Tyler, L.K. & Wessels, J. (1983). Quantifying contextual contributions to word recognition processes. *Perception and Psychophysics, 34,* 409-420.

Tyler, L.K. & Wessels, J. (1985). Is gating an on-line task? Evidence from naming-latency data. *Perception and Psychophysics, 38,* 217-222.

Van Petten, C. (1993). A comparison of lexical and sentence-level context effects in event-related potentials. *Language and Cognitive Processes, 8,* 485-532.

Van Petten, C. & Kutas, M. (1987). Ambiguous words in context: An event-related potential analysis of the time course of meaning activation. *Journal of Memory and Language, 26,* 188-208.

Van Petten, C. & Kutas, M. (1991). Electrophysiological evidence for the flexibility of lexical processing. In G.B. Simpson (ed.), *Understanding word and sentence.* Amsterdam: North-Holland.

Walley, A.C. & Metsala, J.L. (1990). The growth of lexical constraints on spoken word recognition. *Perception and Psychophysics, 47(3),* 267-280.

Warren, R.M. (1970). Perceptual restoration of missing speech sounds. *Science, 167,* 392-393.

Warren, R.M. (1976). Auditory illusions and perceptual processes. In N.J. Lass (ed.), *Contemporary issues in experimental phonetics.* New York: Academic Press.

Zwitserlood, P. (1989a). The locus of the effects of sentential-semantic context in spoken word processing. *Cognition, 32,* 25-64.

Zwitserlood, P. (1989b). *Words and sentences: The effects of sentential semantic context on spoken word processing.* Nijmegen, Netherlands: Stichting Studentenpers.

Zwitserlood, P. (1994). Access to phonological form representations in language comprehension and production. In C. Clifton, L. Frazier & K. Rayner (eds.), *Perspectives on sentence processing.* Hillsdale, NJ: Lawrence Erlbaum.

Zwitserlood, P. & Schriefers, H. (1995). Effects of sensory information and processing time in spoken-word recognition. *Language and Cognitive Processes, 10(2),* 121-136.

Chapter 4

Morphology and Word Recognition

Herbert Schriefers

4.1 Introduction

Besides syntax and phonology, morphology is one of the traditional research areas in linguistics. Morphology is the branch of linguistics studying the internal structure of words. So, for example, a word like *modernizes* is composed of three building blocks or so-called morphemes, the *modern*, *ize* and -*s*. The present article gives an overview of experimental psycholinguistic research and psycholinguistic models on the role of morphological structure in word recognition.

The article is structured as follows. In Section 4.2, we will introduce some key concepts from linguistic morphology. We will focus on those concepts that have been used in psycholinguistic research, leaving out detailed discussions of specific linguistic theories and their recent development (see for example, Anderson, 1992; Halle & Marantz, 1993; Lieber, 1992; Steele, 1995). In Section 4.3 we will introduce the main research issues and an overview of psycholinguistic theories of the recognition of morphologically complex words. In Sections 4.4 to 4.8, we will review the relevant empirical evidence against the background of the corresponding theories. Finally, in Section 4.9, we will summarize the lessons to be drawn about the role of morphology in word recognition. As will already become evident in Sections 4.4 to 4.8, the main conclusion will be that there are a number of factors determining whether and how morphological structure influences word recognition, undermining proposals according to which a given type of morphological complexity is consistently processed in the same way.

4.2 Linguistic Concepts

Linguistic morphology is concerned with the internal structure of words. Morphologically complex words can be decomposed into parts, with each part carrying some independent meaning. These parts are called morphemes and are defined as the smallest elements carrying meaning (e.g., Crystal, 1995). Within the domain of morphology, one distinguishes inflectional morphology from derivational (or lexical) morphology. Inflectional morphology is concerned with the way of how words are modified (or inflected) in order to express grammatical contrasts in sentences (e.g., plural formation on nouns, like *word, word-s*, and inflection of verbs, like *I walk, he walk-s, he walk-ed*). Derivational morphology is concerned with word formation, that is the principles determining the construction of morphologically complex words, without considering the specific syntactic role the word is going to take in a sentence (e.g., *modern, modern-ize, luck, un-luck-y*). In addition inflectional and derivational morphology there is compounding which refers to the construction of new words by combining words (e.g., *ballpark* or *housewife*). In the present article, we will concentrate primarily on inflectional and derivational morphology. Research on the processing of compound words will be discussed only occasionally.

Inflectional and derivational morphology differ in a number of aspects. First, inflectional morphology is syntactically motivated and obligatory (but see Section 4.8 below). Second, inflection usually does not change the syntactic class of a word (e.g., *walk - walks*) whereas derivation frequently does (e.g., *success* (noun) - *successful* (adjective)). Third, a given inflectional process can be applied to all members of a syntactic class of words (except inflectionally irregular forms, e.g., *think - thought*) whereas a given derivational affix usually can be applied only to some words of a given syntactic class (e.g., *success-ful*, but not *friend-ful*). Fourth, the meaning of a derived complex word is not necessarily predictable from the meaning of its components (contrast, for example, *confess - confessor* with *success - successor*). Fifth, at least in English and Dutch (the languages which have been most frequently investigated in psycholinguistics), derivational affixes precede inflectional affixes (e.g., *modern - ize* (derivational suffix) - *s* (inflectional suffix).

The following categories of morphemes are usually distinguished. First, there is the difference between free morphemes and bound morphemes. Free morphemes can occur as words on their own whereas bound morphemes cannot. The majority of bound morphemes are affixes. Affixes can be categorized along two dimensions. The first one concerns their position relative to the stem. Here, one distinguishes between prefixes, suffixes and infixes. The second one concerns the distinction between derivational and inflectional affixes (e.g., *walk - walk-er* vs. *walk - walked*).

Morphological complex words also differ with respect to formal-phonological and semantic transparency. With respect to phonological transparency, the addition of a suffix to a stem might or might not change the phonological form of the stem (e.g., *serene - serenity* vs. *friend - friendly*). With respect to semantic transparency, morphologically complex words are said to be semantically opaque if there is no straightforward way for predicting the meaning of the complex word from the meaning of its parts (e.g., *success - success-or*). For semantically transparent words, in contrast, the meaning of the complex word is highly predictable from the meaning of its parts (e.g., *success -successful*).

The world's languages differ considerably in the role and patterns of morphology (e.g., Crystal, 1995). In so-called isolating or analytic languages (e.g., Chinese, Vietnamese) words have (almost) no internal morphological structure. Syntactic relations are primarily reflected in word order. In so-called synthetic languages (e.g., Latin), syntactic relations are almost exclusively coded by the internal structure of words. In so-called agglutinative languages, words are composed of long sequences of morphemes with each morphological constituent carrying a particular syntactic function (e.g., Turkish). Finally, so-called polysynthetic languages show properties of agglutinative and synthetic languages (e.g., Eskimo). Despite the considerable variability in morphology between languages, the majority of psycholinguistic research has been conducted in English, a language with only a small set of inflectional affixes, which, according to Crystal (1995) resembles somewhat the so-called isolating languages. Although more recently other languages have been investigated as well, the body of psycholinguistic research is far from covering the range of the different types of morphological phenomena encountered in the world's languages. But even this small set of crosslanguage comparisons suggests that languages presumably differ in the role of morphology in word recognition. Whether these differences can eventually be accounted for by the different factors affecting the processing of morphologically complex words (see Sections 4.4 through 4.8) will form a central issue for future research.

Before turning to psycholinguistic research on the processing of morphologically complex words one additional remark is necessary. Psycholinguistic research in this area is concerned with the processing and representation of morphologically complex words in a listener's or reader's mental lexicon. Therefore, words which from the perspective of linguistics or historical linguistics may count as morphologically complex (e.g., words like *complex* or *perplex*) might turn out to be processed like monomorphemic words. Therefore, not every word that counts as morphologically complex from a linguistic perspective has to be treated as morphologically complex by the language processing system studied by psycholinguists. As we will see in the course of the present article, it is indeed the case that the distinctions drawn in linguistic morphology do not map directly on the distinctions that have to be drawn in 'mental' psycholinguistic morphology.

4.3 Recognition of Morphologically Complex Words: Psycholinguistic Theories

Does morphology play any role at all in language processing? Intuition, as well as systematic observation, tells us that morphology does play some role in language processing. So, for example, we are able to understand morphologically complex novel words we have never encountered before (e.g., computerization), indicating that we can compute the meaning of such words from the combination of morphemes they contain. Furthermore, in some speech errors in language production, morphemes exchange places (e.g., *funny to get your model renosed* instead of *funny to get your nose remodelled*), indicating that morphemes have some status as processing units in language production.

In order to provide the background for the following discussion of experimental research on the role of morphology in word recognition, we will first introduce the necessary basic concepts from the psycholinguistics of word recognition. Theories of word recognition distinguish between so-called modality specific access representations and modality free representations in a central lexicon. The modality specific access representations mediate the mapping from the (orthographic or spoken) input onto lexical representations in the central lexicon. If this mapping has occurred, that is if a specific entry in the central lexicon has been selected, lexical access is said to have occurred (though see Seidenberg, 1990, for a critical discussion of the concept of lexical access).

With respect to the role of morphological structure in word recognition, we first have to ask whether access representations reflect morphological structure. There are three possible positions in regard to this question. First, all words, whether morphologically simple or complex, have their own full access representation. Second, only morphemes, that is stem and affixes, have their own access representations. Third, access representations exist for full forms as well as for morphological components like stems and affixes.

If only affixes and stems, but not full word forms, have access representations, morphologically complex words have to be decomposed or parsed into their morphological constituents prior to lexical access, i.e. before the word's lexical entry can be located in the central lexicon. That is, prelexical morphological parsing becomes an obligatory part of the word recognition process. In Section 4.4, we will review the empirical evidence on these issues: Does prelexical morphological decomposition occur? Is it an obligatory or an optional process? Does it occur equally for different types of morphologically complex words (inflections versus derivations; prefixed versus suffixed words)? What type of access representation is the product of morphological parsing?

The next set of questions concerns the central lexicon. Is the morphological structure of morphologically complex words stored in the central lexicon, and if so, how? For models assuming that morphological structure is somehow represented in the central lexicon, we can, in a first approximation, distinguish two main positions, so-called shared entry models and so-called separate entry models. According to shared entry models, all members of a morphological family (i.e. all words with the same stem or root morpheme) share a single lexical entry. Shared entry models come in different variants, the two most important ones being listing models and network models. In listing models, all morphological relatives of a stem are listed in the same entry, in morphologically decomposed form. In network models, the stem functions as a lexical entry which is positively linked to the affixes with which it can combine (and negatively linked to affixes with which it can not combine (e.g., in the case of irregular forms).

According to separate entry models, each morphological complex word is fully represented as a separate lexical entry in the central lexicon. Morphological relatedness between words is reflected in the way in which the nodes representing different members of a morphological family are connected to each other.

In the following, we will briefly introduce psycholinguistic models of the role of morphology in word recognition which commit themselves to these different theoretical options concerning the modality specific access representations and the central lexicon. However, it should be stressed that most of these models are only verbally stated, that is they are not specified and formalized to a degree that an actual implementation of the models would allow for simulation and prediction of experimental data. This also implies that they are often not specified to a level of detail that allows one to derive contrasting predictions (see also Baayen & Schreuder, 1996).

The first model, the so-called full listing model assumes that each morphological variant of a given stem or base form has its own access representation and its own separate entry in the central lexicon. Potential relations between morphological relatives are assumed to be associative or semantic. Therefore, morphology does not play any genuine role in word recognition (e.g., Butterworth, 1983). This model commits itself to a position without prelexical morphological parsing and with separate entries for morphologically related words.

On the other extreme, we have models subscribing to an obligatory prelexical morphological parsing process. Taft and Forster (1975; see also Taft, 1979a, 1981; Taft, Hambley & Kinoshita, 1986) introduced such a model under the term prefix-stripping model. Affixes (in fact, in their original model Taft and Forster focussed on prefixed words) are stripped off from the stem by an obligatory prelexical parsing process. The remaining string corresponding to the irreducible root morpheme of the morphologically complex word functions as the access code for a search in the central lexicon. If a matching stem entry is found in the central lexicon all morphological complex variants of this stem are listed under this stem entry. This model commits itself to an obligatory prelexical morphological parsing procedure and to the assumption of shared lexical entries in the central lexicon. In this model, potential effects of morphological structure on word recognition are localized in the obligatory prelexical morphological parsing process.

By contrast, the so-called satellite entries model and so-called network models locate morphological effects in word recognition in the structure of the central lexicon. According to the satellite entries model (Feldman & Fowler, 1987; Günther, 1988; Lukatela et al., 1980; but see Kostic, 1995, for critical discussion), each morphologically complex word has a separate lexical entry in the central lexicon. For each cluster of morphologically related words, one word forms the so-called nucleus (defined as the morphological form with fastest recognition as measured by, for example, lexical decision, see Lukatela et al., 1978, 1980). All morphologically related words are linked to this nucleus, but they are not directly linked to each other.

In similar ways, the class of so-called network models (e.g., Andrews, 1986; Fowler, Napps & Feldman, 1985; Grainger, Cole & Segui, 1991; Schreuder et al., 1990; Schriefers, Zwitserlood & Roelofs, 1991; Schriefers, Friederici & Graetz, 1992) assume the existence of separate lexical entries for each morphologically complex word. Morphological relations between words are represented by corresponding connections in a lexical network. So, for example, Fowler, Napps and Feldman (1985) propose (following Dell, 1986), that the central lexicon consists of a network of interconnected nodes for words, morphemes, syllables and phonemes. Furthermore, they assume that there are word nodes for each morphological variant of a given stem. Each word node is connected to a morpheme node representing its stem. Therefore, morphological variants of a stem are closely connected to each other via a common morpheme node, without sharing a lexical entry. The satellite entries model and the network models agree with the full listing model (e.g., Butterworth, 1983) in the assumption that each morphological variant of a word has a separate entry in the lexicon. However, in contrast to the full listing hypothesis, they assume that the mental lexicon contains information about the morphological relations between words. It is obvious that separate entry models of this type do not require prelexical morphological parsing. Rather, potential effects of morphological structure on word recognition can be accounted for by morphological relations which are specified in the central lexicon.

Finally, there is the class of so-called dual route models. These models assume that morphologically complex words can either be recognized via a route using prelexical morphological parsing or via a direct route accessing morphologically complex words as full forms. Which route is used depends on a number of processing factors (see below). The two most prominent examples of dual route models are the Augmented Addressed Morphology Model (AAM, e.g., Burani & Caramazza, 1987; Caramazza, Laudanna & Romani, 1988), and the Morphological Race model (MRM, Frauenfelder & Schreuder, 1992; see also Schreuder & Baayen, 1995, for further development of MRM).

According to AAM, all known words (be they morphologically complex or simple) have their own full access representation (even for an inflectionally rich language like Italian for which the model was originally developed). These access representations are connected to central representations consisting of a network containing stems which are positively linked to the affixes they can combine with, and negatively linked to affixes they cannot combine with. The latter is the case for irregular inflectional forms. In the central lexicon the representation of a complex word is computed on-line.

In addition to accessing the central lexicon via the full form access representations, the model also allows for access to the central lexicon via a morphological parsing process which decomposes the orthographic input string into its morphological components. In the original version of AAM this parsing route is only used for novel complex words which are morphologically regular. In more recent versions (e.g., Chialant & Caramazza, 1995) the possibility is left open that words with a low frequency of occurrence consisting of morphological components with a high frequency of occurrence might also be processed via the parsing route.

In AAM the recognition of morphologically complex words via full-form access representations (i.e. the direct route) is assumed to be faster than the parsing route. Therefore the latter route can only be demonstrated in special cases in which the full form access code route is particularly slow, or not available, as in the case of novel morphologically complex words. Furthermore, in AAM the parsing route is not only slower, but only comes into play if the direct route has failed. Therefore, following Baayen, Dijkstra & Schreuder (in press) one can refer to this model as a cascaded dual route model. By contrast, the morphological race model, to be discussed next (see Frauenfelder & Schreuder, 1992; Schreuder & Baayen, 1995) assumes that the direct route and the parsing route are operating in parallel.

According to the morphological race model, the mental lexicon is a spreading activation network with three layers. The first layer consists of access codes for full forms as well as for stems and affixes. The second layer consists of central representations of stems and affixes and so-called integration nodes (also called lemmas) coding possible combinations of stems and affixes. Finally, the third level contains semantic and syntactic representations of words.

On encountering a morphologically complex word the access representations of stems and affixes, as well as the full-form access representations, become activated. The direct route maps the full-form access representations directly onto the corresponding lemma representations. On the parsing route, the access representations of stems and affixes will activate their corresponding central representations. Following this step a so-called licensing procedure checks the compatibility of the activated morphemic constituents. Thus, the direct route and the parsing route are active in parallel from the very beginning of word processing. In further developments of MRM (Schreuder & Baayen, 1995) the model is further specified quantitatively by assuming that the relative speed of both routes varies stochastically, with overlapping distribution of completion times.

In addition, the model incorporates a dynamic component in so far as the strength of the access representations, i.e. the resting level activation of the nodes representing the access codes for full forms, stems and affixes, can vary as a function of the frequency of usage of the respective nodes. If, for a given morphologically complex word, the direct route completes before the parsing route, then the corresponding full form access representation is slightly strengthened; its resting level activation is increased such that the chance that this word will be recognized via the direct route in the future will be increased. If, by contrast, the morphological parsing route completes before the full form route, the access representations of the corresponding stem and affixes will be strengthened. As a consequence, low frequency, transparent forms with highly productive (and thus highly frequent) affixes are good candidates for morphological parsing.

In summary, in dual route models, prelexical morphological decomposition is attempted on all words. But the operation of this route will affect word recognition only when the direct route is slow or fails. In the MRM, the outcome of the race between the direct route and the parsing route will be affected by factors like word frequency, productivity and frequency of affixes, and semantic transparency. Below we will see that the available empirical evidence strongly suggests that such factors have an important influence on the processing of morphologically complex words.

A central aspect of the models discussed so far concerns the relation between storage and computation. At one extreme, there is exhaustive storage of full forms of all morphologically complex words, thus requiring only a minimal amount of computation in recognizing and accessing the meaning of such words. At the other extreme, storage requirements are minimized by assuming that only morphemes are stored. So, for example, in shared entry models, the central lexicon is relieved of the burden of replicating the stem for each morphologically complex word in which the stem participates. However, this storage economy in the central lexicon comes at the price of additional computational burden like the need for morphological decomposition in the word recognition process. Two aspects of this computation versus storage issue should be kept in mind, however. First, it is not always simple to determine and assess storage economy (cf., Henderson 1989). Second, there is no apriori reason to assume that the storage versus computation issue is resolved in the same way for a complete cognitive domain. So, for example, it appears that in solving arithmetic problems like the addition or subtraction of digits, single digit problems are solved by a direct fact retrieval from memory whereas other operations require computation instead of retrieval of stored information. Below we will see that the available empirical evidence suggests that the storage versus computation issue is not solved in one uniform way for all morphologically complex words.

4.4   Morphological Decomposition

Taft and Forster (1975; see also Taft et al., 1986) introduced the notion of an obligatory prelexical decomposition process for morphologically complex words. This so-called prefix stripping model was originally developed for the recognition of derived prefixed words. According to the prefix stripping models, readers first detect potential prefixes and strip these prefixes from the presented word. The remaining part of the word is used in an attempt to locate a corresponding stem morpheme in the central lexicon. If such a stem entry is found the list of all morphological complex forms found under this stem can be checked as to whether the morphologically complex word is contained in this list. If it is not contained in this list, the full word form has to be used as an access code and it has to be determined whether this form has a corresponding stem entry in the mental lexicon.

This proposal is primarily based on two types of empirical evidence, the nonword interference effect and the pseudoprefixation effect. The nonword interference effect comes in two versions. First, nonwords consisting of a bound stem (e.g., the nonword *vive* which is the bound stem morpheme of a word like *revive*) are identified as nonwords in a lexical decision task more slowly than nonwords which are so called pseudostems, i.e. which do not constitute a possible stem (e.g., *lish* from *relish*). Second, nonwords consisting of an existing prefix and an existing stem (e.g., *dejoice*) take more time to reject in a lexical decision task than nonwords containing a pseudostem (e.g., *dejouse*, see Taft et al., 1986, who provide evidence for a nonword interference effect in visual as well as spoken word recognition). These results are explained as being due to the fact that bound stems have an access representation and thus, via this access code, make contact with the central lexicon whereas pseudostems do not make contact with the central lexicon and can therefore be rejected immediately.

Henderson (1985), however, argued that the inference from results obtained with nonwords to normal word recognition is at the very least problematic. So it might be, for example, that morphological decomposition of nonwords is only attempted when access to the mental lexicon based on the full word form has failed, which is, by definition, the case for the type of nonword materials used in the nonword interference effect.

In this respect the so-called pseudoprefixation effect (e.g., Rubin, Becker & Freeman, 1979; see also Bergman, Hudson & Eling, 1988, for comparable results in Dutch) is more convincing as it concerns the processing of words instead of nonwords. The pseudoprefixation effect concerns the fact that lexical decisions to pseudoprefixed words (e.g., *misery*, consisting of a pseudo-prefix *mis* plus a pseudo-stem *ery*) are slower than lexical decisions to real prefixed words (e.g., *misplace*, consisting of the prefix *mis* and the stem *place*). According to the prefix stripping model, pseudoprefixed words are first decomposed in (pseudo-) prefix and (pseudo-) stem, but as no corresponding central representation of the pseudostem can be found in the central lexicon the full form of the pseudoprefixed word has to be used in a second attempt for accessing the central lexicon.

However, the generality of the pseudoprefixation effect is controversial. Rubin et al. (1979) observed the pseudoprefixation effect only if the experimental materials also contained prefixed nonwords. Similarly, Henderson, Wallis and Knight (1984) did not obtain a pseudoprefixation effect if the proportion of potentially prefixed words and nonwords in the experimental materials was low. Taft (1981), by contrast, in a word naming task, obtained longer word naming latencies for pseudoprefixed words than for monomorphemic unprefixed control words in the absence of any nonwords and any prefixed words. In summary, evidence that is taken as support for morphological decomposition appears to depend on additional factors favoring or disfavoring a subject's attempt to perform morphological decomposition, and thus suggests that decomposition is an optional rather than an obligatory process.

For derived suffixed words, the combined evidence points in the same direction. Manelis and Tharp (1977) asked subjects to give lexical decisions on two simultaneously presented words. Lexical decision latencies to pairs of pseudosuffixed words (e.g., *fancy - nasty*) did not take any longer than lexical decisions to pairs of suffixed words (e.g., *bulky - dusty*). Lexical decisions to pairs consisting of one pseudosuffixed word and one suffixed word (e.g., *fancy - dusty*), however, had longer lexical decision latencies than the former two types of pairs. Feldman, Frost and Pnini (1995; see also Feldman, 1994) presented subjects with pairs of words, with part of one of the two words being underlined (e.g., hard*en* - bright or gard*en* - bright). Subjects were instructed to combine the second word of a pair with the underlined part of the first word and to say this word aloud. This task was easier when the underlined part had the status of a morpheme (e.g., hard<u>en</u>) than when it had not (e.g., gard*en*). Bergman et al. (1988) and Henderson et al. (1984), by contrast, did not find any difference in lexical decision times to suffixed and pseudosuffixed forms when these were presented in isolation.

Caramazza et al. (1988) demonstrated a nonword interference effect for inflected (suffixed) verb forms in Italian. The critical four conditions were the following: (a) an existing verb stem (e.g., *cant* from *cantare, to sing*) combined with an existing suffix which, however, given the verb stem inappropriate because verb stem and inflection belong to different conjugation types, (b) an existing verb stem combined with a non-existing inflectional (pseudo-) suffix, (c) a nonexisting stem combined with an existing inflectional suffix, and (d) a nonexisting stem combined with a nonexisting inflectional (pseudo-) suffix. Lexical decision times to (a) were longer than to (b) and (c) which did not differ, reflecting a nonword interference effect similar to the one obtained by Taft and Forster (1975) for prefixed derived words. However, lexical decision times to (b) were longer than to (d). Caramazza et al. argue that the latter result indicates that even with nonwords, morphological decomposition is not mandatory. If it were mandatory, (b) and (d) should have given the same lexical decision times because both conditions comprise a nonexisting suffix which can not be stripped off from the potential stem prelexically. Given these results, they propose that morphological decomposition is not obligatory, as assumed in their AAM dual route model (see above).

In general, the available evidence appears to converge on a position in which morphological decomposition is optional instead of obligatory. This proposal receives further support from studies showing that different types of affixes have different effects in word recognition. So, for example, some evidence suggests that results congruent with the assumption of morphological decomposition are more likely to obtain for orthographic strings which on the majority of their occurrences form a real prefix rather than a pseudoprefix (Laudanna, Burani & Cermele, 1994; see also Laudanna & Burani, 1995).

The view that morphological decomposition is not obligatory for all morphologically complex words with an orthographic string forming a potential affix is also supported by considerations concerning the computational tractability of an obligatory morphological decomposition process. If an attempt at decomposition would be made on every word that, given its orthographic make up, could be affixed, this would imply a substantial processing cost for all pseudo-affixed words (e.g., *relish*, where orthographically *re* is a potential prefix although the word is monomorphemic). In a corpus analysis, Schreuder and Baayen (1994) showed that 30% of Dutch words in this corpus began with orthographic strings that could be prefixes, but actually were not prefixed. For a corresponding analysis of an English corpus, the corresponding figure is even higher with 80%. Given these figures, an obligatory decomposition process would be highly inefficient.

In summary, the evidence reviewed so far speaks against an obligatory morphological decomposition. Rather, whether a complex word is decomposed in its morphological components or not appears to depend on additional processing factors such as the relative frequency with which a given orthographic string functions as real prefix as opposed to a pseudoprefix. Furthermore, these processing factors do not divide up the domain of morphological phenomena along the lines suggested by distinctions drawn in linguistic theory. So, for example, it is not the case that decomposition only occurs for prefixed words, or only for inflected forms. Taken together, the relevant data are more in line with some type of dual route model than a model committing itself to either obligatory decomposition or exclusively to access via full form representations.

Let us conclude this Section with two final remarks. First, the research reviewed so far suggests an optional decomposition process, but it does not necessarily imply that decomposition occurs prelexically, that is at early stages of perceptual identification. Second, the evidence presented so far refers exclusively to visual word recognition. In Section 4.8 we will discuss the few existing studies on the role of morphology in auditory word recognition. As we will see there, McQueen and Cutler (1997, in press) have argued that the evidence from processing spoken morphologically complex words in particular is more compatible with a view that morphological decomposition occurs during lexical access rather than prelexically.

4.5   Evidence for Representation of Morphological Relationships

The second main set of experimental evidence concerns the question whether and how morphological relationships are represented in the central lexicon. Many of these studies use a morphological repetition priming paradigm. Stanners, Neisser,

Hernon and Hall (1979) presented their subjects with either a monomorphemic stem form (e.g., lend) or an inflected variant of this form (e.g., lending) as the prime, and the stem form as the target. Prime and target were separated by 9 intervening words and nonwords in this experiment. Stanners et al. obtained a pattern of results that has been labelled full priming (e.g., Fowler et al., 1985). The lexical decision latencies for the stem forms did not differ in the two priming conditions suggesting that an inflected form is as effective as a prime for the stem form as the stem itself. Stanners et al. (1979a) interpreted full priming to indicate repeated access to a lexical entry that is shared by the different morphological relatives of a stem or base form. Partial priming, by contrast, is thought to reflect separate lexical entries that are closely related in the central lexicon.

In contrast to regularly inflected forms, Stanners et al. (1979a,b) obtained so-called partial priming for irregularly inflected forms and for derived forms. That is, the lexical decision to the target (the stem form) was slower after presentation of derivationally related words or irregularly inflected forms as primes (e.g., prime: *thought*, target: *think*) than after the stem form itself as prime (e.g., prime: *think*, target: *think*). However, Fowler et al. (1985) reported full priming for regularly inflected, irregularly inflected and derived primes if the lag between primes and targets was increased to 49 intervening words (see also Stanners, Neisser & Painton, 1979). According to Fowler et al. (1985), the full priming for irregularly inflected words in particular suggests that these priming effects are due to a morphological structuring of the central lexicon rather than to some prelexical decomposition because irregularly inflected forms should not be accessible to a prelexical surface decomposition. According to Fowler et al. (1985), these results also speak against the assumption of shared lexical entries because this would mean that inflectional *and* derivational variants of a stem would have to share the same entry irrespective of the high degree of irregularity of derivational morphology as compared to inflectional morphology.

Nevertheless, the results from repetition priming converge on the conclusion that morphological structure is somehow represented in the mental lexicon. However, before such a conclusion can be accepted, it has to be shown that the corresponding priming effects are genuinely morphological in nature. That is, it has to excluded that the priming effects are due to orthographic and/or semantic relations between prime and target (for discussion see Feldman & Fowler, 1987; Fowler et al., 1985; Henderson 1985).

With respect to influences from associative semantic priming Henderson et al. (1984) showed that morphological priming can be obtained with prime-target intervals of 1 sec and 4 sec whereas associative semantic priming is only obtained at the short interval. Similarly, Bentin and Feldman (1990) showed, for Hebrew, that morphological priming can be obtained with 0 and 15 words intervening between prime and target whereas again semantic priming was not obtained with long lags of

15 intervening items. Thus, priming effects between morphologically related words obtained with long prime-target distances are not contaminated by associative semantic priming effects.

A similar pattern of results holds for priming due to orthographic relatedness (e.g., *balloon - saloon*) as opposed to morphological relatedness (*submit - permit*). That is, morphological priming and orthographic priming have different properties (e.g., Feldman & Moskolievic, 1987; Napps & Fowler, 1987). So, for example studies using masked priming (i.e. the prime which is immediately followed by the target is masked such that subjects are not consciously perceiving the prime) have shown that orthographic overlap between prime and target without a morphological relation between prime and target leads to inhibitory effects while the presence of a morphological relation leads to facilitatory effect (see Drews & Zwitserlood, 1995; Grainger, Cole & Segui, 1991). Corresponding results have also been obtained with unmasked priming (e.g., Drews & Zwitserlood, 1995; Henderson, Wallis & Knight, 1984). Furthermore, Feldman and Moskolievic (1987) conducted a study of morphological repetition priming in Serbo-Croatian, a language which uses two different alphabets (Cyrillic and Roman). These authors showed that morphological repetition priming was about as large when prime and target were printed in different alphabets as when they were printed in the same alphabet.

Additional evidence for a representation of morphological structure independent from orthographic relations comes from a study by Schreuder et al. (1990) on the processing of prefixed Dutch verbs. This study combined a word naming task (name a printed word aloud as quickly as possible) with a partial priming technique. In this technique, part of the to-be-named word is displayed briefly before presentation of the whole word. If the part presented first corresponded to the stem or prefix, naming latencies were significantly reduced. This morphological priming effect differed from the effect obtained with a preview of parts of monomorphemic words. However, the morphological priming effect was only obtained for verbs with separable prefixes, that is prefixes that can be detached from their stems in certain syntactic constructions (e.g., *opstaan - to get up*, but: *hij staat op - he gets up*). For prefixed verbs with nonseparable prefixes, no morphological priming effect was obtained (see also Frazier, Flores d'Arcais & Coolen, 1993, for further discussion of the processing of verbs with separable prefixes). This latter result suggests that not all morphologically complex words of a given type (e.g., all prefixed verbs) are processed in the same way.

In summary, these studies converge on the conclusion that morphological relations are represented in the central lexicon independent of orthographic and semantic associative relations between morphologically related words. The question then arises whether these and related results can also reveal more detail about how morphological relations are represented in the central lexicon. As stated above, originally Stanners et al. (1979a) interpreted the pattern of full priming for inflectionally related words as evidence for a shared entry model of morphological organization in the central lexicon. According to this view all inflectional variants of a stem are listed under the entry for the corresponding stem. However, the results of Fowler et al. (1985), i.e. full priming for derived and irregularly inflected words, appears to contradict this claim. Further evidence against a shared entry model comes from the finding of asymmetrical repetition priming effects between morphologically related words. Most studies investigating morphological repetition priming use exclusively stem forms as targets, comparing the priming of these stem forms by either the stem form (identical repetition priming) or a morphological variant of the stem form. Full priming is assumed to reflect a shared entry organization; recognizing an inflected form activates the stem entry as much as presenting the stem itself because the inflected form is recognized via the shared stem entry. But then, by the same argument, the reverse should also hold; a given inflected form as target should also be primed by its stem form. However, this is not what corresponding experiments reveal. For example, Schriefers et al. (1992), using case inflected adjectives in German, showed that the dative singular form of an adjective primed its stem, but that the stem form did not prime the dative singular form (see also Feldman & Fowler, 1987, and Feldman, 1991, for related results). These results speak for internally structured morphological representations in which morphological relatives have bidirectional facilitatory connections with the stem form and / or to each other. These facilitatory connections are not necessarily symmetrical and can vary in strength. Alternatively, one might assume a network organization with morphologically decomposed representations. In such a network, nodes represent stems and affixes, and there are connections of variable strength between stems and affixes and between affixes (e.g., Marslen-Wilson et al. 1994; see also the AAM model discussed in Section 4.3 for a related proposal).

Although it will be difficult to provide experimental evidence ultimately distinguishing between these different possibilities for representing morphological relations in such network models (see, for example, Burani, 1993), this family of models has the advantage that one does not have to assume anymore that a given type of morphological relation is always represented in the same way, and that different types of morphologically complex words like derived versus inflected words, are represented in principally different ways. This gives more freedom for accommodating some of the conflicting results in the literature in one theoretical framework. On the other hand, however, these models force the researcher to specify the factors that are responsible for the variability in connections between morphologically related words and / or their morphological constituents. Recent research has therefore focussed more on determining these factors instead of searching for a one-to-one correspondence between linguistic morphology and 'mental' morphology. In the next Sections we will review some of the research aiming at identifying the factors and variables that are relevant for the lexical representation of morphological relations.

4.6 Frequency

The so-called word frequency effect is one of the most robust findings in the psycholinguistics of visual word recognition. High frequency words, that is words that occur very frequently in language use, are processed faster than low frequency words (e.g., Gernsbacher, 1984; Rubenstein & Pollack, 1963; Scarborough, Cortese & Scarborough, 1977). For morphologically complex words, however, the question of which frequency (i.e., frequency of the morphological complex word as a whole versus frequency of its morphological constituents) determines processing speed arises. Frequency effects have been used frequently as a diagnostic tool for uncovering the processes underlying the recognition of morphologically complex words. For example, if morphological structure does not play a role in word recognition, then the frequency of the morphological components of a complex word should not affect processing speed. Before embarking on a review of studies on frequency effects in the processing of morphologically complex words, we will first give some definitions of different types of frequency counts and discuss some methodological aspects playing a role in this type of research.

First, when using frequency as a predictor for the speed of visual word processing (e.g., when computing correlations between word frequency and lexical decision RTs), researchers usually use the logarithm of the frequency count rather than absolute frequency. The reason is that log-frequency is more linearly related to processing speed than absolute frequency. Second, when using frequency counts computed on the basis of corpora the possibility of sampling errors has to be kept in mind. In particular when relatively small corpora are used for determining the frequency of use of words, the frequencies in the lower frequency ranges may be underestimated (see Gernsbacher, 1984). Third, in the study of processing of morphologically complex words, different frequency measures have to be distinguished. The most important ones are the following. Surface frequency, defined as the frequency of occurrence of a particular inflected form. Combined stem frequency, defined as the frequency of occurrence of a stem across all inflectional forms and/or across all derived words and compounds in which this stem occurs. Affix frequency, defined as the frequency with which a given affix occurs. With respect to affix frequency a further distinction is of importance. Some affixes can occur in different functions (e.g., in Dutch, -en can be a nominal affix or a verbal affix, see Baayen, Dijkstra & Schreuder, in press). Therefore, one can distinguish the frequency of the affix per se and the frequencies of this affix in its different functions. Finally, there is the so-called morphological family size, defined as the number of words in which a given stem occurs, irrespective of their individual frequency of occurrence (e.g., Baayen, Dijkstra & Schreuder, in press).

Forth, at the theoretical level, frequency effects have often been interpreted as being located at the level of access representations. The resting level activation of access representations is assumed to be higher for frequently encountered words, stems or affixes than for less frequently encountered ones. However, frequency effects are sometimes also interpreted as being located at the level of representations in the central lexicon (see also McQueen & Cutler, in press). So, for example, Baayen, Dijkstra and Schreuder (in press) point out that different versions of AAM locate cumulative stem frequency effects either exclusively at the level of central representations (e.g., Laudanna, Badecker & Caramazza, 1992) or consider the possibility of two sources, access representations and central representations (e.g., Caramazza et al., 1988).

With these preliminaries, we can look at research on frequency effects in the recognition of morphologically complex words. Taft (1979) showed that lexical decision latencies to monomorphemic (uninflected) English words (nouns and verbs) were codetermined by the frequencies of the inflected variants of this word. Similarly, lexical decisions to inflected words were also codetermined by their combined stem frequency (see also Burani, Salasmo & Caramazza, 1984, for a replication in Italian). Originally, these combined stem frequency effects were interpreted as evidence that the stem functions as access representation for all inflected variants of that stem instead of separate access representations for each inflected form (Taft, 1979b). However, this conclusion has theoretical as well as empirical problems. On the theoretical side, the finding of combined stem frequencies does indicate that morphological information plays a role in word recognition, but it does not necessarily indicate that the combined stem frequencies are due to stems functioning as access representations. As McQueen and Cutler (in press) point out "these results are also consistent with any model in which morphological information is represented in the central lexicon in which lexical entries are frequency sensitive. If representations of stems are linked to those of whole-word forms in a cluster, either within a shared entry or in a network, then recognition of any word in that cluster should be sensitive both to combined stem frequency and its own surface frequency".

On the empirical side, combined stem frequency effects have not been found in a number of other studies, or combined stem frequency effects only apply to certain inflectional forms but not to others. Katz, Rexer and Lukatela (1991) obtained only a surface frequency effect for uninflected English verbs (see also Sereno & Jongman, 1992, cited in McQueen & Cutler, in press). Taken together, the emerging picture as to combined stem frequency effects appears to be unclear. One might suspect that other factors are involved in addition to combined stem frequency and surface frequency. In a recent series of studies Schreuder and Baayen (in press, see also Baayen, Dijkstra and Schreuder, in press) systematically investigated of combined stem frequency and surface frequency effects, taking into account a number of variables that might also be of relevance.

Baayen, Dijkstra and Schreuder (1997) investigated the processing of singular and plural forms of Dutch nouns and verbs. They made systematic use of the fact that for some nouns the singular form has a higher surface frequency than the plural noun (so-called singular dominant nouns, e.g., *nose*) while for other nouns the plural form has a higher surface frequency than the singular noun (so-called plural dominant nouns, e.g., *shoes*). When keeping the cumulative stem frequency (i.e. the summed frequency of the singular and plural form of the nouns) constant, singular dominant singular nouns were processed equally fast as plural dominant singular nouns, despite the fact that the former singular nouns had a higher surface frequency than the latter singular nouns. In contrast to the singular nouns, processing speed for plural nouns was determined by their surface frequency such that plural dominant plurals were processed faster than singular dominant plurals. Similarly, if the surface frequency of singular nouns is kept constant, response latencies to these singular nouns vary as a function of the frequency of the surface frequency of the corresponding plural nouns. In summary, it appears that the processing of singular nouns in Dutch is determined by the summed frequency of their singular and plural forms whereas processing of Dutch plural nouns is primarily determined by their surface frequency (see also Baayen, Burani & Schreuder, in press, for corresponding results in Italian, and Baayen, Lieber & Schreuder, in press, for corresponding results in English). In terms of the dual route morphological race model (e.g., Schreuder & Baayen, 1995), it therefore appears that plural nouns are processed by the direct access route.

The Dutch affix *-en* does not only occur as a nominal affix, but also as a verbal affix indicating plural verb forms. In contrast to plural nouns which were processed according to their surface frequency, however, low frequent verb plurals were processed as fast as their corresponding high frequent verb singulars (Baayen, Dijkstra & Schreuder, in press), indicating that both singular and plural verb forms were accessed through their high frequency singular form, i.e. in terms of the morphological race model via the parsing route. This difference between nominal and verbal plural forms has presumably its origin in a frequency difference of the *-en* suffix as nominal and a verbal suffix. In Dutch, *-en* occurs about twice as often as a verbal than as nominal suffix, suggesting that the distributional properties of a particular affix have an impact on the processing of morphologically complex words with this affix (for details of how these results can be embedded in the MRM model, see Baayen, Dijkstra & Schreuder, in press; for further evidence on the role of distributional properties of affixes see also Laudanna & Burani, 1995).

When the processing times for monomorphemic words (like monomorphemic singular nouns) are codetermined by the frequency of occurrence of these nouns in their inflectional variants, the question arises whether their occurrence in other derived words and compound words (that is their derivational morphological family) also influences the processing of these monomorphemic words. Schreuder & Baayen (in press) showed this indeed to be the case. Lexical decision RTs to singular Dutch nouns were faster and subjective frequency ratings were higher for nouns with a large morphological family size than for nouns with a small morphological family size. The cumulative summed frequency of the words in the morphological family, however, did not affect lexical decision speed and subjective frequency ratings (but see Burani, Dovetto, Thornton & Laudanna, 1996). Furthermore, the effect of morphological family size was not obtained with the progressive demasking task, a task which taps primarily into early identification stage of word processing (e.g., Grainger & Segui, 1990; Grainger & Jacobs, 1996). Thus it appears that the effect of morphological family size is a late semantic effect. Further analyses suggested that the effect of morphological family size is primarily carried by semantically transparent members of the morphological family (i.e., morphologically complex words whose meaning can be predicted from the meaning of its morphological components), and not by the semantically opaque members. Baayen, Lieber and Schreuder (in press) propose that the effect of morphological family size is due to spreading of semantic activation to the other members of the morphological family. This leads to an overall higher level of activation in the mental lexicon which will, according to the Grainger and Jacobs (1996) multiple read-out model of visual word recognition, lead to faster positive (word-) responses in the lexical decision task. The role of semantic transparency in morphological processing will be discuss in more detail in the next Section.

Until now we have focussed on the processing of monomorphemic words and inflected words. We have seen that the overall results are plagued by inconsistencies which are presumably due to additional factors beyond surface frequency and cumulative stem frequency which have presumably not been controlled adequately in earlier investigations of frequency effects in the processing of morphologically complex words. The situation is no better for research on the processing of derivationally complex words. For derived prefixed words which were matched with respect to their surface frequency, Taft (1979b) obtained faster lexical decisions for words with high combined root frequency than for words with low combined root frequency (combined root frequency being defined as the summed frequency of all derived and inflected words in which the root occurs, see also Holmes and O'Reagan, 1992, for related results with gaze durations as the dependent variable). However, Cole, Beauvillain and Segui (1989) did not obtain a corresponding effect for French prefixed words. For suffixed words, the same authors obtained evidence that surface frequency and combined root frequency codetermine processing speed (see also Burani & Caramazza, 1987, for Italian). However, in an experiment comprising a high proportion of words with the same suffix, Bradley (1980) did not obtain an effect of surface frequency for the processing of suffixed English words. Even if we assume that the high proportion of words with the same suffix has induced a morphological decomposition of these words (e.g., McQueen & Cutler, in press), this would imply that the word recognition system has different processing routes, a direct one and a so-called parsing route. Which route will eventually be used for a given word appears to depend on a number of factors, some of them being within experiment factors (like the composition of the list of experimental materials) and some of them being independent of the experimental setting, like frequencies of full forms and stems, distributional properties of the affixes and semantic transparency. Therefore, anticipating the general conclusions, it appears that we need more detailed research identifying the particular factors influencing the processing of morphologically complex words. This also means that, on the theoretical side, we need models that are able to include these factors. Dual route models with an internal structure reflecting the morphological relations between words in dependence of the relevant processing factors appear to be the most promising framework for achieving this goal.

4.7 The Role of Semantic Transparency

Morphologically complex words differ in their semantic transparency. A morphologically complex word is assumed to be semantically transparent if its meaning can be predicted on the basis of the meaning of its morphological constituents (e.g., *confess + er = confessor*). This contrasts with semantically opaque words (e.g., "success-or"). Although the role of semantic transparency has been investigated primarily for derived words, some of the above mentioned results on inflectional morphology can also be related to the issue of semantic transparency.

Baayen, Dijkstra and Schreuder (in press) have provided evidence that Dutch plural nouns are accessed via a direct route using full form representations, whereas verb plurals with the same inflectional suffix are accessed via the parsing route (see above). Referring to Booj (1993), these authors (see also Baayen, Burani & Schreuder, in press) argue that this difference can be related to a distinction between two types of inflections, which are related to a difference in the semantics. On the one hand, the so-called inherent inflection (e.g., the plural of nouns, or the tense marking on verbs) is assumed to express a change in meaning of the corresponding monomorphemic word. On the other hand, the so-called contextual inflectional (e.g., agreement marking) is assumed to be semantically redundant. Rather, its function is to make syntactic structure explicit. From this perspective, it appears that inflectional variants of a word tend to be processed via the direct route if they differ from the corresponding monomorphemic word in meaning. It appears that some languages explicitly reflect such semantic factors in their morphology. So, for example, Dimmendaal (1987, cited in Baayen, Burani & Schreuder, in press) refers to Bari, an Eastern Nilotic Language. In singular dominant nouns, the singular can be seen as the semantically unmarked form, referring to the canonical number of denoted objects as encountered in daily life. In plural dominant nouns, by contrast, the plural can be seen as the semantically unmarked form, referring to the canonical number of denoted objects. In a language like Bari, the semantically unmarked form is always monomorphemic, irrespective of whether it expresses a singular or plural concept, indicating that semantic factors can have an influence on the morphological system of a language (for more discussion see Baayen, Burani & Schreuder, in press, and references therein).

Marslen-Wilson, Tyler, Waksler and Older (1994) investigated the role of semantic transparency in the processing of derived words. In a cross modal priming paradigm, they measured the lexical decision times to written words which were presented immediately after the offset of spoken prime words. Priming effects between morphologically related words were only obtained for semantically transparent rime-target pairs like *confessor - confess*, but not for semantically opaque ones like *successor - success* (semantic transparency being defined by subjective ratings of semantic relatedness between primes and targets; for more details on this study see Section 4.8). On the basis of their results, Marslen-Wilson et al. (1994) argue that morphological relatedness cannot be defined on pure formal grounds. Furthermore, since most studies on the processing of derivationally complex words did not control for semantic transparency, this might account for some of the inconsistencies in other studies (see also Henderson 1985, 1989).

Semantic transparency also plays a role in the processing of compounds. Sandra (1990) reports evidence that in particular semantically opaque compounds have separate whole word representations. In addition, however, the relation between a compound and its morphological components also appears to be coded in the mental lexicon (e.g., Zwitserlood, 1994). In summary, the available evidence shows that semantic transparency affects the processing of morphologically complex words such that semantically opaque words are more likely to be processed via a direct route than semantically transparent words.

4.8   Morphological Structure in Spoken Word Recognition

Until now, we have primarily been referring to studies of visual word recognition. As compared to the number of studies in the visual domain, the number of studies on the role of morphology in spoken word recognition is relatively small. This situation is surprising as in the first couple of years the language learning child is obviously only confronted with spoken language input. Therefore, one might expect that properties of spoken language have a considerable influence on the structure of the mental lexicon as it develops in the course of language acquisition.

In considering the potential role of morphology in spoken word recognition, we have to keep in mind that in spoken word recognition, the acoustic signal is coming in continuously from a word's beginning to its end. Although some authors have proposed a left-to-right processing in the processing of morphologically complex words in the visual domain (e.g., Bergman, 1988; Libben, 1994), the left-to-right processing in the auditory domain is directly imposed onto the language processing system by the very nature of the acoustic signal.

First, we can ask whether the dissociation of form related priming and morphological priming as demonstrated for the visual domain (see Section 4.5 above) can also be demonstrated for the domain of auditory word recognition. Kempley & Morton

(1982) showed that the recognition of spoken words presented in noise can be primed by regular inflectional relations between prime and target (e.g., *hedge - hedges*), but not by purely phonological relations (*pledge - hedge*; see also Emmeroy, 1989, for related results). These results converge with the evidence obtained in the visual modality, that is at some level of representation morphological information appears to be represented independent of phonological and orthographic form.

With respect to the left-to-right nature of spoken word recognition, Tyler, Marslen-Wilson, Rentoul & Hanney (1988) and Schriefers, Zwitserlood & Roelofs (1991) investigated the processing of spoken prefixed words. If such words are identified via a prelexical decomposition in stem and prefix, and if the stem serves as access representation, the recognition of prefixed words should be determined by the uniqueness point of the stem (i.e. the point in the acoustic signal at which the stem of the prefixed word deviates from all other competitor words in the language). However, their results show that the recognition of prefixed word is primarily determined by the uniqueness point of the prefixed word as a whole, and not by the uniqueness point of its stem. That is, recognition of prefixed spoken words is primarily a continuous left-to-right process.

Such a continuous left-to-right processing of spoken words can account for the differences between the processing of spoken suffixed and prefixed words in the study by Marslen-Wilson et al. (1994) which has already been mentioned above in the context of the semantic transparency issue. Marslen-Wilson et al. showed that, in a cross-modal priming paradigm (see above), derived suffixed forms (e.g., *friendly*) primed and were primed by their corresponding stems (e.g., *friend*). The same pattern was obtained for derived prefixed words and their stems (e.g., *fasten - unfasten*). However, whereas two prefixed forms also primed each other (*refasten - unfasten*), such priming was not obtained for two suffixed words (see also Beauvillain, 1996, for evidence for different processing of prefixed and suffixed words in the domain of visual word recognition). This overall pattern of results was modulated by semantic transparency, that is any priming effects only obtained for pairs of words that had been judged as having a strong semantic relation between the respective prime and target (see Section 4.7).

Marslen-Wilson et al. (1994) propose a lexical organization similar to that proposed by Caramazza et al. (1988). Lexical entries consist of stem morphemes and affixes, with stems being connected to the affixes they can combine with. Accessing a complex derived word therefore always implies access to a central representation of its stem, and as a consequence all derived forms should prime each other. The absence of priming between suffixed forms is explained by the assumption of inhibitory connections between the different suffixes of a given stem which is motivated by the requirements of spoken word recognition. Recognition of a spoken suffixed word starts with the recognition of its stem. This stem will send activation to all suffixes forming possible completions of the stem. When the information of the actual suffix comes in, the activation of the other suffixes has to be suppressed. It should be noted that Marslen-Wilson et al.'s proposal does only concern derivational morphology. However, as pointed out by McQueen and Cutler (in press), the assumption of a stem with affixes clustering around them with different connection strengths might also provide a general account for asymmetries in repetition priming (e.g., Schriefers et al., 1992; Feldman et al., 1987).

An additional aspect of the study of Marslen-Wilson et al. (1994) concerns phonological transparency. For some derivations, the phonological realization of the stem changes (e.g., *serene - serenity*) whereas for others the phonological realization of the stem does not change (e.g., *bulk - bulky*). Marslen-Wilson et al (1994) showed that phonological transparency does not matter for the pattern of priming effects suggesting that the priming effects have their origin at a level of representation which has abstracted from the specific input modality (see also Fowler et al., 1985; Downie, Milech & Kirsner, 1985). This also converges with the above mentioned results of Kempley and Morton (1982) and Emmeroy (1989) and supports the conclusion that morphological priming effects in spoken word recognition are not located at the level of modality specific access representations.

The research on recognition of morphologically complex words in the auditory domain thus converges in the assumption of a continuous left-to-right processing. Cutler, Hawkins and Gilligan (1985) have proposed that this continuous left-to-right processing might also provide an explanation of the so-called suffixing preference, that is the fact that the world's languages have a preference towards suffixing. From a continuous left-to-right processing perspective this might reflect the fact that listeners prefer to process stems before affixes. As pointed out by McQueen and Cutler (in press), temporally continuous access also gives a different perspective on the discussion about prelexical decomposition. If the central lexicon represents stems with links to their possible affixes, a complex word will be decomposed during lexical access, that is while the continuous input activates the representations of stems and affixes, and not prior to lexical access.

On the other hand, however, the assumption of temporally continuous left-to-right processing of morphologically complex words also poses a challenge for models of spoken word recognition subscribing to this assumption (Baayen, personal communication). This becomes obvious when one compares the processing of monomorphemic and morphologically complex words in one of the most advanced models of spoken word recognition, the Shortlist model (Norris, 1994). According to the Shortlist model, a given input word will not only activate its corresponding entry in the mental lexicon, but also the lexical entries of so-called embedded words if present. So, for example, the Dutch word *trompet* (trumpet) will also activate the words *trom* (drum) and *pet* (cap). A lateral inhibition mechanism then takes care of the problem of eventually selecting the target word *trompet* instead of the embedded words. This is achieved by having the lateral inhibition mechanism such that longer input strings matching the inut inhibit the shorter (embedded) strings. Although this is what should happen for monomorphemic words, the situation looks quite different for morphologically complex words. If morphologically complex words are decomposed in its constituents during lexical access by activating representations of its morphological constituents, then these constituents and, if present, the full form representation of the corresponding word should compete with each other just as in the case of monomorphemic words with embedded words. Although this possibility cannot be excluded, it is theoretically unappealing and empirically difficult to reconcile with the results on the role of morphology in word recognition. As a consequence, it appears to be an important challenge to consider how models of spoken word recognition which have pimarily focussed on the recognition of monomorphemic words can be reconciled with models and results concerning the role of morphology in word recognition. This important topic has until now received rather little attention in psycholinguistics.

4.9 Conclusion

Looking back at the psycholinguistic research on the role of morphology in word recognition, one can identify two main issues that keep reappearing in this line of research. The first one concerns the issue of storage versus computation. Following Baayen, Dijkstra and Schreuder (in press), one can identify a continuum of theoretical proposals. At the one end of this continuum, we find proponents of pervasive storage of morphologically complex words (e.g., Butterworth, 1983; Seidenberg, 1987; see also Stemberger & MacWhinney, 1986, 1988). At the other end of the continuum we find proposals that pervasive storage of regular morphologically complex words is completely absent (Pinker, 1991; Taft & Forster, 1975). Only words with irregular morphology or mother idiosyncratic properties are assumed to be stored.

In balance, the corresponding studies strongly suggest that neither of these two extreme positions is correct. Rather, the word recognition system appears to be structured in much more flexible ways allowing for both storage and computation. The constraints provided by the relevant empirical evidence therefore suggest a model in which morphologically complex words can either be accessed via a direct route or a parsing route. Furthermore, the mental lexicon appears to contain information about morphological structure in such a way that different morphological relations between words are coded in different ways. The available evidence suggests that an adequate model should either take the form of a network model with separate full-form representations which are linked with variable connections to their stem, or the form of a model with morphologically decomposed entries with variable connections between stems and affixes (and, perhaps, between affixes). An interesting consequence of such models is that one does not need to assume a qualitatively different representation for inflectional and derivational morphology. Rather, inflectional and derivational morphology could be represented in the same basic architecture, with factors like semantic transparency determining the connection strength between the different representations.

This leads to the second issue. Early studies on the role of morphology in word recognition tried to uncover general principles of morphological organization that should hold for all morphologically complex words of a language in the same way, or that should at least systematically reflect distinctions proposed in linguistics. So, for example, a central question was whether inflectional and derivational morphology were represented in qualitatively different ways. Again, on balance, the relevant evidence strongly suggests that this is not the appropriate question to ask. Rather, it appears that a number of factors determine the recognition and representation of morphologically complex words. That is, linguistic morphology does not have a direct one-to-one correspondence in "mental" morphology (see also McQueen & Cutler, in press).

Above we have discussed a number of the factors that are of relevance. First, semantic transparency appears to play an important role. This factor is of primary importance for derived words, and it appears that high semantic transparency favors computation over storage. However, semantic considerations might also play a role in the domain of inflectional morphology (e.g., Baayen, Burani & Schreuder, in press). Second, the order of occurrence of affixes (prefixes versus suffixes) appears to be important, in particular in spoken word recognition. Third, the frequency and productivity of affixes is important. Fourth, the relative surface frequencies of different inflectional variants of a stem as well as the size of the morphological family have an effect on processing of morphologically complex words. All of these factors and their potential interactions (e.g., highly productive affixes are more likely to occur in semantically transparent complex words) have to be taken into account in order to derive an adequate model of the recognition of morphologically complex words. This also means that adequate lexical data bases and lexical statistics will become increasingly important tools for designing experiments as well as for model construction.

Besides these factors, evidence is accumulating that processing of morphologically complex words is also dependent on the experimental context in which the critical words occur. So, for example, it appears that morphological decomposition is an optional process which can be triggered by the set of words and nonwords used in an experiment. Whether such context influences also play a role outside experimental settings with lists of isolated words remains to be seen.

Finally, as langages differ in the complexity of their morphology, one should not generalize from the few languages that have been investigated to other languages. Rather, systematic cross-linguistic research is needed to pinpoint the differences and commonalities in the processing of morphologically complex words between languages. So, for example, Hankamer (1989) argues that in agglutinative languages like Turkish morphological parsing is a necessary part of the processing of morphologically complex words. Whether cross-language differences in the processing of morphologically complex words can ultimately be accounted for by the factors discussed above is an additional important issue for future research. Note, however, that crosslinguistic research might be hampered by the fact that for many languages we do not have the adequate lexical databases that allow to perform the lexical statistics that are needed for a careful investigation of the above mentioned factors.

In light of combined evidence, none of the currently available models receives unequivocal empirical support. However, the combined results clearly constrain adequate models. First, the models should allow for a direct route and a parsing route in the processing of morphologically complex words. Therefore, some version of a dual route model appears to be the adequate choice. Second, the models should allow the incorporation of the relevant processing factors by differences in the connection strength between full forms, stems, and affixes. Third, because there are a number of factors beyond and above morphological structure affecting the processing of morphologically complex words, corresponding models require a computational implementation which also reflects the relevant lexical statistics. And fourth, future research should devote more work to an integration of models that primarily aim at the recognition of monomorphemic words with models concerned with morphological factors in word recognition.

References

Anderson, S.R. (1992). *A-morphous morphology*. Cambridge: Cambridge University Press.

Andrews, S. (1986). Morphological influences on lexical access: Lexical or nonlexical effects? *Journal of Memory and Language, 25*, 726-740.

Baayen, R.H., Burani, C. & Schreuder, R. (in press). Effects of semantic markedness in the processing of regular nominal singular and plurals in Italian. In G.E. Booj & J. van der Marle (eds.), *Yearbook of Morphology 1996*. Dordrecht: Kluwer.

Baayen, R.H., Dijkstra, T. & Schreuder, R. (in press). Singulars and plurals in Dutch: Evidence for a parallel route model. *Journal of Memory and Language*.

Baayen, R.H., Lieber, R. & Schreuder, R. (in press). The morphological complexity of simplex nouns. *Linguistics*.

Baayen, R.H. & Schreuder, R. (1996). Modelling the processing of morphologically complex words. In T. Dijkstra & K. deSmedt (eds.), *Computational Psycholinguistics* . Taylor & Francis: London.

Beauvillain, C. (1996). The integration of morphological and whole-word form information during eye fixations on prefixed and suffixed words. *Journal of Memory and Language, 35*, 801-820.

Bentin, S. & Feldman, L.B. (1990). The contribution of morphological and semantic relatedness to repetition priming at short and long lags: Evidence from Hebrew. *Quarterly Journal of Experimental Psychology, 42A*, 693-711.

Bergman, M.W. (1988). *The visual recognition of word structure: Left-to-right processing of derivational morphology*. Doctoral Dissertation, University of Nijmegen.

Bergman, M.W., Hudson, P.T.W. & Eling, P.A.T.M. (1988). How simple complex words can be: Morphological processing and word representation. *Quarterly Journal of Experimental Psychology, 40A*, 41-72.

Booij, G.E. (1993). Against split morphology. In G.E. Booij & J. van Marle (eds.), *Yearbook of Morphology 1993*. Dordrecht: Kluwer Academic Publishers.

Bradley, D. (1980). Lexical representation of derivational relation. In M. Aronoff & M.-L. Kean (eds.), *Juncture* . Saratoga, CA: Anma Libri.

Burani, C. (1993). What determines morphological relatedness in the mental lexicon? Comments on the chapter by Tyler, Waksler, and Marslen-Wilson. In G. Altmann & R. Shillcock (eds.), *Cognitive models of speech processing.* Hillsdale, NJ: Erlbaum.

Burani, C. & Caramazza, A. (1987). Representation and processing of derived words. *Language and Cognitive Processes, 2,* 217-227.

Burani, C., Dovetto, F.M., Thornton, A.M. & Laudanna, A. (1996). Accessing and naming suffixed pseudo-words. In G.E. Booij & J. van Marle (eds.), *Yearbook of Morphology 1996.* Dordrecht: Kluwer Academic Publishers.

Booij & J. van Marle (eds.), *Yearbook of Morphology 1996.* Dordrecht: Kluwer Academic Publishers.

Burani, C., Salasmo, D. & Caramazza, A. (1984). Morphological structure and lexical access. *Visible Language, 18,* 342-352.

Butterworth, B. (1983). Lexical representation. In B. Butterworth (ed.), *Language Production, Vol. II.* London: Academic Press.

Caramazza, A., Laudanna, A. & Romani, C. (1988). Lexical access and inflectional morphology. *Cognition, 28,* 297-332.

Chialant, D. & Caramazza, A. (1995). Where is morphology and how is it represented? The case of written word recognition. In L.B. Feldman (ed.), *Morphological aspects of language processing.* Hillsdale, NJ: Erlbaum.

Cole, P., Beauvillain, C. & Segui, J. (1989). On the representation and processing of prefixed and suffixed derived words: A differential frequency effect. *Journal of Memory and Language, 28,* 1-13.

Crystal, D. (1995). *Die Cambridge Enzyklopädie der Sprache.* Frankfurt, New York: Campus.

Cutler, A., Hawkins, J.A. & Gilligan, G. (1985). The suffixing preference: A processing explanation. *Linguistics, 23,* 723-758.

Dell, G.S. (1986). A spreading activation theory of retrieval in sentence production. *Psychological Review, 93,* 283-321.

Dimmendaal, G.J. (1987). Drift and selection mechanisms in morphological change: The Eastern Nilotic case. In A.G. Ramat, O. Carruba & G. Bernini (eds.), *Papers from the 7th international conference on historic linguistics.* John Benjamins: Amsterdam.

Downie, R., Milech, D. & Kirsner, K. (1985). Unit definition in the mental lexicon. *Australian Journal of Psychology, 37,* 141-155.

Drews, E. & Zwitserlood, P. (1995). Morphological and orthographic similarity in visual word recognition. *Journal of Experimental Psychology: Human Perception and Performance, 21,* 1098-1116.

Emmeroy, K.D. (1989). Auditory morphological priming in the mental lexicon. *Language and Cognitive Processes, 4,* 73-92.

Feldman, L.B. (1991). The contribution of morphology to word recognition. *Psychological Research, 53,* 33-41.

Feldman, L.B. (1994). Beyond orthography and phonology: Differences between inflections and derivations. *Journal of Memory and Language, 33,* 442-470.

Feldman, L.B. & Fowler, C.A. (1987). The inflected noun system in Serbo-Croatian: Lexical representation of morphological structure. *Memory & Cognition, 15,* 1-12.

Feldman, L.B., Frost, R. & Pnini, T. (1995). Decomposing words in their constituent morphemes: Evidence from English and Hebrew. *Journal of Experimental Psychology: Learning, Memory and Cognition, 21,* 947-960.

Feldman, L.B. & Moskolievic, J. (1987). Repetition priming is not purely episodic in origin. *Journal of Experimental Psychology: Learning, Memory and Cognition, 13,* 573-581.

Fowler, C.A., Napps, S.E. & Feldman, L.B. (1985). Relations among regular and irregular morphologically related words in the lexicon as revealed by repetition priming. *Memory and Cognition, 13,* 241-255.

Frauenfelder, U.H. & Schreuder, R. (1992). Constraining psycholinguistic models of morphological processing and representation: The role of productivity. In G.E. Booj & J. van Marle (eds.), *Yearbook of Morphology 1991.* Dordrecht: Kluwer.

Frazier, L., Flores d'Arcais, G.B. & Coolen, R. (1993). Processing discontinuous words: On the interface between lexical and semantic processing. *Cognition, 47,* 219-249.

Gernsbacher, M.A. (1984). Resolving 20 years of inconsistent interactions between familiarity and orthography, concreteness, and polysemy. *Journal of Experimental Psychology: General, 113,* 256-281.

Grainger, J. & Jacobs, A. (1996). Orthographic processing in visual word recognition: A multiple read-out model. *Psychological Review, 103,* 518-565.

Grainger, J. & Segui, J. (1990). Neighborhood effects in visual word recognition: A comparison of lexical decision and masked identification latencies. *Perception and Psychophysics, 47,* 191-198.

Grainger, J., Cole, P. & Segui, J. (1991). Masked morphological priming in visual word recognition. *Journal of Memory and Language, 30,* 370-384.

Günther, H. (1988). Oblique word forms in visual word recognition. *Linguistics, 26,* 583-600.

Halle, M. & Marantz, A. (1993). Distributional morphology and the pieces of inflection. In K. Hale & S.J. Keyser (eds.), *The view from building 20: Essays in honor of Sylvain Bromberger.* Cambridge, Mass: MIT Press.

Hankamer, J. (1989). Morphological parsing and the lexicon. In W. Marslen-Wilson (ed.), *Lexical representation and process.* Cambridge, MA: MIT Press.

Henderson, L. (1985). Toward a psychology of morphemes. In A.W. Ellis (ed.), *Progress in the Psychology of Language, Vol. I.* London: Erlbaum.

Henderson, L. (1989). On mental representation of morphology and its diagnosis by measures of visual access speed. In W. Marslen-Wilson (ed.), *Lexical representation and process.* Cambridge, MA: MIT Press.

Henderson, L., Wallis, J. & Knight, D. (1984). Morphemic structure and lexical access. In H. Bouma & D. Bouwhuis (eds.), *Attention and Performance X.* Hillsdale, NJ: Erlbaum.

Holmes, V.M. & O'Reagan, J.K. (1992). Reading derivationally affixed French words. *Language and Cognitive Processes, 7,* 163-192.

Katz, L., Rexer, K. & Lukatela, G. (1991). The processing of inflected words. *Psychological Research, 53,* 25-32.

Kempley, S.T. & Morton, J. (1982). The effects of priming with regularly and irregularly related words in auditory word recognition. *British Journal of Psychology, 73,* 441-454.

Kostic, A. (1995). Information load constraints on processing inflectional morphology. In L.B. Feldman (ed.), *Morphological aspects of language processing.* Hillsdale, NJ: Erlbaum.

Laudanna, A., Badecker, W. & Caramazza, A. (1992). Processing inflectional and derivational morphology. *Journal of Memory and Language, 31,* 333-348.

Laudanna, A. & Burani, C. (1995). Distributional properties of derivational affixes: Implications for processing. In L.B. Feldman (ed.), *Morphological aspects of language processing.* Hillsdale, NJ: Erlbaum.

Laudanna, A., Burani, C. & Cermele, A. (1994). Prefixes as processing units. *Language and Cognitive Processes, 9,* 295-316.

Libben, G. (1994). How is morphological decomposition achieved? *Language and Cognitive Processes, 9,* 369-391.

Lieber, R. (1992). *Deconstructing morphology: Word formation in syntactic theory.* Chicago: Chicago University Press.

Lukatela, G., Manic, Z., Gligorijevic, G., Kostic, A., Savic, M. & Turvey, M.T. (1978). Lexical decision to inflected nouns. *Language and Speech, 21,* 166-173.

Lukatela, G., Gligorijevic, G., Kostic, A. & Turvey, M.T. (1980). Representation of inflected nouns in the mental lexicon. *Memory & Cognition, 8,* 415-423.

Manelis, L. & Tharp, D.A. (1977). The processing of affixed words. *Memory & Cognition, 5,* 690-695.

Marslen-Wilson, W., Tyler, L.K., Waksler, R. & Older, L. (1994). Morphological and meaning in the English mental lexicon. *Psychological Review, 101,* 3-33.

McQueen, J.M. & Cutler, A. (in press). Morphology in word recognition. In A.M. Zwicky & A. Spencer (eds.), *The Handbook of Morphology.* Oxford: Blackwell.

Napps, S.E. & Fowler, C.A. (1987). Formal relationships among words and the organization of the mental lexicon. *Journal of Psycholinguistic Research, 16,* 257-272.

Norris, D. (1994). Shortlist: A connectionist model of continuous speech recognition. *Cognition, 52,* 309-331.

Pinker, S. (1991). Rules of language. *Science, 153,* 530-535.

Rubenstein, H. & Pollack, I. (1963). Word predictability and intelligibility. *Journal of Verbal Learning and Verbal Behavior, 2,* 147-158.

Rubin, G.S., Becker, C.A. & Freeman, R.H. (1979). Morphological structure and its effect on visual word recognition. *Journal of Verbal Learning and Verbal Behavior, 18,* 757-767.

Sandra, D. (1990). On the representation and processing of compound words: Automatic access to constituent morphemes does not occur. *Quarterly Journal of Experimental Psychology, 42A,* 529-567.

Scarborough, D.L., Cortese, C. & Scarborough, H.S. (1977). Frequency and repetition effects in lexical memory. *Journal of Experimental Psychology: Human Perception and Performance, 3,* 1-17.

Schreuder, R. & Baayen, R.H. (1994). Prefix stripping re-revisited. *Journal of Memory and Language, 33,* 357-375.

Schreuder, R. & Baayen, R.H. (1995). Modelling morphological processing. In L.B. Feldman (ed.), *Morphological aspects of language processing.* Hillsdale, NJ: Erlbaum.

Schreuder, R. & Baayen, R.H. (in press). How complex simplex words can be. *Journal of Memory and Language.*

Schreuder, R., Grendel, M., Poulisse, N., Roelofs, A. & van der Voort, M. (1990). Lexical processing, morphological complexity and reading. In D.A. Balota, G.B. Flores d'Arcais & K. Rayner (eds.), *Comprehension processes in reading*. Hillsdale, NJ: Erlbaum.

Schriefers, H., Friederici, A.D. & Graetz, P. (1992). Inflectional and derivational morphology in the mental lexicon: Symmetries and asymmetries in repetition priming. *Quarterly Journal of Experimental Psychology, 44A*, 373-390.

Schriefers, H., Zwitserlood, P. & Roelofs, A. (1991). The identification of morphologically complex spoken words: Continuous processing or decomposition. *Journal of Memory and Language, 30*, 26-47.

Seidenberg, M. (1987). Sublexical structure in visual word recognition: Access units or orthographic redundancies. In M. Coltheart (ed.), *Attention and Performance XII*. Hove: Lawrence Erlbaum.

Seidenberg, M. (1990). Lexical access: Another theoretical soupstone? In D.A. Balota, G.B. Flores d'Arcais & K. Rayner (eds.), *Comprehension processes in reading*. Hillsdale, NJ: Erlbaum.

Sereno, J.A. & Jongman, A. (1992). *The processing of inflectional morphology in English*. Presented at the 5th Annual CUNY Conference on Human Sentence Processing, March 1992.

Stanners, R.F., Neisser, J.J., Hernon, W.P. & Hall, R. (1979a). Memory representations for morphologically related words. *Journal of Verbal Memory and Verbal Behavior, 18*, 399-412.

Stanners, R.F., Neisser, J.J. & Painton, S. (1979b). Memory representations for prefixed words. *Journal of Verbal Memory and Verbal Behavior, 18*, 733-743.

Steele, S. (1995). Towards a theory of morphological information. *Language, 71*, 260-309.

Stemberger, J.B. & MacWhinney, B. (1986). Frequency and the lexical storage of regularly inflected forms. *Memory and Cognition, 14*, 17-26.

Stemberger, J.B. & MacWhinney, B. (1988). Are lexical forms stored in the lexicon? In H. Hammond & M. Noonan (eds.), *Theoretical morphology: Approaches in linguistics*. London: Academic Press.

Taft, M. (1979a). Lexical access via an orthographic code: The Basic Orthographic Syllable Structure (BOSS). *Journal of Verbal Learning and Verbal Behavior, 18*, 21-39.

Taft, M. (1979b). Recognition of affixed words and the word frequency effect. *Memory & Cognition, 7*, 263-272.

Taft, M. (1981). Prefix stripping revisited. *Journal of Verbal Learning and Verbal Behavior, 20*, 263-272.

Taft, M. (1985). The decoding of words in lexical access: A review of the morpho-graphic approach. In D. Besner, T.G.Waller & G.E. Mackinnon (eds.), *Reading research: Advances in theory and practice, Vol. V*. New York: Academic Press.

Taft, M. & Forster, K.I. (1975). Lexical storage and retrieval of prefixed words. *Journal of Verbal Memory and Verbal Behavior, 14*, 630-647.

Taft, M., Hambly, G. & Kinoshita, S. (1986). Visual and auditory recognition of prefixed words. *Quarterly Journal of Experimental Psychology, 38A*, 351-366.

Tyler, L.K., Marslen-Wilson, W., Rentoul, J. & Hanney, P. (1988). Continuous and discontinuous access in spoken word recognition: The role of derivational pre-fixes. *Journal of Memory and Language, 27*, 368-381.

Zwitserlood, P. (1994). The role of semantic transparency in the processing and rep-resentation of Dutch compounds. *Language and Cognitive Processes, 9*, 341-368.

Chapter 5

The Architecture of the Mental Lexicon

Johannes Engelkamp
Ralf Rummer

5.1   Introduction

The original subject of research on the mental lexicon is the subjective representation of word meanings. Just as in linguistics words are allocated their meanings in the lexicon, words were allocated a mental representation in the psychology of the 1970's. This position could, however, not be maintained. Assumptions regarding representation have become increasingly differentiated, so that now the mental lexicon must be understood as a part of the whole cognitive architecture.

In describing this development we are guided by two basic assumptions: (1) In the course of the phylogenetic and ontogenetic development, our central nervous system has developed specialization with respect to the processing of various linguistic and non-linguistic informational aspects of stimuli. Particular regions of the brain have become specialized to particular information processing procedures. (2) The processing of stimuli is characterized by a high degree of *flexibility*. In this way, for instance, objects are named differently according to the communication situation and words are understood differently according to the context.

In the following treatment both assumptions will be taken into consideration. On one hand, a cognitive architecture will be postulated which is to be thought of as neuro-anatomically fixed and consists of several (at least) partially independent subsystems. On the other hand, it will be assumed that this cognitive architecture is used flexibly according to the purpose to which it is applied. A further basic assumption is that stimulus representations are distributed within the specific processing system. Before we give a summary of this paper, a few basic remarks should be made about the conception of the system and about the status of empirical research relating to the notion of system. When we speak of a cognitive subsystem, we mean that the links within a system are significantly more frequent than the links between systems. Systems are in our opinion not fully encapsulated (see e.g., Zimmer, 1993). The degree of connectedness between subsystems differs. With this assumption we take into account of neurological conceptions according to which our context is organized in a modular fashion in the form of so-called neuronal maps (e.g., Spitzer, 1996). These subsystems are partly hierarchically organized. The structure of these subsystems should manifest itself in observable behavioral phenomena. The proposals made here on the subdivision of the cognitive system should be seen as temporary. Further subdivisions are probable.

In the following Section (Section 5.2) we will proceed from a holistic conception in sketching the distinctions made in the assumption about the system which have been made in the last 25 years. We successively introduce differentiations, until an architecture is left which corresponds to the modular theory of memory (Engelkamp, 1990; Engelkamp & Zimmer, 1994a). The Section ends with a discussion of the causes making finer and finer distinctions between subsystems the conception of the system assumed here.

In Section 5.3 the various (postulated) subsystem will be compared with each other. Empirical results will be cited which justify each of the distinctions. We will appeal to results from diverse sources. We distinguish experimental results from *general psychology,* from *neuropsychology* and from the *neurological sciences.* The interpretation of these results is based on a comparable logic. In experimental cognitive psychology separate systems are assumed when the performances attributed to particular systems can be dissociated (for example, on the basis of the paradigm of selective interference). The neuropsychological equivalent to this consists in the observation of double dissociations. Such double dissociations exist, when two patients show opposing performance deficits in two tasks, that is when, for instance, patient 1 is impaired in task A but not in task B and patient 2 is impaired in task B but not in task A. In neuroimaging techniques the basic methods of cognitive neuroscience, one assumes separate systems when different areas of the brain are activated in dealing with different tasks. The interpretation of one of these data sources is (for various reasons) problematic (the validity of neuropsychological data is discussed e.g., by Kelter, 1994). For this reason, subdivisions of the cognitive system are particularly convincing when the various sources show convergent results. Finally, in Section 5.4 we show how the mental lexicon can be described in a modular framework of memory and which functions it has. In this connection we will also discuss the flexible use of the architecture postulated in Section 5.2. In doing so we will distinguish between word production and word comprehension.

5.2   From the Lexicon in an Unitary Cognitive System to the Lexicon in a Composed Cognitive Architecture

5.2.1   The Development of System Assumptions

Assuming a mental lexicon serves to explain certain observable phenomena. The necessity of this assumption becomes evident, when one considers behaviorist linguistic psychology (e.g., Skinner, 1957). In this theoretical paradigm the attempt was made to work without assuming internal stimulus representations (e.g., Hörmann, 1978). However, at the beginning of the sixties it had to be concluded that a number of linguistic phenomena (such as the fact that we are able to understand utterances which are completely new to us) could not be adequately explained if one dispensed with mentalist assumptions. (The failure of behaviorism in the explanation of human language processing was a major reason for the emergence of cognitive psychology which began in the 1960's.) This result led to the assumption that we represent meanings mentally.

As mentioned at the outset, mental representations were in the psychology of the 1970's allocated to meanings in the same way as words were allocated meanings in dictionaries in lexicography. The basic assumption that knowledge of meaning is mentally, or, as we also said, subjectively, represented was such an innovation in comparison with the behaviorist view and was such a theoretical advance that problems which were connected with this relatively simple approach of meaning went unnoticed. Of central importance was the assumption that words which one sees or hears activate the appropriate meanings in the reader or hearer. Researchers spoke of *concepts* instead of word meanings. In this they were interested in the internal structure of meanings or concepts (e.g., Deese, 1970; Engelkamp, 1973; Hörmann, 1967; Slobin, 1971) as well as their organization, that is the relations between concepts (Collins & Quillian, 1969; Kintsch, 1972; Schank, 1972, 1975; Rumelhart, Lindsay & Norman, 1972). The internal structure of concepts was often described using semantic features (for an overview, see Strube, 1984), while the relations between concepts were modeled in semantic networks (for an overview, see Engelkamp, 1985).

Nearly ten years elapsed before it was recognized that in this concern for semantic features and semantic networks the function of word use had been forgotten (Johnson-Laird, Herrmann & Chaffin, 1984). In semantic network conceptions researchers *speculated* which meaning is connected with a word and how one should best represent this, but they overlooked the fact that words (via their meanings) also refer to things in the world. Many words refer to *something*. 'Stat aliquid pro aliquo' has been the motto since as early as the times of classical rhetoric, in which, in trying to find out about the origin of words, the question was asked as to whether that which is named has an influence on the name itself. The fact that a speaker informs a partner about something in the world, which was discussed as long ago as Bühler's Organon model (1934), had been lost sight in the early years of cognitive psychology. This referential aspect of language only became a subject of theoretical importance as a distinction between word representation and object representation began to be made.

Unimpressed by the endeavors of those who were constructing semantic networks, Paivio (1969, 1971) had in his dual code theory distinguished between non-linguistic and linguistic representations. This theory makes explicit reference to the fact that one can refer to pictorial stimuli with linguistic stimuli. The semantic conception of the dual code theory takes the specificity of the stimulus experience into account. It is assumed that experience with the nonverbal (especially visually perceived) world leads to nonverbal semantic representations, while verbal semantic representations develop through experience with language. Paivio's (1971) dual code theory differed in two ways from the theoretical positions which were then popular. (1) Linguistic and non-linguistic knowledge representations were distinguished, both representations having semantic content. (2) The connection between both types of representations was conceived as associative. Thus, a word (e.g., the word *bottle*) activates a verbal representation. This verbal representation could then activate the corresponding nonverbal representation via its associative connection with the non-verbal-imaginal representation and vice versa. Seeing of an object (e.g., a bottle) should lead to the activation of a nonverbal-imaginal representation, and by its associative connection this could activate the verbal representation.

A problem which Paivio (1969, 1971) with his dual code theory was confronted with was, that the verbal and the nonverbal representation had no inherent common features, but were merely associated with each other. In the same way that the representation of the word bottle could be associated with the representation of the object 'bottle', it could also be associated with that of the objects 'cork', 'glass', 'beer' etc. The Paivio theory did not allow a distinction between these cases. A further criticism can be directed at the lack of cognitive economy of the model. The assumption to different semantic representations for words and pictures is theoretically uneconomic, since here a large portion of the conceptual information is doubly represented, on one hand as conceptual (language independent) information and on the other hand as word meaning (e.g., Herrmann, 1994). Theses problems were not solved until the model proposals of the end of the 1970's, which distinguished between stimulus representations and semantic representations.

Suggestions were made for instance by Glass, Holyoak and Santa (1979), Nelson (1979), Snodgrass (1984) and Warren and Morton (1982). All these studies distinguished between the representation of forms of stimuli and their meanings. The general structure of these proposals is depicted in figure 1.

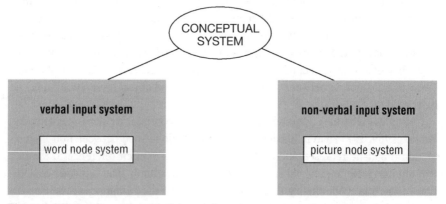

Figure 1. Word node system and picture node system as entry to the conceptual system.

The crucial difference to Paivio (1969, 1971) was that these models represented the forms in which stimuli appeared independently from their meanings. The word form and the picture form - we call them word node (see Klix, 1980, 1985) and, by analogy, picture node - are presemantic representations. They preserve sensorial information which activates a particular concept. The concept contains the knowledge which is associated with the stimuli. This knowledge is not directly given with the stimulus currently present, but is connected with it associatively through learning processes (Prinz, 1983). This basic idea has in large part been accepted. The conceptual system contains abstract information. As a rule, the information represented in the conceptual system is information which in the course of ontogenesis has been shown to be instrumental for the attainment of goals (Hoffmann, 1996).

In the 1980's the following distinctions were introduced: Instead of a single word node for words, a *visual* and *acoustic word node* were postulated, depending on the modality of presentation (e.g., Morton & Patterson, 1980). The previous remarks refer to the reception of words. We also (re)act with language, and the phenomena observable in the production of words differ in many ways from the corresponding findings regarding reception. In order to be able to explain these processing differences, two linguistic *output systems* were assumed together with the two *input systems* for words which are heard or read. One of the output systems is for written and the other is for oral language production (Morton & Patterson, 1980; Warren & Morton, 1982). Engelkamp (1990) speaks of *speaking-* and *writing programs*. At the same time it was postulated that both output systems can be accessed either directly from the word nodes or via the corresponding concept (e.g., Ellis & Young, 1989; Morton & Patterson, 1980; Riddoch et al., 1988).

Until now only object concepts have been referred to. These correspond to nouns which refer to entities which can be experienced sensoricly (mainly visually). Such object concepts are acquired in ontogenesis earlier than abstract concepts. In this respect the nouns corresponding to object concepts can in a certain sense be characterized as prototypical for this word class. Object concepts are connected with picture nodes in a special way.

While physical objects can be seen as the prototypical referents of nouns, Lyons (1977) suggests that verbs correspond in a comparable manner to open physical actions (see Engelkamp, 1990). As a prototypical case which arises particularly early in language acquisition, simple motoric activities like DRINK, LIFT; CARRY can be mentioned. Thus, in a manner similar to the way in which object concepts are connected with picture nodes, it can be assumed that this class of verb concepts corresponds to motoric representations.

Engelkamp and Zimmer (e.g., 1983) included such motor representations in their framework of memory for actions. They call the motoric representation for simple actions *motoric programs*. Later they introduced the verbal-motoric output systems along with the verbal-motoric one (Engelkamp, 1990, 1991a; Engelkamp & Zimmer,

1994a). At the same time, they pointed out that the nonverbal motoric output system can (analogously to linguistic processing) be directly accessed via the picture nodes as well as via the conceptual system. Figure 2 summarizes this distinction between verbal and nonverbal input and output systems.

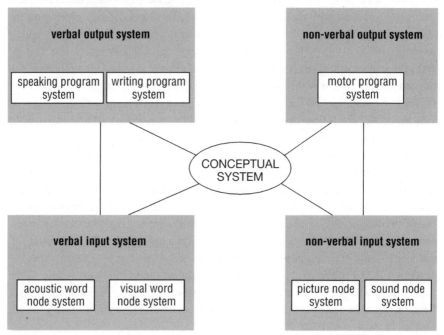

Figure 2. Input- and output system for verbal and non-verbal information. The lines mark the possible pathways through cognitive system.

The significant aspect of this proposal is that, although there are direct paths from the nodes to the programs (direct in the sense that they do not have to pass through the conceptual system), this only occurs in the case that there is no change of modality. If the modality is changed (verbal -> nonverbal or vice versa) from the input to the output system, passage through the conceptual system is unavoidable (Engelkamp, 1991a).

Remembering that it is possible to hear and read not only words, but also a number of objects (e.g., telephone and its ringing), it is not surprising that a visual and an acoustic input system is also distinguished in the nonverbal area (Riddoch et al., 1988). (We will call the units of the acoustic input system sound nodes.) It is natural to postulate further input systems throughout the other sense modalities.

Another distinction concerns not so much the separation of various input systems (the horizontal level) as the time course (the vertical level). With respect to the vertical level proposals have been described until now which distinguish three levels in the temporal passage through the system: The level of the input system, the conceptual level and the level of the output system (cf., figure 2). It seems to be justifiable to distinguish various levels of representation as early as at the input systems, that is in the analysis of a stimulus. Let us discuss two examples of this. Engelkamp (1990; see also Engelkamp & Zimmer, 1994a) assumed for instance words that are not only represented in a modality-specific manner as acoustic and visual word nodes. It is also postulated, along with modality-specific word nodes on a higher level, abstract word nodes, which represent what acoustic and visual word nodes have in common (figure 3). These abstract word nodes contain information about the word class to which the concept is assigned. Grammatically relevant information is also represented here (in the case of verbs, e.g., argument structure and theta roles; e.g., Bierwisch & Schreuder, 1992; Schwarz, 1992).

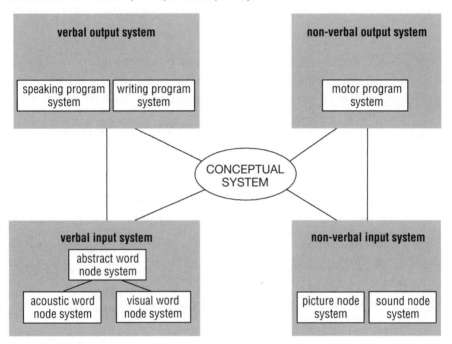

Figure 3. General survey of the cognitive architecture of the system.

Since Marr (1982) it has been assumed that objects are analyzed and represented on at least two levels, a viewer-centered and an object-centered level. The former is specific to a particular perspective; the latter makes generalizations about various perspectives and is thus independent of perspective (for an overview, see Ellis & Young, 1989; Humphreys & Bruce, 1989). Although distinguishing further levels is plausible , we will content ourselves with this classification.

It should be remarked at this point that, despite their relative complexity, the distinctions made here ignore important aspects which should be considered in the context of a mental lexicon. These involve syntactic information. Content words, as discussed here, occur embedded in syntactic structures. The information which governs this embedding (such as gender information in nouns or the argument structure of verbs) should be integrated into a comprehensive conception of the mental lexicon.

5.2.2   Reasons for the Trend Towards Assuming Increasingly Differentiated Systems

Until a few years ago, there were intensive discussions as to whether differentiations within the system are justified or not. Particularly controversial was the discussion about the whether a separate visual systems besides a conceptual system should be postulated (e.g., Kosslyn, 1981; Pylyshyn, 1981). Finally it was concluded that the controversy could not be decided in one way or the other (Anderson, 1978 talks of a 'structure-process-tradeoff'). If one compares the result of this discussion with the models which are currently generally accepted, the in this point relatively uniform development of recent theoretical approaches is surprising. Not only is the assumption of a visual system hardly the subject of controversial discussion any more. It is also true that further system distinctions such as those described here are generally accepted in current research.

One of the reasons why no decision was reached in the so-called imagery debate can be seen in the failure of those involved to go beyond individual experimental paradigms. A typical paradigm for the examination of representation types was the comparison of the processing of words and pictures (see the special edition of the Journal of Verbal Learning and Verbal Behavior, 1984). In this paradigm the task was constant but the stimulus was varied (word vs. picture) and the reaction time was measured (e.g., Potter & Faulconer, 1975; Potter, So, Eckart & Feldman, 1984). It was found e.g., that words are read aloud more quickly than pictures are named. Such a result can be explained just as well by models which assume one system (concepts are accessed more quickly from words than from pictures) as by those which assume several systems (the concept could be accessed e.g., via the word node more quickly than via the picture node (Engelkamp, 1987).

The apparent equality of the possible explanations is reduced when the reaction times for words and pictures are measured using different tasks. An observation which emerges from this is that, although words are read more quickly than pictures are named, pictures can be more quickly categorized semantically (Smith & Magee, 1980; see also Glaser & Glaser, 1989). Such a reversal of the results under the influence of the type of task cannot be explained as simply on the basis of the assumption of a unitary system approach (Engelkamp, 1994, reports on this in more detail). It is significant for our subject that the variations in the task are a factor which gave impetus to the system approach.

The distinction of systems was justified in the 1980's by the attempt to show that a further factor (e.g., two tasks) had a different effect on differing stimulus types like words and pictures. A similar logic underlies the paradigm of structural (i.e. system-specific) interference. Here the attempt is made to show in double task experiments that two main or primary tasks (e.g., word processing and picture processing) are differentially influenced by two secondary tasks (with regard to which it is also assumed that one utilizes the verbal system and the other the visual system). Experiments which are based on such interference paradigms yielded convincing evidence for assuming different cognitive systems (but see Howe, Rabinowitz & Grant, 1993).

A further factor which gave impetus to the system approach was the increasing attention paid to neuropsychological research results (see Ellis & Young, 1989; McCarthy & Warrington, 1990). In neuropsychology it has been known for a long time that there are specific impairments. For instance patients with a visual agnosia are unable to recognize objects through visual perception, but they recognize objects via other sense channels (e.g., feeling, smell). Other patients can recognize objects presented visually, but not through other sense channels. Such double dissociation (see Ellis & Young, 1989) likewise support the assumptions of different systems. The assumption of various systems allows a more plausible explanation of the observed disturbances than the assumption of a single system. Perhaps the strongest impetus was given to the system approach through the progress of the cognitive neurosciences in the last ten years. In many cognitive theories, including the older ones, it is assumed that certain brain structures are specialized to the processing of specific types of information (see Posner & Raichle, 1994). These assumptions, however, could not be convincingly proved. Not enough attention was paid to the fact that many parts of the brain are involved in most tasks. Moreover, technical possibilities were initially lacking with which the activity of the brain in very simple cognitive tasks could be recorded. This situation has changed fundamentally. We now know that in most tasks (including those which are seen as elementary) many parts of the brain work together, and we are now able to analyze fairly well the effect of individual components of tasks (thanks to the various neuroimaging techniques). The online research of brain activity (during the performance of individual tasks) is still in its initial stages. (An introductory overview of this research area is given by Posner & Raichle, 1994 and Spitzer, 1996, see also Friederici, this volume). The present paper deals mainly with the results of experimental psychology and neuropsychology. Before evidence for the system assumptions introduced above is compiled, we will in the next Section give a more precise description of how the terms representation and system are used here.

The terms 'cognitive system' and 'mental representation' describe separate entities. The assumption of subsystems is more general than that of types of representations. Representations refer to individual stimuli (e.g., words) which are stored in the subsystems allocated to them. (In choosing this formulation we are not adopting the neurologically implausible assumption that the systems we are postulating are a sort of container for a special type of information). In our view the representational assumption is problematic to the extent that is supposed that there are fixed structures for individual stimuli. When one remembers the construction of the nervous system, it becomes clear that this idea is oversimplified. Generally, whole cell assemblies are activated in processing a stimulus (this was known as early as Hebb, 1949). Which neuronal structures can be activated in this process can vary considerably from situation to situation (e.g., depending on the context). The necessity of this 'flexibility assumption' is the result of functional studies and everyday observations. According to the context and the goal of the communication a word can activate different concepts. The word *bank* activates differing concepts depending on whether it is presented in conjunction with the word *river* or the word *money*. Analogously, an object can in a naming task activate differing speaking programs via the different concepts according to the context and the goal (see also Herrmann, Grabowski, Schweizer & Graf, 1996; Mangold-Allwinn, Barattelli, Kiefer & Koelbing, 1995). Thus, a robin would be referred to as a 'bird' when a child is addressed and, depending on circumstances, as 'erithacus rubecula' when speaking to an ornithologist. The explanation of such phenomena will be the subject of Section 5.4. Here we may note that, in principle, representation assumptions are able to take these flexibility requirements into account.

The activation of a stimulus representation can be seen as the activation structure of a local network. When we speak of nodes, concepts, and programs, we mean that certain activation patterns within a subsystem are repeated with repeated presentation of a stimulus. Our idea of representation is in principle in agreement with connectionist ideas. It is, however, crucial that the representations are allocated to systems which are also distinguished in the hardware of brain.

5.3 Empirical Evidence for the System and Representation Assumptions

In this Section we summarize some empirical evidence for the system assumptions formulated in Section 5.2.1. The evidence is based on the processing of individual stimuli and thus on the activation of certain representations as representatives of certain subsystems. The proposal to distinguish subsystems is thus indirectly supported through the representation types allocated to them. We will present separately the various empirical arguments for each of the different systems proposed in Section 5.2.

5.3.1 Word Nodes and Concepts

Even everyday phenomena support distinguishing a word node and a conceptual system. Thus, it occasionally happens that we know words without being able to recall their meaning, or, in reverse, we know meanings without knowing the appropriate terms. Since Brown and McNeill (1966) we also know that word node information can be partially available in the tip-of-the-tongue phenomenon, i.e. when we basically know the term for a particular meaning but are unable to recall it. The tip-of-the-tongue phenomenon thus shows that there can be separate access to meanings and terms.

Further support for the distinction between word nodes and concepts comes from neuropsychological data. Sartori, Masterson and Job (1987) report on patients who are able to read words but cannot understand their meaning (see also Schwartz, Saffran & Marin, 1980). Nevertheless, these patients can recall the meanings in other ways (e.g., when objects are presented visually). Thus, the conceptual system of these patients is intact as a rule.

The separation of a word node and a conceptual system is also supported by studies in which the method of the positron emission tomography (PET) was used. This method reflects topographic differences in the activity of the brain. It allows the comparison of the brain activity in particular tasks and with particular stimuli. It could be shown experimentally that the processing of visual word information mainly takes place in the extrastriate occipital cortex, while the processing of conceptual information must be attributed to other regions lying further to the frontal areas (e.g., Peterson, Fox, Posner, Mintun & Raichle, 1989).

Results from the so-called *semantic priming* also lead to the distinction between word nodes and concepts. In these studies, a prime stimulus and a target stimulus are presented, generally shortly after each other. A semantic priming experiment consists of a number of such prime-target presentations. The prime-target-relation is varied. A prime stimulus can be in a semantic relationship with the target stimulus (e.g., *dog-cat*). That is, the prime stimulus is semantically related to the target stimulus and differs from it in form. It is also possible that the prime stimulus is neither semantically related to the target stimulus nor related to it on the surface (*church*). The task of the subject can be, for instance, to judge in a lexical decision task whether the presented target stimulus is a word or a nonword. In such semantic priming experiments it becomes clear that the lexical decision can be made more quickly after semantically related prime stimuli than after nonrelated prime stimuli. This semantic priming effect has been documented many times (e.g., Lorch, 1982; Lupker, 1988; Meyer & Schvanefeldt, 1971; Neely, 1977).

The usual explanation for this effect is that the prime word activates its concepts and spreads this activation to associated concepts (e.g., Anderson, 1996; Collins & Loftus, 1975). Thus, the concept of a semantically related word is already preactivated when it appears. This accelerates its processing relative to those prime-target-combinations in which the target stimulus is preceded by an unrelated prime word.

Incorporating the semantic priming effect into the conceptual system and distinguishing word nodes are the same time is also supported by the absence of a priming effect when the prime is formally similar to the target word (e.g., graphemically) but differs from it semantically (Martin & Jensen, 1988; McNamara & Healy, 1988). Without assuming separate systems for word nodes and concepts, it would be difficult to explain why similarity leads to priming effects and formal similarity does not. That under certain conditions phonological priming effects can occur (e.g., in subliminal prime presentation or controlled prime-target-presentation) (Humphreys, Evett, Quinlan & Besner, 1987) does not concern the conclusion drawn here (for more detail see Engelkamp, 1990).

Further relevant data were collected on the basis of the so-called *repetition priming*. Here we are dealing with processing effects which are attributed to the repetition of the stimulus or the repeated processing of the same stimulus. Dannenbring and Briand (1982) and Den Heyer, Goring and Dannenbring (1985) were able to show that semantic priming effects are distinct from repetition effects. The authors observed that the repeated presentation of the same target words in a semantic priming experiment does reduce the decision time, but that this reduction is independent from the semantic priming effect. Thus, the repeated activation of a representation improves the access to the representation.

In order to find out more exactly whether the access to the word node, to the concept, or to both representations is improved by repetition, the processing of forms was varied by changing the surface characteristics from the first to the second presentation of a word. The assumption that the word node is (at least partly) responsible for the repetition effect could be supported by the observation that a change in the word form reduces the repetition effect in comparison with an identical repetition (an overview is given in Kirsner, Dunn & Standen, 1989; and Schacter, 1990). Admittedly, it cannot be excluded solely on the basis of this result that the conceptual system is also involved in the repetition effect.

However, an attribution of this repetition effect to word nodes is supported through the inclusion of cross-linguistic studies. If the effect was due to concept repetition, then a repetition effect should occur despite a change of language (e.g., from German to English) from the first presentation to the second. Here the form of the first stimulus is changed completely. Should repetition effects occur, then these would be clearly attributable to the conceptual system. The fact that no such repetition effects occur (Durso & Johnson, 1979) can be adduced as evidence that repetition priming is a pure word node effect.

Additional support for this view comes from experiments in which the repetition effect under different processing instructions is examined. From experiments on the explicit recall and recognition it has been known since Craik & Lockhart (1972) that semantic (so-called 'deep') processing improves the memory performances in comparison with non-semantic ('shallow') processing (e.g., Craik & Tulving, 1975). Manipulating the depth of processing does not effect repetition priming (Bowers & Schacter, 1990; Graf & Mandler, 1984; Roediger, Weldon, Stadler & Riegler, 1992).

These observations also apply to perceptual implicit tests such as word stem completion, word fragment completion, or word identification. On the other hand, in conceptual implicit tests which are expressly aimed at conceptual information, an effect of processing depth becomes noticeable (e.g., Weldon & Coyote, 1996; see also Engelkamp & Wippich, 1995). In some studies which are based on perceptual implicit tests, a slight positive influence of the semantic processing on the perceptual repetition priming was admittedly observed (e.g., Bowers & Schacter, 1990; Challis & Brodbeck, 1992). However, it is generally assumed that these slight effects are due to the confounding with explicit (i.e. concept-related) recall processes (Bowers & Schacter, 1990).

The distinction between word nodes and concepts is also supported by the fact that the performance in simple word recognition tasks is on one hand dependent on factors which are generally attributed to the conceptual representation level (e.g., concreteness) (Boles, 1983; Hines, 1976; Shanon, 1979). On the other hand, performance in word recognition tasks is systematically influenced by surface characteristics which are usually attributed to word nodes (e.g., word length) (for a summary, see Solso, 1979).

A separation of the word node system from the conceptual system is also supported by experimental results from research into bilingual memory. According to the asymmetry-model, the translation of one language into another can take place either via the conceptual system or a direct connection of both verbal input systems. Words presented in the first language should be more strongly connected with the conceptual system and words from the second should be more strongly connected with the input system of the first language. In accordance with these assumptions it could be shown that the translation of a word from the first language into a second takes longer than the reverse translation direction (e.g., de Groot, Danneburg & van Hell, 1994), while the opposite effect appears in a naming task (Chen, Cheung & Lau, in press).

Generally the results reported here support the distinction between a word node and a conceptual system.

5.3.2 Picture Nodes

Repetition effects can be demonstrated for picture processing which are similar to those found in word processing. If pictures - beginning with a subliminal or masked presentation - are presented for an increasing length of time or increasingly clearly until they are recognized, a repetition effect is noticeable. Pictures are recognized in their second presentation, even after days, better than comparable pictures in their first presentation (for an overview, see Schacter, Delany & Merikle, 1990). Wippich et al. (1995) presented objects embedded and hidden in geometrical patterns. They found a repetition effect in the detection rate of these objects. In the second presentation the detection rate was greater than in the first. Zimmer (1996) manipulated the form of object stimuli from the first to the second presentation and also found a repetition effect.

Analogous to the distinction between word node and concept, the question arises as to whether the effects are really due to picture nodes and not concepts. The same logic can be used in researching this question as in distinguishing between word nodes and concepts. It is assumed that picture nodes (like word nodes and unlike concepts) represent surface characteristics - here those of pictures. If repetition effects in picture identification are (analogously to that in words) based on surface representation then variations in form should influence repetition effects from the first to the second presentation and meaning variations should not do so.

Bartram (1976) was able to show that a variation in form reduces the picture repetition effect. He distinguished three different types of experimental conditions: (1) The picture presented first was identical to that presented second; (2) the picture presented second showed the same object but from a different perspective; and (3) the objects pictured were different but belonged to the same semantic category (e.g., different types of clocks). The repetition effect was most significant when the same object was shown twice from the same perspective and was least significant when both pictures represented different objects with the same name. Biederman and Cooper (1991; 1992) replicated this result with line drawings, i.e. with pure outline drawings which had only information about forms but no information about texture.

These results show that form information is significant for the repetition effect in the case of objects, but they do not exclude that conceptual information is also partly responsible for the repetition effect. Conceptual information was kept constant in the studies cited above. That the picture repetition effect is independent of conceptual information was shown by e.g., Caroll, Byrne and Kirsner (1985). In the first presentation they presented pictures either without requesting conceptual processing or with the task of conceptually processing the pictures in a specific way (e.g., to judge them according to particular features). The difference in the conceptual processing depth did not influence the repetition effect. Schacter, Cooper and Delany (1990) were even able to show a disordinal interaction for an object decision task (Is this a possible object?) and a recognition task. A semantic orientation task in the first word presentation improved (in comparison with a non-semantic task) the performance in recognition, but reduced the performance in the object decision task.

Studies on repetition priming supported the distinction between picture nodes and concepts. This distinction is also supported by experiments on explicit remembering. The results show that sensoric picture characteristics (e.g., color information; realized by the variation of black and white vs. color photographs) influence the retention performance when concepts remain unchanged (e.g., realized by the fact that a photograph depicts the same object) (e.g., Homa & Viera, 1988; Madigan, 1983).

This distinction finds further support through neuropsychological observations. Humphreys and Riddoch (1987a) describe a patient who in an object decision task could not distinguish real objects (e.g., a hen) from non-objects (e.g., a hen with four legs). Although the patient did not recognize visually presented object stimuli, he was able to describe the meaning of objects without problems if the term for the object was given to him. Thus, he had no access to concepts via the word nodes. Obviously, his conceptual system was intact but he was unable to activate the appropriate concepts via the picture nodes. Another possible explanation is the assumption that the picture nodes themselves were damaged.

Humphreys and Riddoch (1987b) describe a patient who showed considerable impairments in naming visually presented objects while the categorization of the corresponding objects on the basis of their terms caused him no difficulty. The conceptual system of this patient was also intact, but he could not access concepts via picture nodes, although he could do so via word nodes. Thus, both cases show along with the experimental results reported in the next Section that distinguishing picture nodes and word nodes is necessary.

5.3.3   Picture Nodes and Word Nodes

Distinguishing between picture nodes and word nodes can also be supported by experimental data. Results on repetition priming show that perceptual repetition effects of words do not apply to pictures and vice versa. Roediger and Weldon (1987) were able to show that the performance in word completion tasks (in comparison with a control condition) did improve if the appropriate words were visually presented beforehand, but not when the test subjects had seen the picture of the reference objects before. Analogously, a repetition effect was observable in picture completion when the pictures had been seen before, but not when their terms had been seen before.

An analogous result had been reported by Watkins, Peynircioglu and Brems (1984). They presented their test subjects with objects and their terms. They varied the type of encoding and the rehearsal of the item. In a verbal group, the subjects had to concentrate for 15 seconds on the name of the object (e.g., repeat it mentally). In the visual group, on the other hand, they had to try to imagine the picture as precisely as possible for 15 seconds. As in Roediger and Weldon (1987), a word and picture completion test followed. The result was that the subjects in the verbal group performed better in word completion than in the control, while the subjects in the visual group did better in the picture completion than in the control.

With another method, Pair Association Learning, Nelson had found evidence for the necessity of studying distinguishing word nodes and picture nodes as early as the 1970's. These experiments showed that in word-word pairs the performance in cued recall (stimulus word as cue for the response word) was impaired when the stimulus words of the pairs where phonologically similar (e.g., if they all began with the same prefix). If the stimulus words were replaced by their reference objects (e.g., the word *broom* by the picture of a broom), the performance was not impaired. (Nelson & Brooks, 1973). In another study, the visual similarity among the stimulus objects was varied. In this experiment, the performance was impaired through visual similarity when the subjects were confronted with picture stimuli, but this was not so with word stimuli. If terms instead of pictures were presented as stimuli, there was thus no impairment (Nelson, Reed & Walling, 1976). Nelson and his coworkers were finally able to show that the effects of conceptual similarity were different from both acoustic and visual similarity and were equally significant for both words and pictures (Nelson & Reed, 1976; Nelson, Reed & Walling, 1976). These results are also in agreement with our assumption that picture nodes, word nodes and concepts must be distinguished.

As a last point relevant in connection with this Section we cite the results on selective interference of words and pictures (Dhawan & Pellegrino, 1977; Pellegrino, Siegel & Dhawan, 1975; Warren, 1977; Wells, 1972). Even if the experiments individually have weakness, as a whole they demonstrate in an impressive manner that the retention of words is impaired by verbal-acoustic secondary tasks carried out simultaneously, while interference in the retention of pictures comes about when at the same time visual interference tasks are performed. In support of this it was shown in other experiments that verbal encoding strategies (of verbal material) were selectively impaired by word processing and visual strategies through picture processing (Logie, 1986). These results also speak for the distinction of a verbal and a visual memory system.

As a whole, the results reported thus far in this Section show that word nodes, picture nodes and concepts are different as mental representations. Accordingly, three subsystems should be postulated for these representation types.

5.3.4   Acoustic, Visual and Abstract Word Nodes

As has become clear, there are convincing proofs that picture processing generally does not include the term of the picture, i.e. the processing of the corresponding word node. The reverse is also true: word processing does not include the activation of picture nodes. Repetition effects are not, for example, transferred from pictures to words and from words to pictures in implicit perceptual tests (e.g., Roediger & Weldon, 1987; Roediger, 1990). This is different in a modality change of words. If a word is visually presented in the learning phase, test subjects benefit, even if the word is presented acoustically in an implicit perceptual test and vice versa. This cross-modal repetition priming has been demonstrated for various implicit tests like word identification, word stem completion, word fragment completion and lexical decision (for an overview, see Kirsner, Dunn & Standen, 1989). This cross-modal priming effect is, however, uniformally smaller than the priming effect in the repetition of the word stimulus in the same modality. From this can be concluded that acoustically and visually presented words have a common element, the repetition of which induces the cross-modal priming. Yet this 'common element' is clearly not the meaning of the word, for otherwise a repetition effect should occur in a change of language (e.g., *dog - Hund*), but it does not do so (e.g., Durso & Johnson, 1979).

Engelkamp (1990) and Engelkamp and Zimmer (1994a) assume an abstract, modality-independent word representation (abstract word node) to be the basis of the cross-modal priming effect.

This assumption and the preconceptual nature of the abstract word nodes is also supported by the fact that the cross-modal priming effect depends on word frequency (Kirsner, Dunn & Standen, 1989). That is, the cross-modal priming effect increases with decreasing word frequency (see also Engelkamp, Zimmer & Kurbjuweit, 1995); the specific priming effect, which goes back to the repetition of the same modality, is, however, independent of word frequency (Kirsner, Milech & Stunpfel, 1986). This effect could also be attributed to conceptual processing procedures. However, the fact that word frequency in recognition has an effect independent of the variation of the semantic processing (e.g., of processing depth), speaks against this assumption (e.g., Mandler, Goodman & Wilkes-Gibbs, 1982; Gorman, 1961; Gardiner, Gregg & Hampton, 1988). The reported data thus support the assumption of abstract word nodes.

However, along with an abstract word node there must also be modality-specific word node as the data mentioned above on cross-modal repetition priming suggest. The repetition of words within a modality leads to significantly larger priming effects than the repetition of words when the modality is changed. This effect was previously mostly demonstrated with a visual stimulus presentation in tests. If a word is presented visually in both the learning and the test phase, the repetition effect is larger than if it is presented acoustically in learning and visually in testing (e.g., Kirsner, Dunn & Standen, 1989). There are far fewer studies on acoustic word priming than on visual word priming (for an overview, see Schacter & Church, 1992). But here also there is evidence for the assumption that acoustic word repetition effects are presemantic effects and their significance depends on acoustic features of the word presentation.

Schacter and Church (1992) dealt specially with acoustic word priming. In their work they manipulated the processing depth e.g., in the first (acoustic) word presentation. Their subjects either had to estimate the number of meanings which they associated with words (semantically deep processing), or judge how clearly the words were spoken (semantically shallow processing). Both a word identification task (under white noise) and a stem completion task (where the first syllable was given) were used as implicit tests. Furthermore, an explicit test was also used. As expected, the explicit retention performance was better after 'deep' processing than after 'shallow' processing. The implicit retention performances were, on the other hand, slightly influenced or not influenced at all by the processing depth, yet there was a significant priming effect. This result shows that acoustic priming also is not based on conceptual processing procedures and that acoustic priming is based on word node information. That the word nodes in question are acoustic can be shown when in learning visually presented words are tested acoustically. Such a change of modality reduces the priming effect in the same way as a modality change in the opposite direction (Bassili, Smith & MacLeod, 1989; Jackson & Morton, 1984).

Interestingly, the acoustic word priming effect does not depend on the specific characteristics of the speaker's voice and is not dependent on whether or not the voice changes from the learning to the testing stage (Jackson & Morton, 1984; Schacter & Church, 1992). This effect suggests that the acoustic word node is a relatively abstract representation. Nevertheless, Schacter and Church point out that effect of the change of voice from the learning to the testing phase does depend on how the test is carried out. If the word processing is made more difficult (e.g., by white noise), no effect of the voice change is observable. If, however, words are offered in a test without masking noise, the size of the effect is reduced by the change of voice. This suggests that (as in visual object processing) several levels of representation should be distinguished for acoustic nodes (see Harley, 1995).

In addition, experiments on acoustic word priming show that acoustic and visual word nodes should be distinguished. They also show that the visual as well as the acoustic word nodes should be seen as presemantic representations.

The distinction between acoustic and visual word nodes is also supported by neuropsychological results, as made clear above. Ellis and Young (1989) report on patients who understand spoken and not written words and vice versa.

PET-studies also suggest that the processing of acoustic word forms takes place in specific parts of the brain. While regions of the temporal lobes of both hemispheres are activated when words are presented acoustically, several regions in the back of the brain are involved in visual presentation (and the task of examing words superficially) (Peterson et al., 1989). It is to be emphasized that there is no overlap of the areas respectively activated in these cases.

In conclusion, the report results support the distinction of visual, acoustic and abstract word nodes.

5.3.5   Word Nodes and Speaking and Writing Programs

With the distinction between on one hand word nodes and speaking and writing programs on the other, an input and output system for linguistic stimuli is postulated. Convincing proofs for the assumption of separate output and input systems come from neuropsychology. In the relevant literature patients are described who are able to recognize pictures without difficulty and to understand their spoken and written terms. They can say e.g., whether an object or a word belongs in a semantic category (e.g., fruit) and they can determine which pictures belong with which words and judge sentences according to whether they make sense. But the same patients are incapable of reading words aloud or naming objects. They often produce neologisms (Caramazza, Berndt & Bassili, 1983; Ellis, 1983). This suggests that the acoustic and visual word nodes as well as the access to concepts via the word nodes is intact. On the other hand, access to the speaking program is impaired.

An especially interesting case is the patient EST (Kay & Ellis, 1987). He exhibited massive disturbances in finding words although he understood them well in reading and hearing and knew their meanings. His word finding impairments are furthermore restricted to terms for objects and actions. If he e.g., was introduced to name a snowman he would say "it is cold, a man, frozen ...". Patients such as EST show that word nodes and the access to concepts from word nodes can be intact while at the same time access from the concepts to the word labels is impaired in spontaneous language production and in object naming. Such results suggest the systematic distinction of word nodes and speaking programs.

The distinction of word nodes and speaking programs is also supported by a case with the opposite symptom. As already mentioned, there are patients who, despite having an intact hearing capacity, are unable to understand words which they hear. Here one speaks of 'word deafness'. The spontaneous language of these patients is, however, intact, as is their ability to name objects (Ellis & Young, 1989). Hemphill and Stengel (1940) report e.g., on a patient who after a brain injury could neither understand nor repeat linguistic utterances. At first it was supposed that the man was deaf. But audiometric tests showed completely normal values. This patient spoke fluently and without grammatical mistakes.

The occurrence of these two complementary deficits (impaired comprehension of language but intact language production and impaired language production but intact language comprehension) suggests that a linguistic input system should be distinguished from a linguistic output system (Ellis & Young, 1989; Engelkamp, 1994; Mohr & Engelkamp, 1996).

In the previous Section (5.3.4) we showed that two input systems should be distinguished, one for acoustic and one for visual word nodes. Which results can be cited in favor of an analogous modality-specific differentiation of the output systems in speaking and writing programs? Such a distinction is supported by a study by Levine, Calvanio, and Popovics (1982, cited following Ellis & Young, 1989). The authors report on a 54 year-old engineer who had lost his language after a stroke. Despite great effort he could only produce a few undifferentiated sounds. Yet he could understand written and spoken language and write long texts without help. The opposite case is reported by Rosati and Bastiani (1979, cited following Ellis & Young, 1989). The patient described by them was able to speak after a stroke and could understand written and spoken language but could no longer write. The fact that there are patients with severe word-finding difficulties in writing but whose ability to speak is unimpaired at the same time is evidence that these are not necessarily peripheral writing disturbances (Bub & Kertesz, 1982a,b; Hier & Mohr, 1977). The cited (double) dissociations support the assumption of two modality-specific speech output systems, one for speaking and one for writing programs.

5.3.6   Concepts and Motor Programs

The role of nonlinguistic response production in information processing, especially in the processing of linguistic stimuli is largely underestimated. This is due among other things to problems of method in measuring motor behavior. It is thus not surprising that in research of human motor performance very simple movements (like grasping, key pressing, tracking) are generally the subject of study (e.g., Heuer, 1983, 1990). However, it is generally assumed that movement patterns and movement sequences must be represented in the brain on various levels. For example, other brain areas are involved in the planning of a movement than in actually carrying it out (for an overview, see Rosenbaum, 1991). The representational bases of a specific movement or sequence of movements are here referred to as a 'motor program'. We will not discuss which information is represented by such a program and whether programs should be distinguished on various levels of abstraction (see Schmidt, 1975). Here it is merely important that we have motoric representations for movement patterns and that these are not part of the conceptual system. We will thus confine ourselves to the case especially important in discussing the mental lexicon, the fact that we can call up particular movement patterns through linguistic stimuli.

The prototypical case in this context are linguistic requests to perform simple actions like 'open the door please'. In work on language psychology, these requests have been studied e.g., with respect to the question as to which situative conditions lead to which specific form of request is most likely to be followed by the hearer (e.g., Engelkamp & Mohr, 1986; Engelkamp, Mohr & Mohr, 1985; Herrmann, 1982; Herrmann & Grabowski, 1994; Mohr, 1989). At this point, we are interested in the question as to whether a hearer has motoric action programs as well as action concepts.

This question was studied at the beginning of the 1980's in several research groups. The experimental studies generally proceeded as follows: the subjects were presented, mainly acoustically, with simple action requests (e.g., 'lift up the pen') or simple action phrases ('lifting up the pen'). They were instructed to perform the respective activities. Finally, they were asked to reproduce the items learned. Compared with a control group who had heard and not performed the items, these subjects consistently performed better in retention (e.g., Bäckman & Nilsson, 1985; Cohen, 1981, 1983; Engelkamp & Krumnacker, 1980; Engelkamp & Zimmer, 1983). This effect we will call here the *enactment-effect*. Now these results do not entitle us to judge whether a semantically richer concept or additionally a motor program or both were activated by the additional performance of the action. To clarify this question, further experiments were carried out (Engelkamp, 1997a gives an overview). As a result of these experiments it can be stated that the enactment-effect is likely not due to conceptual processes. It turns out that retention after performance of the activity is independent of the processing depth while it does depend on the processing depth after only hearing the phrases (Cohen, 1983; Zimmer, 1984; Helstrup, 1987).

The assumption that motor programs are involved in the enactment-effect is supported by the fact that similarity of movement has an effect on recognition after carrying out the action even though the concept remains the same (Engelkamp & Zimmer, 1994b, 1995) analogous to the visual similarity with a constant concept in pictures (Homa & Viera, 1988; Madigan, 1983). However, unlike in the experiments on pictures, Engelkamp and Zimmer did not use identical, but rather similar concepts (e.g., 'picking apples' and 'picking peaches' were compared). In this it was found that controlling the conceptual similarity, especially when at the same time the motoric similarity was varied, is extremely difficult (see Engelkamp, 1997a). For this reason it is more informative to vary the motoric similarity while keeping the concepts the same. Since recognition testing after hearing and after performing the action is generally done verbally (i.e. action phrases are to be judged) the question arises as to whether carrying out the actions in the recognition test improves performance in learning after carrying them out (and only then). This is the case, as Engelkamp, Zimmer, Mohr and Sellen (1994) were able to show. If one compares recognition performance after hearing and carrying out the tasks in a verbal recognition test (in which only phrases are presented) and in a motoric recognition test (in which the activities are also carried out), an improvement in performance in the motoric test compared to the verbal test is observable only after learning by enacting. This result is evidence for the assumption that the enactment-effect is also due to the activation of motor programs.

Further arguments can be adduced for this assumption. The effect of motoric testing after doing reduces when one changes the motoric movement from learning stage to the testing stage, but without changing the concept (e.g., by performing an action one time with the left and the other time with the right hand). If, after a learning phase in which actions were performed with one hand (e.g., waving), a motoric recognition test is carried out once with the same hand as that used in the learning stage and once with the other hand, performance is worse when a different hand is used (Engelkamp et al., 1994). Besides these experimental results there are also neuropsychological proofs for the existence of motor programs which are largely independent of the conceptual system.

As early as the beginning of this century, different forms of apraxia were distinguished by Liepman (1905/08; cited following Rothi & Heilman, 1996). For the context of our argument, the distinction between ideational and ideomotor apraxia is of special interest. Patients who suffer from ideational apraxia are unable to perform complex, goal-directed motoric actions but can imitate the individual components which constitute these actions. Ideomotor apraxia is the reverse case. Patients are able to imitate particular motoric actions but they do not succeed in carrying out complex, goal-directed actions. We will not discuss these results in detail nor summarize the (sometimes very controversial) discussion about the classification of apraxia. Here it is significant that goal-directed and non-goal-directed motoric actions can also be dissociated on the basis of neuropsychological findings. Taken together. The results support assumption of a motoric representation independent of action concepts.

5.3.7 Picture Nodes and Motor Programs

A frequent objection against the assumption that the motoric system is involved in the retention of actions was that the enactment was an effect of the visual system. In order to counter this objection various experiments were carried out in the 1980's within the paradigm of selective interference (Saltz & Donnenwerth-Nolan, 1981; Cohen, 1989; Zimmer & Engelkamp, 1985; Zimmer, Engelkamp & Sieloff, 1984). Although the results are not consistent with regard to selective interference after visual-imaginal encoding, all experiments are in agreement in showing that there is a selective interference after motoric encoding. Learning by performing actions is more strongly impaired by a motoric interference task than by a visual or visual-imaginal interference task. This speaks for a distinction between visual and motoric processes. The observation that no differential effects through motoric and visual-imaginal interference tasks result after visual-imaginal encoding can be traced back to flaws in method, as Engelkamp (1997a) showed in a detailed analysis.

The assumption that the effects of carrying out the action are motoric and not visual in nature is given further support through the following observation: In the selective interference experiments of Zimmer & Engelkamp (1985) and Zimmer, Engelkamp and Sieloff (1984), selective motoric interference was observable only for the verb recall but not for the object recall of action phrases or sentences. This supports the assumption that motor programs are part of verb representations.

This assumption is also supported by the studies of Engelkamp and Zimmer (1983, 1996). They were able to show that the presentation of real objects under motor encoding of action phrases does improve the retention in comparison with a symbolic performance of the denoted actions (without real objects) but that the extent of the improvement is just as large in the enactment as in the control condition: If one varies the seeing vs. the carrying out of actions and, orthogonally, the use of real vs. imaginary objects, both effects are additive. Observable is an object effect which is independent of the enactment-effect and which goes back to haptic information. The independence of both effects speaks against the assumption that the enactment-effect is due to visual processing of action objects (picture nodes). The enactment-effect occurs when the subjects are unable to observe the performance of the action (i.e. when they perform it blindfolded) (Engelkamp, Zimmer & Biegelmann, 1993). On the other hand, the enactment-effect fails to occur when the subjects imagine visually how the action is carried out by themselves or another person (Denis, Engelkamp & Mohr, 1991; Engelkamp, 1991b, 1995). Clearly, the visual or visual-imaginal encoding has no significance for the enactment-effect. That even imagining performing an action one self does not lead to a retention rate comparable to that of actually performing it makes it clear that carrying out actions is what causes the enactment-effect. This is underscored by the fact that even the planning of an action does not lead to the 'full' effect seen when it is completed (Engelkamp, 1997b). The distinction between picture nodes and motor programs is also supported by functional neurophysiological results. In a EEG-study, Marks and Isaak (1995) found different activation patterns according to whether the subjects imagined performing an action themselves (motoric representation) or whether they imagined observing themselves in performing the same action (pictorial representation).

In summary, it may be stated that the distinction of picture nodes and motor programs can be well documented by studies on remembering actions. The studies also show that in the visual system picture nodes for static objects should distinguished from those picture nodes (they could be called event nodes) which refer to actions or events, i.e. to dynamic stimuli.

5.3.8   The Internal Structure of the Conceptual System

In this Section we go beyond the system differentiations made in Section 5.2. We report on results which suggest a further subdivision of the conceptual system. However, the results discussed thus far do not entitle us to make any precise proposals about the internal structure of the conceptual system. Neuropsychological dissociations can also observed with respect to certain features of conceptual information. In the neuropsychological literature it is for instance often reported that some patients have serious deficits in naming tasks when presented with animate objects but not in the case of inanimate objects (e.g., Warrington & McCarthy, 1983; De Renzi & Lucchelli, 1994). For example, Caramazza et al. (1994) report on patients who are not able to name animals and on other patients who only display deficits in naming when they are presented with artefacts (in the sense of artificially produced objects). Spitzer (1996) lists as a result of a literature survey a number of typical deficit phenomena in naming pictures. Deficit phenomena are particularly common with inanimate objects, animate objects, animals, objects in the home (e.g., furniture), tools and kitchen utensils, body parts and artificially produced objects.

These neuropsychological results suggest that the conceptual subsystem is to be seen as a system which itself consists of a large number of different subsystems. This view is also supported by the results of the two experimental studies which we will now describe.

In a semantic priming experiment, Flores d'Arcais, Schreuder and Glazenborg (1985) tested the extent to which the presentation of categorially and perceptually similar items leads to a preactivation of the corresponding target. For instance, if test subjects are offered the word *banana* as a prime and must then in a lexical decision task judge whether the word *cherry* is a word or a nonword, a priming effect is able to be demonstrated as expected. However, a similar priming effect also occurs if instead of the word *banana* the word *ball* is offered as a prime for the target *cherry*.

In the case of prime-target combinations which correspond to the first example, the authors speak of categorially related words; prime-target combinations corresponding to the second example are referred to as perceptually related words. Flores d'Arcais et al. (1985) found that an interesting change occurs when a time limit is introduced in the lexical decision task: While the priming effect is reduced in the case of categorial similarity, it is increased in the case of perceptual similarity. Mangold-Allwinn (1993) was able to demonstrate similar results when subjects are instructed to carry out similarity ratings of visually presented word pairs. He had his subjects make similarity judgments with a time limit and without (in a control condition). This study, too, showed that the information which is less abstract, and nearer to perception was more likely to be taken into account under time pressure than in the control.

It is important for the interpretation of both experiments that the results reported above can only with difficulty be explained through the assumption of an additional activation of picture node information. Since the activation of picture nodes in the presentation of linguistic stimuli presupposes the prior activation of a concept, similarity judgments which are made on the basis of picture information should take more time than judgments which are made via the abstract conceptual information (Zimmer, 1988).

There is thus reason to assume that conceptual information is not represented in a homogenous subsystem but rather that various conceptual subsystems must be distinguished. Instead of assuming that concepts belonging to a particular category are represented in special conceptual subsystems (Caramazza et al., 1994), it is conceivable that certain characteristics of objects are connected with certain cognitive subsystems (Spitzer, 1996). A more exact specification of these subsystems is at the moment extremely difficult, however. Nevertheless, the existent results suggest that the degree of abstraction of the information or its proximity to perception are in this respect an important dimension. In Section 5.4.1 we will come back to the problems sketched here.

5.4 On the Function of the Mental Lexicon in a System Approach

Our point of departure was the assumption that the meanings of words are represented in the mental lexicon. Meanings are in this view those mental representations which are activated by words. This view has turned out to be too simple, as we showed in the previous Sections. Firstly, it was shown to be necessary to distinguish word nodes and concepts. Secondly, the representations in the comprehension of language (word nodes) must be distinguished from those involved in the production of language (speaking programs and writing programs). Thirdly, words can activate not only concepts but also picture nodes and motor programs in the cognitive system. And fourthly, it can be assumed that the conceptual system is not a homogeneous system.

These distinctions force a new definition of the mental lexicon. There appear to be two reasonable views. Either one considers the mental lexicon to consist of the output representations (speaking and writing programs) and the input representations (word nodes) which have direct reference to language or one includes the concepts corresponding to the word nodes and speaking and writing programs. As the following remarks show, both positions are found in the literature on word recognition.

The search model of Forster (e.g., 1976, 1989; Forster & Davis, 1984; Taft & Forster, 1976) considers word nodes and concepts as the mental lexicon. In this model, the lexicon is searched serially until a lexical entry for the incoming visual or acoustic linguistic stimulus is found. For written words this search takes place in an orthographic lexicon (which contains visual word nodes in our terminology) and for spoken words it does so in a phonological lexicon (which contains acoustic word nodes in our terminology). The lexical nodes allow access to the 'lexicon proper' (the master file), in which the whole information about a word, especially its meaning, is represented (concepts in our terminology).

The logogen model of Morton (e.g., 1969; Warren & Morton, 1982) not only makes a sharper distinction between the lexicon and the conceptual system, but also distinguishes between an input lexicon and an output lexicon. Morton speaks of input logogens instead of word nodes and of output logogens instead of language programs. Both types of logogens are separated according to visual and acoustic modality. The logogen model and Forster's search model also differ in their assumptions about processes. Two points may be made. Firstly, the logogens search actively for stimulus evidence. The logogens more strongly activated when they are given more evidence by the stimulus event. Once a particular threshold is reached, the appropriate word is cognitively available. Secondly, the logogen activates on one hand information in the cognitive system and is on the other hand stimulated by this information. The conceptual system contains semantic and syntactic word characteristics in Morton's view.

The interactive-activation model of McClelland and Rumelhart (e.g., McClelland, 1987; McClelland & Elman, 1986; McClelland & Rumelhart, 1981) is clearly presemantic. Although it was not originally intended as a lexicon model, the description is appropriate because the model tries to explain what occurs between the visual presentation of words and their identification. The model is in this respect a further development of the logogen model. However, unlike in the logogen model, word meaning has no influence on word recognition. Moreover, McClelland and Rumelhart o not assume an output lexicon.

We believe that the following idea is the most appropriate. Like Morton (1979) and McClelland and Rumelhart (1981) we separate the conceptual system from the lexicon and see the lexicon as a presemantic linguistic system. As Morton (1979) does we do, however, distinguish an input and an output lexicon. Figure 4 depicts this.

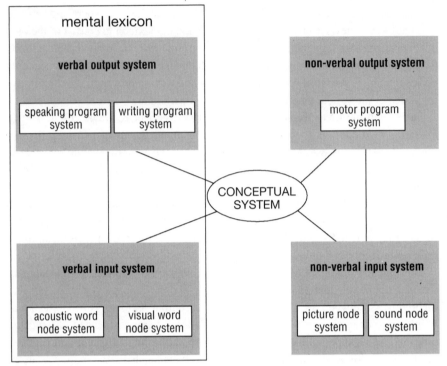

Figure 4. The mental lexicon as part of the cognitive architecture of the system.

In principle, an individual can have several such mental lexicons for different individual languages (e.g., de Groot et al., 1994; Kroll & Stewart, 1994). The subsystems of the individual languages are in each case connected both to each other and to the conceptual system (see also Section 5.3.1).

In the following paragraph we ill describe the input lexicon (Section 5.4.1) and the output lexicon (5.4.2), emphasizing the aspect of the flexibility and goal-dependency of linguistic stimulus processing.

5.4.1   The Mental Input Lexicon

Following what we have already said, the process of comprehending visually or acoustically presented words can be sketched as follows. Firstly, a (concrete) word node represented in the word node system is activated on the basis of the visually or acoustically presented information. Here it is sufficient to observe that the activation of the word nodes is (in healthy individuals) largely determined by stimuli. A concept is activated through the appropriate word node (via the activation of an abstract word node). We see this concept activation as a dynamic process. From the source concept, the activation in the conceptual system spreads directly to other concepts. A spreading of activation in the conceptual system occurs (e.g., Collins & Loftus, 1975;

Meyer & Schvanefeldt, 1971). This spreading of activation is the basis of semantic priming. The course of the spreading activation depends on the structure of the semantic system which has developed in the learning history of an individual. The interindividually constant portions of this structure are described approximately in semantic network theories (Engelkamp, 1985). We will not pay particular attention to these intersituational aspects of spreading activation but rather to the specific influence of the current task or goal of the individual (in everyday life naturally also to the linguistic context). As a rule, the goals lead to inhibiting processes which focus the conceptual activation (this has not been discussed and proven here; see Engelkamp, 1990; or 1997a). Generally, a specific activation pattern can be build up in the conceptual system for each specific goal (e.g., Neely, 1977).

Barclay et al. (1974) demonstrated in a cued recall experiment that the context in which words are offered has influence on certain aspects of the semantic representation. They presented subjects with words in different contexts and measured in the test phase the extent to which the context influences the meaning activated in each case. For example, subjects were presented with the word *piano* either in the context (a) *the man smashes the piano to pieces* or in the context (b) *the man carries the piano*. In the test phase it became evident that in the case of (a) the word *wooden* worked better as a cue for the word *piano* than the word *heavy*. The reverse effect occurred with subjects who were given the word in context (b). Thus, the information activated differs according to the context.

In another experiment Barsalou (1982) was able to show that the influence of the context did not extend to all perception-based meaning aspects to the same degree. He also presented his subjects with words (e.g., *roof*) which were embedded in different sentence contexts (e.g., *the roof was renovated shortly before the rain* or *the roof creaked under the weight of the roof worker*). In a so-called feature verification task, the subjects had to decide whether particular characteristics (e.g., 'people can walk around on it' or 'it is covered') are true of the word in question or not. The decision times were measured. The result was that the sentence context did not influence the decision times with respect to each characteristic. With reference to the above mentioned example, for instance, it could be shown that the decision time for the characteristic 'it is covered' was independent of the context while the decision time for the characteristic 'people can walk around on it' turned out to be sensitive to the context. Accordingly, Barsalou distinguished between context dependent and context independent perception-based meaning aspects.

However, beyond the specific patterns, the activation of certain nodes can also be dependent on the task situation. The dependent activation of picture nodes is illustrated by a study by Zimmer (1988). In this study the subjects had to verify the characteristics of nouns (e.g., bullseye - round). Zimmer was able to show that (1) the verification time correlated with the time which the subjects needed in order to be able to imagine the corresponding reference object (here a bullseye), and that (2) an embedded secondary task in which visually presented stimuli were to be judged increased the verification time. Both effects could only be observed when the subjects had to verify stimulus characteristics which required the activation of a picture node.

Here we can conclude that the various subsystems and representation types are used flexibly and with reference to the goal. That is, there is a fixed system architecture but it is used flexibly. The fact that the architecture is used flexibly can also be illustrated by the following considerations.

When words are presented, the same path through the cognitive architecture is not always chosen. The following examples show that the path from the input lexicon to the output lexicon does not necessarily proceed via the conceptual system. For instance, we can read words for which we have no conceptual representation or can read a page of a text aloud without having understood its 'content'. Also, neuropsychological results show that there is a direct path between the input lexicon and the output lexicon. Ellis and Young (1989) report for instance on a patient who had to say or write down words she had heard in order to understand them. The patient is thus able to write words she has heard without activating the appropriate concept. Thus, there must be a connection between the word node system and the speaking program which does not pass through the conceptual system. It is important to ask which paths through the system are possible.

It remains to observe that we have not examined sentence processing. Sentence processing is in the sense of the model suggested here to be seen as a specific task. A special characteristic of a sentence is that in relations between concepts and, as a rule, nonverbal nodes and programs are discussed. This leads to very complex mental representation structures which can likewise be described on the basis of the subsystems postulated here.

5.4.2   The Mental Output Lexicon

The subject of this book is the comprehension of language. Thus, this treatise emphasizes the reception of words. Since the global cognitive structure also includes an output lexicon (which is a component of the mental lexicon), some remarks should be made on the use of the output lexicon. Here we also want to underscore the flexible use of the cognitive architecture. An important aspect in the naming of objects is e.g., that this can take place at various levels of abstraction. An example is the fact that we can call a dachshund a dachshund, a dog or an animal. The level of abstraction on which an object is named depends on the particular goal of the speaker. This influences how (and how long) the object is analyzed, which picture node is activated and which concept is activated (Hoffmann, 1993; Mangold-Allwinn et al., 1995; Zimmer, 1988).

Grosser, Pobel, Mangold-Allwinn and Herrmann (1989) were also able to demonstrate an effect of the speaker's goal on the specificity of object naming. They instructed their subjects to tell partners (either children or adults) the names of objects presented in drawings in such a way that (1) the names make an impression on the partners or (2) the objects are identified by the partner as easily as possible. When (1) was the goal, more specific terms were produced than when (2) was the goal. Comparable effects could also be demonstrated for the production of texts. Kiefer, Barattelli and Mangold-Allwinn (1993) instructed their subjects either to describe the assembly of an object made of several parts of a box of building blocks, or they asked the subjects to give instructions on how the object was to be assembled. When the goal was the description of the building process, more objects were introduced at a specific level, while more objects were introduced at basic level when the goal was giving instructions. Both experiments show that communicative goals play an important role in determining lexical specificity.

However, object names vary not only with respect to their lexical specificity, but also in a connotative dimension. This is illustrated by the fact that we can speak of a dog, a cur or a mangy hound according to our intentions. In the case of connotative naming, the choice of the term is determined by the affective reaction to the object stimulus. Here certain affective features which the speaker focuses on lead to the activation of certain concepts (Herrmann, 1985; Herrmann & Deutsch, 1976). Experimental evidence for the influence of the speaker's goal on this aspect of object naming is reported by Pobel (1991).

In most experiments on object naming, subjects are instructed to name objects presented via a computer screen. Which processes occur in the cognitive system in the processing of such a naming task? With reference to the cognitive architecture presented above four phases may be distinguished: (1) the perceptual analysis of the object, (2) the activation of a picture node, (3) the activation of a concept and (4) the triggering of a speaking or writing program which leads to the articulation of the appropriate word (or to the motoric performance of a writing program). The successful completion of an object naming task is, unlike a reading task (Secton 5.4.1) impossible without the involvement of the conceptual system.

One point which should be mentioned in connection with the first processing stage (and which is directly related to the lexical specificity of object naming) is that not all object information can be processed with the same degree of speed. Thus, global features of an object (such as information about the profile or contours of the object) can generally be processed more quickly than local features (Navon, 1977). Color information is processed more quickly than information about size (Zimmer, 1984). Target objects which are not similar to the context objects around them are recognized more quickly than those which are similar to their context objects (Treisman & Gormican, 1988; Nothdurft, 1992). To us it seems important to point out that the communicative goals in which the naming of an object takes place influence the perceptual analysis through the type of information search. A speaker whose aim it is to name an object at a high level of specification (e.g., in order to distinguish it from other categorially similar objects) should accordingly carry out a more comprehensive perceptual object analysis than a speaker whose goals suggest the naming of the object at a basic level (Kiefer et al., 1995). The communicative requirements can thus have influence as soon as the search for information begins. Moreover, it can be stated that perceptual analysis can also determine the lexical specificity of the term chosen for an object (Zimmer, 1984). This is supported e.g., by the fact that shortening the time in which an object is presented leads to a reduction of the number of specific terms and at the same time an increase in the number of basic level terms (Mangold-Allwinn et al., 1995). Comparable changes can occur when black and white illustrations are presented in the place of color illustrations (Zimmer & Biegelmann, 1990).

These remarks show that, in the use of the output lexicon as well, a fixed cognitive structure is used flexibly with reference to the communicative task. The communicative goals influence (by directing the individual's attention to particular aspects) not only the intake of perceptual information but also the information processing which take place in the conceptual system.

References

Anderson, J. R. (1978). Arguments concerning representations for mental imagery. *Psychological Review, 85,* 249-277.

Anderson, J. R. (1996). *Kognitive Psychologie.* Heidelberg: Spektrum Akademischer Verlag.

Bäckman, L. & Nilsson, L.-G. (1985). Prerequisites for lack of age differences in memory performance. *Experimental Aging Research, 11,* 67-73.

Barclay, J.R., Bransford, J.D., Franks, J.J., McCarrell, N.S. & Nitsch, K. (1974). Comprehension and semantic flexibility. *Journal of Verbal Learning and Verbal Behavior, 13,* 471-481.

Barsalou, L.W. (1982). Context-independent and context-dependent information in concepts. *Memory & Cognition, 10,* 82-93.

Bartram, D. J. (1976). Levels of coding in picture-picture comparison tasks. *Memory & Cognition, 4,* 593-602.

Bassili, J. N., Smith, M. C. & MacLeod, C. M. (1989). Auditory and visual word-stem completion: Separating data-driven and conceptually driven processes. *Quarterly Journal of Experimental Psychology, 41A,* 439-453.

Biederman, I. & Cooper, E. E. (1991). Priming contour-deleted images: Evidence for intermediate representations in visual object recognition. *Cognitive Psychology, 23,* 393-419.

Biederman, I. & Cooper, E. E. (1992). Size invariance in visual object priming. *Journal of Experimental Psychology: Human Perception and Performance, 18,* 121-133.

Bierwisch, M. & Schreuder, R. (1992). From concepts to lexical items. *Cognition, 42,* 23-60.

Boles, D. B. (1983). Dissociated imageability, concreteness, and familiarity in lateralized word recognition. *Memory & Cognition, 11,* 511-519.

Bowers, J. S. & Schacter, D. L. (1990). Implicit memory and test awareness. *Journal of Experimental Psychology: Learning, Memory and Cognition, 16,* 404-416.

Brown, R. W. & McNeill, D. (1966). The "tip of the tongue"-phenomenon. *Journal of Verbal Learning and Verbal Behavior, 5,* 325-337.

Bub, D. & Kertesz, A. (1982a). Evidence for lexicographic processing in a patient with preserved written over oral single word naming. *Brain, 105,* 697-717.

Bub, D. & Kertesz, A. (1982b). Deep agraphia. *Brain and Language, 18,* 128-174.

Bühler, K. (1934). *Sprachtheorie: Die Darstellungsfunktion der Sprache.* Jena: Fischer.

Caramazza, A., Berndt, R. S. & Basili, A. G. (1983). Autobiographical memory and perceptual learning: A developmental study using picture recognition, naming latency, and perceptual identification. *Memory and Cognition, 13,* 273-279.

Caramazza, A., Hillis, A., Leek, E. C. & Miozzo, M. (1994). The organization of lexical knowledge in the brain: Evidence from category- and modality-specific deficits. In L. A. Hirschfeld & S. A. Gelman, (eds.), *Mapping the Mind.* Cambridge University Press, Cambridge.

Caroll, M., Byrne, B. & Kirsner, K. (1985). Autobiographical memory and perceptual learning: A developmental study using picture recognition, naming latency, and perceptual identification. *Memory & Cognition, 13,* 273-279.

Challis, B. H. & Brodbeck, D. R. (1992). Level of processing affects priming in word fragment completion. *Journal of Experimental Psychology: Learning, Memory and Cognition, 18,* 595-607.

Chen, H.-C., Cheung, H. & Lau, S. (in press). Examining and reexamining the structure of Chinese-English bilingual memory. *Psychological Research.*

Cohen, R. L. (1981). On the generality of some memory laws. *Scandinavian Journal of Psychology, 22,* 267-281.

Cohen, R. L. (1983). The effect of encoding variables on the free recall of words and action events. *Memory and Cognition, 11,* 575-582.

Cohen, R. L. (1989). Memory for action events: The power of enactment. *Educational Psychological Review, 1,* 57-80.

Collins, A. M. & Loftus, E. F. (1975). A spreading-activation theory of semantic processing. *Psychological Review, 82,* 407-428.

Collins, A. M. & Quillian, M. R. (1969). Retrieval time from semantic memory. *Journal of Verbal Learning and Verbal Behavior, 8,* 240-247.

Craik, F. I. M. & Lockhart, R. S. (1972). Levels of processing: A framework for memory research. *Journal of Verbal Learning and Verbal Behavior, 11,* 671-684.

Craik, F. I. M. & Tulving, E. (1975). Depth of processing and the retention of words in episodic memory. *Journal of Experimental Psychology: General, 104,* 155-158.

Dannenbring, G. L. & Briand, K. (1982). Semantic priming and the word repetition effect in a lexical decision task. *Canadian Journal of Psychology, 36,* 435-444.

Deese, J. (1970). *Psycholinguistics.* Boston: Allyn & Bacon.

de Groot, A. M. B., Danneburg, L. & van Hell, J. G. (1994). Forward and backward word translation. *Journal of Memory and Language, 33,* 600-629.

Den Heyer, K., Goring, A. & Dannenbring, G. L. (1985). Semantic priming and word repetition: The two effects are additive. *Journal of Memory and Language, 24,* 699-716.

Denis, M., Engelkamp, J. & Mohr, G. (1991). Memory of imagined actions: Imagining oneself or another person. *Psychological Research, 53,* 246-250.

De Renzi, E. & Lucchelli, F. (1994). Are semantic systems separately represented in the brain? The case of living category impairment. *Cortex, 30,* 3-25.

Dhawan, M. & Pellegrino, J. W. (1977). Acoustic and semantic interference effects in words and pictures. *Memory & Cognition, 5,* 340-346.

Durso, F. T. & Johnson, M. K. (1979). Facilitation in naming and categorizing repeated pictures and words. *Journal of Experimental Psychology: Human Learning and Memory, 5,* 449-459.

Ellis, A. W. & Young, A. W. (1989). *Human cognitive neuropsychology.* Hillsdale, N. J.: Erlbaum.

Ellis, A. W. (1983). Syndromes, slips and structures. *Bulletin of the British Psychological Society, 36,* 372-374.

Engelkamp, J. (1973). *Semantische Struktur und die Verarbeitung von Sätzen.* Bern: Huber.

Engelkamp, J. (1985). Die Repräsentation der Wortbedeutung. In C. Schwarze & D. Wunderlich (eds.), *Handbuch der Lexikologie.* Königstein/Ts.: Athenäum.

Engelkamp, J. (1987). Arguments for a visual memory system. In J. Engelkamp, K. Lorenz & B. Sandig (eds.), *Wissensrepräsentation und Wissensaustausch.* St. Ingbert: Röhrig.

Engelkamp, J. (1990). *Das menschliche Gedächtnis.* Göttingen: Hogrefe.

Engelkamp, J. (1991a). Memory of action events: Some implications for memory theory and for imagery. In C. Cornoldi & M. McDaniel (eds.), *Imagery and cognition.* New York: Springer.

Engelkamp, J. (1991b). Imagery and enactment in paired-associate learning. In R. H. Logie & M. Denis (eds.), *Mental images in human cognition.* Amsterdam: Elsevier.

Engelkamp, J. (1994). Mentale Repräsentationen im Kontext verschiedener Aufgaben. In H.-J. Kornadt, J. Grabowski & R. Mangold-Allwinn (eds.), *Sprache und Kognition - Perspektiven moderner Sprachpsychologie.* Heidelberg: Spektrum Akademischer Verlag.

Engelkamp, J. (1995). Visual imagery and enactment of actions in memory. *British Journal of Psychology, 86,* 227-240.

Engelkamp, J. (1997a). *Das Erinnern eigener Handlungen.* Göttingen: Hogrefe.

Engelkamp (1997b). Memory for to-be-performed tasks versus memory for performed tasks. *Memory and Cognition, 25,* 117-124.

Engelkamp, J. & Krumnacker, H. (1980). Imaginale und motorische Prozesse beim Behalten verbalen Materials. *Zeitschrift für experimentelle und angewandte Psychologie, 27,* 511-533.

Engelkamp, J. & Mohr, G. (1986). Legitimation und Bereitschaft bei der Rezeption von Aufforderungen. *Sprache und Kognition, 3,* 127-139.

Engelkamp, J., Mohr, G. & Mohr, M. (1985). Zur Rezeption von Aufforderungen. *Sprache und Kognition, 4,* 65-75.

Engelkamp, J. & Wippich, W. (1995). Current issues in implicit and explicit memory. *Psychological Research, 57,* 143-155.

Engelkamp J. & Zimmer, H. D. (1983) Zum Einfluß von Wahrnehmen und Tun auf das Behalten von Verb-Objekt-Phrasen. *Sprache & Kognition, 2,* 117-127.

Engelkamp, J. & Zimmer, H. D. (1994a). *The human memory. A multi-modal approach.* Seattle: Hogrefe & Huber.

Engelkamp, J. & Zimmer, H. D. (1994b). Motor similarity in subject-performed tasks. *Psychological Research, 57,* 47-53.

Engelkamp, J. & Zimmer, H. D. (1995). Similarity of movement in recognition of self-performed tasks. *British Journal of Psychology, 86,* 241-252.

Engelkamp, J., Zimmer, H. D. & Biegelmann, U. (1993). Bizarreness effects in verbal tasks and subject-performed tasks. *European Journal of Cognitive Psychology, 5,* 393-415.

Engelkamp, J., Zimmer, H. D. & Kurbjuweit, A. (1995). Verb frequency and enactment in implicit and explicit memory. *Psychological Research, 57,* 242-249.

Engelkamp, J., Zimmer, H. D., Mohr, G. & Sellen, O. (1994). Memory of self-performed tasks: Self-performing during recognition. *Memory & Cognition, 22,* 34-39.

Flores d'Arcais, G. B., Schreuder, R. & Glazenborg, G. (1985). Semantic activation during recognition of referential words. *Psychological Research, 47,* 39-49.

Forster, K. I. (1976). Accessing the mental lexicon. In R. J. Wales & E. C. T. Walker (eds.), *New Approaches to language mechanisms.* Amsterdam: North Holland.

Forster, K.I. (1989). Basic issues in lexical processing. In W. D. Marslen-Wilson (ed.), *Lexical representation and process.* Cambridge, MA: MIT-Press.

Forster, K.I. & Davis, C. (1984). Repetition priming and frequency attenuation in lexical access. *Journal of Experimental Psychology: Learning, Memory and Cognition, 10,* 680-698.

Gardiner, J. M., Gregg, V. H. & Hampton, J. A. (1988). Word frequency and generation effects. *Journal of Experimental Psychology: Learning, Memory and Cognition, 14,* 687-693.

Glaser, W. R. & Glaser, M. O. (1989). Context effects in stroop-like word and picture processing. *Journal of Experimental Psychology: General, 118,* 13-42.

Glass, A. L., Holyoak, K. J. & Santa, J. L. (1979). *Cognition.* London: Addison-Wesley.

Gorman, A. M. (1961). Recognition memory for nouns as a function of abstractness and frequency. *Journal of Experimental Psychology, 61,* 23-29.

Graf, P. & Mandler, G. (1984). Activation makes words more accessible, but not necessarily more retrievable. *Journal of Verbal Learning and Verbal Behavior, 23,* 553-568.

Grosser, Ch., Pobel, R., Mangold-Allwinn, R. & Herrmann, Th. (1989). *Determinanten des Allgemeinheitsgrades von Objektbenennungen* (Arbeiten der Forschergruppe "Sprechen und Sprachverstehen im sozialen Kontext" Heidelberg/Mannheim, Bericht Nr. 24). Universität Mannheim: Lehrstuhl Psychologie III.

Harley, T. A. (1995). *The psychology of language: From data to theory.* Erlbaum: Psychology Press.

Hebb, D. O. (1949). *Organization of Behavior.* New York.

Helstrup, T. (1987). One, two or three memories? A problem-solving approach to memory for performed acts. *Acta Psychologica, 66,* 37-68.

Hemphill, R. E. & Stengel, E. (1940). A study on pure word deafness. *Journal of Neurology, Neurosurgery and Psychiatry, 3,* 251-262.

Herrmann, Th. (1982). *Sprechen und Situation.* Berlin: Springer.

Herrmann, Th. (1985). *Allgemeine Sprachpsychologie. Grundlagen und Probleme.* München: Urban & Schwarzenberg. (2. Aufl.- Weinheim: Beltz, Psychologie-Verlags-Union, 1994.).

Herrmann, Th. (1994). Psychologie ohne "Bedeutung"? Zur Wort-Konzept-Relation in der Psychologie. *Sprache & Kognition, 13,* 126-137.

Herrmann, Th. & Deutsch, W. (1976). *Psychologie der Objektbenennung.* (Studien zur Sprachpsychologie 5). Bern: Huber.

Herrmann, Th. & Grabowski, J. (1994). *Sprechen: Psychologie der Sprachproduktion.* Heidelberg: Spektrum Akademischer Verlag.

Herrmann, Th., Grabowski, J., Schweizer, K. & Graf, R. (1996). Die mentale Repräsentation von Konzepten, Wörtern und Figuren. In J. Grabowski, G. Harras & T. Herrmann (eds.), *Bedeutung, Konzepte, Bedeutungskonzepte: Theorien und Anwendung in Linguistik und Psychologie.* Opladen: Westdeutscher Verlag.

Heuer, H. (1983). *Bewegungslernen.* Stuttgart: Kohlhammer.

Heuer, H. (1990). Psychomotorik. In H. Spada (ed.), *Allgemeine Psychologie.* Bern: Huber.

Hier, D. B. & Mohr, J. P. (1977). Incongruous oral and written naming: Evidence for a subdivision of the syndrome of Wernicke's aphasia. *Brain and Language, 4,* 115-126.

Hines, D. (1976). Recognition of verbs, abstract nouns, and concrete nouns from the left and right visual half-fields. *Neuropsychologia, 14,* 211-216.

Hoffmann, J. (1993). *Vorhersage und Erkenntnis.* Göttingen: Hogrefe.

Hoffmann, J. (1996). Die Genese von Begriffen, Bedeutungen und Wörtern. In J. Grabowski, G. Harras & T. Herrmann (eds.), *Bedeutung, Konzepte, Bedeutungskonzepte: Theorien und Anwendung in Linguistik und Psychologie.* Opladen: Westdeutscher Verlag.

Homa, D. & Viera, C. (1988). Long-term memory for pictures under conditions of thematically related foils. *Memory & Cognition, 16,* 411-421.

Hörmann, H. (1967). *Psychologie der Sprache.* Heidelberg.

Hörmann, H. (1978). *Meinen und Verstehen. Grundzüge einer psychologischen Semantik.* Frankfurt/M.: Suhrkamp.

Howe, M. L., Rabinowitz, F. M. & Grant, M. J. (1993). On measuring (in-)dependence of cognitive processes. *Psychological Review, 100,* 737-747.

Humphreys, G. W. & Bruce, V. (1989). *Visual cognition.* Hillsdale, N. J.: Erlbaum.

Humphreys, G. W. & Riddoch, M. J. (1987a). *To see but not to see: A case study of visual agnosia.* London: Erlbaum.

Humphreys, G. W. & Riddoch, M. J. (1987b). *Visual object processing: A cognitive neuropsychological approach.* London: Erlbaum.

Humphreys, G. W., Evett, J. L., Quinlan, P. T. & Besner, D. (1987). Orthographic priming: Qualitative differences between priming from identified and unidentified primes. In M. Coltheart (ed.), *Attention and Performance XII. The psychology of reading* . Hillsdale, N. J.: Erlbaum.

Jackson, A. & Morton, J. (1984). Facilitation of auditory word recognition. *Memory & Cognition, 12,* 568-574.

Johnson-Laird, P. N., Herrmann, D. J. & Chaffin, R. (1984). Only connections: A critique of semantic networks. *Psychological Bulletin, 96,* 292-315.

Journal of Verbal Learning and Verbal Behavior (1984). Special edition.

Kay, J. & Ellis, A. W. (1987). A cognitive neuropsychological case study of anomia: Implications for psychological models of word retrieval. *Brain, 110,* 613-629.

Kelter, S. (1994). Kognitive Semantik und Aphasieforschung. Zur Unterscheidung zwischen Bedeutungen und Konzepten. In M. Schwarz (ed.), *Kognitive Semantik/ Cognitive Semantics. Ergebnisse, Probleme, Perspektiven* (Tübinger Beiträge zur Linguistik, 395). Tübingen: Narr.

Kiefer, M., Barattelli, S. & Mangold-Allwinn, R. (1993). *Kognition und Kommunikation: Ein integrativer Ansatz zur multiplen Determination der lexikalischen Spezifität der Objektklassenbezeichnung* (Arbeiten aus dem Sonderforschungsbereich 245 "Sprache und Situation" Heidelberg/Mannheim, Bericht Nr. 51). Universität Mannheim: Lehrstuhl Psychologie III.

Kiefer, M., Barattelli, S. & Mangold-Allwinn, R. (1995). Vom generierten Konzept zum enkodierten Wort: Zur Determination der lexikalischen Spezifität von Objektbenennungen. *Linguistische Berichte, 159,* 381-408.

Kintsch, W. (1972). Notes on the structure of semantic memory. In E. Tulving & W. Donaldson (eds.), *Organization of memory.* New York: Academic Press.

Kirsner, K., Dunn, J. C. & Standen, P. (1989). Domain-specific resources in word recognition. In S. Levandowsky, J. C. Dunn & K. Kirsner (eds.), *Implicit memory.* Hillsdale, N. J.: Erlbaum.

Kirsner, K., Milech, D. & Stunpfel, V. (1986). Word and picture identification: Is representational parsimony possible? *Memory & Cognition, 14,* 398-408.

Klix, F. (1980). Die allgemeine Psychologie und die Erforschung kognitiver Prozesse. *Zeitschrift für Psychologie, 188,* 117-139.

Klix, F. (1985). Über Basisprozesse für geistige Dispositionen. *Zeitschrift für Psychologie, 193,* 27-50.

Kosslyn, S. M. (1981). The medium and the message in mental imagery: A theory. *Psychological Review, 88,* 46-66.

Kroll, J. F. & Stewart, E. (1994). Category interference in translation and picture naming: Evidence for asymmetric connections between bilingual memory representations. *Journal of Memory and Language, 33,* 149-174.

Levine, D. N., Calvanio, R. & Popovics, A. (1982). Language in the absence of inner speech. *Neuropsychologia, 20,* 391-409.

Liepmann, H. (1905/8). *Drei Aufsätze aus dem Apraxiegebiet.* Berlin: Karger.

Logie, R. H. (1986). Visuo-spatial processing in working memory. *Quarterly Journal of Experimental Psychology, 38A,* 229-247.

Lorch, R. L. (1982). Priming and search processes in semantic memory: A test of three models of spreading activation. *Journal of Verbal Learning and Verbal Behavior, 21,* 468-492.

Lupker, S. J. (1988). Picture naming: An investigation of the nature of categorical priming. *Journal of Experimental Psychology: Learning, Memory, and Cognition, 14,* 444-455.

Lyons, J. (1977). *Introduction to Theoretical Linguistics.* Cambridge: Cambridge University Press.

Madigan, S. (1983). Picture memory. In J. C. Yuille (ed.), *Imagery, memory and cognition.* Hillsdale, N. J.: Erlbaum.

Mandler, G., Goodman, G. O. & Wilkes-Gibbs, D. L. (1982). The word-frequency paradox in recognition. *Memory & Cognition, 10,* 33-42.

Mangold-Allwinn, R. (1993). *Flexible Konzepte: Experimente, Modelle, Simulationen.* Frankfurt/M.: Lang.

Mangold-Allwinn, R., Barattelli, S., Kiefer, M. & Koelbing, H.-G. (1995). *Wörter für Dinge.* Opladen: Westdeutscher Verlag.

Marks, D. F. & Isaak, A. R. (1995). Topographical distribution of EEG activity accompanying visual and motor imagery in vivid and non-vivid images. *British Journal of Psychology, 86,* 271-282.

Marr, D. (1982). *Vision.* San Francisco: Freeman.

Martin, R. C. & Jensen, C. R. (1988). Phonological priming in the lexical decision task: A failure to replicate. *Memory & Cognition, 16,* 505-521.

McCarthy, R. A. & Warrington, E. K. (1990). *Cognitive neuropsychology.* New York: Academic Press.

McClelland, J. L. (1987). The case for interactions in language processing. In M. Coltheart (ed.), *Attention and Performance XII: The psychology of reading.* Hove, UK: Lawrence Erlbaum Associates Ltd.

McClelland, J. L. & Elman, J. O. (1986). The TRACE model of speech perception. *Cognitive Psychology, 18,* 1-86.

McClelland, J. L. & Rumelhart, D. E. (1981). An interactive activation model of context effects in letter perception. Part 1: An Account of Basic Findings. *Psychological Review, 88,* 375-407.

McNamara, T. P. & Healy, A. F. (1988). Semantic, phonological, and mediated priming in reading and lexical decisions. *Journal of Experimental Psychology: Learning, Memory, and Cognition, 14,* 398-409.

Meyer, D. E. & Schvaneveldt, R. W. (1971). Facilitation in recognizing pairs of words: Evidence of a dependence between retrieval operations. *Journal of Experimental Psychology, 90,* 227-234.

Mohr, G. (1989). *Auffordern und Begründen. Die Integration verstehens- und entscheidungsrelevanter Informationen.* Saarbrücken: Dadder.

Mohr, G. & Engelkamp, J. (1996). Neuropsychologische und allgemein-psychologische Evidenzen für die Modularität des Sprachsystems. In A. Gather & H. Werner (eds.), *Semiotische Prozesse und natürliche Sprache.* Stuttgart: Steiner.

Morton, J. (1969). Interaction of information in word recognition. *Psychological Review, 76,* 165-178.

Morton, J. (1979). Facilitation in word recognition: Experiments causing change in the logogen model. In P. A. Kolers, M. E. Wrolstad & H. Bouma (eds.), *Processing of visible language I.* New York: Plenum Press.

Morton, J & Patterson, K.E. (1980). A new attempt at an interpretation or an attempt at a new interpretation. In M. Coltheart, K. E. Patterson & J. C. Marshall (eds.), *Deep dyslexia .* London: Routledge & Kegan Paul.

Navon, D. (1977). Forest before trees. The precedence of global features in visual perception. *Cognitive Psychology, 9,* 353-383.

Neely, J. H. (1977). Semantic priming and retrieval from lexical memory: Roles of inhibitionless spreading activation and limited capacity attention. *Journal of Experimental Psychology: General, 106,* 226-254.

Nelson, D. L. (1979). Remembering pictures and words: Appearance, significance and name. In L. Cermak & F. I. M. Craik (eds.), *Levels of processing in human memory.* Hillsdale, N. J.: Erlbaum.

Nelson, D. L. & Brooks, D. H. (1973). Independence of phonetic and imaginal features. *Journal of Experimental Psychology, 97,* 1-7.

Nelson, D. L. & Reed, V. (1976). On the nature of pictorial encoding: A levels-of-processing analysis. *Journal of Experimental Psychology: Human Learning and Memory, 2,* 49-57.

Nelson, D. L., Reed, V. & Walling, J. R. (1976). Pictorial superiority effect. *Journal of Experimental Psychology: Human Learning and Memory, 2,* 523-528.

Nothdurft, H. (1992). Feature analysis and the role of similarity in preattentive vision. *Perception & Psychophysics, 52,* 355-375.

Paivio, A. (1969). Mental imagery in associative learning and memory. *Psychological Review, 76,* 241-263.

Paivio, A. (1971). *Imagery and verbal processes.* New York: Holt, Rinehard & Winston.

Pellegrino, J. W., Siegel, A. W. & Dhawan, M. (1975). Short-term retention of pictures and words: Evidence for dual coding systems. *Journal of Experimental Psychology: Human Learning and Memory, 104,* 95-102.

Peterson, S. E., Fox, P. T., Posner, M. I., Mintun, M. & Raichle, M. E. (1989). Positron emission tomographic studies of the processing of single words. *Journal of Cognitive Neuroscience, 1 (2),* 153-170.

Pobel, R. (1991). *Objektrepräsentation und Objektbenennung. Situative Einflüsse auf die Wortwahl beim Benennen von Gegenständen.* Regensburg: Roderer.

Posner, M. I. & Raichle, M. E. (1994). *Images of mind.* New York: Scientific American Library.

Potter, M. C. & Faulconer, B. A. (1975). Time to understand pictures and words. *Nature, 253,* 437-438.

Potter, M. C., So, K. F., von Eckart, B. & Feldman, l. B. (1984). Lexical and conceptual representation in beginning and proficient bilinguals. *Journal of Verbal Learning and Verbal Behavior, 23,* 23-28.

Prinz, W. (1983). *Wahrnehmung und Tätigkeitssteuerung.* Berlin: Springer.

Pylyshyn, Z. W. (1981). The imagery debate: Analogue media versus tacit knowledge. *Psychological Review, 88,* 16-45.

Riddoch, M. J., Humphreys, G. W., Coltheart, M. & Funnell, E. (1988). Semantic systems or system? Neuropsychological evidence re-examined. *Cognitive Neuropsychology, 5,* 3-25.

Roediger, H. L. (1990). Implicit memory. Retention without remembering. *American Psychologist, 45,* 1043-1056.

Roediger, H. L. & Weldon, M. S. (1987). Reversing the picture superiority effect. In M. McDaniel & M. Pressley (eds.), *Imagery and related mnemonic processes.* New York: Springer.

Roediger, H. L., Weldon, M. S., Stadler, M. L. & Riegler, G. L. (1992). Direct comparison of two implicit memory tests: Word fragment and word stem completion. *Journal of Experimental Psychology: Learning, Memory and Cognition, 18,* 1251-1269.

Rosati, G. & de Bastiani, P. (1979). Pure agraphia: A discrete form of aphasia. *Journal of Neurology, Neurosurgery and Psychiatry, 42,* 266-269.

Rosenbaum, D. A. (1991). *Human motor control.* San Diego: Academic Press.

Rothi, L. J. G. & Heilman, K. M. (1996). Liepmann (1900 and 1905): A definition of apraxia and a model of praxis. In C. Code, C.-W. Walesch, Y. Joanette & A. R. Lecours (eds.), *Classic cases in Neuropsychology.* Hove: Taylor & Francis.

Rumelhart, D. E., Lindsay, P. H. & Norman, D. A. (1972). A process model of long term memory. In E. Tulving & W. Donaldson (eds.). *Organization of memory.* New York.

Saltz, E. & Donnenwerth-Nolan, S. (1981). Does motoric imagery facilitate memory for sentences? A selective interference test. *Journal of Verbal Learning and Verbal Behaviour, 20,* 322-332.

Sartori, G., Masterson, J. & Job, R. (1987). Direct-route reading and the locus of lexical decision. In M. Coltheart, G. Sartori & R. Job (eds.), The cognitive neuropsychology of language. London: Erlbaum.

Schacter, D. L. (1990). Perceptual representation systems and implicit memory: Toward a resolution of the multiple memory systems debate. In A. Diamond (ed.), *Development and neural bases of higher cognitive functions .* Annals of the New York Academy of Sciences, 608.

Schacter, D. L. & Church, B. (1992). Auditory priming: Implicit and explicit memory for words and voices. *Journal of Experimental Psychology: Learning, Memory and Cognition, 18,* 915-930.

Schacter, D. L., Cooper, L. A. & Delany, S. M. (1990). Implicit memory for unfamiliar objects depends on access to structural descriptions. *Journal of Experimental Psychology: General, 119,* 5-24.

Schacter, D. L., Delany, S. M. & Merikle, E. P. (1990). Priming of nonverbal information and the nature of implicit memory. *The Psychology of Learning and Motivation, 26,* 83-123.

Schank, R. C. (1972). Conceptual dependency: A theory of natural language understanding. *Cognitive Psychology, 3,* 552-631.

Schank, R. C. (1975). *Conceptual information processing.* Amsterdam: North Holland.

Schmidt, R. A. (1975). A schema theory of discrete motor skill learning. *Psychological Review, 82,* 225-260.

Schwartz, N. F., Saffran, E. M. & Marin, O. S. M. (1980). Fractionating the reading process in dementia: Evidence for word-specific print-to-sound-associations. In M. Coltheart, K. E. Patterson & J. C. Marshall (eds.), *Deep dyslexia.* London: Routledge.

Schwarz, M. (1992). *Kognitive Semantiktheorie und neuropsychologische Realität. Repräsentationale und prozedurale Aspekte der sematischen Kompetenz.* Tübingen: Niemeyer.

Shanon, B. (1979). Lateralization effects in response to words and nonwords. *Cortex, 15,* 541-549.

Skinner, B. F. (1957). *Verbal Behavior.* New York: Appleton-Century-Crofts.

Slobin, D. J. (1971). *Psycholinguistics.* London: Scott, Foresman.

Smith, M. C. & Magee, L. E. (1980). Tracing the time course of picture-word processing. *Journal of Experimental Psychology: General, 109,* 373-392.

Snodgrass, J. G. (1984). Concepts and their surface representation. *Journal of Verbal Learning and Verbal Behavior, 23,* 3-22.

Solso, R. L. (1979). *Cognitive psychology.* New York: Harcourt, Brace, Janovich.

Spitzer, M. (1996). *Geist im Netz. Modelle für Lernen, Denken und Handeln.* Heidelberg: Spektrum Akademischer Verlag.

Strube, G. (1984). *Assoziation. Der Prozeß des Erinnerns und die Struktur des Gedächtnisses.* Berlin: Springer.

Taft, M. & Forster, K. J. (1976). Lexical storage and retrieval polymorphemic and polysyllabic words. *Journal of Verbal Learning and Behavior, 15,* 607-620.

Treisman A. & Gormican, S. (1988). Feature analysis in early vision: Evidence from search asymmetries. *Psychological Review, 95,* 15-48.

Warren, R. E. (1977). Time and spread of activation in memory. *Journal of Experimental Psychology: Human Learning and Memory, 3,* 458-466.

Warren, R. E. & Morton, J. (1982). The effects of priming of picture recognition. *British Journal of Psychology, 73,* 117-129.

Warrington, E. K. & McCarthy, R. (1983). Category specific access dysphasia. *Brain, 106,* 859-878.

Watkins, M. J., Peynircioglu, Z. F. & Brems, D. J. (1984). Pictorial rehearsal. *Memory & Cognition, 12,* 553-557.

Weldon, M. S. & Coyote, K. C. (1996). Failure to find the picture superiority effect in implicit conceptual memory tests. *Journal of Experimental Psychology: Learning, Memory and Cognition, 22,* 670-686.

Wells, J. E. (1972). Encoding and memory for verbal and pictorial stimuli. *Quarterly Journal of Experimental Psychology, 24,* 242-252.

Wippich, W., Mecklenbräucker, S., Weidmann, H. & Reichert, A. (1995). Priming-Effekte beim Bilderrätseln: Erste Lösungsvorschläge. *Zeitschrift für experimentelle Psychologie, 42,* 324-352.

Zimmer, H. D. (1984). Blume oder Rose? Unterschiede in der visuellen Informationsverarbeitung bei Experten und Laien. *Archiv für Psychologie, 136,* 343-361.

Zimmer, H. D. (1988). Formkonzepte und Bildmarken: Zwei verschiedene Repräsentationen für visuell-sensorische Merkmale? *Sprache & Kognition, 7,* 40-50.

Zimmer, H. D. (1993). Modalitätsspezifische Systeme der Repräsentation und Verarbeitung von Informationen. *Zeitschrift für Psychologie, 201,* 203-235.

Zimmer, H. D. (1996). Memory for spatial location and enactment. *Psychologische Beiträge, 38,* 404-418.

Zimmer, H. D. & Biegelmann, U. E. (1990a). *Die Herausbildung und Beurteilung von Basisbegriffen in einer artifiziellen Farbhierarchie* (Arbeiten der Fachrichtung Psychologie, Bericht Nr. 151). Saarbrücken: Universität des Saarlandes.

Zimmer, H. D. & Engelkamp, J. (1985). An attempt to distinguish between cinematic and motor memory components. *Acta Psychologica, 58,* 81-106.

Zimmer, H. D., Engelkamp, J. & Sieloff, U. (1984). Motorische Gedächtniskomponenten als partiell unabhängige Komponenten des Engramms verbaler Handlungsbeschreibungen. *Sprache & Kognition, 3,* 70-85.

Chapter 6

The Reading of Words and Sentences

Evelyn Ferstl
Giovanni Flores d'Arcais

6.1 Introduction

Reading is a complex skill that requires the interplay of various information sources, and that involves a number of psychological processes. Readers must possess knowledge about the writing system, they must have a lexicon of the words existing in their language, and they must have access to some representation of the syntactic rules used to build acceptable sentences. Based on the knowledge representations on these different levels, cognitive processes can be postulated for identifying words and accessing their lexical properties, and for processing of word sequences, i.e., mapping syntactic structures onto semantic interpretations.

Until recently, these processes have been neatly divided into separate research areas. In the last few years, however, more emphasis has been put on comparing and contrasting lexical processing of isolated words, and the syntactic processing of isolated sentences. The reasons for this development are twofold. First, it has become increasingly clear that recognizing words in isolation is very different from reading them within a sentence context, and in turn, that the ease of processing a sentence depends strongly on the lexical properties of its individual words. At first glance, this does not seem surprising. However, careful analyses of the syntactic features of sentence contexts, and of lexical features of words in syntax studies have only recently started. Second, in both areas, the modularity hypothesis (Forster, 1979; Fodor, 1983, 1987) has been a driving force in the empirical world. However, the specific translations of this hypothesis into testable models were decidedly different.

In this chapter, we present an overview over the most important results and theories in both word recognition and sentence processing during reading. For both areas, excellent comprehensive reviews are already available (e.g., Balota, 1994; Seidenberg, 1995; Tanenhaus & Trueswell, 1995; Simpson, 1994; Mitchell, 1994). Instead of attempting to provide an exhaustive treatment of these areas, we concentrate on those issues which help elucidating the interface between words and sentences. The outline of the chapter is as follows. In the first Section we will briefly summarize the most pertinent effects established in word recognition research. Without

going into detail about discussions of the empirical limits and theoretical interpretations, we present the basic findings as they pertain to the subsequent Sections on sentence
processing. In the second Sections, we will give an introduction to models of parsing
and review empirical results from three areas. Finally, we try to reevaluate whether
lexical and syntactic disambiguation reflect the same cognitive processes.

6.2   Word Recognition

Recognizing a word means making available phonological, syntactic, semantic and
pragmatic information. When we read a word, usually we know how to pronounce it,
we might have in mind other words that are phonetically similar or associatively related,
we know whether it is a noun or a verb, we might think of an appropriate use for it, and
we can decide quickly whether a presented letter string is a word of our native language.
The goal of visual word recognition research has been twofold. The first line of research
is to investigate how we proceed from letters to a representation of the word, and the
second line of research is to use word recognition results to shed light on the structure
of the internal lexicon and the processes used to access information stored in this lexicon.
To address the first issue, we discuss word level effects and the most important models
of word recognition from this area. To address the second issue, we will then proceed
to summarize results from the investigation of sentence level effects on word recognition.

6.2.1   Word Level Effects
One of the first results motivating the development of models of word recognition
was the frequency effect. Words that occur more often in written language are usually recognized faster than words that occur only rarely (e.g., Forster & Chambers,
1973; Balota & Chumbley, 1984; Inhoff & Rayner, 1986). The cause for this effect is
assumed to be the familiarity of a reader with the words. High frequency words have
been encountered more often and are thus processed more easily. However, the correspondence of the number of times a reader has been exposed to a word with counts
from written frequency norms is far from perfect. Other variables, such as the subjective familiarity with a word (Gernsbacher, 1984; Connine et al., 1990), the concreteness of a word (e.g., Bleasdale, 1987), or its contextual availability (Schwanenflugel
et al., 1988) are highly correlated with frequency, and have been shown to influence
word recognition measures over and above frequency.

   The *frequency effect* has been accounted for by two types of models. Search models (e.g., Forster, 1976, 1994) assume that the lexicon is organized in ordered lists,
with high frequency words being on top of the list. When encountering a word, a
serial search is initiated that compares the input to each entry in turn. Thus, high
frequency words are encountered before low frequency words, and therefore accessed more quickly. Activation based models, such as the Logogen model (Morton,
1969), assume that each word is represented by a unit, called a logogen, whose

recognition threshold is determined by its frequency. Lexical access is conceptualized as the accumulation of activation until the recognition threshold is reached. Each letter contributes activation to the logogens representing the words in which it occurs. For more frequent words with lower recognition threshold, raising activation to reach the threshold requires less support from the input, which is thus accomplished more quickly than for words with a higher threshold.

A second effect, which had already been observed at the end of the 19th century, is what is now called the *word superiority effect* (Cattell, 1885; cited in Balota, 1994). Although letters were thought to be the basic units for reading words, perceptual identification of single letters was shown to be easier when the letter was presented within a word than when it was presented in isolation or embedded in a non-word letter string (Reicher, 1969; Wheeler, 1970). Paradoxically, even when subjects are explicitly shown in which position the target letter will appear, their performance is still worse than when they are instructed to read the whole word (Johnston & McClelland, 1974). Further evidence for the resulting view, that the letter is not the basic unit for word recognition, but that words can be directly accessed from their written form, comes from the letter detection paradigm (Healy, 1976). In this task, subjects are asked to circle a target letter whenever it occurs in connected text. The finding was that letters are missed reliably more often when they are part of high frequency words.

To account for the word superiority effect, McClelland and Rumelhart (1981) developed a connectionist model in the tradition of Morton's logogen model. In their interactive activation model, three levels of processing are postulated: a feature level (which we will ignore for the present discussion), a letter level, and a word level. As in the logogen model, each letter unit is connected to the nodes representing the words in which the letter occurs, and recognition takes place when a recognition threshold has been reached. In addition, inhibitory connections are assumed between different words, and feedback is allowed from the word units back to the letter level. The word superiority effect can thus be explained by assuming that, after activation from the letter level reached the word level, the feedback connections in turn raise the activation levels of the individual letters. Although none of the word units might have reached its recognition threshold, the top-down feedback reinforces the letter units and thus helps them to reach their recognition threshold more quickly than with bottom-up activation from the feature level alone.

In both the search model and the activation based models, localist representations for lexical entries are used. The lexical entries are assumed to have associated information about orthography, phonology, syntactic and semantic features of the words. In Forster's (1976) model, for instance, these different information types are represented in various slave files containing access codes, in addition to a master file containing entries for each word. The representational assumption maps onto the process assumption that word recognition entails an all-or-none process in which a lexical entry is accessed. Effects of lexical, semantic, or contextual variables can then be analyzed according to whether they occur before or after this uniquely defined access point, the 'magic moment' (Balota, 1990). This has led to the distinction of pre-lexical and post-lexical processes in word recognition (cf., Seidenberg, 1990). Traditionally, these two stages have been empirically distinguished using naming and lexical decision tasks, with the former being considered sensitive to pre-lexical processes, and the latter more susceptible to post-lexical decision and integration processes (cf., Balota, 1990, 1994; Schwanenflugel, 1991).

Tests of the modularity hypothesis in lexical processing must then target the pre-lexical stage. Influences of non-lexical information on word recognition during a post-lexical integration or checking stage, are still consistent with a modular account. The first finding challenging a modular theory of lexical access is the well-documented priming effect. When a word (the target) is presented after an appropriately selected, related word (the prime), word recognition is facilitated. Orthographic priming by a similarly spelled word (e.g., Evett & Humphreys, 1981; Sereno, 1991), or phonological priming by a similarly sounding word (e.g., Meyer, Schvaneveldt & Ruddy, 1974; Evett & Humphreys, 1981) can easily be accommodated within the lexical assumptions outlined above. However, Meyer and Schvaneveldt (1971) also found priming effects for associatively or semantically related primes. Lexical decision times were shorter when, let's say, *dog* was preceded by *cat*, than when it was preceded by *pen*. It has been argued that this effect might be due to a post-lexical bias which utilizes the associative relationship during the decision stage (e.g., Neely, Keefe & Ross, 1989). This account cannot explain similar, albeit smaller, priming effects in naming tasks (e.g., Schreuder et al., 1984).

The more prevalent account uses the notion of spreading activation, originally proposed for the representation of semantic memory (e.g., Anderson, 1976; Posner & Snyder, 1975). When a word is activated, it automatically transmits activation to associatively related words. Under the additional assumption that these associative relationships are encoded within the lexical representations, rather than on a conceptual, non-lexical level, the modularity of lexical processing can be maintained.

The alternative, interactive view abandons this distinction. Based on the notion of distributed representations in connectionist networks, Seidenberg and McClelland (1989) have proposed that the lexicon does not contain entries for each word. Instead, lexical and semantic information is represented on the subsymbolic level, that is, in the form of a large network of nodes representing microfeatures (Smolensky, 1988). The connections between these features, determined by exposure, can be approximated using a learning algorithm, so that no assumptions about the internal organization of the lexicon are needed. According to this framework, accessing a word consists of computing an activation pattern distributed across the nodes in the network. Since this computation proceeds continuously, the notion of a 'magic moment' cannot be preserved. Thus, the distinction of a pre-lexical from a post-lexical stage, and the notion of modularity of lexical processing become void.

6.2.2   Sentence Level Effects

The question of whether sentence context can have an effect on word recognition has been studied using two types of contexts. First, it has been studied how coherence and predictability influence lexical access. Second, lexical ambiguities have been used to study whether biasing information influences the access of the different meanings associated with homonyms.

In early studies on context effects, associative priming could account for facilitation of lexical decision and naming times. For instance, West and Stanovich (1982) showed that a sentence fragment like *The skier was buried in the...* primed the target word *snow*. However, similar priming effects have been obtained with sentence contexts that did not contain lexical associates of the target words (e.g., Stanovich & West, 1983). More importantly, some studies have shown that presumably automatic associative priming effects disappear when the sentence fragment is scrambled (Foss, 1982), or when the sentence context implies an semantic feature irrelevant to the associative relationship between the prime and the target (Williams, 1988). Evidence for the importance of featural restrictions was also provided by Schwanenflugel and Shoben (1985). They showed that high constraint sentences, i.e., sentences in which the target word is highly predictable, prime the expected word, but not a semantically related, unexpected word. This sensitivity to the strength of sentence constraint is also apparent in eye fixation times (Ehrlich & Rayner, 1981) and evoked brain potentials (Kutas & Hillyard, 1984). Thus, it is clear that intra-lexical associative priming cannot account for sentence level effects in word recognition.

A similar conclusion comes from studies on syntactic priming. While an appropriate syntactic context, such as *my house* or *he sleeps*, facilitates lexical decision times (e.g., Goodman, McClelland & Gibbs, 1981), it does not facilitate naming times (e.g., Seidenberg, et al., 1984). Again, this task difference has been interpreted as implying that the syntactic coherence influences post-lexical integration, but not lexical access. In contrast, syntactic priming does occur in both naming and lexical decision, when a full sentence context is used (e.g., West & Stanovich, 1986, Tanenhaus, Dell & Carlson, 1987).

Somewhat inconsistent with these findings are studies on lexical disambiguation. In this domain, the target words consist of homonyms, and the question of interest is whether biasing sentence contexts influence access to the meaning alternatives. Interactive models, in this domain also called selective access models, postulate that only the contextually appropriate meaning becomes activated if the sentence bias is sufficient. Exhaustive access or multiple access models hold that lexical access is modular, and thus all meanings of a homonym are activated, as long as the sentence level context does not contain lexical associates of one of the meanings. Selection of the appropriate meaning is a post-lexical process which takes place after the initial activation.

The empirical evidence supporting the latter theory has been abundant (e.g., Tanenhaus, Leiman & Seidenberg, 1979; Kintsch & Mross, 1985; Till, Mross &

Kintsch, 1988). For example, using a cross-modal paradigm, Swinney (1979) showed exhaustive access for equi-biased homonyms, for which both meanings are equally frequent. Exhaustive access occurs even for homonyms whose alternative meanings involve different lexical classes (Seidenberg et al., 1982). For instance, even after the sentence fragment *John began to...* which unambiguously requires a verb continuation, both the appropriate verb meaning and the inappropriate noun meaning of the target word *tire* were initially facilitated. After a delay as short as 200 ms, the facilitation for the inappropriate meaning was no longer observed. Multiple access was also shown for biased homonyms, which have a dominant and a subordinate meaning (Onifer and Swinney, 1981).

Evidence for selective access has since been provided in a series of studies by Tabossi and colleagues (1988; 1991; Tabossi et al., 1987; Tabossi & Zardon, 1993; see also Kellas et al., 1991). In these studies, contexts were designed to make salient a central feature of the dominant meaning of the homonym. These contexts yielded selective access. However, similar contexts biasing towards the subordinate meaning led to activation of both meanings. In a series of eye movement studies, Rayner and colleagues (e.g., Duffy, Morris & Rayner, 1988; Rayner & Frazier, 1989) confirmed these differences between dominant and subordinate meanings. Equi-biased homonyms were fixated longer than biased homonyms, indicating that in the latter case only the dominant meaning was accessed. When prior context information biased towards the subordinate meaning, the opposite pattern was obtained. Thus, context information was used to select the subordinate meaning for equi-biased homonyms, and rendered processing difficulties when it was conflicting with the dominant meaning of biased homonyms. These results were interpreted as consistent with a reordered access model. In this model, the meanings are accessed in the order of their frequency. Thus, without context information, the dominant meaning is available sooner. Context can then speed access for the subordinate meaning, without affecting the contextually inappropriate dominant meaning.

Finally, Van Petten and Kutas (1987) used event-related potentials to study lexical disambiguation. At a short delay, both meanings showed facilitation, as evidenced by smaller N400 amplitudes (a component which is sensitive to priming effects - see Kutas and van Petten, 1988). However, the latency was shorter for the appropriate meaning than for the inappropriate meaning. Thus, while the appropriate meaning seemed to be initially activated, van Petten and Kutas argued that the effect for the inappropriate meaning was due to a post-lexical backward checking process.

Taken together, these and similar results still seem to indicate that alternative meanings are activated in parallel. However, additional factors also exert their influence. In particular, sentence level variables, such as the salience of semantic features, and lexical variables, such as the relative frequency of alternative meanings do influence the time course of lexical disambiguation.

6.3 Sentence Processing

Just like word recognition research poses the question of how letters are combined to enable accessing a lexical entry, sentence processing investigates the question of how words are combined into meaningful, interpretable statements. In contrast to word recognition, however, it is clear that sentence processing requires the interplay of at least two information sources. Besides syntactic information, such as word order, inflectional morphology, and the lexical functions of the individual words in the sentence, the semantic, thematic and pragmatic relationships between the content words have to be taken into account. Thus, the relative contributions of syntactic and non-syntactic information and the processes utilizing this information are heart of sentence processing research.

Throughout the history of psycholinguistics, the focus on one or the other of these issues has shifted repeatedly. In the Sixties, syntactic processes were on center stage. Miller (1962, Miller & Isard, 1963) observed that even a semantically senseless sentence such as *Colorless green ideas sleep furiously* could relatively easily be syntactically analyzed. However, the attempt to empirically establish the psychological relevance of the then prevalent transformational grammar (Chomsky, 1957) failed (see Fodor, Bever & Garrett, 1974; Clark & Clark, 1977).

At the same time, experimental studies addressing the use of semantic and pragmatic knowledge in language comprehension provided strong evidence against the representation of sentences on a linguistic or structural level. For instance, Bransford and Franks (1971) found that after hearing the sentence *Three turtles rested on a log and the fish swam beneath them* listeners could not recall whether the fish swam beneath the log or beneath the turtles. This was taken as evidence for language processing mechanisms which extract the general meaning of a sentence, rather than analyzing its structure. Bever (1970) observed that Garden Path sentences, i.e., sentences in which the initial syntactic interpretation turns out to be incorrect, could be avoided by using appropriate semantic and pragmatic information. For example the sentence *The horse raced past the barn fell* is almost impossible to understand, because *raced* is interpreted as the main verb of the sentence, so that the following verb *fell* does not seem to make sense. This so-called reduced relative clause ambiguity, ("reduced" refers to the missing relative pronoun), does not pose much problem when it occurs in the structurally similar sentence *The articles read in the garden were boring.* Supported by ideas from the artificial intelligence community, these and similar observations led to the rather extreme semantically oriented view that syntactic analysis might not be necessary at all. Rather, it was suggested, sentence processing consists of conceptually analyzing the thematic relationships between content words (e.g., De Jong, 1982; Riesbeck & Schank, 1978).

The compromise between the radical syntax and the radical semantics view was to try to identify perceptual strategies in sentence comprehension (e.g., Bever, 1970;

Fodor et al., 1974; Clark & Clark, 1977; Kimball, 1973). These principles or heuristics included semantic as well as syntactic variables. For instance, a strategy might be syntactic ("whenever you find a determiner, begin a noun phrase"), or thematic ("interpret the noun preceding the verb as the agent"). Empirical research tried to identify the generality and limits of such strategies.

In this tradition, and again based on linguistic theory (Chomsky, 1965; 1981), Frazier (1979; Frazier and Fodor, 1978) developed her theory of syntactic processing. She postulated two principles which were sufficient to capture a larger number of more specific strategies proposed previously. The first principle is the Principle of Minimal Attachment. This principle states that the interpretation is chosen which leads to the simplest structure consistent with the rules of grammar, or, in other words, to the interpretation whose phrase structure contains the fewest nodes. The second principle is the Principle of Late Closure, which states that a new word is preferably integrated into the current phrase. These two principles cover a wide range of syntactic preferences, including the reduced relative / main clause ambiguity mentioned above. Prepositional phrases are preferably attached to the verb, as in *The janitor cleaned the room with the broom*, compared to the object noun, as in *The janitor cleaned the room with the hardwood floor* (Rayner, Carlson & Frazier, 1983). Direct object interpretations are preferred over sentence complements (*The mathematician knew the solution would not be easy*), and over clause boundaries (*After the doctor visited the patient sneezed*) (e.g., Mitchell, 1989), and sentence complements are preferred over relative clauses (*Mary told the man that she had danced with a story*).

Based on these principles, Frazier developed a modular parsing theory which is now called the Garden Path model (Frazier, 1979; Frazier & Rayner, 1982). The basic assumption is that processing proceeds serially and only one alternative is considered at a time. The principles of Minimal Attachment and Late Closure determine the first pass parse. Since syntactic processing is postulated to be informationally encapsulated, non-syntactic information cannot influence the first pass interpretation. Semantic and pragmatic information, as well as discourse context, enter the picture during a second stage. The so-called 'thematic processor' evaluates the output of the syntactic analysis with respect to its consistency with the non-syntactic information. In case this plausibility check fails, or in case of syntactically incompatible inputs, a revision process is initiated.

Another influential serial model of parsing was developed by Bresnan (1978; Bresnan and Kaplan, 1982; Ford, Bresnan & Kaplan, 1982). While this theory also assumes that only one interpretation is constructed at a time, the first pass parse is based on lexical information associated with verbs, rather than with structural principles. We will return to this model later.

The alternative view to the serial account is represented by interactive models. In this class of models, alternative interpretations of syntactic ambiguities are assumed to be activated in parallel. Depending on the assumptions about the processes for selection of one of these alternatives, Altmann and Steedman (1988) distinguished weakly interactive from strongly interactive models. In weakly interactive models (e.g., Altmann & Steedman, 1988; Kintsch, 1988), the initial activation of syntactic structures is not influenced by non-syntactic information. However, the selection of the appropriate alternative does use this information and it is fast and efficient. Of course, these assumptions are perfectly consistent with the modularity hypothesis. In fact, this description of weakly interactive models is almost identical to the multiple access account of word recognition. Thus, the term 'interactive' is somewhat of a misnomer.

Strongly interactive models, on the other hand, do allow for the influence of non-syntactic information to propose a syntactic interpretation, instead of only using it for the disposal of an inappropriate interpretation. In these models, the language comprehension process is considered a constraint-satisfaction process in which multiple sources of information are used in parallel. No restrictions as to the flow of information are postulated (e.g., MacDonald et al., 1994; MacWhinney & Bates, 1989; McClelland, 1987; Marslen-Wilson, 1975; Trueswell & Tanenhaus, 1994; Waltz & Pollack, 1985). In this account, it is possible that pragmatic knowledge, contextual constraints or lexical frequency information propose an analysis to the syntactic processor. For instance, the order of application of grammatical rules could be influenced by co-occurrence frequencies of words, or the rules could contain conditions which are context-dependent. These empirically observable interactions between different types of constraints can be modeled in a constraint-satisfaction network.

While it has proven difficult to empirically distinguish weakly interactive theories from the Garden-Path model, strongly interactive theories make qualitatively different predictions. In contrast to the garden-path model, strongly interactive models predict no difference in the time course of processing syntactic and non-syntactic information, since there is no principled distinction between these two. On the other hand, strongly interactive models do predict that preferences can be reversed when appropriately selected conflicting constraints are present.

With these predictions in mind, we will now review research on three selected areas within recent sentence processing research. The first issue is the influence of lexical class ambiguity on structural processing. Although this question has not been central, and only few studies are available, we include this Section with a look back at the previous Section on word recognition. The second issue is the question of when lexical information, in particular syntactic or thematic information associated with verbs, enters the parsing process. This issue has first been studied in the attempt to distinguish serial, lexical models from the structurally based garden-path model. More recently, constraint-satisfaction models have led to the search for interactions of lexical factors with other variables. Finally, we conclude with a relatively detailed review of studies on discourse context effects in parsing. Although this issue is not as directly related to word recognition and lexical processes, the question of when contextual information is used during parsing seems to be the most stringent test for the modularity hypothesis.

6.3.1   Lexical Category Ambiguities

Due to its sparse morphology, English contains many lexical class ambiguities. For example, almost any noun can be used as an adjectival modifier in a compound noun, and many words can be used both as a verb and a noun. As we have seen in the previous Section, multiple meanings of ambiguous words seem to be activated even when they involve different lexical classes.

Of course there are sentences in which the lexical function of a word determines the syntactic structure rather than the other way around. The first study investigating the effect of lexical category assignment on parsing was conducted by Tyler and Marslen-Wilson in 1977. In their experiment, sentence contexts were varied prior to a subject noun phrase such as *flying planes*. If *flying* is interpreted as the gerundive verb form and planes as its associated object, subject-verb agreement requires the following verb to be singular. If *flying* is interpreted as an adjective modifying the head noun planes, a plural verb form is required. Using a cross-modal naming task, Tyler and Marslen-Wilson (1977) found evidence for the sentence bias influencing lexical class decisions. Naming times were shorter for the verb form that was consistent with the sentence bias. This result was taken as evidence for an interactive parsing system in which contextual information is used immediately for lexical disambiguation, and in turn for deriving a consistent syntactic structure. Subsequently, these results were replicated with similar materials using a self-paced reading paradigm (Farrar & Kawamoto, 1993).

In contrast, Frazier and Rayner (1987) found no effects of bias inherent in the ambiguous materials. Using a sentence continuation task, they classified the ambiguous combinations according to whether they were more likely to be used as an adjective-noun combination (e.g., *moving trains*) or a gerundive-noun combination (*hanging curtains*). This variable had no effect on eye fixations during the ambiguous region, and did not interact with ambiguity in the disambiguating region. Compared to disambiguated control sentences, reading times in the ambiguous region were shorter, and in the disambiguating region longer. This finding paralleled those for ambiguities such as *warehouse fires* which can either be interpreted as a plural compound noun or a noun-verb combination. The fact that reading times during the ambiguous region were shorter than in control sentences, was taken to suggest that the different lexical classes are not activated in parallel - which would lead to an increase in reading time during the ambiguous region -, but that lexical class assignment is delayed until disambiguating information is encountered. This explanation seems to conflict with the multiple access view from the word recognition literature, as well as with the claim that syntactic attachment decisions are made immediately. Since attachment requires the use of lexical class information, it cannot take place before lexical ambiguities are resolved.

MacDonald (1993) put forth an alternative explanation for these results. Frazier and Rayner (1987) disambiguated their control sentences using deictic determiners, instead of definite articles. For instance, the sentence fragment *These warehouse fires...* biases towards the compound noun reading. Reading times showed that sentences with deictic determiners took longer to read even in the absence of lexical category ambiguities. Moreover, she showed in a second experiment that ambiguity effects for noun-noun combinations were only obtained when the compound noun reading was pragmatically plausible. Reading times for the ambiguous region correlated with corpus frequencies of the compound noun reading, as well as with frequencies of the first noun being used as an adjectival modifier.

While in all of these studies, the resolution of the lexical class ambiguities had an impact on the constituents, it did not interact with the complexity of the resulting global sentence structure. Ferstl (1994b) reported an experiment designed to study this interaction. Compound nouns were used in prepositional phrase attachment sentences that could be interpreted with either of the two nouns alone. Consider the sentence *Catherine cut the shirt with the pocket knife*, which requires the preferred minimal attachment reading. If the lexical class ambiguity of *pocket* was immediately resolved towards the preferred noun reading, and attachment of the prepositional phrase also occurred immediately, a garden-path on the subsequent word *knife* would be expected. Counter to the intuition, both the noun phrase and the PP-attachment would have to be reanalyzed. Of course, this is not what reading times from a self-paced reading task showed. Processing difficulties were observed for the non-preferred sentences (using *pocket* alone), but the compound noun sentences were equally easy as the preferred sentences (*knife* alone). This finding is consistent with the proposal of delayed category assignment. However, in this case, it also has to be assumed that attachment is delayed until the lexical category is unambiguously identified. Alternatively, the result can be explained by a process which delays global attachments until additional information signals the end of the constituent (Perfetti, 1990).

6.3.2 Effects of Verb Information

The first studies concerned with the limits of the structural account of parsing, investigated the influence of lexical information. In particular, the development of Lexical Functional Grammar (Bresnan, 1978; Bresnan & Kaplan, 1982) influenced psycholinguistics. In this theory, the lexical entries of verbs include information on the subcategorization frames, that is, the syntactic contexts in which they can appear. For example, intransitive verbs, such as *sleep*, have only one subcategorization frame (e.g., *John slept*). A verb like *tell*, on the other hand, has several subcategorization frames. For instance, *tell* can appear with a direct object (e.g., *John told the truth*), with an indirect object (*John told Mary*), or with a complement sentence (*John told Mary that he was tired*). Related is the notion of thematic grid. In this representation, it is specified that a sentence using a verb like *give* has to specify an agent, a recipient, and a theme, even though these thematic roles might be realized using different subcategorization frames (e.g., *John gave Mary the book* or *John gave the book to Mary*). For these thematic grids, selection restrictions are specified which constrain the possible categories for each role. For instance, recipients of give are usually animate. Thus, when the sentence fragment *John gave the book...* is read, this selection restriction strongly suggests that *book* is the theme of the sentence, and a prepositional phrase specifying the recipient will follow.

A number of studies have investigated whether these types of lexical information are immediately available during parsing, and whether they can override structural parsing preferences. According to the garden-path model, the effects of verb information are expected to be observed after initial structural decisions have been made. Lexical theories, on the other hand, predict that verb information guides parsing decisions.

Ferreira and Henderson (1990) used reduced complement ambiguities which either biased towards a direct object interpretation, as in *He wished Pam needed a ride with him*, or towards a complement interpretation, as in *He forgot Pam needed a ride with him*. Compared with unreduced control sentences including the complementizer *that*, these sentences were more difficult to process. However, verb bias had an effect on eye fixation durations not in the disambiguating region, but only later. Thus, they concluded that the structural preference for a direct object could not be influenced by verb bias. However, the verb preferences in this study did not seem very strong, and some of the noun phrases following the verb were implausible direct objects. Using more carefully selected verbs, both Trueswell, Tanenhaus and Kellows (1993) did find immediate verb effects, and Garnsey et al. (1997) showed that plausibility of the second noun as a direct object had only an effect for those verbs that did not have a preference for one of the two subcategorization frames. Further evidence for the immediate use of subcategorization preference was provided in an experiment using evoked brain potentials (Osterhout, Holcomb & Swinney, 1994).

The contributions of argument structure to parsing have been studied using prepositional phrase attachment ambiguities. For these sentences, minimal attachment predicts a preference for verb attachment over noun attachment. Ford (1989) contrasted sentences of the form *The secretary owned/stuck the paintings in the office* using a continuous grammaticality judgment paradigm. In contrast to *owned*, *stuck* requires a locative argument, so that the prepositional phrase is expected to be processed more easily after this verb. Of course, the same prediction is made by a purely structure based account. However, Ford (1989) found longer decision times not only on the noun filler (*office*), the location where the garden-path theory predicts reanalysis to occur, but also on the preposition itself. Thus, she concluded, verb information influenced processing even before attachment decisions were postulated.

A similar prediction was tested by Clifton, Speer and Abney (1990). They independently varied the attachment of the prepositional phrase and its argument status. For instance, in the noun-attachment sentence *The man expressed his interest in a wallet*, the prepositional phrase is an argument of the noun *interest*. On the other hand, the sentence *The man expressed his interest in a hurry* requires a verb attachment, but the prepositional phrase is not an argument of the verb, but an adjunct. The results showed that although total reading times confirmed the preference of arguments over adjuncts, first pass reading times confirmed the structural preference of verb attachments over noun attachments. Thus, the predictions of the lexical account could not be confirmed.

Without making this strict distinction between arguments and adjuncts, Taraban and McClelland (1988) also argued that thematic information affects parsing of prepositional phrase ambiguities. Using highly constrained sentence contexts, they first established that there was no effect of syntactic preference, but that the sentence bias determined reading times. In addition, they found significant increases in reading times not only for attachment preference violations, but also for thematic role violations. Taraban and McClelland interpreted these results as evidence for an interactive parsing model, in which thematic role information and sentence context contribute to the ease of processing.

Finally, there are a number of studies on the influence of selection restrictions on immediate parsing decisions (e.g., Stowe, 1989). As with subcategorization information, the first results seemed to support a structure based account. Ferreira and Clifton (1986) used reduced relative clause ambiguities and varied the animacy of the subject. For the verb *examined*, for instance, an animate subject is required. If selection restrictions are used to guide the parsing process, no garden-path effects are expected in the sentence *The evidence examined by the lawyer turned out to be unreliable*. Eye movement data confirmed that the reduced relative sentences were harder than unreduced control sentences. Animacy information was immediately available, as indicated by longer reading times on the verb following an inanimate subject. However, this information did not facilitate disambiguation. Using similar materials, Just and Carpenter (1992) argued that the use of lexical information is dependent on individuals' reading skills. They assessed subjects' reading spans, a language specific measure for working memory capacity (Daneman & Carpenter, 1980), and found that readers with a high reading span did indeed benefit from animacy information during disambiguation. Low span readers, on the other hand, did not have sufficient memory capacity to keep track of multiple information sources. Finally, Trueswell, Tanenhaus and Garnsey (1994) varied the strength of the animacy constraint. Animacy did facilitate reading of the disambiguating region, but only for nouns with a strong constraint against being the agent of the verb.

Although this latter result provided evidence for the use of co-occurrence information, it seems to argue against the notion of categorical selection restrictions. Rather, the plausibility of a given word in a given context seems to be crucial. Selection restrictions are all-or-none (e.g., animate or not), whereas plausibility can be considered a continuous variable. Plausibility alone, which usually is a weaker constraint than selection restrictions, does not seem to influence parsing. For instance, in a study by Rayner, Carlson and Frazier (1983) the typicality of the subject as an agent of the verb (*The florist sent the flowers...* vs. *The performer sent the flowers...*) did not eliminate the Garden Path for reduced relative clauses. Similarly, Mecklinger et al., (1995) did not find facilitative effects of plausibility. In this study, evoked brain potentials were measured during reading of German relative clause ambiguities.

6.3.3   Effects of Discourse Context

Leaving aside sentence level factors such as syntactic structure or lexical biases, the strongest test of the impenetrability of the parser is to study context effects. By embedding sentences in appropriately designed discourse paragraphs, the lexical content as well as the syntactic structure is held constant. Potentially confounding lexical variables, as discussed in the previous Sections, are avoided. Moreover, most lexical effects might be originating within the syntactic module, given the appropriate assumptions about the structure of the lexicon. This is not the case for discourse information. This distinction is analogous to the distinction between word level and sentence level priming effects in the area of word recognition.

In contrast to the domain of word processing, where in the earlier work not much attention has been paid to the features of biasing sentences, empirical studies on context effects in parsing are closely linked to a theoretical proposal about what type of discourse information is expected to influence parsing decisions, and why. Steedman and colleagues (Crain & Steedman, 1985; Altmann & Steedman, 1988) instigated a large number of empirical investigations by proposing their Referential Theory. The underlying assumption was that language serves a communicative purpose, and speakers restrict their utterances to information needed for establishing a coherent discourse model. Consequently, parsing is not assumed to be based on structural principles for the construction of an interpretation, but on two discourse principles for selection of an appropriate interpretation. The Principle of Parsimony states that a reading which carries fewer unsupported presuppositions will be favored over one that carries more (Altmann & Steedman, 1988). A corollary of this principle is the Principle of Referential Support, which states that referentially supported noun phrases will be favored. For isolated sentences, these discourse principles predict that modified noun phrases (e.g., by a prepositional phrase, or by a relative clause) are unpreferred. It follows that verb attachments are preferred over noun attachments in prepositional phrase ambiguities, that complement clause interpretations are preferred over relative clause interpretations (e.g., of a sentence fragment *The counselor told the woman that...*), and that main clause interpretations are preferred over reduced relative clause interpretations. In contrast to structure based models, these preferences can and must be influenced by appropriate discourse information. If the current discourse model contains more than one referent for a noun phrase mentioned in the target sentence (for instance, *two women speaking to a counselor*), a unique referent needs to be identified. In this case a noun modification becomes felicitous, and renders the syntactically preferred alternative structure more difficult.

In an early study on contextual effects on parsing, Ferreira and Clifton (1986) used biasing contexts and neutral contexts in an eye movement paradigm. Prepositional phrase attachment ambiguities of the form *Sam loaded the boxes on the cart...* were continued as either a noun attachment (i.e., continued with *onto the van*), or as a verb attachment (*before the coffee break*). Reduced relative clauses were also used and embedded in contexts containing either one or two possible referents for the modified subject noun phrase. No evidence for facilitating context effects for the non-preferred readings were found. Altmann and Steedman (1988) pointed out that the contexts might have differed on more than one dimension. In addition, the neutral contexts seemed to induce unwanted biases. They suggested to use minimally different contexts changing only one crucial piece of information, and to cross sentence types with context types. Using this paradigm, confounding context variables can be avoided, and the effect of an infelicitous context on the syntactically preferred reading can be evaluated.

Using this design, Altmann and Steedman (1988) reported two experiments on prepositional phrase attachment ambiguities. Verb attachment sentences of the form *The burglar blew open the safe with the dynamite* were read more quickly after a context paragraph containing only one safe than after a context mentioning two safes. More importantly, the non-preferred noun attachment sentences, such as *The burglar blew open the safe with the new lock*, were facilitated by a two-safe context, compared to the one-safe context. These results obtained for both sentence reading times, as well as for phrasal reading times from a cumulative presentation.

Britt et al. (1992) replicated the effects of referential support using word-by-word reading and eye movement monitoring. Moreover, their context paragraphs were longer and avoided the verbatim repetition of the complex noun phrase. For instance *the child with the doll* was introduced early in the prior discourse by the sentence *The child was hanging on to a doll*. Single word and phrasal self-paced reading times, as well as eye fixation patterns, showed that the biasing contexts eliminated the Garden Path for the noun attachment sentences. In contrast, an experiment using reduced relative clauses did not yield immediate context effects. As in the Ferreira and Clifton (1986) study, the paragraphs used different scenarios, and target sentences and context types were not fully crossed.

A phrasal reading paradigm was used by Mitchell, Corley and Garnham (1992) in a study of contextual override for relative clause / complement clause ambiguities. Although they manipulated the number of referents in the discourse paragraphs, they could confirm the predictions of referential theory. However, a variety of methodological objections have been raised (e.g., small global effects of context, and the particular segmentation), so that the results are difficult to interpret. Using similar ambiguities, Altmann, Garnham and Dennis (1992) employed eye movement monitoring. Sentence fragments of the form *He told the builder that he'd arranged to pay...* were either continued as a complement clause or as a relative clause. These sentences were then embedded in one-referent and two-referent contexts. The results were not clear-cut. Even in the biasing context, residual syntax effects were found (in number of regressions or reading times). Only when the trials in which a regression occurred were eliminated from the analysis, did contextual override take place.

Rayner, Garrod and Perfetti (1992) reported two eye movement studies that clearly confirmed the predictions of the Garden Path model. For both reduced relative ambiguities and prepositional phrase ambiguities, biasing contexts were written which contained information facilitating the non-minimal interpretation. Furthermore, by inserting intervening information between the referential information and the target sentence, the referential information was either in the discourse focus or not. The results were identical for the two types of ambiguity. First pass reading times showed clear effects of syntactic structure. In contrast, total reading times were sensitive to the discourse manipulation. In the disambiguating region, total reading times were shorter when the referential information was foregrounded in the discourse. These late context effects were interpreted as evidence for facilitation of the reanalysis process by appropriate referential information. Inspection of the discourse contexts shows, like in Britt et al. (1992, Experiment 3), that they differed not only with respect to the referential information, but also in many other ways. Thus, it is not clear how to evaluate the strength of the discourse bias and the availability of discourse information during disambiguation.

A more controlled study, again following the design of Altmann and Steedman (1988), was conducted by Murray and Liversedge (1994). They first confirmed the context bias using a sentence completion study. While after the one-referent context almost no modifications of the noun phrase were produced, the two-referent contexts were almost always completed with a noun modification, and often with a relative clause. First and second pass reading times showed processing difficulties for reduced relative clauses compared to unambiguous control sentences. Surprisingly, no effects of context were found, not even in second pass measures. A post-hoc explanation might be that additional inference requirements in the two-referent condition counteracted the biasing effects. For instance, the *man dressed as a woman* had to be identified as the *man who was playing the old witch* in a play. Even when a noun attachment is expected, this inference might induce additional processing costs.

A study providing evidence for context effects for the processing of reduced relative clause ambiguities was conducted by Spivey-Knowlton, Trueswell and Tanenhaus (1993). Using one- and two-referent contexts, they studied processing of reduced relative clauses, such as *The prisoner removed by...* . Unambiguous clauses containing the relative pronoun and reduced relative clauses disambiguated by the verb form (e.g., *taken*) were used as control sentences. In all sentences, the word after the participle was the preposition *by*, which disambiguated the syntactic structure immediately. As expected, processing difficulties for the reduced relative sentences were observed only in the one-referent context. This result seems to support contextual penetrability, but a methodological trick was needed to obtain it. The sentences were presented in a self-paced reading task with a two-word window, so that the verb and the following disambiguating preposition *by* were presented at once. When the same materials were displayed in the usual word-by-word fashion, interactions between context and sentence type were no longer significant. Spivey-Knowlton et al. (1993) justify this paradigm by noting that in normal reading, as evidenced in eye movement studies, peripheral vision plays a role. Thus, the availability of the short function word after the crucial verb is also given in natural reading conditions.

Trueswell and Tanenhaus (1991) could also successfully diminish processing difficulties for reduced relative clauses. Using sentences similar to those of Spivey-Knowlton et al. (1993), they argued that the interpretation of a past participle does not require temporal coherence, but a main clause reading does. When the context establishes a scenario taking place in the future, the past tense main verb reading is not supported, and the reduced relative reading becomes more available. After presenting short context paragraphs of the form *The students will take an exam tomorrow. The proctor will notice one of them cheating*, they found that the Garden Path for the reduced relative reading was diminished. However, as in Spivey-Knowlton et al. (1993), this result was obtained with presentation of two words at once, so that the processing of the agentive preposition *by* combined with the contextual information.

While Spivey-Knowlton et al. (1993) suggested that this feature of their experimental materials and procedure might be crucial, a more recent study found context effects without these constraints on the materials. Ni, Crain and Shankweiler (1996) studied reduced relative clauses in still another type of context (also first suggested by Trueswell & Tanenhaus, 1991). When a noun phrase is introduced by the prenominal *only*, a contrast set needs to be established. For example, the sentence *Only children play* implies that there are other some other people, and they don't play. If the contrast set has not been part of the discourse, an inference is needed. In contrast, a restrictive noun modification is referentially supported. By default, the contrast set for *Only children with blond hair play* is given by all the other children. Using this context manipulation in an eye movement paradigm provided evidence for such a referential effect. Increased first pass reading times were found on the disambiguat-

ing main verb in *The businessmen loaned money were told...*, but not in the sentence
Only businessmen... . This provides clear evidence for contextual effects on reduced
relatives. In contrast to the previous two studies, the ambiguous region contained
several words, and the sentences were not disambiguated using the agentive preposition *by*. However, the referential information was provided within the target sentences, not in an extra-sentential context paragraph.

In the same study, Ni et al. (1996) also used prepositional phrase attachment ambiguities to test the effects of the focus operator *only*. Again, the Garden Path for the
non-preferred noun attachment disappeared due to the referential information, as
evidenced in first pass reading times of the prepositional phrase. In addition, this
experiment used the crossed design, so that it could also be tested whether the preferred verb attachment would be rendered more difficult after *only*. This was not the
case in the analysis of the data from all subjects. When grouping them into high and
low span readers, a different pattern emerged. First pass reading times did show
increased processing times for this condition in the high span group. In contrast, for
low span subjects processing difficulties manifested themselves in the number of
regressions out of the disambiguating region. Thus, it seemed that the prediction of
the referential support theory were confirmed for high span readers. Low span readers were sensitive to the same contextual information, but they could not apply it as
efficiently.

Finally, two recent studies showed interactions between verb information and discourse context. Britt (1994) distinguished verbs with obligatory arguments from verbs
with optional arguments. For instance, *put* requires a locative prepositional phrase,
while *drop* does not. In a self-paced reading paradigm she found referential context
effects only for sentences containing verbs with optional arguments. The remaining
Garden Path for sentences in which the verb required an argument slot to be filled
was interpreted as evidence for the immediate use of verb information and its preference over contextual information.

Spivey-Knowlton and Sedivy (1995), on the other hand, distinguished action verbs
(e.g., *cut*) from psychological or perception verbs (e.g., *see*). Corpus counts and
sentence completion results showed that the preference for verb attachment is much
stronger for the former than for the latter. Although Spivey-Knowlton and Sedivy
(1995) do not agree with this interpretation, this could be accounted for by assuming
that verb attachments to action verbs fill an argument role, while verb attachments to
psych verbs are adjuncts. In their study, they manipulated referential support by
either using a definite or an indefinite article in the object noun phrase (e.g., *a safe
with a new lock* vs. *the safe with the new lock*). Since a definite article presupposes
the existence of a not yet mentioned but well-defined referent, a noun attachment is
more likely when the noun phrase carries an indefinite article. Similar to the interaction found in the Britt (1994) study, Spivey-Knowlton and Sedivy found referential
context effects in a self-paced reading paradigm only for the psych verbs, but not for

the action verbs. Once more, the conclusion was that multiple constraints are used simultaneously, and that verb information takes precedence over discourse information. Although both of these studies seem to provide strong evidence for a modulated effect of context information, a replication using eye movement monitoring might be desirable.

Recently, a study on context effects using the method of event-related potentials has been conducted. Ferstl and Friederici (1997) used German relative clause ambiguities, which are due to identical word order for both subject and object relative clauses. In contrast to English, the verbatim translation of the complex noun phrase *the student who the professor saw* can, depending on case information and subject-verb agreement, either mean that the student saw the professor (a subject relative clause) or that the professor saw the student (an object relative clause). Context information was provided in the form of two questions biasing either toward a subject relative or an object relative. The questions included information on the thematic roles as well as on the case of the ambiguous relative pronoun. While behavioral data confirmed the efficacy of these contexts, the ERP patterns showed a more differentiated picture. A large positivity for inconsistent trials was found as early as 250 ms after onset of the disambiguating word, independent of syntactic structure. This shows clearly that context information was immediately available. However, it did not override the syntactic preference. At around 350 msec a positivity for the unpreferred object relative reading was found, independent of context condition. Finally, an interaction between these two factors in a later window suggested that the processes involved in reanalyzing the syntactic structure differed as a function of context condition. Thus, it seems that syntactic information and context information make initially independent contributions to parsing.

The results from a decade of research on discourse context effects in parsing during reading are by no means conclusive. While several studies provided evidence for contextual override of syntactic preferences, there are others which could not find immediate context effects. Explanations have been based on three distinct arguments (cf., Tanenhaus & Trueswell, 1995). First, there seems to be a task dependence. Studies using self-paced reading have been more likely to provide evidence for immediate context effects than studies using eye-movement monitoring. Second, it appears that prepositional phrase attachment preferences are more susceptible to contextual override than other syntactic preferences. This explanation is also confirmed in the studies reviewed here. The reason might either be the comparable availability of the two structures (MacDonald et al., 1994), or the fact that these ambiguities are not disambiguated by a syntactic mismatch, but rather by pragmatic information (cf., Perfetti, 1990). And third, although most context studies are inspired by Referential Theory, there are considerable differences with respect to the content of the discourse paragraphs. The effects of these differences cannot be properly evaluated without controlling for text level processes, such as inferences.

Taken together, the small but growing literature on discourse effects in syntactic processing has not provided a conclusive answer to the question of whether syntactic processing is contextually impenetrable. Although a considerable number of studies provided evidence for the immediate facilitation of the non-preferred reading, almost none have documented a context induced Garden Path for the preferred reading (cf., Frazier, 1995).

6.3.4   Lexical versus Syntactic Processing

Now that we have summarized issues and results in both the word recognition and the sentence processing literature, we can return to a discussion of the *lexical approach* to syntactic parsing, and discuss the notion of modularity once more.

MacDonald et al. (1994) offered a unified, constraint-satisfaction account of lexical and syntactic ambiguity resolution (see also Trueswell & Tanenhaus, 1994, for a similar model). Instead of considering word recognition and syntactic parsing as two qualitatively different mechanisms, they argue that these two processes are just two sides of the same coin. The main arguments for this theory are the following. First, many syntactic ambiguities are in fact due to ambiguities on the lexical level. For example, the relative clause ambiguity arises from the lexical ambiguity between participles and past tense verbs. Second, an increasing number of studies, some reviewed here, seem to indicate that factors such as verb information, discourse context, and most prominently, frequency information have an impact on syntactic disambiguation. MacDonald et al. (1994) propose an architecture in which all these types of information are conceptualized as lexical constraints that the language processing system tries to fulfil simultaneously when interpreting a sentence.

This approach is by no means novel. Waltz and Pollack (1985) and Kintsch (1988; see Ferstl, 1994a) are just two examples for models similar in spirit. However, the advantage over these early models is that MacDonald et al. (1994) theory could be grounded in a quite extensive body of empirical literature. Moreover, the proposal about how linguistic knowledge is represented and what kinds of constraints enter the network is more specific. The major contribution of this approach is that it has put emphasis on extending traditional investigations of syntactic processing to considering previously neglected factors. By now there is overwhelming empirical evidence for interactions between different factors, such as syntactic structure, verb information, frequency counts, plausibility measures, and text level processes. Although it is less clear that all these interactions are operating during the first stages of processing, they need to be taken into account by all models of language processing. To date, the constraint-satisfaction approach has been the most explicit in trying to formulate a mechanism for explaining these interactions.

Of course, there are criticisms of the constraint satisfaction approach as well. These include methodological issues, lack of falsifiability, generalizability to complex syntactic structures, and the ill-defined problem of grain size over which lexical frequencies are computed. We will not discuss these arguments here, but refer the interested reader to Frazier (1995). Instead, we would like to return for a moment to methodological issues.

In research on lexical access, frequency has been shown to have large effects that often smother more subtle differences. Frequency has also been shown to modulate a large number of effects due to other variables (cf., Balota, 1994). Therefore, it has long been common practice to use frequency as a control dimension, on which other, presumably psychologically more interesting conditions are matched. An even stronger control, which is also standard practice in the priming literature, is to use identical targets in different prime contexts. Syntactic processing research, in contrast, is only now starting to establish the predictiveness as well as the limits of frequency (see Mitchell, 1994; Gibson, Schütze & Salomon, 1996). We hope that in the future syntactic processing research, just like lexical access research, will move on to effects beyond frequency.

The second issue where syntactic processing research might benefit from the experiences of word recognition researchers is the careful evaluation of the paradigms used. In the priming literature, it has been standard to compare results from lexical decision and naming tasks, and to interpret differences as reflecting systematic, psychologically valid distinctions between pre- and post-lexical processes. Although task differences have been noted in the syntax research as well, theoretically motivated task comparisons are still rare (see Spivey-Knowlton et al., 1993; Ferreira & Henderson, 1990). Moreover, a convincing mapping of empirical results to theoretical proposals has not been accomplished. Even in eye movement monitoring, which is the most sensitive and most readily accepted paradigm (cf., Rayner et al. 1989),, it is not yet clear which of the many possible measures truly reflects first pass parsing processes. However, alternative methods have been introduced recently to dissociate syntactic from non-syntactic processing (e.g., speed-accuracy analyses, McElree, 1993, McElree & Griffith, 1995; compressed speech presentation, Fodor et al., 1996).

These analogies from lexical to syntactic processing research can only hold if they indeed do involve the same psychological process. To conclude, we briefly discuss two selected arguments for why lexical and syntactic disambiguation might involve different processes after all.

The first argument concerns individual differences in lexical processing and syntactic processing. In one of the first studies documenting the relationship between reading span and comprehension skill, Daneman and Carpenter (1980) showed that high span readers are better able to assign the correct referent to a pronoun, in particular when a larger distance in the discourse has to be bridged. As we have seen above, Just and Carpenter (1992; King & Just, 1991) have argued that high span readers are able to consider alternative syntactic representations in parallel (Pearlmutter & MacDonald, 1995). Moreover, they seem to have sufficient working memory capacity available for immediately taking into account non-syntactic plausibility information. Similarly, in an ERP study using German relative clause ambiguities, Mecklinger et al. (1995) found good readers to be more sensitive to syntactic preferences than poor readers (as defined by question answering speed). These findings are consistent with the vew that syntactic processing requires considerable resources.

For lexical processing, there are also numerous findings on individual differences. However, the results seem not consistent with the resuts from the syntactic processing literature. First, poor readers are *more* context sensitive than good readers. For instance, contextual constraints, as defined by cloze probability, have larger benefits for children, elderly subjects, and various patient populations (Cohen & Faulkner, 1983; Fischler, 1985). Second, in the area of lexical ambiguity resolution, Gernsbacher, Varner and Faust (1990) obtained the opposite pattern from that observed in the area of syntactic ambiguity resolution. Using a comprehension test battery for grouping subjects, they studied how reading skill influences processing of homonyms. Like good readers, poor readers were able to immediately activate alternative meanings. However, after a delay of 850 ms, only good readers had deactiated the inappropriate meaning. Thus, in contrast to the failure to activate alternative interpretations, poor readers had problems with using contextual information for suppressing the inappropriate meaning (but, see Friederici et al., in pres, for a similar finding in syntactic disambiguation).

While these results suggest that reading skill has differential effects in lexical and syntactic ambiguity resolution, they are not yet conclusive. In the aforementioned studies a variety of different operationalizations of reading skill were used. Further research is needed to replicate the patterns of individual differences in both areas of language processing within the same subject population.

The second line of evidence comes from neuropsychological research. This evidence falls into two categories (see Friederici, this volume). The first is the well-documented dissociation of lexical, semantic and syntactic processes found in some brain-injured patients (see Caplan, 1992; Linebarger, 1989). In fact, traditional neurolinguistic theories have classified aphasia subtypes according to selective disturbances of one of these areas. In particular, agrammatism has been defined as the selective loss of syntactic knowledge, and numerous patients seem unimpaired in syntactic processing while having severe word finding difficulties. Empirical findings have recently challenged this simplified view, and interactive or resource based theories have been proposed (Bates & Wulfeck, 1989; Miyake, Carpenter & Just, 1995). However, it seems that studies on language processing y brain-injured patients can shed light on the claim that lexical and syntactic processing share the same underlying mechanism.

The second contributio of neurosychology hasbeen the development of methodologies that circumvent the need to draw inferences from behavioral data. As we have seen, some of the traditional measures, suc as reading times, naming, or even eye movement patterns, do not readily enable to separate diferent processes. In contrast, evoked potentials have been used successfully to provide evidence for different brain reactions to lexical and syntactic variables (e.g., Garnsey et al., 1989; Hagoort, Brown & Groothusen, 1993; Münte, Heinze & Mangun, 1993; Neville et al., 1991; Osterhout & Holcomb, 1992; Rösler et al., 1993). There is still considerable debate about the functional relevance of the observed components. In particular, there is much debate about whether the late positivities observed in response to syntactic violations or syntactic preference violations are syntax or even language specific (e.g., Coulson, King & Kutas, 1995; Gunter, Vos & Mulder, 1996). Nevertheless, at this point it is difficult to see how a constraint satisfaction account, in which all processing difficulties are conceptualized by uni-dimensional activation levels, can account for qualitatively different, multi-dimensional ERP components. Finally, with the development of more sophisticated methods for brain imaging, it might soon be possible to directly assess the effects of lexical and syntactic processing on brain activity.

But what about modularity? Empirical psycholinguistics have concentrated on two defining characteristics of a module: automaticity and contextual impenetrability. Particularly the latter criterion has produced mixed results in both word recognition studies and sentence processing studies. The answer to whether sentence context or discourse context influences lexical access or parsing decisions seems to be that it depends on a variety of modulating variables. In fact, many researchers in both areas agree that it has become more fruitful to identify these variables than to focus on the notion of modularity (e.g., Tabossi, 1991). Thus, in order to provide strong evidence for or against modularity it might be necessary to take more seriously some of the other criteria defined by Fodor (1983). Given the recent developments in neuropsychological methods, the criterion of a module being associated with a fixed neural architecture might become a viable candidate in future research.

6.4 Summary and Conclusions

In this chapter we reviewed some recent developments in sentence processing research. This field has been dominated by attempts to test the modularity hypothesis in the domain of language processing. We outlined similarities and differences between word recognition and parsing. While in both areas the empirical results are less than conclusive, we have come closer to an understanding of the human language processing system. The influence of constraint-satisfaction theories has highlighted the various factors contributing to sentence interpretation, and the linguistic materials under study have become more differentiated than in the early days of psycholinguistics. Unfortunately, at this time it seems that this work has posed more questions than provided answers. We can only hope that the accumulation of further empirical results will help to focus and to unify theories of sentence comprehension. Moreover, new methodological developments, in particular the increased use of evoked potentials as a measure of parsing diffculties, is expected to shed light on the architecture of the language processing system.

References

Altmann, G.T.M. & Steedman, M.J. (1988). Interaction with context during human sentence processing. *Cognition, 30,* 191-238.

Altmann, G.T.M., Garnham, A. & Dennis, Y. (1992). Avoiding the garden path: Eye movements in context. *Journal of Memory and Language, 31,* 685-712.

Anderson, J.R. (1976). *Language, memory and thought.* Hillsdale, NJ: Erlbaum.

Balota, D.A. (1990). The role of meaning in word recognition. In D.A. Balota, G.B. Flores d'Arcais & K. Rayner (eds.), *Comprehension Processes in Reading.* Hillsdale, NJ: Lawrence Erlbaum.

Balota, D.A. (1994). Visual word recognition: The journey from features to meaning. In M.A. Gernsbacher (ed.), *Handbook of Psycholinguistics.* San Diego, CA: Academic Press.

Balota, D.A. & Chumbley, J.I. (1984). Are lexical decisions a good measure of lexical access? The role of word frequency in the neglected decision stage. Journal of Experimental Psychology: *Human Perception and Performance, 10,* 340-357.

Bates, E. & Wulfeck, B. (1989). Crosslinguistic studies of aphasia. In B. MacWhinney & E. Bates (eds.), *The crosslinguistic study of sentence processing.* New York: Cambridge University Press.

Bever, T.G. (1970). The cognitive basis for linguistic structures. In J.R. Hayes (ed.), *Cognition and the development of language.* New York: John Wiley and Sons.

Bleasdale, F.A. (1987). Concreteness-dependent associative priming: Separate lexical organization for concrete and abstract words. *Journal of Experimental Psychology: Learning, Memory & Cognition, 13,* 582-594.

Bransford, J.D. & Franks, J.J. (1971). The abstraction of linguistic ideas. *Cognitive Psychology, 2,* 331-350.

Bresnan, J. (1978). A realistic transformational grammar. In M. Halle, J. Bresnan & G. Miller (eds.), *Linguistic Theory and Psychological Reality.* Cambridge, MA: MIT Press.

Bresnan, J. & Kaplan, R.M. (1982). Introduction: Grammars as mental representations of language. In J. Bresnan (ed.), *The mental representation of grammatical relations*. Cambridge, MA: MIT Press.

Britt, M.A. (1994). The interaction of referential ambiguity and argument structure in the parsing of prepositional phrases. *Journal of Memory and Language, 33,* 251-283.

Britt, M.A., Perfetti, C.A., Garrod, S. & Rayner, K. (1992). Parsing in discourse: Context effects and their limits. *Journal of Memory and Language, 31,* 293-314.

Caplan, D. (1992). *Language: Structure, processing and disorders*. Cambridge, MA: MIT Press.

Chomsky, N. (1957). *Syntactic Structures*. The Hague: Mouton.

Chomsky, N. (1965). *Aspects of the Theory of Syntax*. The Hague: Mouton.

Chomsky, N. (1981). *Lectures on Government and Binding*. Dordrecht: Foris.

Clark, H.H. & Clark, E.V. (1977). *The psychology of language: An introduction to psycholinguistics*. New York: Harcourt Brace Jovanovich.

Clifton, C., Speer, S. & Abney, S.P. (1991). Parsing arguments: Phrase structure and argument structure as determinants of initial parsing decisions. *Journal of Memory and Language, 30,* 251-271.

Cohen, G. & Faulkner, C. (1983). Word recognition: Age differences in contextual facilitation effects. *British Journal of Psychology, 74,* 239-251.

Connine, C. , Mullennix, J., Shernoff, E. & Yelens, J. (1990). Word familiarity and frequency in visual and auditory word recognition. *Journal of Experimental Psychology: Learning, Memory & Cognition, 16,* 1084-1096.

Coulson, S., King, J.W. & Kutas, M. (1995). In search of: Is there a syntax-specific ERP component? *Cognitive Neuroscience Society Second Annual Meeting Poster Abstracts, 9*. Davis, CA: Congitive Neuroscience Society.

Crain, S. & Steedman, M.J. (1985). On not being led up the garden-path: The use of context by the psychological parser. In D. Dowty, L. Karttunen & A. Zwicky (eds.), *Natural language parsing*. Cambridge: Cambridge University Press.

Daneman, M. & Carpenter, P.A. (1980). Individual differences in working memory and reading. *Journal of Verbal Learning and Verbal Behavior, 19,* 450-466.

De Jong, G. (1982). An overview of the FRUMP system. In W.G. Lehnert & M.H. Ringle (eds.), *Strategies for natural language parsing*. Hillsdale, NJ: Lawrence Erlbaum Associates.

Duffy, S.A., Morris, R.K. & Rayner, K. (1988). Lexical ambiguity and fixation times in reading. *Journal of Memory and Language, 27,* 429-446.

Evett, L.J. & Humphreys, G.W. (1981). The use of abstract graphemic information in lexical accesss. *Quarterly Journal of Experimental Psychology, 33A,* 325-350.

Ehrlich, S.F. & Rayner, K. (1981). Contextual effects on word perception and eye movements during reading. *Journal of Verbal Learning and Verbal Behavior, 20,* 641-655.

Farrar, W. & Kawamoto, A. (1993). The return of „visiting relatives": Pragmatic effects in sentence processing. *Quarterly Journal of Experimental Psychology, 46A,* 463-487.

Ferreira, F. & Clifton, C. (1986). The independence of syntactic processing. *Journal of Memory and Language, 25,* 348-368.

Ferreira, F. & Henderson, J.M. (1990). The use of verb information in syntactic parsing: A comparison of evidence from eye movements and word-by-word self-paced reading. *Journal of Experimental Psychology: Learning, Memory and Cognition, 16,* 555-568.

Ferstl, E.C. (1994a). The construction-integration model: À framework for studying context effects in sentence processing. In A. Ram & K. Eiselt (eds.), *Proceedings of the Sixteenth Annual Conference of the Cognitive Science Society,* Hillsdale, NJ: Lawrence Erlbaum Associates.

Ferstl, E.C. (1994b). Context effects in syntactic ambiguity resolution: The location of prepositional phrase attachment. In A. Ram & K. Eiselt (eds.), *Proceedings of the Sixteenth Annual Conference of the Cognitive Science Society.* Hillsdale, NJ: Lawrence Erlbaum Associates.

Ferstl, E.C. & Friederici, A.D. (1997). Inter-sentential context effects on parsing: A study using event-related potentials. *Presentation at the 10th Annual CUNY Conference of Sentence Processing.* Santa Monica, CA, März 1997.

Fischler, I. (1985). Word recognition, use of context, and reading skill among deaf college students. *Reading Research Quarterly, 20,* 203-218.

Fodor, J.A. (1983). *Modularity of mind.* Cambridge, MA: MIT Press.

Fodor, J.A. (1987). Modules, frames, fridgeons, sleeping dogs and the music of the spheres. In J.L. Garfield (ed.), *Modularity in knowledge representation and natural-language understanding. The psychology of language: An introduction to psycholinguistics and generative grammar.* New York: McGraw-Hill.

Fodor, J.D. (1988). On modularity in syntactic processing. *Journal of Psycholinguistic Research, 17,* 125-168.

Fodor, J.D., Ni, W., Crain, S. & Shankweiler, D. (1996). Tasks and timing in the perception of linguistic anomaly. *Journal of Psycholinguistic Research, 25,* 25-57.

Ford, M. (1989). Parsing complexity and a theory of parsing. In G.N. Carlson & M.K. Tanenhaus (eds.), *Linguistic Structure in Language Processing*. Dordrecht: Kluwer Academic.

Ford, M., Bresnan, J. & Kaplan, R.M. (1982). A competence-based theory of syntactic closure. In J. Bresnan (ed.), *The mental representation of grammatical relations*. Cambridge, MA: MIT Press.

Forster, K.I. (1976). Accessing the mental lexicon. In R.J. Wales & E.W. Walker (eds.), *New approaches to language mechanisms*. Amsterdam: North Holland.

Forster, K.I. (1979). Levels of processing and the structure of the language processor. In W.E. Cooper & E.C.T. Walker (eds.), *Sentence processing: Psycholinguistic studies presented to Merrill Garrett*. Hillsdale, NJ: Erlbaum.

Forster, K.I. (1994). Computational modeling and elementary process analysis in visual word recognition. *Journal of Experimental Psychology: Human Perception and Performance, 20*, 1292-1310.

Forster, K.I. & Chambers, S.M. (1973). Lexical access and naming time. *Journal of Verbal Learning and Verbal Behavior, 12*, 627-635.

Foss, D.J. (1982). A discourse on semantic priming. *Cognitive Psychology, 14*, 590-607.

Frazier, L. (1979). *On comprehending sentences: Syntactic parsing strategies*. Bloomington: Indiana University Linguistics Club.

Frazier, L. (1987). Theories of sentence processing. In J.L. Garfield (ed.), *Modularity in knowledge representation and natural-language understanding*. Cambridge, MA: MIT Press.

Frazier, L. (1995). Constraint satisfaction as a theory of sentence processing. *Journal of Psycholinguistic Research, 24*, 437-468.

Frazier, L. & Clifton, C. (1996). *Construal*. Cambridge, MA: MIT Press.

Frazier, L. & Fodor, J.D. (1978). The sausage machine: A new two-stage parsing model. *Cognition, 6*, 291-325.

Frazier, L. & Rayner, K. (1982). Making and correcting errors during sentence comprehension: Eye movements in the analysis of structurally ambiguous sentences. *Cognitive Psychology, 14*, 178-210.

Frazier, L. & Rayner, K. (1987). Resolution of syntactic category ambiguities: Eye movements in parsing lexically ambiguous sentences. *Journal of Memory and Language, 26*, 505-526.

Friederici, A.D., Steinhauer, K., Mecklinger, A. & Meyer, M. (in press). Working memory constraints on syntactic ambiguity resolution as revealed by electrical brain responses. *Biological Psychology*.

Garnsey, S.M., Pearlmutter, N.J., Myers, E. & Lotocky, M.A. (1997). The contributions of verb bias and plausibility to the comprehension of temporarily ambiguous sentences. *Journal of Memory and Language, 37,* 58-93.

Garnsey, S.M., Tanenhaus, M.K. & Chapman, R.M. (1989). Evoked potentials and the study of sentence comprehension. *Journal of Psycholinguistic Research, 18,* 51-60.

Gernsbacher, M.A. (1984). Resolving 20 years of inconsistent interactions between lexical familiarity and orthography, concreteness and polysemy. *Journal of Experimental Psychology: General, 113,* 256-280.

Gernsbacher, M.A., Varner, K.R. & Faust, M. (1990). Investigating differences in general comprehension skill. *Journal of Experimental Psychology: Learning, Memory and Cognition, 16,* 430-445.

Gibson, E., Schütze, C.T. & Salomon, A. (1996). The relationship between the frequency and the processing complexity of linguistic structure. *Journal of Psycholinguistic Research, 25,* 59-92.

Goodman, G.O., McClelland, J.L. & Gibbs, R.W. (1981). The role of syntactic context in word recognition. *Memory & Cognition, 9,* 580-586.

Gunter, T.C., Stowe, L.A. & Mulder, G. (1997). When syntax meets semantics. *Psychophysiology, 34,* 660-676.

Hagoort, P., Brown, C. & Grothusen, J. (1993). The syntactic positive shift as an ERP- measure of syntactic processing. *Language and Cognitive Processes, 8,* 439-483.

Healy, A.F. (1976). Detection errors on the word the: Evidence for reading units larger than letters. *Journal of Experimental Psychology: Human Perception and Performance, 2,* 235-242.

Holmes, V.M., Stowe, L. & Cupples, L. (1989). Lexical expectations in parsing complement-verb sentences. *Journal of Memory and Language, 28,* 668-689.

Inhoff, A.W. & Rayner, K. (1986). Parafoveal word processing during eye fixations in reading: Effects of word frequency. *Perception & Psychophysics, 34,* 49-57.

Johnston, J.C. & McClelland, J.L. (1974). Perception of letters in words: Seek not and ye shall find. *Science, 184,* 1192-1194.

Just, M.A. & Carpenter, P.A. (1992). A capacity theory of comprehension: Individual differences in working memory. *Psychological Review, 99,* 122-149.

Kellas, G., Paul, S.T., Martin, M. & Simpson, G.B. (1991). Contextual feature activation and meaning access. In G.B. Simpson (ed.), *Understanding word and sentence.* Amsterdam: North-Holland.

Kimball, J. (1973). Seven principles of surface structure parsing in natural language. *Cognition, 2,* 15-47.

King, J. & Just, M.A. (1991). Individual differences in syntactic processing: The role of working memory. *Journal of Memory and Language, 30,* 580-602.

Kintsch, W. (1988). The role of knowledge in discourse comprehension: A construction-integration model. *Psychological Review, 95,* 163-182.

Kintsch, W. & Mross, E.F. (1985). Context effects in word identification. *Journal of Memory and Language, 24,* 336-349.

Kutas, M. & Hillyard, S.A. (1984). Brain potentials during reading reflect word expectancy and semantic association. *Nature, 307,* 161-163.

Kutas, M. & van Petten, C. (1988). Event-related brain potential studies of language. In P.K. Ackles, J.R. Jennings & M.G.H. Coles (eds.), *Advances in psychophysiology (Vol. 3).* Greenwich, CT: JAI Press.

Linebarger, M.C. (1989). Neuropsychological evidence for linguistic modularity. In G.N. Carlson & M.K. Tanenhaus (eds.), *Linguistic structure in language processing.* Dordrecht: Kluwer Academic.

MacDonald, M.C. (1993). The interaction of lexical and syntactic ambiguity. *Journal of Memory and Language, 32,* 692-715.

MacDonald, M.C. (1994). Probabilistic constraints and syntactic ambiguity resolution. *Language and Cognitive Processes, 4,* 35-56.

MacDonald, M.C., Just, M.A. & Carpenter, P.A. (1992). Working memory constraints on the processing of syntactic ambiguity. *Cognitive Psychology, 24,* 56-98.

MacDonald, M.C., Pearlmutter, N.J. & Seidenberg, M.S. (1994). The lexical nature of syntactic ambiguity resolution. *Psychological Review, 101,* 676-703.

MacWhinney, B. & E. Bates (eds.) (1989). *The crosslinguistic study of sentence processing.* New York: Cambridge University Press.

Marslen-Wilson, W.D. (1975). Sentence perception as an interactive parallel process. *Science, 189,* 226-228.

Marslen-Wilson, W.D., Brown, C. & Tyler, L.K. (1988). Lexical representations in language comprehension. *Language and Cognitive Processes, 3,* 1-16.

McClelland, J.L. (1987). The case for interactionism in language processing. In M. Coltheart (ed.), *Attention and Performance XII: The psychology of reading.* Hillsdale, NJ: Lawrence Erlbaum Associates.

McClelland, J.L. & Rumelhart, D.E. (1981). An interactive activation model of context effects in letter perception: Part 1. An account of basic findings. *Psychological Review, 86,* 287-330.

McElree, B. (1993). The locus of lexical preference effects in sentence comprehension: A time-course analysis. *Journal of Memory and Language, 32,* 536-571.

McElree, B. & Griffith, T. (1995). Syntactic and thematic processing in sentence comprehension: Evidence for a temporal dissociation. *Journal of Experimental Psychology: Learning, Memory and Cognition, 21,* 134-157.

Mecklinger, A., Schriefers, H., Steinhauer, K. & Friederici, A.D. (1995). Processing relative clauses varying on syntactic and semantic dimensions: An analysis with event-related potentials. *Memory & Cognition, 23,* 477-494.

Meyer, D.E. & Schvaneveldt, R.W. (1971). Facilitation in recognizing words: Evidence of a dependence upon retrieval operations. *Journal of Experimental Psychology, 90,* 227-234.

Meyer, D.E., Schvaneveldt, R.W. & Ruddy, M.G. (1974). Functions of graphemic and phonemic codes in visual word recognition. *Memory & Cognition, 2,* 309-321.

Miller, G.A. (1962). Some psychological studies of grammar. *American Psychologist, 17,* 748-762.

Miller, G. & Isard, S. (1963). Some perceptual consequences of linguistic rules. *Journal of Verbal Learning and Verbal Behavior, 2,* 217-228.

Mitchell, D.C. (1989). Verb-guidance and other lexical effects in parsing. *Language and Cognitive Processes, 4,* 123-154.

Mitchell, D.C. (1994). Sentence parsing. In M.A. Gernsbacher (ed.), *Handbook of Psycholinguistics.* San Diego, CA: Academic Press.

Mitchell, D.C., Corley, M.M.B. & Garnham, A. (1992). Effects of context in human sentence parsing: Evidence against a discourse-based proposal mechanism. *Journal of Experimental Psychology: Learning, Memory and Cognition, 18,* 69-88.

Miyake, A., Carpenter, P.A. & Just, M.A. (1995). Reduced resources and specific impairments in normal and aphasic sentence comprehension. *Cognitive Neuropsychology, 12,* 651-679.

Morton, J. (1969). Interaction of information in word recognition. *Psychological Review, 76,* 165-178.

Münte, T.F., Heinze, H.J. & Mangun, G.R. (1993). Dissociation of brain activity related to syntactic and semantic aspects of language. *Journal of Cognitive Neuroscience, 5,* 335-344.

Murray, W.S. & Liversedge, S.P. (1994). Referential context effects on syntactic processing. In C. Clifton, L. Frazier & K. Rayner, (eds.), *Perspectives on Sentence Processing.* Hillsdale, NJ: Erlbaum.

Neely, J.H., Keefe, D.E. & Ross, K.L. (1989). Semantic priming in the lexical decision task: Role of prospective prime-generated expectancies and retrospective semantic matching. *Journal of Experimental Psychology: Learning, Memory and Cognition, 15,* 1003-1019.

Neville, H.J., Nicol, J., Barss, A., Forster, K. & Garrett, M. (1991). Syntactically based sentence processing classes: Evidence from event-related potentials. *Journal of Cognitive Neuroscience, 3,* 155-170.

Ni, W., Crain, S. & Shankweiler, D. (1996). Sidestepping garden paths: Assessing the contributions of syntax, semantics and plausibility in resolving ambiguities. *Language and Cognitive Processes, 11,* 283-334.

Norris, D. (1990). Connectionism: A case for modularity. In D.A. Balota, G.B. Flores d'Arcais & K. Rayner (eds.), *Comprehension Processes in Reading.* Hillsdale, NJ: Lawrence Erlbaum.

Onifer, W. & Swinney, D.A. (1981). Accessing lexical ambiguity during sentence comprehension: Effects of frequency of meaning and contextual bias. *Memory & Cognition, 9,* 225-236.

Osterhout, L. & Holcomb, P.J. (1992). Event-related brain potentials elicited by syntactic anomaly. *Journal of Memory and Language, 31,* 785-806.

Osterhout, L., Holcomb, P.J. & Swinney, D. (1994). Brain potentials elicited by garden path sentences: Evidence of the application of verb information during parsing. *Journal of Experimental Psychology: Learning, Memory and Cognition, 20,* 786-803.

Pearlmutter, N.J. & MacDonald, M.C. (1995). Individual differences and probabilistic constraints in syntactic ambiguity resolution. *Journal of Memory and Language, 34,* 521-542.

Perfetti, C.A. (1990). The cooperative language processors: Semantic influences in an autonomous syntax. In D.A. Balota, G.B. Flores d'Arcais & K. Rayner (eds.), *Comprehension Processes in Reading.* Hillsdale, NJ: Lawrence Erlbaum.

Posner, M.I. & Snyder, C.R.R. (1975). Attention and cognitive control. In R. Solso (ed.), *Information processing and cognition: The Loyola symposium.* Hillsdale, NJ: Erlbaum.

Rayner, K. & Duffy, S.A. (1986). Lexical complexity and fixation times in reading: Effects of word frequency, verb complexity and lexical ambiguity. *Memory & Cognition, 12,* 191-201.

Rayner, K., Carlson, M. & Frazier, L. (1983). The interaction of syntax and semantics during sentence processing: Eye movements in the analysis of semantically biased sentences. *Journal of Verbal Learning and Verbal Behavior, 22,* 358-374.

Rayner, K. & Frazier, L. (1989). Selection mechanisms in reading lexically ambiguous words. *Journal of Experimental Psychology: Learning, Memory and Cognition, 15,* 779-790.

Rayner, K., Garrod, S. & Perfetti, C.A. (1992). Discourse influences during parsing are delayed. *Cognition, 45,* 109-139.

Rayner, K., Sereno, S.C., Morris, R.K., Schmauder, A.R. & Clifton, C. (1989). Eye movements and on-line language comprehension processes. *Language and Cognitive Processes, 4,* 21-50.

Reicher, G.M. (1969). Perceptual recognition as a function of meaningfulness of stimulus material. *Journal of Experimental Psychology, 81,* 24-280.

Riesbeck, C. & Schank, R. (1978). Comprehension by computer: Expectation-based analysis of sentences in context. In W.J.M. Levelt & G.B. Flores d'Arcais (eds.), *Studies in the perception of language.* New York: Wiley.

Rösler, F., Friederici, A.D., Pütz, P. & Hahne, A. (1993). Event-related brain potentials while encountering semantic and syntactic constraint violations. *Journal of Cognitive Neuroscience, 5,* 345-362.

Schreuder, R., Flores d'Arcais, G.B. & Glazenborg, G. (1984). Effects of perceptual and conceptual similarity in semantic priming. *Psychological Research, 45,* 339-354.

Schriefers, H., Friederici, A.D. & Kühn, K. (1995). The processing of locally ambiguous relative clauses in German. *Journal of Memory and Language, 34,* 499-520.

Schwanenflugel, P.J. & Shoben, E.J. (1985). The influence of sentence constraint on the scope of faciliation for upcoming words. *Journal of Memory and Language, 24,* 232-252.

Schwanenflugel, P.J., Harnishfeger, K.K. & Stowe, R.W. (1988). Context availability and lexical decisions for abstract and concrete words. *Journal of Memory and Language, 27,* 499-520.

Schwanenflugel, P.J. (1991). Contextual constraint and lexical processing. In G.B. Simpson (ed.), *Understanding word and sentence.* Amsterdam: North-Holland.

Seidenberg, M.S. (1990). Lexical access: Another theoretical soupstone? In D.A. Balota, G.B. Flores d'Arcais & K. Rayner (eds.), *Comprehension Processes in Reading.* Hillsdale, NJ: Lawrence Erlbaum.

Seidenberg, M.S. (1995). Visual word recognition: An overview. In J.L. Miller & P.D. Eimas (eds.), *Speech, Language and Communication.* San Diego, CA: Academic Press.

Seidenberg, M.S. & McClelland, J.L. (1989). A distributed, developmental model of visual word recognition and naming. *Psychological Review, 96,* 523-568.

Seidenberg, M.S., Tanenhaus, M.K., Leiman, J.M. & Bienkowski, M. (1982). Automatic access of the meanings of ambiguous words in context: Some limitations of knowledge-based processing. *Cognitive Psychology, 14,* 489-537.

Seidenberg, M.S., Waters, G.S., Sanders, M. & Langer, P. (1984). Pre- and post-lexical loci of contextual effects on word recognition. *Memory & Cognition, 12,* 315-328.

Sereno, J.A. (1991). Graphemic, associative and syntactic priming effects at a brief stimulus onset asynchrony in lexical decision and naming. *Journal of Experimental Psychology: Learning, Memory and Cognition, 17,* 459-477.

Simpson, G.B. (1994). Context and the processing of ambiguous words. In M.A. Gernsbacher (ed.), *Handbook of Psycholinguistics.* San Diego, CA: Academic Press.

Smolensky, P. (1988). On the proper treatment of connectionism. *Behavioral and Brain Sciences, 11,* 1-74.

Spivey-Knowlton, M. & Sedivy, J. (1995). Parsing attachment ambiguities with multiple constraints. *Cognition, 55,* 227-267.

Spivey-Knowlton, M., Trueswell, J. & Tanenhaus, M.K. (1993). Context effects in syntactic ambiguity resolution: Discourse and semantic influences in parsing reduced relative clauses. *Canadian Journal of Experimental Psychology, 37,* 276-309.

Stanovich, K.E. & West, R.F. (1983). On priming by sentence context. *Journal of Experimental Psychology: General, 112,* 1-36.

Stowe, L.A. (1989). Thematic structures and sentence comprehension. In G.N. Carlson & M.K. Tanenhaus (eds.), *Linguistic structure in language processing.* Dordrecht: Kluwer Academic.

Swinney, D.A. (1979). Lexical access during sentence comprehension: (Re)consideration of context effects. *Journal of Verbal Learning and Verbal Behavior, 18,* 645-659.

Tabossi, P. (1988). Accessing lexical ambiguity in different types of sentential context. *Journal of Memory and Language, 27,* 324-340.

Tabossi, P. (1991). Understanding words in context. In G.B. Simpson (ed.), *Understanding word and sentence.* Amsterdam: North-Holland.

Tabossi, P. & Zardon, F. (1993). Processing ambiguous words in context. *Journal of Memory and Language, 32,* 359-372.

Tabossi, P., Colombo, L. & Job, R. (1987). Accessing lexical ambiguity: Effects of context and dominance. *Psychological Research, 49,* 161-167.

Tanenhaus, M.K. & Trueswell, J.C. (1995). Sentence comprehension. In J.L. Miller & P.D. Eimas (eds.), *Speech, Language and Communication.* San Diego, CA: Academic Press.

Tanenhaus, M.K., Dell, G.S. & Carlson, G. (1987). Context effects and lexical processing: A connectionist approach to modularity. In J.L. Garfield (ed.), *Modularity in knowledge representation and natural language understanding.* Cambridge, MA: MIT.

Tanenhaus, M.K., Leiman, J.M & Seidenberg, M.S. (1979). Evidence for multiple stages in the processing of ambiguous words in syntactic contexts. *Journal of Verbal Learning and Verbal Behavior, 18,* 427-440.

Taraban, R. & McClelland, J.L. (1988). Constituent attachment and thematic role assignment in sentence processing: Influences of context-based expectations. *Journal of Memory and Language, 27,* 597-632.

Till, R.E., Mross, E.F. & Kintsch, W. (1988). Time course of priming for associate and inference words in a discourse context. *Memory and Cognition, 16,* 283-298.

Trueswell, J.C. & Tanenhaus, M.K. (1991). Tense, temporal context and syntactic ambiguity resolution. *Language and Cognitive Processes, 6,* 303-338.

Trueswell, J.C. & Tanenhaus, M.K. (1994). Towards a constraint-based lexicalist approach to syntactic ambiguity resolution. In C. Clifton, L. Frazier & K. Rayner (eds.), *Perspectives on sentence processing.* Hillsdale, NJ: Erlbaum.

Trueswell, J.C., Tanenhaus, M.K. & Garnsey, S.M. (1994). Semantic influences on parsing: Use of thematic role information in syntactic disambiguation. *Journal of Memory and Language, 33,* 285-318.

Trueswell, J.C., Tanenhaus, M.K. & Kellows, C. (1993). Verb-specific constraints in sentence processing: Separating effects of lexical preference from garden-paths. *Journal of Experimental Psychology: Learning, Memory and Cognition, 19,* 528-553.

Tyler, L.K. & Marslen-Wilson, W.M (1977). The on-line effects of semantic context on syntactic processing. *Journal of Verbal Learning and Verbal Behavior, 16,* 683-692.

van Petten, C. & Kutas, M. (1987). Ambiguous words in context: An event-related potential analysis of the time course of meaning activation. *Journal of Memory and Language, 26,* 188-208.

Waltz, D.L. & Pollack, J.B. (1985). Massively parallel parsing: A strongly interactive model of natural language interpretation. *Cognitive Science, 9,* 51-74.

West, R.F. & Stanovich, K.E. (1982). Source of inhibition in experiments on the effect of sentence context on word recognition. *Journal of Experimental Psychology: Learning, Memory & Cognition, 8,* 395-399.

West, R.F. & Stanovich, K.E. (1986). Robust effects of syntactic structure on visual word processing. *Memory & Cognition, 14,* 104-112.

Wheeler, D.D. (1970). Processes in word recognition. *Cognitive Psychology, 1,* 59-85.

Williams, J.N. (1988). Constraints upon semantic activation during sentence comprehension. *Language and Cognitive Processes, 3,* 165-206.

Chapter 7

Sentence Parsing

Gerard Kempen

7.1 Introduction

The printed words you are reading now are the perceptible cornerstones of an otherwise invisible grammatical edifice that is automatically reconstructed in your mind. According to many psycholinguists, comprehending spoken, written or signed sentences involves building grammatical structures. This cognitive activity, usually called syntactic analysis or sentence parsing, includes assigning a word class (part-of-speech) to individual words, combining them into word groups or 'phrases', and establishing syntactic relationships between word groups. All these parsing decisions should harmonize not only with rules of grammar but also with the message intended by speaker, writer or signer. Although usually proceeding effortlessly and automatically, the parsing process may slow down, err, or even break down completely when the sentence is very long or contains difficult grammatical constructions. Characterizing the exact nature of such problems and explaining them in terms of underlying cognitive mechanisms are important objectives of the subfield of psycholinguistics called Human Sentence Processing (HSP).

Developing a working model of sentence parsing is impossible without adopting a grammatical formalism and the structure building operations specified in it. Nevertheless, a survey of the psycholinguistic parsing literature need not spell out these operations *in extenso* because the behaviorally important processing issues can be stated without a great deal of linguistic jargon.

Section 7.2 outlines the cognitive architecture responsible for sentence comprehension; various modules are distinguished, and the control structure of the sentence parser is characterized. Section 7.3 presents an overview of the key factors that have been shown to affect the parser's functioning and provide clues to its inner workings. Section 7.4 addresses two cross-linguistic issues that have stimulated a great deal of empirical work. Finally, Section 7.5 offers some conclusions and directions for future research.

For details concerning experimental methodology, which are beyond the scope of this chapter, I refer to the psycholinguistic handbook edited by Gernsbacher (1994). Friederici's chapter in this volume deals with electrophysiological and brain-imaging methods in particular.

7.2 Sentence Parsing and Sentence Comprehension

The sentence comprehension task is usually dissected into subtasks that correspond to linguistic levels of description:

- auditory and visual word recognition (phonological/orthographic level; see chapters by Zwitserlood, by Frauenfelder & Floccia, by Cutler, by Zwitserlood, all this volume)
- lexical and morphological processes (morphological level; see chapters by Schriefers, by Engelkamp & Rummer and by Ferstl & Flores d'Arcais, all in this volume)
- parsing (syntactic level; see chapter by Ferstl & Flores d'Arcais and this chapter, both this volume)
- conceptual interpretation (semantic level; see chapter by Engelkamp & Rummer, in this volume for conceptual processes at the lexical level)
- referential processes (discourse or pragmatic level; see chapter by Vonk & Noordman, this volume).

As evidenced by an increasing body of empirical data, the cognitive modules that take care of these subtasks operate in parallel rather than sequentially, and exchange information in bottom-up and top-down directions. These interactions usually promote efficiency and accuracy but may be detrimental at times, namely, when different modules happen to compute and distribute conflicting pieces of information. The latter is exemplified by sentences that lead the reader or listener up the garden-path, such as the classic example *The horse raced past barn fell*. One of the factors contributing to the 'garden-path' character of this sentence is lexical in nature, namely, the rare usage of *raced* as past-participle in passive voice, causing a bias in favor of *raced* interpreted—incorrectly—as a past-tense main verb. A conceptual factor conspiring against the past-participle reading of *raced* is the information that horses make particularly good 'agents' of racing events. The garden-path character of this sentence can probably be alleviated by embedding it in a discourse that introduces two or more horses, only one of which being chased past a shed. Such a context promotes the interpretation of *raced past the barn* as a modifier serving to single out one of the story characters—a referential factor. Numerous experimental studies can be cited in support of the sensitivity of the sentence parser to lexical, conceptual, and referential factors. This example illustrates a key feature of the control structure of the human sentence parser: *interactivity*. Interactive parsers are the counterparts of 'autonomous' parsers, which at first rely on syntactic and word-class information alone, and only subsequently allow their initial decisions to be modified in view of detailed lexical, conceptual and referential information. The psychological reality of an autonomous syntactic parsing stage is extensively debated in the literature (e.g., see Frazier & Clifton,

1996; Tanenhaus & Trueswell, 1995; see also Mitchell, 1994; Garrod & Sanford, 1994; and Section 7.3.1 below).

The second central feature of the control structure of human parsing is *incrementality*. Parsing a sentence does not wait for an end-of-sentence signal but starts immediately upon recognition of the first input word. From there, the parser 'consumes' every new input word without unnecessary delay, exploiting extrasyntactic information as much as possible (Marslen-Wilson, 1975). The syntactic structure computed for a sentence therefore grows basically from left to right in a word-by-word fashion—in contrast with clause-by-clause parsing schedules that many psycholinguists adhered to in the sixties, in the early days of modern psycholinguistics (see the surveys by Fodor, Bever & Garrett, 1974, and Levelt, 1978).

The third feature is *bounded parallelism*. Natural languages tend to have a large number of vocabulary items whose word-class membership is indeterminate. Moreover, their grammars often allow a given string of words to be combined into several different syntactic configurations. (A wide-spread type of 'syntactic ambiguities' is called 'attachment ambiguity'; the classic example is *The man saw the woman with the binoculars*, where the prepositional phrase can be attached as a modifier to *saw* or *woman*.) In sentential contexts, many ambiguities are ultimately resolved thanks to the filtering effect of grammatical constraints. In actual practice, though, a considerable proportion of sentences is left with multiple word-class or syntactic ambiguities. How does the sentence parser deal with this problem? Three theoretical alleys have been explored in the literature: (1) serial parsing, (2) parallel parsing, and (3) minimal-commitment parsing. (For a detailed discussion of the theoretical and empirical merits of these parsing models, see Mitchell, 1994; computational versions are reviewed by Kempen, 1996.)

A *serial* parser commits itself to one of the available options as soon as a choice point presents itself; if, further down the sentence, a problem is encountered, the parser backtracks to an earlier choice point, selects another option from the available set, and proceeds from there. This strategy economizes working memory capacity because at no point in time is there a need to store more than one syntactic structure. However, this advantage entails the risk of delays due to frequent backtracking and structure revision operations ('reanalysis'). A *parallel* parser refuses to make a selection from among the alternative options offered at a choice point and computes several different syntactic configurations, one for each of the options. This parallel strategy taxes working memory capacity but obviates time consuming structure revisions. A *minimal-commitment* parser attempts to combine the best of both worlds. It computes only a single syntactic configuration at any choice point; however, like non-deterministic parsers, it avoids backtracking and reanalysis. To this purpose it resorts to a wait-and-see strategy: any decision or computation that runs the risk of having to be undone, is postponed in anticipation of disambiguating information downstream. Upon arrival of such information it catches up on any outstanding work.

The well-attested phenomena of garden-path sentences and revisions reveal the human parser's liability to premature decisions and rule out minimal commitment as a viable model of human sentence parsing[1]. This also applies to extreme versions of parallel parsing models, which compute and store *all* syntactic configurations compatible with the current input string and therefore never need to retract any decisions. However, a weak version of parallelism cannot be ruled out—a parser that, at some or all choice points, explores more than one alternative reading and carries these for at least a brief period of time. This strategy entails a certain risk of backtracking—although smaller than in case of a strictly serial model—but reduces the probability of overtaxing the parser's working memory (in comparison with a fully parallel model). MacDonald, Just & Carpenter (1992) provide experimental evidence in support of a limited form of parallelism in parsing. For the time being I conclude that *bounded parallelism* is best viewed as the human parser's response to word-class and syntactic ambiguity[2].

Characterized in folkpsychological parlance, the sentence parser is an eager beaver ('incrementality'), sensitive to multifarious impressions ('interactivity') but also somewhat impetuous ('bounded parallelism', reanalysis)—indeed, it's only human!

7.3 Phenomena and Explanations

In this Section I present an overview of three groups of empirical phenomena that have been studied extensively. The explanations substantiate the control structure of the sentence parser as outlined in the previous Section and add further details.

7.3.1 Syntactic Complexity and Processing Overload

One of the earliest parsing phenomena to draw systematic psycholinguistic attention was the remarkable difference in processing complexity between center-embedded clauses and their right-branching counterparts (e.g., Miller & Isard, 1964). Single embeddings of both types present no particular problems—compare (1a) and (1b)—, nor do doubly-embedded right-branching clauses (2a). But doubly center-embedded clauses tend to become incomprehensible (2b), unless conceptual factors help to sort out which roles are assigned to which referents (3).

> *(1a) The intern who was supervised by the nurse had bothered the administrator.*
> *(1b) The nurse supervised the intern who had bothered the administrator.*

---

[1] These phenomena are not incompatible with the presence of 'deterministic' components *within* the parser—components that never retract their initial decisions, not even in case of garden-path sentences that force drastic reanalysis. Marcus (1980) and Gorrell (1995) have proposed minimal-commitment models for parsing sentences that do not give rise to conscious garden-path effects.

[2] A probabilistic model of bounded-parallel parsing was recently proposed by Jurafsky, 1996.

(2a)   *The intern who the nurse supervised had bothered the administrator who*
         lost the medical reports. (Gibson, 1997)
(2b)   *The administrator who the intern who the nurse supervised had bothered*
         lost the medical reports.
(3)   *The vase that the maid that the agency hired dropped on the floor broke into*
         a hundred pieces. (Stolz, 1967)

A third type of embedded clauses, so-called cross-serial dependencies, has been studied by Bach, Brown & Marslen-Wilson (1986). An example from Dutch is given in (4a). The German translation equivalent (4b) contains a doubly center-embedded structure, whereas the English counterpart is right-branching. Bach et al. (1986) presented sentences like (4a) and (4b) to native speakers of Dutch and German, respectively, and obtained various measures of comprehensibility. The cross-serial structures turned out to be easier than the center-embeddings.

(4a)   *Jeanine heeft de mannen Hans de   paarden helpen leren voeren.*
         Joanna has   the men   Hans the horses   help·   teach feed
(4b)   *Johanna hat die Männer Hans die Pferde füttern lehren helfen.*
                                                feed   teach   help
(4c)   *Joanna (has) helped the men teach Hans to feed the horses.*

Very recently, Gibson (1997) has proposed a complexity metric that is in remarkably good agreement with processing loads as measured for a wide range of sentence structures. The metric follows from his Syntactic Prediction Locality Theory (SPLT), which assumes a limited pool of computational resources that is shared by two kinds of processes[3]:

- integrating new input into the syntactic and referential (discourse) structures that have already been built for earlier parts of the current input string, and
- storing syntactic predictions, that is, syntactic categories that are needed to complete the current input string as a grammatical sentence.

The 'cost' associated with both types of computations increase monotonically over time. More precisely, the cost is incremented each time a new discourse referent is introduced. Only NPs (objects) and verbs of VPs (events) count as referents. Therefore, when many discourse referents intervene between a new to-be-integrated input word (the source) and an older element (the target), the cost is high. Similarly, the memory cost of retaining the syntactic category of a prediction depends on the number of novel discourse referents intervening between the input word that originally gave rise to the prediction, and the current input word.

---

[3]   Just & Carpenter (1992) were the first to propose a parser model (CC-READER) where processing and storage activities draw from the same, limited source of working memory capacity.

(5a)   The reporter who the senator attacked admitted the error.
(5b)   The reporter who attacked the senator admitted the error.
(5c)   De reporter die de senator aanviel gaf de fout toe.

Consider the examples in (5a) and (5b), containing an object and subject relative clause, respectively. The integration cost profiles of for these sentences are similar, except at the position of the embedded verbs *(attacked)*. Simplifying somewhat, integration of this verb in case of (5a) implies attaching to it a subject *(the senator)* and an object *(who)*. In (5b), only the subject *(who)* needs to be attached; moreover, the latter action is less costly than establishing the link between *who* and *attacked* in (5a), where a new referent *(the senator)* intervenes. Likewise, (5a) taxes the storage capacity more heavily than (5b) does: the important difference is the prediction, launched by the relative pronoun *who*, of an embedded verb. This prediction has to be carried over intervening discourse referent *the senator* in case of (5a), but not (5b). Various experiments have indeed shown that object relatives are somewhat harder to understand than subject relatives.

Surprisingly, this empirical finding applies not only to English but to German and Dutch, although in both latter languages object and subject relatives have the same word order (for a detailed survey, see Kaan, 1997). Sentence (5c), for instance, the translation equivalent of both (5a) and (5b), is preferably interpreted as (5b). Gibson accounts for this bias by making the additional assumption that, at a point of ambiguity, the parser opts for storage economy and selects the simplest set of predictions. In case, of (5c), the interpretation of relative pronoun *die (who)* as the object, entails the prediction of both an embedded verb and a subject, whereas the subject reading of *die* only implies the prediction of a verb[4].

The SPLT model predicts substantial processing load differences between doubly center-embedded and right-branching clauses (2a/b). Gibson's 1997 paper gives detailed computations for these cases, for the contrast between (4a) and (4b), and for quite a few other constructions.

(6a)   The Republicans who the senator who I voted for chastised were trying to cut all benefits for veterans.
(6b)   The Republicans who the senator who Ann/she/the citizens voted for chastised were trying to cut all benefits for veterans.

---

[4]   However, alternative explanations of the preference for subject interpretation of ambiguous relative clauses cannot be ruled out as yet. The effect could originate, not from complexity *per se*, but from a 'configurational bias' to take the first NP of a clause to be the grammatical subject (see the list of processing strategies in Section 7.3.2 below), and/or from a conceptual bias to interpret the (animate) referent of the first NP as the thematic agent.

Before leaving SPLT , I should point out Gibson's empirical motive for measuring distance in terms of *new discourse referents* denoted by NPs and VPs rather than the NPs and VPs themselves. It has been observed in various studies that double center-embeddings (in a null context) tend to become somewhat easier when the most deeply embedded subject is replaced by an indexical pronoun (e.g., *you* or *I*). Gibson verified this in an as yet unpublished experiment with sentences such as (6a), which were rated as easier understandable than their counterparts (6b) with either a short name (*Ann*), a third-person pronoun (*she*) or a full NP (*the citizens*) substituting for *I*. The argument is that referents of indexical pronouns—namely, the speaker and the hearer—are always included in the discourse model and can be mentioned without processing cost.

7.3.2   Parsing Preferences and Garden-Path Sentences

The mechanisms underlying the interpretation of structural ambiguities have occupied a prominent position on the psycholinguistic research agenda ever since Bever's seminal 1970 paper. The stage for both theory formation and experimentation was set in influential papers by Kimball (1973) and Frazier & Fodor (1978). They proposed a set of perceptual strategies ('parsing principles') responsible for guiding the human sentence parser towards its initial choices, in particular, towards determining how to integrate new input into the current syntactic configuration. These syntax-oriented perceptual strategies together with further proposals about a limited-capacity processing architecture, were assumed to constitute the first stage of sentence comprehension. Extrasyntactic (conceptual, discourse, context) information could exert its influence only in a second stage, possibly leading to reanalysis of the input and revision of earlier choices. Over the past ten years, this two-stage model has been seriously challenged by experimental data, collected by means of increasingly refined and sensitive techniques, indicating that the parser is affected by extrasyntactic information immediately upon receiving new syntactic input. The most likely conclusion from this work is that, even if a short purely syntactic initial parsing stage exists, it is relatively inconsequential. A more fruitful research strategy is predicated on the assumption that syntactic and non-syntactic factors can operate concurrently and determine parsing preferences in mutual interaction, with garden-paths and reanalysis as possible outcomes (cf., McClelland, 1987; MacDonald, Pearlmutter & Seidenberg, 1994; Tanenhaus & Trueswell, 1995).

(7a)   The horse raced past the barn fell. (Bever, 1970)

(7b)   The boat floated down the river sank.

(7c)   The land mine buried in the sand exploded.

(7d)   The cop arrested by the detective was guilty of taking bribes. (McRae et al., 1997)

(7e)   The crook arrested by the detective was guilty of taking bribes.

The famous Main Clause versus Reduced Relative Clause (MC/RRC) ambiguity exemplified in (7) serves to illustrate the kinds of syntactic and extrasyntactic factors that are thought to steer the course of the sentence parsing process. The first item on the list below represents an elaborate system of syntactic processing strategies worked out by Frazier and her associates (see Frazier & Fodor, 1978; Frazier & Clifton, 1996). Items 2 through 5 have recently been used in a model simulation study by McRae, Spivey-Knowlton & Tanenhaus, (in press). I refer to these publications for discussions of, and pointers to, the supporting experimental literature.

1. *Parsing principles.* One of the key processing strategies proposed by Frazier is called Minimal Attachment. While attempting to integrate new input into the current syntactic tree, the processor initially prefers the attachment with the smallest number of syntactic nodes. Within the grammatical formalism underlying Frazier's model, this is the analysis where the ambiguous verb (*raced, floated*) is finite verb in the main clause. Another important principle is Late Closure (see below).

2. *Thematic fit.* In terms of (7d/e), crooks are more likely to play the thematic role of patient in an arrest event than that of agent.

3. *Relative morphological frequency.* Certain ambiguous verb forms (including *raced* and *floated*) are more frequently used as past-tense main verbs, others as past participles.

4. *Bigram frequency.* The string Verb+*ed* followed by the preposition *by* supports the passive RRC construction.

5. *Configurational bias.* The first NP + finite-verb string in a sentence is preferably interpreted as opening a main clause.

6. *Relative frequency of argument structure (lexical frame).* Verbs like *race* and *float* are more frequently used as intransitive verbs (lacking a direct object argument) than as transitive verbs (Trueswell, 1996).

7. *Referential ambiguity.* A referentially ambiguous discourse context tends to bias the parser toward an analysis that resolves the ambiguity. For instance, a RRC analysis of *raced past the barn* or *floated down the river* may help to determine a unique referent for *the horse* or *the boat* in a context of several horses or boats (Crain & Steedman, 1985; Altmann & Steedman, 1988).

8. *Syntactic priming.* When two or more exemplars of a problematic grammatical construction, e.g., a garden-path, occur in close temporal succession, the parsing process tends to become progressively easier (see experimental demonstrations by Frazier, Taft, Roeper, Clifton & Ehrlich, 1984, and by Branigan, Pickering, Liversedge, Stewart & Urbach, 1995).

Reanalysis. When the parser hits upon information signaling that the current string has been misparsed, reanalysis will be attempted. However, very little is known about the parser's diagnostic and recovery strategies, about the time course of the structure revision process and about the resources it consumes (see Mitchell, 1994, and Gorrell, 1995, for some discussion). Frazier & Rayner (1982), in a pioneering study, explored eye-movements as cues to the reanalysis process. Friederici (1997; see also her chapter in this volume) presents electrophysiological data relevant to reanalysis.

An important class of hypotheses relates the difficulty of recovery from a misparse to certain configurational similarities between the original and the revised structure. Consider the examples in (8), and assume—in line with most two-stage parsing models—that the parser produces no more than one analysis at a time.

(8a) *Ian knew the answer to the problem was complex.* (Gorrell, 1995)

(8b) *As soon as he had phoned his wife started to prepare for the journey.* (Mitchell, 1994)

The second NP in (8a) is initially attached as the direct object of *knew*. This decision follows from the parsing principle of Late Closure, telling the parser to attach new input to the most recently posited clause or phrase (if allowed by the grammar), rather than opening a new phrase or clause. However, application of this heuristic in (8a) precludes the subsequent integration of finite verb *was*. The solution involves three steps:

(a)   de-attaching the direct object NP

(b)   positing a complement clause (with *was* as its finite verb), and

(c)   reattaching the NP as subject of the new clause.

Reanalysis of (8b) proceeds along similar lines:

(a')   de-attaching the direct object NP

(b')   positing a *main* clause (with *started* as its finite verb), and

(c')   reattaching the NP as subject of the new clause.

However, the second step contains a critical difference. In case of (8a), the dominance relationships between the leftmost verb (*knew/phoned*) and the problematic NP are left intact: *knew* dominates this NP both before and after the revision, but *phoned* does so only before the revision. (For precise definitions of 'dominates', see Gorrell, 1995, and Pritchett, 1992.) Formal and informal empirical evidence indeed confirms that (8b) typically causes a boggle effect ('conscious garden-path') whereas the reanalysis in (8a) often goes unnoticed[5].

7.3.3   Aphasic Parsing Deficits

A source of syntactic processing evidence outside the normal range is provided by the comprehension performance of *aphasic* patients, in particular those affected by agrammatism (see also Friederici, this volume). Caplan, Baker & Dehaut (1985; see

---

[5]   Within the framework of a bounded-parallelism parser one might postulate, alternatively, that both analyses are made concurrently in case of (8a), but not of (8b). However, this assumption has to be justified as well.

also Caplan & Hildebrandt, 1988) present the data of an extensive study of sentence comprehension in a large group of aphasics. The patients were presented with spoken sentences of varying grammatical make-up and had to show their understanding by manipulating toy animals (enacting the thematic role assigned to each of the animals). Table I shows examples of the nine sentence types and the percentages of correct understanding.

Computational models of sentence parsing developed for normal language users should be able to simulate data like these by tuning some of their parameters. Two models have recently taken up this challenge: CC-READER (Haarmann, Just & Carpenter, in press) and the Unification Space (Vosse & Kempen, submitted). Both simulations yielded rank correlations of over .90 between the observed scores and the output parameter in the models. This result was obtained, in both cases, by artificially lowering the parser's working memory capacity. This suggests that a similarly adapted version of Gibson's (1997) SPLT model should give at least an equally satisfactory fit with the data in Table I. Even better approximations may be possible when the models take additional factors into account, e.g., frequency differences between active and passive verbs.

Table I. Examples of stimulus sentences and comprehension scores in the Caplan, Baker & Dehaut (1985) study. The sentences were taken from Table 1 in Caplan et al.; the numerical data are percentages correct, averaged over the three sets of data reported in Tables 3, 9, and 15 of Caplan et al..

A	Active	*The elephant hit the monkey*	81.9
CS	Cleft-subject	*It was the elephant that hit the monkey*	80.2
P	Passive	*The elephant was hit by the monkey*	59.2
D	Dative	*The elephant gave the monkey to the rabbit*	58.7
CO	Cleft-object	*It was the elephant that the monkey hit*	51.1
C	Conjoined	*The elephant hit the monkey and hugged the rabbit*	45.0
OS	Object-subject relative	*The elephant hit the monkey that hugged the rabbit*	41.4
DP	Dative Passive	*The elephant was given to the monkey by the rabbit*	37.7
SO	Subject-object relative	*The elephant that the monkey hit hugged the rabbit*	25.9

7.4 Unresolved Cross-Linguistic Issues

After repeatedly having touched on the major HSP debate in the literature—between two-stage (syntax-first, garden-path) models and single-stage (interactive, constraint-satisfaction) models—I now turn to two more fine-grained and as yet undecided issues where cross-linguistic comparisons figure prominently.

Head-driven parsing strategies. Many grammatical formalisms assume that word groups or phrases derive their identity from one of its members, called the head. For example, in noun phrases a noun or pronoun functions as head; prepositional phrases are headed by a preposition, and clauses by main verbs. Other members of those phrases—e.g., determiners and modifiers of NPs, direct and indirect objects in clauses—are supposed to be somehow dependent on their head. Several parsing models, beginning with those developed by Abney (1989) and Pritchett (1991), assign a prominent role to heads of phrases in the parser's processing strategies. More specifically, they postulate parsing principles which cause the attachment of novel input to be postponed until a suitable head has been processed. For instance, an NP that could play the role of direct object in a clause, is left unattached until a transitive verb is seen at an appropriate position in the string. This principle does not delay attachment as long as the NP comes after such a verb; but in verb-final clauses— e.g., in German, Dutch and Japanese—the NP will dangle for a while. On the additional assumption that dangling phrases consume more computational resources than integrated ones, a head-driven parser is predicted to incur a processing problem at the direct object position in verb-final clauses. Quite a few experiments have been conducted in order to test predictions along these lines (e.g., Bader & Lasser, 1994; Konieczny, Hemforth, Scheepers & Strube, 1997). Although the results disconfirm strictly head-driven parsing models, they are compatible with milder versions (see Konieczny *et al.* for a concrete proposal).

Exposure-based parsing strategies. That statistical properties of individual words, including the relative frequencies of alternative readings of ambiguous words, affect the parser, is incontrovertible. This raises the question whether parsing performance is also sensitive to frequency effects of a non-lexical nature. A case in point is the attachment pattern in complex noun phrases such as in (9), which offer several alternative landing sites for the relative clause.

(9)   Someone shot the brother of the actress who was on the balcony.

Cuetos & Mitchell (1988) observed that native speakers of English tend to attach the relative clause to the nearest noun (*actress*, N2), in agreement with the parsing principle of Late Closure. However, this (weak) preference failed to show up in Spanish readers, who manifested a (rather strong) bias in favor of N1 attachment (with the *brother* being the person on the balcony) when reading the translation equivalent of (9). Meanwhile, this pattern has been confirmed in further experiments, and several additional European languages have been taken into consideration as well. It turns out that the N2 bias in English is an exception; German, Dutch and French go along with the Spanish N1 bias.

An obvious place to look for an explanation of this cross-linguistic difference is the frequency of occurrence of both attachment patterns in the languages studied. If the parser is capable of tuning its processing strategies to the preponderant syntactic patterns, then one expects parsing preferences to mirror usage frequencies. However, the statistical tuning hypothesis has not met with a great deal of success. Attachment frequencies counted in written and spoken corpora for several languages often contradict human parsing preferences (see Brysbaert, Mitchell & Grondelaers, 1997, for data on Dutch and for a cross-linguistic overview).

An important methodological problem, recognized by the investigators, is that the 'grain-size' chosen in the corpus analyses may have been suboptimal. For instance, should only occurrences of the preposition *of* and its translation equivalents be included in the counts? Should animacy or personhood of the referent of N1 and/or N2 be taken into consideration? Tabor, Juliano & Tanenhaus (1997) suggest that connectionist neural networks (in particular so-called Simple Recurrent Nets: see Elman, 1995, and Christiansen & Chater, 1997) may provide a way out of the grain-size problem by virtue of their sophisticated statistical learning capacity. Therefore, despite the disappointing results reported to date, it seems premature to give up the statistical tuning hypothesis.

7.5   Some Conclusions and Questions

Three decades of research on human sentence processing have made the psycholinguistic community aware of the multitude of external influences—lexical, morphological, conceptual, referential—to which the syntactic parser is exposed. This enables us, not only to design more accurately targeted experiments, but also to gain a better understanding of the structure building operations going on within the parser, and to develop sentence processing architectures that do justice to the complex causation of parsing performance. Advanced process modeling tools, such as are under construction within 'computational psycholinguistics' (Dijkstra & De Smedt, 1996; Crocker, 1996), will prove indispensable. Other computational techniques are already helping us to collect and analyze large corpora of spontaneously produced language utterances, and to put them through sophisticated pattern discovery algorithms (neural nets, memory-based learning). These recent developments enable us to launch innovative research projects into important but neglected HSP questions such as the following:

(a)   How does the parser deal with ill-formed utterances?
(b)   Which relationships exist between syntactic processing in language comprehension and production?

The liability of the human sentence processor to all sorts of parsing preferences is paralleled by its remarkable robustness - its ability to ignore major construction errors in a grammatical edifice, and to carry on its re-construction effortlessly. This feat seems inexplicable without postulating intimate relationships between sentence parsing and sentence production mechanisms.

References

Abney, S.P. (1989). A computational model of human parsing. *Journal of Psycholinguistic Research, 18,* 129-144.

Altmann, G.T.M. & Steedman, M. (1988). Interaction with context during human sentence processing. *Cognition, 30,* 191-238.

Bach, E., Brown, C. & Marslen-Wilson, W. (1986). Crossed and nested dependencies in German and Dutch: A psycholinguistic study. *Language and Cognitive Processes, 4,* 249-262.

Bader, M. & Lasser, I. (1994). German verb-final clauses and sentence processing: Evidence for immediate attachment. In C. Clifton, L. Frazier & K. Rayner (eds.), *Perspectives on sentence processing.* Hillsdale NJ: Erlbaum.

Bever, T.G. (1970). The cognitive basis for linguistic structures. In J.R. Hayes (ed.), *Cognition and the development of language.* New York: Wiley.

Branigan, H.P., Pickering, M.J., Liversedge, S.P., Stewart, A.J. & Urbach, T.P. (1995). Syntactic priming: Investigating the mental representation of language. *Journal of Psycholinguistic Research, 24,* 489-506.

Brysbaert, M., Mitchell, D.C. & Grondelaers, S. (submitted). Cross-linguistic differences in modifier attachment biases: Evidence against Gricean an tuning accounts.

Caplan, D. , Baker, C. & Dehaut, F. (1985). Syntactic determinants of sentence comprehension in aphasia. *Cognition, 21,* 117-175.

Caplan, D. & Hildebrandt, N. (1988). *Disorders of syntactic comprehension.* Cambridge, MA: MIT Press.

Christiansen, M.H. & Chater, N. (in press). Connectionist natural language processing: The state of the art. *Cognitive Science.*

Crain, S. & Steedman, M. (1985). On not being led up the garden path: The use of context by the psychological syntax processor. In D. Dowty, L. Karttunen & A. Zwicky (eds.), *Natural language parsing: Psychological, computational and theoretical perspectives.* Cambridge, UK: Cambridge University Press.

Crocker, M.W. (1996). *Computational psycholinguistics: An interdisciplinary approach to the study of language.* Dordrecht: Kluwer.

Cuetos, F. & Mitchell, D.C. (1988). Cross-linguistic differences in parsing: Restrictions on the use of the late closure strategy in Spanish. *Cognition, 30,* 73-105.

Dijkstra, T. & De Smedt, K. (1996). *Computational psycholinguistics: Symbolic and subsymbolic models of language processing.* London: Taylor & Francis.

Elman, J.L. (1995). Representation and structure in connectionist models. In G.T.M. Altmann (ed.), *Cognitive models of speech processing: Psycholinguistic and computational perspectives.* Cambridge, MA: MIT Press.

Fodor, J.A., Bever, T.G. & Garrett, M.F. (1974). *The psychology of language.* New York: McGraw-Hill.

Frazier, L. & Clifton, C. (1996). *Construal.* Cambridge MA: MIT Press.

Frazier, L. & Fodor, J.D. (1978). The sausage machine: A new two-stage parsing model. *Cognition, 6,* 291-325.

Frazier, L. & Rayner, K. (1982). Making and correcting errors during sentence comprehension: Eye movements in the analysis of structurally ambiguous sentences. *Cognitive Psychology, 14,* 178-21.

Frazier, L., Taft, L., Roeper, T., Clifton C. & Ehrlich, K. (1984). Parallel structure: A source of facilitation in sentence comprehension. *Memory and Cognition, 12,* 421-430.

Friederici, A.D. (1997). Diagnosis and reanalysis: Two processing steps the brain may differentiate. In J.D. Fodor & F. Ferreira (eds.), *Reanalysis in sentence processing.* Dordrecht: Kluwer.

Garrod, S.C. & Sanford, A.J. (1994). Resolving sentences in a discourse context: How discourse representation affects language understanding. In M.A. Gernsbacher (ed.), *Handbook of psycholinguistics.* San Diego: Academic Press.

Gernsbacher, M.A. (1994). *Handbook of psycholinguistics.* San Diego: Academic Press.

Gibson, E. (1997). Linguistic complexity: Locality of syntactic dependencies. MIT manuscript.

Gorrell, P. (1995). *Syntax and parsing.* Cambridge, UK: Cambridge University Press.

Haarmann, H.J., Just, M.A. & Carpenter, P.A. (in press). Aphasic sentence comprehension as a resource deficit: A computational approach. *Brain and Language.*

Jurafsky, D. (1996). A probabilistic model of lexical and syntactic access and disambiguation. *Cognitive Science, 20,* 137-194.

Just, M.A. & Carpenter, P.A. (1992). A capacity theory of comprehension: Individual differences in working memory. *Psychological Review, 99*, 122-149.

Kaan, E. (1997). *Processing subject-object ambiguities in Dutch.* PhD Thesis, University of Groningen. [Groningen Dissertations in Linguistics 20].

Kempen, G. (1996). Computational models of syntactic processing in human language comprehension. In T. Dijkstra & K. De Smedt (eds.), *Computational psycholinguistics: Symbolic and subsymbolic models of language processing.* London: Taylor & Francis.

Kimball, J. (1973). Seven principles of surface structure parsing in natural language. *Cognition, 2,* 15-47.

Konieczny, L., Hemforth, B., Scheepers, C. & Strube, G. (1997). The role of lexical heads in parsing: Evidence from German. *Language and Cognitive Processes, 12,* 307-348.

Levelt, W.J.M. (1978). A survey of studies in sentence perception: 1970-1976. In W.J.M. Levelt & G.B. Flores d'Arcais (eds.), *Studies in the perception of language.* Chicester: Wiley.

MacDonald, M.C., Just, M.A. & Carpenter, P.A. (1992). Working memory constraints on the processing of syntactic ambiguity. *Cognitive Psychology, 24,* 56-98.

MacDonald, M.C., Pearlmutter, N.J. & Seidenberg, M.S. (1994). Lexical nature of syntactic ambiguity resolution. *Psychological Review, 101,* 676-703.

Marcus, M.P. (1980). *A theory of syntactic recognition for natural language.* Cambridge, MA: MIT Press.

Marslen-Wilson, W. (1975). Sentence perception as an interactive parallel process. *Science, 189,* 226-228.

McClelland, J.L. (1987). The case for interactions in language processing. In M. Coltheart (ed.), *Attention and performance XII: The psychology of reading.* Hove UK: Erlbaum.

McRae, K., Spivey-Knowlton, M.J. & Tanenhaus, M.K. (in press). Modeling the influence of thematic fit (and other constraints) in on-line sentence comprehension. *Journal of Memory and Language.*

Miller, G.A. & Isard, S.D. (1964). Some perceptual consequence of linguistic rules. *Journal of Verbal Learning and Verbal Behavior, 2,* 217-228.

Mitchell, D.C. (1994). Sentence parsing. In M.A. Gernsbacher (ed.), *Handbook of psycholinguistics.* San Diego: Academic Press.

Pritchett, B.L. (1991). Head position and parsing ambiguity. *Journal of Psycholinguistic Research, 20,* 251-270.

Pritchett, B.L. (1992). *Grammatical competence and parsing performance*. Chicago: The University of Chicago Press.

Stolz, W.S. (1967). A study of the ability to decode grammatically novel sentences. *Journal of Verbal Learning and Verbal Behavior, 6*, 867-873.

Tabor, W., Juliano, C. & Tanenhaus, M.K. (1997). Parsing in a dynamical system: An attractor-based account of the interaction of lexical and structural constraints in sentence processing. *Language and Cognitive Processes, 12*, 211-271.

Tanenhaus, M.K. & Trueswell, J.C. (1995). Sentence comprehension. In J.L. Miller & P.D. Eimas (eds.), *Speech language and communication*. San Diego: Academic Press.

Trueswell, J.C. (1996). The role of lexical frequency in syntactic ambiguity resolution. *Journal of Memory and Language, 35*, 566-585.

Vosse, Th. & Kempen, G. (submitted). Syntactic processing in human sentence comprehension: An inhibition-based parser with a lexicalized grammar.

Chapter 8

Discourse Comprehension

Leo Noordman
Wietske Vonk

8.1 Introduction

The human language processor is conceived as a system that consists of several interrelated subsystems. Each subsystem performs a specific task in the complex process of language comprehension and production. A subsystem receives a particular input, performs certain specific operations on this input and yields a particular output. The subsystems can be characterized in terms of the transformations that relate the input representations to the output representations. An important issue in describing the language processing system is to identify the subsystems and to specify the relations between the subsystems. These relations can be conceived in two different ways. In one conception the subsystems are autonomous. They are related to each other only by the input-output channels. The operations in one subsystem are not affected by another system. The subsystems are modular, that is they are independent. In the other conception, the different subsystems influence each other. A subsystem affects the processes in another subsystem. In this conception there is an interaction between the subsystems.

The first subsystem in language understanding is the perceptual subsystem. In the perception of spoken language sound waves are perceived and the representation of theses sound waves are transformed into phonetic representations. In the perception of written language the initial input are the visual shapes and the output a representation of the letter features, letters and letter strings. In the further process of understanding, various subsystems can be identified that deal with phonological decoding, graphemic decoding, syntactic analysis (parsing), semantic analysis and discourse interpretation. Input to the phonological decoder are the phonetic representations; the output consists of a string of lexical elements. The processes in this module are the segmentation of the stimulus and the identification of the lexical elements. These elements are identified in the mental lexicon. In identifying a word, the syntactic and semantic information is retrieved from the mental lexicon. The word is recognized and lexical information is accessed. The input to the graphemic decoder is the visual representation of letter strings; the output is again the representation of the lexical elements. The next subsystem is the parser: on the basis of the syntactic information of the words, the parser makes a syntactic analysis of the sentence. Input to the semantic analysis are the word meanings retrieved form the lexicon. The output is the semantic representation of the words as they relate to each other in the clause (for these subsystems see chapter 1 to 7, this volume). Finally, the clauses are interpreted in relation to other clauses in the discourse. The input to this interpreter subsystem is the representation of the clauses as delivered by the previous subsystems. The output is the representation of the conceptual information expressed in the discourse. This representation is identified as the discourse representation or the mental model of the information in the text. It includes not only the literal meaning of the sentences, but also the information that is left implicit and the intention of the writer as inferred by the reader. The mental model can contain all kinds of inference. These inferences are triggered by the text, but they are derived on the basis of the contextual information and the reader's background knowledge.

In the description given so far, the subsystems are presented in a sequential order; one subsystem is affected only by the output of the other subsystem. But the exact relation between subsystems is still a point of research. The relation that has been quite extensively investigated is the relation between semantic analysis and parsing. There is increasing evidence challenging the position (Frazier, 1987) of the autonomy of the parser. Even with respect to subsystems that are far apart from each other in the present description, there is evidence for interaction. For example, contextual information may play a role very early (Garrod, O'Brien, Morris & Rayner, 1990). Related to the question of the modularity vs. interaction of the subsystems is, of course, the question of the identifiability of the different kinds of representation. If the subsystems are independent modules, there are identifiable representations as outputs of the different subsystems. But if the subsystems interact, there might not be separate representations. For example, if syntactic and semantic analyses interact, there are no sequential and separate syntactic and semantic representations. This issue is not solved yet.

The present paper deals with text understanding. We will be concerned with the representation readers construct of the text. Characteristic of a text is that its sentences are coherently related to each other. Therefore, the description of coherence and the way in which coherence is established are central topics of this chapter. That sentences are related to each other is to a certain degree expressed by linguistic means. For example, the use of a pronoun in a text indicates that that sentence refers to an entity that was mentioned earlier; the use of a conjunction expresses the nature of the relation between sentences. To the extent that relations between sentences are expressed by linguistic means, we talk about cohesion. Cohesion is distinguished from coherence. Coherence refers to the relatedness between sentences as we understand them. The interpretation of a sentence in a text depends on the previous sentences (its context) and on the reader's knowledge of the world. Therefore, contextual information and world knowledge contribute to the coherence of the sentences in the text.

We will use the terms text and discourse as synonyms. Both terms can refer to a set of interrelated sentences or utterances, but the main focus in this chapter will be on written language. We will not deal with discourse in the sense of interactive use of language between different participants.

8.2 Discourse Representation from a Psycholinguistic Point of View

In discourse comprehension three kinds of representation are generally distinguished: a surface representation, a propositional representation and a mental model representation (Fletcher & Chrysler, 1990; van Dijk & Kintsch, 1983). There is empirical evidence for the separability of these kinds of representation. They represent different kinds of information. The representations are generated during comprehension in real time, more or less sequentially. We will discuss these representations in terms of their content as well as their time characteristics. But since a complete model of the comprehension process is not sufficiently spelled out yet, it is not possible to locate these representations in the process of understanding and to indicate when exactly they are constructed. However, it is clear that a particular representation can only be constructed if specific information has been processed. For example, the propositional representation requires that the syntactic and semantic analyses of the sentences have been performed. The mental model representation requires in addition the activation of contextual information and world knowledge. The discourse representation of a text is ultimately a mental model.

Surface representation. The surface representation contains the information about the wording and the surface structure of the sentence and text. It contains the word forms and the order of the words in the sentence. This representation corresponds more or less to the output of the parser. The surface representation is in general rather short lived. Sentences are processed clause by clause. Once a clause has been processed, the surface information in the clause decreases in availability. This has been demonstrated by Jarvella (1971). He presented pairs of sentences as:

(1a) The confidence of Kofach was not unfounded. *To stack the meeting for McDonald, the union had even brought in outsiders.*

(1b) Kofach had been persuaded by the international *to stack the meeting for McDonald. The union had even brought in outsiders.*

The Section in italics was identical in the two conditions, even acoustically. But the clause *to stack the meeting for McDonald* is in (1a) part of the second sentence; in (1b) it is part of the first sentence. After hearing *outsiders* participants had to recall the sentences as completely as possible. Participants were able to recall the last clause (*the union had even brought in outsiders*) almost completely after (1a) and after (1b); recall of the first clause was very poor in both conditions. Interest-

ingly, recall of the clause *to stack the meeting for McDonald* was much better after
(1a) than after (1b): Once a sentence has been understood, the surface form disap-
pears rapidly. The literal form gets lost and the information is stored in a more abstract form.

This point has been demonstrated by Sachs (1967). Participants listened to a series
of sentences, including the sentence (2).

(2)   *He sent a letter about it to Galileo, the great Italian scientist.*

After 0, 80 or 160 syllables of the continuing sentences, a sentence was presented in
a recognition task. This recognition sentence was either the identical sentence, or a
form change (e.g., *A letter about it was sent to Galileo, the great Italian scientist* or *He
sent Galileo, the great Italian scientist, a letter about it*), or a meaning change (*Galileo,
the great Italian scientist, sent him a letter about it*). Immediately after hearing the
critical sentence, the participants made almost no errors. After 80 and 160 syllables,
however, the responses were only slightly better than chance, except for the meaning
changes; these were detected quite accurately. The surface information is lost rapidly
and after some time we have encoded only the meaning of the information.

Propositional representation. The propositional representation contains the meaning of the information expressed in propositions. Propositions are predicate-argu-
ment constructions. The predicate is a relational concept, expressed for example by
a verb or an adjective. The arguments are in general concepts expressed by nouns or
other propositions. They function as semantic roles. An example is the propositional
representation of the sentence *Mary gave John a book*: (Give [agent MARY; recipient
JOHN; object BOOK]), or shorter: (give, Mary, John, book). We follow here the nota-
tion of Kintsch and van Dijk (1978), because we will discuss their model later in this
chapter. Evidence for the existence of the propositional representation is obtained in
a number of experiments, for instance in a priming experiment by Ratcliff and
McKoon (1978). They presented participants with sets of four study sentences and
then tested a list of single words for recognition. Participants had to decide whether
the test words were present or not present in the study sentences. An example of a
sentence is (3).

(3)   *The soldier who intercepted the despatch won a medal.*

This sentence consists of the following propositions: (*intercepted, soldier, despatch*) and (*won, soldier, medal*). A larger priming effect was obtained if the target
word was from the same proposition as the word preceding it than if the target word
was from a different proposition than the word preceding it. For example, the recognition time for *medal* was shorter when it was preceded in the recognition task by the
word *soldier* than when it was preceded by the word *despatch*. On the basis of a
surface representation one would predict the opposite, because the distance between

medal and *despatch* is shorter than between *medal* and *soldier*. This result provides strong evidence for the propositional encoding of sentences.

Mental model representation. The mental model representation is a further elaboration of the propositional representation. It contains not only the information in the propositions, but also information that is inferred on the basis of the context and on the basis of world knowledge. The mental model representation reflects the state of affairs in the world that is described by the text. It is also called situation model (van Dijk & Kintsch, 1983), or mental model (Garnham, 1987; Glenberg, Meyer & Lindem, 1987; Johnson-Laird, 1983). A classic example that illustrates the mental model representation is given by Bransford, Barclay and Franks (1992). Participants were asked to memorize the following sentence:

(4a) *Three turtles rested on a floating log and a fish swam beneath them.*

On a later recognition task participants quite frequently reported erroneously that they had heard sentence (4b).

(4b) *Three turtles rested on a floating log and a fish swam beneath it.*

They did not make this recognition error if the original sentence (4a) had *beside* in stead of *beneath*. The results are difficult to explain if comprehension is considered as the construction of a propositional representation, but easy to explain in terms of a mental model that understanders construct of the situation described by the text.

Potts (1972) demonstrated that the availability of the information depends on properties of the model that is constructed. Participants had to study short stories in which four animals were ranked with respect to intelligence. For example: *the bear was smarter than the hawk, the hawk was smarter than the wolf and the wolf was smarter than the deer.* Participants were tested in a verification task. Responses to remote pairs were more accurate and faster than responses to adjacent pairs. The result leads to the interpretation that readers construct a spatial model of the information in the form of a linear array and that properties of the array, in particular whether an object is an end term, determine the availability of the information.

If such a mental model can be constructed unambiguously, the surface representation of the sentences is forgotten and only an abstract integrated model is retained. If, however, such an integrated model cannot be constructed unambiguously, the surface representation is retained. This has been demonstrated by Mani and Johnson-Laird (1982). In (5) the location of the bed is not uniquely determined.

(5) *The bookshelf is to the right of the chair. The chair is in front of the table. The bed is behind the chair.*

The surface structure information of these sentences is retained.

That mental models are constructed during the understanding of a narrative has been demonstrated by Morrow, Greenspan and Bower (1987). Participants had to memorize the spatial arrangement of the rooms of a particular building that was the setting of the narrative and to memorize four objects in each room. Subsequently they had to read a story. A target sentence in the story was:

(6)   *Wilbur walked from the library into the reception room.*

This sentence was followed by test probes that presented pairs of objects. Participants had to judge whether or not both objects were located in the same room. Decision times were shorter if both objects were in the room that was the current location of the protagonist (in the present example: the reception room) than when they were in another room. This indicates that the reader constructs a situation model in which the protagonist plays an important role (see also Glenberg, Meyer & Lindem, 1987).

It should be noted that the mental model representation may very well be described in terms of propositions, but the propositions are then derived on the basis of world knowledge and not only on the basis of the sentences. The mental model representation is not necessarily an analogue or a picture-like representation. It does not only represent spatial information. Also temporal information (Anderson, Garrod & Sanford, 1983; Bestgen & Vonk, 1995), information about causes (Fletcher & Bloom, 1980; Trabasso & van den Broek, 1985), goals and intentions (Dopkins, 1996; Long, Golding & Graesser, 1992) or characteristics of the protagonist (Myers, O'Brien, Albrecht & Mason, 1994) can be included (see also Zwaan, Magliano & Graesser, 1995).

Distinguishing the three representations. The studies discussed so far support the plausibility of the distinctions between surface, propositional and mental model representations. But is there more direct evidence for the separation of these representations? Several studies have produced such evidence indeed (Fletcher & Chrysler, 1990; Kintsch, Welsch, Schmalhofer & Zimny, 1990; Schmalhofer & Glavanov, 1986). We will discuss one study in somewhat more detail. Fletcher and Chrysler presented participants with texts followed by a sentence recognition task. The recognition data were used to identify the different representations. As an example, one text described an ordering among five objects of art with respect to their costs. In increasing order of their costs, these objects were a carpet (also referred to earlier in the text by its synonym rug), a painting, a necklace, a vase and a statue. An example of a critical sentence in a text is (7).

(7)   *George says that his wife was angry when she found out that the necklace cost more than the carpet.*

There were three kinds of recognition test sentences: the surface, the propositional (called: textbase) and the model test sentences:

(8)   *Surface: George says that his wife was angry when she found out that the*
      necklace cost more than the carpet / rug.
      Textbase: George says that his wife was angry when she found out that the
      necklace cost more than the carpet / painting
      Model: George says that his wife was angry when she found out that the
      necklace cost more than the carpet / vase.

The participant had to decide which of two words occurred in the sentence of the
text. In the surface test sentence the two words (*carpet / rug*) were synonyms. The
surface distractor (*rug*) differs from the word in the critical sentence (*carpet*) in the
surface representation, but not in the propositional representation, nor in the mental
model representation. The textbase distractor differs from the word in the critical
sentence both in the surface representation and in the propositional representation,
but not in the mental model representation. The word *painting* conveys a different
meaning than the original *carpet* and therefore differs propositionally, but the sentence is in agreement with the mental model. The mental model distractor (*vase*)
differs from the critical sentence in all three kinds of representation: the surface
representation, the propositional representation and the mental model. The logic of
the recognition task is that the greater the number of representations on which the
distractor word and the correct word differ, the easier it is to reject the distractor
word. If participants in the surface test select the correct word better than chance,
this is evidence for the psychological plausibility of the surface representation. If
participants perform better on the textbase test than on the surface test, this is evidence for the propositional representation, because in the textbase test the distractor
and the critical sentences differ also in the propositional representation. If the performance on the mental model test exceeds the performance on the textbase test, this
is evidence for the mental model representation, because in the mental model test
the difference between distractor and critical sentence is increased by the discrep-
ancy at the mental model level. The probability of selecting the target in the surface
test was greater than chance, testifying for the psychological plausibility of the surface representation. The probability of selecting the target word in the textbase test
was greater than in the surface test and the probability of selecting the target word in
the mental model test was greater than in the textbase test. These results give evidence for the propositional representation and for the mental model representation.
This interpretation of the results rests on the assumption that the differences between
distractor sentence and critical sentence at the surface representation are equal across
the three test conditions and that the differences at the propositional level are equal
in the textbase and mental model tests. These assumptions have carefully been tested
in separate experiments.

Kintsch (1994) and McNamara, Kintsch, Singer and Kintsch (1996) considered
the construction of the propositional representation and the mental model represen-

tation as two ways of understanding that differ in depth. They found evidence for the propositional representation and the mental model representation in an investigation of the factors that may improve text understanding. High and low knowledge readers studied a text on the functioning of the heart. The students were tested with a free recall task, which depended primarily on a good propositional representation and with problem-solving questions, which depended more on a good mental model representation. The text was presented in two conditions. In one condition the coherence of the text was increased by adding explanations and elaborations, in the other not. The increase of the coherence enhanced the performance of low knowledge students on both tasks. For high knowledge students, however, the increase of coherence led to lower performance on the problem-solving questions. These results demonstrate the separability of propositional representation and mental model representation. In addition, they suggest that increasing the coherence of a text may be detrimental for text understanding at the deeper level of the mental model representation. Readers have to be challenged by the text and the high knowledge readers were not challenged enough by the very coherent text.

8.3   Coherence of the Discourse Representation

Text understanding can be described as the construction of a coherent representation of the information in the text. This representation is object of study also in recent linguistic theories. Several linguists have developed formal theories to describe the meaning of text and discourse, using notions such as discourse representation (Kamp, 1981; Kamp & Reyle, 1993), discourse domain (Seuren, 1985) and mental space (Fauconnier, 1985). The representations given by linguists are interesting from a psychological point of view. They are representations of the meaning of text not just in terms of truth conditions, but claim to be cognitive representations of the information in the text as processed by the reader. Moreover, these linguistic representations are not static, but dynamic, as psychological representations are. Expressions in the text are considered as instructions to construct the discourse representation and to change the representation at each successive input. Finally, these theories point to different aspects of the notion of coherence.

The following short text (Seuren, 1985) can give an illustration of these characteristics: *There was a man called John. There was a chimney. John swept the chimney.* The interpretation of this discourse is considered by Seuren as the construction of a discourse domain. The discourse domain consists of addresses and predicates. An address corresponds to the entities the text deals about. The use of the indefinite article in this example is the instruction to introduce a new entity. The definite article in the third sentence is an instruction to identify an entity that should be already available in the discourse representation constructed so far. The predicates contain the information that is attributed to the addresses. The meaning of a sentence or proposition consists in the changes that the sentence or proposition effectuates in the representation. A characteristic of these representations is that they are coherent. The coherence is achieved both by the addresses and the predicates. Referential expressions that refer to the same address maintain reference in the text. In this way addresses serve to maintain reference in the text and are the basis for what we will call referential coherence. The predicates are the basis for coherence in terms of the content of the sentences. Sentences are related to each other in terms of their content. We will call this relational coherence. Psychological processes with respect to both referential coherence and relational coherence will be discussed.

8.3.1 Referential Coherence

Readers construct a coherent representation by relating incoming information to addresses in the representation. Information is stored with these addresses. The addresses are the discourse referents, for example a specific person introduced in the text. A noun phrase in a sentence may introduce a new discourse referent or may refer to a referent that is already present in the text representation. In the last case, the expression is called an anaphoric expression. In *John phoned Mary up. He needed some advice* the pronoun *he* refers to *John*. In *A bus came roaring round the corner. A pedestrian was nearly killed by the vehicle* (Sanford & Garrod, 1981), the noun phrase *the vehicle* refers to *a bus*. It is by means of these anaphoric expressions that referential coherence is achieved.

A characterization of the process by which referential coherence is established is proposed by Haviland and Clark (1974). They call this process the 'given-new strategy'. (Although this strategy applies both to pronouns and nominal phrases, it has been described mainly for nominal phrases.) The given-new strategy consists of three steps. In the first step the sentence is analyzed in terms of what is given and what is new. Given information is information that has been mentioned in the previous discourse. New information is what the sentence contributes to the current discourse representation. In (9a)

(9a)   Mary got the beer out of the car. The beer was warm.

the nominal phrase *the beer* in the second sentence is given information. The predicate *was warm* is the new information. Writers have specific devices to express what is given and what is new information. Given information is expressed for example by a definite nominal phrase, or a pronoun. New information is expressed, for example, by a cleft construction. In *It is John who was too late* the new information is *John* and the predicate *too late* expresses given information. Once the given and new information have been identified as such, the process enters its second stage. Readers search in their memory representation of the preceding discourse whether there is an antecedent that corresponds to the given information. In the earlier example this is straightforward, since the preceding sentence mentioned *beer* that serves an antecedent of *the beer* in the second sentence. If the first sentence had been *Mary got the picnic supplies out of the car*, the identification of the antecedent would have been more difficult, since it required the inference that there was beer among the picnic supplies. The third step consists of predicating the new information (*was warm*) to the antecedent.

Experimental evidence that readers indeed use this strategy was obtained by Haviland and Clark in reading time experiments. The second sentence in (9b) required more reading time than the identical second sentence in (9a).

(9b)   Mary got the picnic supplies out of the car. The beer was warm.

The difference is nicely predicted by the given-new strategy. This strategy describes that referential coherence for both (9a) and (9b) is obtained and that the construction of referential coherence in (9b) requires an inference and in (9a) not.

Several kinds of referential expression can be distinguished, for example, proper names, definite nominal phrases (*the sixty-year young director*) and pronouns. These expressions differ in lexical specificity. A definite nominal phrase is more specific than a pronoun. The forms are not used interchangeably. The use of a particular referential expression depends on the accessibility of the referent in the discourse context. Referents indeed vary in accessibility. Several factors affect the accessibility. One factor is the distance between the antecedent and the anaphor. The greater the distance, the less accessible in general the discourse referent identified by the antecedent is. The accessibility of a specific discourse referent depends also on whether there are competing candidates, that is other potential referents. Also thematic constraints determine the accessibility: the main protagonist in a narrative is in general more accessible than a subsidiary protagonist. The difference in accessibility is reflected in the form of the referential expressions. The more accessible a discourse referent is, the less the lexical specificity of the referring expression has to be. For example, the protagonist in a story is highly accessible and will be referred to by a pronoun rather than by a full nominal phrase.

The relation between accessibility and form of the expression has been investigated by Givón (1983) in a quantitative way. Givón measured the relation between antecedents and anaphors in texts in terms of, for instance, the distance between antecedent and anaphor in number of clauses and the presence of competing candidates for the anaphor. These quantitative analyses resulted into a scale of topic accessibility. This scale is an ordering of the referential expressions in terms of the accessibility of the referent they denote. In decreasing order of accessibility, this scale is: zero anaphor, unstressed pronoun, stressed pronoun and definite noun. As an example: pronouns have a shorter distance from their antecedents than non-pronominal expressions; the referent to which they refer are more persistent and they occur rarely if there are competing candidates.

Prince (1981) proposes a hierarchy that is based on the assumed degree of givenness of the discourse referents in the text. She classifies discourse referents on a scale from 'brandnew' (the least 'given' referents), via 'inferred' to 'evoked' (the most 'given' referents). As an example, in *John bought a car. The dashboard was made of mahogany. He liked it very much*, the indefinite expression *a car* is brandnew, *the dashboard* is inferred and *he* is evoked. The analysis by Givón started form the form of the referential expressions; the analysis by Prince took as starting point the accessibility of the discourse referents. The conclusions of these studies converge. In general, the less available the referent is, the more explicit and extended is the referential expression.

Sanford and Garrod (1981) describe the difference between pronouns and definite nominal phrases in terms of memory representations. Pronouns refer to a partition of memory they call explicit focus. This contains only a limited number of accessible and relevant antecedents. Consequently, the use of a pronoun in case it does not refer to a focused character should slow down reading as compared to the use of a pronoun that does refer to a focused character. Sanford, Moar and Garrod (1988) demonstrated indeed that pronoun resolution is sensitive to the focus status of the antecedent, but that resolution of a definite nominal expression is not. This result is consistent with the claim that discourse referents for pronouns and definite nominal expressions differ in accessibility.

In the remainder of this Section we will restrict the discussion of referential coherence to pronouns and definite nominal phrases. We will be concerned with the processes in identifying the referents in these two cases.

Processing Pronouns

Because pronouns contain less information than full nominal expressions, one might suppose that the identification of the antecedent of a pronoun is a more complex process than the identification of the antecedent of a full nominal phrase. This suggestion is incorrect, however, since it ignores the specific constraints on the use of pronouns and definite nominal phrases. As has been discussed before, referential expressions differ with respect to the accessibility of the referents. The more accessible the referent is, the more reduced the referential expression can be. Use of a pronoun requires higher accessibility of the referent than use of a definite nominal expression. Therefore, the fact that a pronoun contains less information than a nominal phrase does not imply that the identification process is more difficult for the pronoun than for the definite nominal phrase. It is the higher accessibility of the antecedent in the context that allows for a more parsimonious referential expression.

In understanding a pronoun information from several bottom-up sources may restrict the number of possible antecedents and can in this way help the reader to find the correct antecedent. One source is the lexical information of the pronoun itself: its gender, case and number. Another source of information is the syntactic structure of the sentence. In the sentence *John may scold Bill, because he...* the pronoun is preferentially interpreted as referring to the noun phrase with the same syntactic function in the main clause as the pronoun in the subordinate clause. This strategy is called the parallel function strategy (Grober, Beardsley & Caramazza, 1978; Sheldon, 1974). Another source relates to the meaning of the verb. In sentence (10a)

(10a) Harry won the money from Albert, because he...
(10b) Harry trusted Albert, because he...

the pronoun is perceived to refer to the first noun phase in the main clause. In sentence (10b) the pronoun is perceived to refer to the second noun phrase in the main clause. The implicit causality underlying the main verb is attributed to the subject in (10a) and to object in (10b).

Apart from these local, bottom-up factors, the earlier discussed contextual availability of the antecedent of the pronoun helps the reader to find the correct antecedent. On the basis of the analytic research by Givón and the experimental research by Clark and Sengul (1979) one may assume that pronouns have a preference to refer to an antecedent in the immediately preceding discourse. Ehrlich and Rayner (1983) observed a longer fixation duration on the region of the pronoun when its antecedent was more distant in the preceding discourse. But Clifton and Ferreira (1987) demonstrated that topic-hood rather than the distance between antecedent and anaphor is the crucial factor. Pronouns refer preferably to entities that are the topic of the passage (see also Morrow, 1985).

The factors that have been mentioned can be located with respect to the three kinds of representation that have been distinguished. The lexical morphological information of the pronoun and the parallel function strategy are related to the surface level representation. The effect of the implicit causality is related to the propositional level. The function of topic and protagonist affects the mental model representation.

Considering that several factors may affect pronoun resolution, a question is how these factors operate in real time and how they relate to each other. More specifically, if the antecedent can unambiguously be identified on the basis of one particular factor, for example, on the basis of the gender of the pronoun, do the other factors still play a role? If several factors interact with each other, how do the different factors contribute to the process in real time. And, since the different factors probably do not operate at the same time, does this interaction imply that the interpretation process is postponed until later factors can have their effect? One study will be presented that discusses some of these problems.

Vonk (1985) varied the gender information and the congruency of the *because*-clause with the implicit causality of the main clause for sentences as (10a) and (10b). For sentences as (10a), in which the implicit causality is attributed to the subject of the main clause, examples are (11a) - (11d): the sentences contained a gender cue

(11c and 11d), that is, the pronoun could unambiguously be identified on the basis of its gender information, or not (11a and 11b) and the *because*-clause was congruent with the bias of the main verb (11a and 11c) or not (11b and 11d).

(11a) Albert won the money from Harry, because he played skillfully.
(11b) Albert won the money from Harry, because he played carelessly.
(11c) Albert won the money from Mary, because he played skillfully
(11d) Albert won the money from Mary, because he played carelessly.

Participants read the sentences and were asked to name the antecedent of the pronoun as quickly as possible. The time between the onset of the presentation of the sentence and the voice onset of the answer was measured. There was a huge effect of gender cue. Naming time was much shorter for sentences with a gender cue than for sentences without gender cue. There was also a congruency effect: congruent sentences were quicker than incongruent sentences. There was no interaction between these two factors. This means that even in the case where the antecedent could unambiguously be identified on the basis of the gender information, congruency played a role. In another experiment with only congruent sentences as (11a) and (11c), Vonk (1984) measured the duration of eye fixations in a naming task. As before, naming times were shorter for sentences with a gender cue (11c) than for sentences without a gender cue (11a). However, the fixation duration on the pronoun was longer in (11c) than in (11a). In addition, the pronoun was skipped in (11a) much more frequently than in (11c). Apparently, if the pronoun is not informative, the reader hardly fixates the pronoun.

This result gives some indication about the time course of this process. It is only when readers have discovered that the two names refer to persons of different gender that they know that the relevant information is contained in the pronoun. This decision is taken very rapidly. Maximally it takes the time interval between the onset of the fixation on the second name to fixation on the pronoun, that is about 500 msec. It should be noted that these studies dealt with isolated sentences. Contextual availability of the topic did not play a role in this study; only local factors were investigated.

Processing Definite Nominal Phrases

Another linguistic device that establishes referential coherence is the definite noun phrase. As is the case with pronouns, there are several information sources that are used in identifying the antecedent of a definite nominal phrase. These sources can be related to the three kinds of representation that are constructed during reading. At the surface level, there is the information in the definite article. In the given-new strategy the definite noun phrase was mentioned as an expression of given information. By searching the memory representation of the text, a link of the current sentence with previous text is established. But this linking function of the definite noun phrase is not so straightforward. First, a definite nominal phrase is not always a referential expression. Indeed, there are many instances of definite noun phrases that introduce new entities in the discourse and that have no antecedent in the text (Fraurud, 1990), for example, *The president.. .* Second, definite references are frequently used in the absence of an explicit antecedent (*Keith drove to London. The car kept overheating*; Garrod & Sanford, 1982). This illustrates that the process of referential linking requires not only linguistic analysis of the surface structure of the information, but also the activation of world knowledge. In many cases it is on the basis of a mental model that coreferentiality is obtained. That picnic supplies contain beer (see 9b) is part of world knowledge.

Another factor that is related to the surface structure is the distance between the referential expression and its antecedent. As was the case for pronouns, this distance affects the difficulty of finding the antecedent. Schustack, Ehrlich and Rayner (1987) found that the target referential expression was fixated shorter if the antecedent was in the previous sentence than when it was one sentence further back. According to O'Brien, Plewes and Albrecht (1990), when an antecedent is not immediately available, a search process takes place in which possible antecedents close to the referential expression are searched more quickly than antecedents at a greater distance from the anaphoric expression. As for pronouns, the distance per se is not the determining factor, but whether the antecedent is still the topic or not (Clifton & Ferreira, 1987). A similar illustration is given by Lesgold, Roth and Curtis (1979).

The crucial step in establishing referential coherence is to find an antecedent in the previous discourse. This is the second stage in the given-new strategy. If such an antecedent cannot be found immediately, for example, by means of a straightforward mapping process, then some information from the preceding discourse has to be reactivated or to be 'reinstated' so that a connection with the current noun phrase can be constructed. Two questions with respect to this reinstatement process are: What is reinstated and what is the time course of this reinstatement process?

To answer these questions Dell, McKoon and Ratcliff (1983) presented sentences such as (12) in an item recognition paradigm.

(12)   A burglar surveyed the garage set back from the street.
Several milk bottles were piled at the curb.
The banker and her husband were on vacation.
The$_1$ criminal$_2$ slipped$_3$ away$_4$ from the$_5$ streetlamp$_6$.

The definite noun phrase *the criminal* refers to *a burglar* in the first sentence. Is the concept BURGLAR activated in the representation the reader constructs when reading the definite noun phrase? The sentences were presented in such a way that every 250 msec a new word appeared on the screen. In this way the test word *burglar* could be presented after any word in the text and its activation measured. Participants had to indicate whether the test word occurred in the text. To test the time course of the reinstatement process, the test words were presented in a number of experiments at the places indicated in the example. Some participants saw a different last sentence, *A cat slipped away from the streetlamp*, which did not contain a referential expression. The activation of the test words when processing the sentence with anaphor was compared with the activation when processing a sentence without anaphor.

Response times to the test word *burglar* were more rapid when the last sentence mentioned the anaphor than when it did not. This was true for presentation at places 2 to 6. Apparently, the definite noun phrase *criminal* activated its antecedent *burglar* and did so very rapidly. An alternative explanation is that the activation of *burglar* is due to semantic association with *criminal*; there is no semantic association between cat and burglar. Therefore, the companion test word *garage* was used in addition to the test word *burglar*. When *garage* was presented at position 2 and 3 in the sentence with *criminal*, reaction time was more rapid than when it was presented at the same positions in the sentence with *cat*. So, the speeding up of the recognition is not due to semantic priming, but to the reinstatement process that is initiated by the referential expression. What is reinstated by the anaphor is not just the antecedent (*burglar*), but also other concepts that occur in the same proposition as *burglar*. Presentation of the test words *burglar* and *garage* at later moments (position 5 and 6) showed that the test word *burglar* was still activated by the anaphor, but that the activation of the companion word *garage* faded away. After 1250 msec the referent word is still activated, but the companion word was not. In conclusion, an anaphor gives rise to a very rapid activation of its referent. Other concepts in the same proposition as the referent are activated as well. The referent remains activated through the end of the sentence, but the activation of the other concepts is short lived.

Referential Expressions and Thematic Structure

By identifying antecedents in the discourse representation referential expressions contribute to the coherence of a text. But referential expressions may on top of their identificational function serve other functions as well. This is clear if we consider the constraints imposed on the use of the expressions. As has been said earlier, pronouns refer in general to entities that are topical and in focus. Definite noun phrases refer to entities that are less activated. So the use of referential expressions depends on what is accessible in the context and in particular on the topic and theme at a particular moment in the text. Because of this constraint one can imagine that there is also a reversed dependency: the use of a specific referential expression can have an influence on what is topical and thematic in a text. Suppose that in a particular context some entity is highly available to such an extent that it can be referred to by a pronoun. If the writer then refers to this entity by means of a full nominal phrase, the expression is more specific than what is required for identification. It is called an overspecification. The writer may use an overspecification to indicate a topic shift. This is what Vonk, Hustinx and Simons (1992) hypothesized. In a production study participants had to complete a sentence of a text. Segment (13) is an example.

(13) By five o'clock John came home from his work
He hung his coat on the hallstand.
He/John....

The first word of the sentence was given. If the first word was a proper name or a role description, the continuation sentences expressed in the majority of the cases a topic shift. On the other hand, if the first word was a pronoun that referred to the protagonist, the majority of the continuation sentences were topic continuations.

The influence of anaphoric expressions on the thematic structuring of the text in comprehension was also investigated in a reading study. If an overspecification is used, readers will assume that it constitutes a topic shift. In a text that dealt with the professional life of one single protagonist, the target sentence started either with a full name-with-extension (14a) or with a pronoun (14b). In addition to these target sentences that were a theme continuation, there were theme shift target sentences as control sentences.

(14a) Johnson, a professor of medicine, considers his research important.
(14b) He considers his research important.

Vonk et al. reasoned that if readers make a thematic boundary in their test representation, the availability of a word preceding this boundary should be decreased. Therefore they used a probe recognition task with a word from the sentence preceding the target sentence. The probe was presented after the target sentence (the difference in length of the anaphoric expressions was controlled for). Participants had to indicate whether that word occurred in the text. The probe recognition time was shorter after the pronoun (14b) than after the extended name (14a). So, the extended name as an overspecified referential expression decreased the availability of the previous theme and can be considered as a thematic boundary marker. Anaphoric expressions not only signal a thematic shift; they can affect the thematic structure of the text. Anaphoric expressions have in addition to their identificational function a thematic structuring function.

Referential coherence has received relatively much attention as source of coherence in the experimental research of text understanding. Referential coherence connects sentences to each other by identifying referents that are shared by different propositions. The kind of coherence that is achieved in this way is generally called argument overlap. Some researchers have considered argument overlap as the primary dimension for establishing text coherence. Argument overlap is also the property that plays an important role in models of text processing (Kintsch, 1988; Kintsch

& van Dijk, 1978; Myers & O'Brien, in press). However, argument overlap is not the only contributor to the coherence of text. What is required in addition is that the predicates that are attributed to the addresses are related to each other in terms of their content and meaning. These relations that exist between propositions are, for example, temporal, causal and contrastive relations. Establishing this relational coherence requires in general knowledge of the world. In fact, these relations are ultimately cognitive categories of human knowledge. It is on the basis of this knowledge that we can construct a mental model of the text.

8.3.2   Relational Coherence

This Section deals with coherence not from the point of view of the identity of referents, but from the point of view of the content of what is predicated to the referents. To illustrate this difference, consider (15):

> *(15)   John phoned Pete up. He needed some information.*

The fact that *He* refers (most likely) to *John* connects the two sentences to each other. This is referential coherence. But in addition there is a relation between the contents of the sentences. The second sentence is the reason for John to phone. The fact that there is a causal relation between the two sentences, more specifically in this case a reason relation, is relational coherence. That referential coherence and relational coherence are not independent, is clear from the fact that the knowledge of the causal relation between the predicates of the two clauses is a cue for establishing referential coherence. This has been demonstrated when we discussed the role of the predicates in the two clauses in pronoun resolution (sentences 11a and 11b).

A number of researchers have tried to account for the relational coherence of text by specifying the kinds of relation that exists between sentences in a discourse. Hobbs (1979) distinguishes between elaboration, parallel and contrast relations. Mann and Thompson (1986) give a list of fifteen rhetorical relations, examples being cause, justification, reason, solutionhood, sequence, evidence and elaboration. These relations are not just structuring relations in a discourse, but they reflect cognitive categories. The problem with lists of coherence relations is that it is hard, or perhaps even impossible, to give an exhaustive list with which the coherence of texts can be described. Sanders, Spooren and Noordman (1992), therefore, do not aim at an exhaustive list of relations, but argue that underlying the coherence relations there is a small number of basic cognitive categories. They distinguish four categories. The first is whether the relation is causal or additive (not-causal). The second is whether the relation is semantic (the sentences describe events or states in the world) or pragmatic (the sentences express a conclusion or a speech act). The third is whether the relation expresses basic order (the order the sentences corresponds with the order of events in the world) or not. The fourth is whether the relation is positive or negative (the relation exists between propositions or the negation of a proposition). Sanders et al. present evidence from psycholinguistic experiments for the plausibility of these basic categories. The proposal reflects the idea that coherence relations are ultimately not textual relations but cognitive relations.

Causality is one of the most fundamental categories of human cognition. Knowledge about events implies the belief that they have causes. Understanding events is being able to explain them by specifying their causes and predicting their consequences. The notion of causality develops in our experience in the world. By observing co-occurrences and relations between events in the world, we learn the reasons for these co-occurrences. In this interaction with the world, the concept of causality develops. Therefore causality is both a property of reality and a property of our conceptual system with which we interpret the world. Since causality is a basic dimension of human knowledge, it is not surprising that much experimental research has dealt with the role of causality in the construction of a coherent text representation (Black & Bern, 1981; Keenan, Baillet & Brown, 1984; Myers, Shinjo & Duffy, 1987; Noordman, Vonk & Kempff, 1992; Rumelhart, 1977; Trabasso & van den Broek, 1985; van den Broek, 1990).

The structure of our knowledge has consequences for the way in which we interpret language. It seems plausible that the more closely sentences correspond to the cognitive categories in long term memory, the more easily they will be understood. Some illustrations will be given, restricting ourselves to the processing of causal relations. First we will illustrate that text understanding depends on the structure of human knowledge (Noordman & Vonk, 1992). Experts and novices in the domain of economics read economic texts. The experts were advanced doctoral students in economics; the novices had never had any economics, but were comparable otherwise. First, using a number of knowledge elicitation techniques (Graesser & Clark, 1985), descriptions of relations between familiar economic concepts were obtained (Vonk & Noordman, 1992; Simons, 1993). Analysis of these relations showed that causality played an important role in the descriptions and, in addition, that experts described the relations to a much greater extent in terms of causal relations than novices. The results indicated that expertise in this domain is related indeed to the amount of causal organization. In subsequent reading experiments experts and novices read sentences that expressed causal relations and that required causal inferences, embedded in long texts. As an example of such a sentence is (16).

(16)   *The American export has been suffering a decline in the last few months, because the rising inflation has produced a harmful effect on the competitive position of the U.S.A.*

This sentence requires the inference that deterioration of the competitive position negatively affects the export. The results of the knowledge elicitation experiments had indicated that the concepts *competitive position* and *export* were familiar to both experts and non-experts, but that the relation between these two concepts was familiar only to the experts. The reading time data indicated that the experts made the causal inferences and the novices did not.

This result sheds some light on the nature of the inference process. Words in the text activate concepts in long term memory. If relations between concepts are familiar to the reader, they are activated and applied to the situation described by the text and added to the text representation. If the relation between the concepts is not available, no inference is made. In this way, understanding is essentially a matching process between the input and concepts in long term memory.

If causality is a fundamental category in the human mind, there must be a tendency to make causal interpretations rather than non-causal ones. This is not a trivial claim, since a causal relation is complex. It is more complex than a temporal relation and an additive relation. A cause precedes the consequence; therefore a causal relation implies a temporal relation and is more specific than a temporal relation. A temporal relation implies an additive relation and is more specific than an additive relation. Two contrasting views are possible on the way in which we interpret relations between sentences. If information processing is controlled by a tendency to minimize effort, there should be a tendency for the reader to be satisfied with the most parsimonious interpretation, that is, the additive interpretation. If, on the other hand, processing is controlled by a principle of informativeness, causality is the preferred interpretation. An experiment by Singer, Halldorson, Lear and Andrusiak (1992) is relevant in this respect. They had sequences of sentences expressing a causal relation as in (17a) or a temporal relation as in (17b).

(17a) Mary poured the water on the bonfire. The fire wet out.
(17b) Mary placed the water by the bonfire. The fire wet out.

The mean reading time for the second sentence was shorter in the causal sequence than in the temporal sequence. Apparently, causality speeds up the processing of the sentence. According to Keenan, Baillet and Brown (1984) and Myers, Shinjo and Duffy (1987) difference in the strength of the causal relation between sentences affects the process of understanding. The second sentence in (18a) is more strongly related to its preceding sentence than in (18b).

(18a) Joey's big brother punched him again and again. The next day his body was covered with bruises.
(18b) Joey went to a neighbor's house to play. The next day his body was covered with bruises.

This was reflected in a shorter reading time. The interpretation of a sentence is speeded up the stronger the causal relation with its preceding sentence is.

That sentences are better understood the more they correspond to an underlying causal relation is also demonstrated in experiments where the causality is more or less directly expressed in the sentences. This claim can be considered as an instance of iconicity between language and knowledge: the more closely the linguistic structure corresponds to a cognitive structure, the more easily the linguistic structure is understood. In causal and conditional sentences the subordinate clause is the antecedens and the main clause is the consequence. Conceptually however, the antecedens can express both the cause and the consequence and so can the consequence. Consider the examples (19a) and (19b):

(19a) If John is ill, he is not going to his work.
(19b) If John is not going to his work, he is ill.

In (19a) the antecedens expresses the cause; the consequence expresses the consequence. In (19b) the antecedens expresses the consequence and the consequence expresses the cause. In (19a) two propositions that express events in the world are related to each other. In (19b) however, illocutions are related to each other: If John is not going to his work, we may conclude that he is ill. And we can add the justification for this conclusion: because if he is ill, he is not going to his work. Relations as (19a) are called semantic relations; relations as (19b) are called epistemic (Sweetser, 1990) or pragmatic relations (Sanders, Spooren & Noordman, 1992). The characterization of semantic and epistemic relations makes clear that epistemic relations are more complex. An epistemic relation is based on an underlying semantic relation. Semantic relations express a causal relation more directly than epistemic relations. If the iconicity between the linguistic structure and the conceptual structure affects processing time, it is expected that semantic relations are processed faster than pragmatic relations. Noordman (1979) asked participants to read sentences that expressed causal relations and to judge whether the sentences were in general true or not. The time to verify semantic relations was shorter than the time to verify epistemic relations. This is in agreement with the iconicity principle.

8.4. On the Control of Inferences

In understanding a text readers make inferences. This has been illustrated already in the previous Section. Establishing referential coherence and relational coherence requires inferences that are based on world knowledge. Much research has been conducted on inferences. This Section does not aim to give an overview. Overview articles are Singer (1994) and van den Broek (1994).

In reading, world knowledge is activated and many inferences can in principle be made. This leads to a fundamental problem. Inferences are time-consuming processes. But reading is a very fast process. It is definitely not the case that the more knowledge a reader has about the topic of a text, the more inferences are made and the longer it takes to read the text. There must be a control of the inferences. All kinds of distinction have been made between inferences, in the hope that these distinctions will lead to a specification of the kinds of inference that are and are not made during reading.

One distinction is between necessary and elaborative inferences. Necessary inferences are generally defined as those inferences that are required for comprehension. Inferences that are not necessary for comprehension are called elaborative inferences. The notion of necessary inferences is ambiguous; it can mean at least two things (Vonk & Noordman, 1990). It may refer to the property that an inference follows necessarily from the propositions in the text. For example, from the sentences *John is smarter than Bill; Bill is smarter than Pete* follows that John is smarter than Pete. But necessary can also refer to the property that without that inference no coherent representation is obtained. The inference is then necessary for the coherence. In *John phoned Bill up, because he needed some information*, it is necessary for the coherence that an inference concerning the antecedent of the pronoun is made. Because of this second interpretation of necessary, the distinction between necessary and elaborative inferences is sometimes referred to as the distinction between inferences that establish coherence vs. elaborative inferences. Whether these 'necessary' inferences are made during reading is an empirical question.

Another distinction that is frequently made is between forward and backward inferences. Forward inferences anticipate the subsequent text; backward inferences make a connection of the present input to the preceding text. In general, backward inferences establish coherence with the preceding text. Forward inferences are in general more or less probable expectations about the content of the subsequent text. Therefore, the distinction between forward and backward inferences sometimes coincides with the distinction between coherence and elaborative inferences and consequently, with one interpretation of necessary vs. elaborative inferences.

Some other distinctions are less frequently made. Transient inferences are inferences that are made initially when the current input is processed, but that are not incorporated in the text representation. An example of transient representations is given by Swinney (1979). He demonstrated that in processing an ambiguous word both meanings are initially activated. But after 200 msec only the meaning that is appropriate in the context is retained. Another distinction is between inferences that achieve global coherence vs. local coherence. Local coherence inferences establish coherence of the current input with only one or two preceding sentences. Finally, distinctions have been made with respect to the content of the inferences. The question is: what is inferred? This may be a cause, a consequence, a motive, an instrument, a means, a time, etc.

The different distinctions are made with the aim to specify which inferences are made on-line during reading and which inferences are not. There is some consensus that backward inferences that contribute to the coherence of the representation are made on-line and elaborative and forward inferences are not. The most articulated theory is the minimalist theory proposed by McKoon and Ratcliff (1992). According to this theory, only those inferences are made spontaneously during normal reading that are based on easily available information and those that are required to achieve local coherence. Information may be easily available on the basis of explicit statements in the text or on the basis of general knowledge. Local coherence refers to propositions that are not farther apart in the text than one or two sentences. Elaborative inferences and global inferences are generally not made. A question, which is certainly not specific for the minimalist theory, is how to define coherence. If in understanding (16) the inference 'the deterioration of the competitive position leads to a decrease of the export' is not made, why is the resulting representation not coherent? A possible answer is that a coherent representation requires that the use of *because* is justified and that this requires that the causal relation is checked against the reader's knowledge.

McKoon and Ratcliff are certainly correct in claiming that inferences depend on the availability of the information. But how does one determine what "easily available information" is? Consider the inference about the instrument spoon in *Mary stirred her coffee* (Dosher and Corbett, 1982). It is commonly assumed that these instrumental inferences are not made on-line. McKoon and Ratcliff (1981) showed that these instrumental inferences were made on-line when the instrument was mentioned several sentences before the inference sentence. This supports indeed the claim of the minimalist position that increasing the availability of the information leads to the encoding of the inference. But do we have to say that the fact that coffee is stirred with a spoon is not "easily available information...from general knowledge" (McKoon & Ratcliff, 1992, p. 440)? One certainly does not want to define what "easily available information from general knowledge" is on the basis of results on inferencing. Another illustration of the same problem is that, according to McKoon and Ratcliff, the concepts of *sitting* is available after the description of someone approaching a chair, but that the concept *hurt* is not available after the description of a diver who jumps, spurs and hit the cement. This illustrates the need to specify independently what is readily available information from general knowledge.

McKoon and Ratcliff contrast their theory with a constructionist view of inference processing. According to a constructionist point of view the reader constructs a mental model of what the text is about. Such a model contains a rich variety of inferences. The problem for a constructionist view is, obviously, to specify which inferences are made and which ones are not made. The crucial point here is to specify what knowledge is necessary for establishing coherence. Graesser, Singer and Trabasso (1994) describe a constructionist theory that accounts for knowledge-based inferences in narratives. The basic principle in this theory is that reading is a search after meaning. This principle is specified in the following assumptions: reading depends on the reader's goal in reading; readers try to establish both local and global coherence; and readers attempt to explain the actions and events in the text. According to the explanation assumption, inferences about superordinate goals and causal antecedents are made on-line, while inferences about causal consequences are not. The reason why inferences about causal consequences are not made, is that they do not explain the events and that there are too many possible causal consequences. It would be too difficult and too time consuming for the reader to make them. An attractive characteristic of this model is the explanation assumption: readers try to explain the events in the text. Indeed, understanding can be considered as an explanation process. This process is essentially a process in which information in the text is matched to the reader's world knowledge. However, the theory claims that inferences about causal consequences are not made. This is not convincing. A fundamental aspect of intelligent and adaptive behavior is the ability to anticipate the consequences of one's own behavior and to predict the consequences of the behavior of others. That we anticipate consequences of the behavior of others is also illustrated in reading narratives. An narrative is entertaining if actions have unexpected consequences. Suspense implies the expectation about (un)desired outcomes.

Two kinds of inferences will be discussed that were generally assumed not to be made: global inferences and predictive inferences. Some recent studies indicate that these inferences are made. Results of these studies point to some blind spots in inference research and suggest that the question about the control of inferences has been conceived in a too narrow way.

The minimalist theory predicts that global inferences are made only in specific circumstances, for example if they are required to achieve local coherence. However, there is experimental evidence that readers do attempt to achieve global coherence even when there is no local incoherence (Albrecht & O'Brien, 1993; Myers, O'Brien, Albrecht & Mason, 1994; O'Brien & Albrecht, 1992). The studies used texts that contained a description of the protagonist early in the passage, for example, *Mary was a vegetarian.* Later in the text a sentence described an action carried out by the protagonist that was incompatible with the earlier description, in this example *Mary ordered a cheeseburger.* That sentence was locally coherent with its preceding context. In addition, at the moment of reading this sentence, the information about Mary being a vegetarian was no longer readily available. Nevertheless, the inconsistency increased the reading time for the critical sentence, testifying for a global inference. According to Albrecht and O'Brien (1993) these results seem to contradict the minimalist theory of inferences. Global inferences were made, although there was no local coherence break and the critical information was not immediately available. However, it is not sure whether these results are in conflict with the minimalist position. The problem is that it is not quite clear what is meant by "easily available information" in the minimalist theory (Myers et al. 1994). One might argue that the critical information (*Mary was a vegetarian*) becomes immediately available as soon as Mary is mentioned again. It seems very likely that the hierarchical structure and the thematic organization of the text determine what is "readily available information" (Vonk, Hustinx & Simons, 1992).

Also research on predictive inferences is relevant for the question about the control of inferences. It is generally agreed that readers make backward inferences, but not forward, predictive inferences (Potts, Keenan & Golding, 1988; Singer & Ferreira, 1983). The reason why predictive inferences are not made is that it is too difficult and time-consuming for the reader to correctly predict future events. However, one cannot maintain that forward inferences are not made. McKoon and Ratcliff (1986) presented short texts containing a sentence such as (20).

(20) The director and the cameraman were ready to start shooting when suddenly the actress fell from the 14th floor.

A predictable inference is that the actress will be dead. After studying several texts, participants performed a speeded recognition test. The critical test word in the present example was *dead*. The correct response to this test word was no. If the inference that the actress will be dead is made, it will interfere with the correct answer no and more errors will be made relative to a control condition in which the actress did not fell from the 14th floor. In the recognition test the critical word was preceded by a priming word. If this prime was the neutral word *ready*, no effect was observed on the number of errors on the test word. This result indicates that the forward inference was not made. However, if the target word was preceded by a word from the text, for instance, *actress*, participants made more errors when they had read the predicting text than a text in a control condition. McKoon and Ratcliff consider this result as evidence for the partial encoding of the inference. The increase in errors when the prime was a word from the text indicates that the inference was encoded to some degree. The theoretical upshot is that we turn away from a conception in which inferences are either made or not made. Murray, Klin and Myers (1993) demonstrated that forward inferences are made under specific conditions, for example, if the event to be inferred is very predictable and if the relevant information is in focus. Participants read short texts of two sentences. An example of a last sentence is (21a).

(21a) One day, no longer able to control his anger, he threw a delicate porcelain vase against the wall.

(21b) One day, unable to control his impulses, he went out and purchased a delicate porcelain vase

The naming latency for the target word *break* was shorter after sentence (21a) than after the control sentence (21b). Similar evidence for forward inferences is obtained by Keefe and McDaniel (1993) who in addition demonstrated that forward inferences are initially encoded, but that they are gradually deactivated.

In the beginning of this paragraph the question was raised which inferences are made during reading and which inferences are not made. Initially there seemed to be some consensus: only backward inferences are made that construct local coherence, no predictive inferences are made, nor elaborative inferences. But this conclusion should be qualified. The research discussed in this Section makes clear that the question which inferences are made and which ones are not made is too simplistic. That question abstracts away from the question what in fact an inference process is in reading. Current research makes clear that we have to consider more closely what it constitutes to make an inference. It is impossible to choose between contrasting theories, such as the minimalist theory and the constructionist theory, as long as we have not spelled out yet the varieties of inference processes and their determinants. In general, the yes-no question regarding inference making should be replaced by more specific questions regarding the nature of the inference process. One question concerns the time course of the inference process. What is encoded over time? It is possible that many inferences are encoded for a short period of time, but that they get deactivated (Keefe & McDaniel, 1993). Whether inferred information deactivates or not, will no doubt depend on the function of that information in the subsequent text. Inferences play a role in the construction of the text representation that is continuously modified by the new incoming clauses and sentences. A related aspect of inferences that should be incorporated in a theory about inferences is that inferences may differ in their degree of activation. This was demonstrated in the case of the partially made predictive inferences (McKoon & Ratcliff, 1986). One may even hypothesize that the notion of graded inference is necessary to account for the difference between forward and backward inferences. The issue that probably deserves the most attention in a theory about inferences is how the text-based inferences depend on the reader's knowledge. The inference process has to be specified in terms of the activation of knowledge by propositions in the text. Since inferences are an interaction between the text propositions and the reader's knowledge, attention should be paid to the representation of the reader's knowledge. Differences between high-knowledge and low-knowledge readers are interesting, but also general principles that structure human knowledge. An illustration was given in the Section on relational coherence. If causality is a fundamental concept in human cognition, then this explains why causal inferences are a preferred kind of inference. These considerations indicate some ways in which a theory of inferences has to be developed. Bearing in mind that the reader's goals and the text genre affect the inference process, it is clear that our understanding of inferences is still minimal.

8.5   Modeling Text Comprehension

Several models of text comprehension have been developed (e.g., Just & Carpenter, 1992; Kintsch, 1988; Kintsch & van Dijk, 1978; Myers & O'Brien, in press). In studies on discourse processing much attention has been paid to the construction-integration model (Kintsch, 1988) and its predecessor (Kintsch & van Dijk, 1978). We will focus on these models.

The Kintsch and van Dijk model takes as input the propositions in which the text has been analyzed. As has been discussed earlier, a proposition consists of a relational predicate and one or more arguments. Relational predicates are in general verbs, adjectives and adverbs; arguments are in general nouns that express specific cases or another proposition which is then an embedded proposition. As an example, the sentence *The lawyer discussed the case with the judge* is expressed by the proposition: (discuss, lawyer, judge, case). Processing takes place in a cyclical way. In each cycle only a limited number of propositions from the current text is put into working memory. This reflects the fact that working memory has a limited capacity. The number of propositions in each cycle is a parameter in the model. In general it corresponds to the number of propositions in a sentence. In the first cycle the propositions of the first sentence are put into working memory. The process consists in connecting propositions on the basis of common elements, in particular common arguments. The result of the first cycle is a connected network of the propositions. A small number of propositions of the first cycle remains in working memory when the second cycle starts. The number of propositions that is retained in working memory is a parameter of the model and reflects again the limited capacity of working memory. The criteria for selecting the propositions are also parameters of the model. The parameters depend on a reader characteristics, text characteristics and reading strategies. In the second cycle, a set of new propositions is put into working memory. The propositions that are retained from the first cycle serve as anchor point for these new propositions. Again, propositions are connected to each other. This cyclical process is iterated until the whole text is processed. If in a particular cycle a proposition cannot be connected to another proposition, a search process takes place to reinstate a proposition from an earlier cycle. Some propositions remain in working memory during several cycles. Each time that a proposition is selected to remain in working memory increases the chance that that proposition is stored in long term memory and can be reproduced. In this way the model predicts text recall.

The successor to the Kintsch and van Dijk model is the construction-integration model (Kintsch, 1988). This model consists of a construction process and an integration process. In the construction process, a representation is constructed that incorporates the concepts and propositions that are expressed by the text. This representation also includes some associations of these elements that are derived from general knowledge, as well as some concepts and propositions that are inferred. This representation has the form of a network is in which the concepts and propositions are the nodes and the connections between these concepts and propositions are the links between the nodes. As in the earlier model, links between concepts and propositions are made if they have common elements, in general common arguments. The links have a particular strength that is determined by the nature of the connections in the text. The strength is a quantitative variable. The connections between the propositions and concepts can be expressed in a connectivity matrix in which each cell express the strengths of the relation. The generation of the propositions in the construction process is not determined by fixed rules. Some associations are allowed. Even wrong or contradictory propositions are incorporated. It is by the integration process that irrelevant propositions are filtered out and that the contextually appropriate representation is obtained. As an example, consider sentence (22)

(22) *The lawyer discussed the case with the judge. He said "I shall send the defendant to prison".*

He is ambiguous; it can refer to the lawyer and to the judge. Possible propositions of the second sentence in (22) are: say (lawyer, argument) and say (judge, argument). Incorporation of the knowledge that judges and not lawyers can send defendants to prison, leads to the following set of propositions of (22):

P1)   discuss (lawyer, judge, case)
P2)   say (lawyer, P 4)
P3)   say (judge, P5)
P4)   send (lawyer, defendant, prison)
P5)   send (judge, defendant, prison)
P6)   sentence (judge, defendant)

Because of the ambiguity of *he*, two say-propositions and two send-propositions are constructed, one with the judge and one with the lawyer as the agent. One interpretation of (22) is P1, P2 and P4; the other interpretation is P1, P3 and P5.

The integration process serves to derive the representation of the correct interpretation. The mechanism in the integration phase is spreading of activation. The nodes in the network have a numerical value. In the beginning of the integration process all nodes have the same value, except the knowledge nodes, that start with the value zero. Each nodes spreads activation to the nodes with which it is connected, in proportion to its own activation and in proportion to the strength of the connection. Technically speaking, this is a series of multiplications of the connectivity matrix (expressing the connections between the propositions) with a vector (expressing the activations of the propositions). This process continues until no appreciable changes in activations occur anymore. The process has then converged to a stable state. The activations of the propositions in that stable state is the mental representation of the processed text. In example (22) the process stabilizes after 19 iterations. The propositions 2 and 4 with lawyer as agent have then activation zero; the propositions 3 and 5 with judge as agent have then activation values of .261 and .283, resp. This is due to the presence of the knowledge proposition 6. Thus, the integration process yields the correct referent.

The model of Kintsch is very influential in research on text processing. It accounts for a variety of results from experimental studies: lexical processes, pronoun disambiguation, sentence recognition, text recall, to name a few. Nevertheless, some aspects deserve further scrutiny. First, the input in the model is a propositional representation. The construction of this representation leaves much freedom for subjective decisions. The claim that it is not so critical which propositions are included in the construction phase, since irrelevant propositions are filtered out in the integration process, seems rather optimistic. The reason is that the nature of the connectivity matrix has a great influence on the result of the integration process. Second, an attractive aspect of the model is that the reader's knowledge and the text are represented in the same format, so that the reading process can be modeled as an interaction between the text and reader's knowledge. But the application of the model requires an independent specification of the reader's knowledge. A third point concerns the incremental construction of the text representation. The text representation is updated and modified by each new incoming sentence. The integration of consecutive sentences in the text representation deserves more study. What happens with the representation of previous sentences? A model that is more explicit in this respect is the so-called resonance model of Myers and O'Brien (in press). This is also a spreading of activation model. Elements in the current input and elements in the previously processed text spread activation to each other. They 'resonate' to each other. The effect is that earlier concepts and propositions increase or decrease in activation depending on the specific conditions in the text. Both decay and reinstatement of earlier information can be accounted for. Experimental data have shown that specific information becomes less accessible after a topic shift and become activated again after a reinstatement. The resonance model has been developed to account for these changes in accessibility of concepts and propositions in the course of processing the text.

The models discussed in this Section illustrate how text understanding is conceived as a memory-based process in which the current text input makes contact with the previously stored text representation as well as with the memory structures in long term memory.

References

Albrecht, J.E. & O'Brien, E.J. (1993). Updating a mental model: Maintaining both local and global coherence. *Journal of Experimental Psychology: Learning, Memory and Cognition, 19,* 1061-1070.

Anderson, A., Garrod, S.C. & Sanford, A.J. (1983). The accessibility of pronominal antecedents as a function of episode shifts in narrative discourse. *Quarterly Journal of Experimental Psychology, 35a,* 427-440.

Bestgen, Y. & Vonk, W. (1995). The role of temporal segmentation markers in discourse processing. *Discourse Processes, 19,* 385-406.

Black, J.B. & Bern, H. (1981). Causal coherence and memory for events in narratives. *Journal of Verbal Learning and Verbal Behavior, 20,* 267-275.

Bransford, J.D., Barclay, J.R. & Franks, J.J. (1992). Sentence memory: A constructive versus interpretative approach. *Cognitive Psychology, 3,* 193-209.

Clark, H.H. & Sengul, C.J. (1979). In search of referents for nouns and pronouns. *Memory & Cognition, 7,* 35-41.

Clifton, C. & Ferreira, F. (1987). Discourse structure and anaphora: Some experimental results. In M. Coltheart (ed.), *The psychology of reading.* Hove, UK.: Erlbaum.

Dell, G.S., McKoon, G. & Ratcliff, R. (1983). The activation of antecedent information during the processing of anaphoric reference in reading. *Journal of Verbal Learning and Verbal Behavior, 22,* 121-132.

Dopkins, S. (1996). Representation of superordinate goal inferences in memory. *Discourse Processes, 21,* 85-104.

Dosher, B.A. & Corbett, A.T. (1982). Instrument inferences and verb schemata. *Memory & Cognition, 10,* 531-539.

Ehrlich, K. & Rayner, K. (1983). Pronoun assignment and semantic integration during reading: Eye movements and immediacy of processing. *Journal of Verbal Learning and Verbal Behavior, 22,* 75-87.

Fauconnier, G. (1985). *Mental spaces: Aspects of meaning construction in natural language*. Cambridge, MA: MIT Press.

Fletcher, C.R. & Bloom, C.P. (1980). Causal reasoning in the comprehension of simple narrative texts. *Journal of Memory and Language, 27*, 235-244.

Fletcher, C.R. & Chrysler, S.T. (1990). Surface forms, textbases and situation models: Recognition memory for three types of textual information. *Discourse Processes, 13*, 175-190.

Fraurud, K. (1990). Definiteness and the processing of noun phrases in natural discourse. *Journal of Semantics, 7*, 395-433.

Frazier, L. (1987). Sentence processing: A tutorial review. In M.Coltheart (ed.), *The psychology of reading*. Hove, UK.: Erlbaum.

Garnham, A. (1987). *Mental models as representations of discourse and text*. Chichester: Horwood.

Garrod, S., O'Brien, E.J., Morris, R.K. & Rayner, K. (1990). Elaborative inferencing as an active or passive process. *Journal of Experimental Psychology: Learning, Memory and Cognition, 16*, 250-257.

Garrod, S. & Sanford, A.J. (1982). Bridging inferences and the extended domain of reference. In J. Long & A. Baddeley (eds.), *Attention and performance, IX*. Hillsdale, N.J.: Erlbaum.

Givón, T. (1983). Topic continuity in discourse: An introduction. In T. Givón (ed.), *Topic continuity in discourse: A quantitative language study*. Amsterdam: Benjamins.

Glenberg, A.M., Meyer, M. & Lindem, K. (1987). Mental models contribute to foregrounding during text comprehension. *Journal of Memory and Language, 26*, 69-83.

Graesser, A.C. & Clark, L.F. (1985). *Structures and procedures of implicit knowledge*. Norwood, NJ: Ablex.

Graesser, A.C., Singer, M. & Trabasso, T. (1994). Constructing inferences during narrative text comprehension. *Psychological Review, 101*, 371-395.

Grober, E.H., Beardsley, W. & Caramazza, A. (1978). Parallel function strategy in pronoun assignment. *Cognition, 6*, 117-133.

Haviland, S.E. & Clark, H.H. (1974). What's new? Acquiring new information as a process in comprehension. *Journal of Verbal Learning and Verbal Behavior, 13*, 512-521.

Hobbs, J.R. (1979). Coherence and coreference. *Cognitive Science, 3*, 67-90.

Jarvella, R.J. (1971). Syntactic processing of connected speech. *Journal of Verbal Learning and Verbal Behavior, 10,* 409-416.

Johnson-Laird, P.N. (1983). *Mental models.* Cambridge: Cambridge University Press.

Just, M.A. & Carpenter, P.A. (1992). A capacity theory of comprehension: Individual differences in working memory. *Psychological Review, 99,* 122-149.

Kamp, H. (1981). A theory of truth and semantic interpretation. In J.A.G. Groenendijk, T.M.V. Janssen & M.B.J. Stokhof (eds.), *Formal methods in the study of language.* Amsterdam: Mathematisch Centrum.

Kamp, H. & Reyle, U. (1993). *From discourse to logic: Introduction to modeltheoretic semantics of natural language, formal logic and discourse representation theory.* Dordrecht: Kluwer.

Keefe, D.E. & McDaniel, M.A. (1993). The time course and durability of predictive inferences. *Journal of Memory and Language, 32,* 446-463.

Keenan, J.M., Baillet, S.D. & Brown, P. (1984). The effects of causal cohesion on comprehension and memory. *Journal of Verbal Learning and Verbal Behavior, 23,* 115-126.

Kintsch, W. (1988). The role of knowledge in discourse comprehension: A construction-integration model. *Psychological Review, 95,* 163-182.

Kintsch, W. (1994). Text comprehension, memory and learning. *American Psychologist, 49,* 294-303.

Kintsch, W. & Van Dijk, T.A. (1978). Towards a model of text comprehension and production. *Psychological Review, 85,* 363-394.

Kintsch, W., Welsch, D., Schmalhofer, F. & Zimny, S. (1990). Sentence memory: A theoretical analysis. *Journal of Memory and Language, 29,* 133-159.

Lesgold, A.M., Roth, S.F. & Curtis, M.E. (1979). *Journal of Verbal Learning and Verbal Behavior, 18,* 291-308.

Long, D.L., Golding, J.M. & Graesser, A.C. (1992). A test of the on-line status of goal-related inferences. *Journal of Memory and Language, 31,* 634-647.

Mani, K. & Johnson-Laird, P.N. (1982). The mental representation of spatial descriptions. *Memory and Cognition, 10,* 181-187.

Mann, W.C. & Thompson, S.A. (1986). Relational propositions in discourse. *Discourse Processes, 9,* 57-90.

McKoon, G. & Ratcliff, R. (1981). The comprehension processes and memory structures involved in instrumental inference. *Journal of Verbal Learning and Verbal Behavior, 20,* 671-682.

McKoon, G. & Ratcliff, R. (1986). Inferences about predictable events. *Journal of Experimental Psychology: Learning, Memory and Cognition, 12*, 82-91.

McKoon, G. & Ratcliff, R. (1992). Inference during reading. *Psychological Review, 99*, 440-466.

McNamara, D.S., Kintsch, E., Songer, N.B. & Kintsch, W. (1996). Text coherence, background knowledge and levels of understanding in learning from text. *Cognition and Instruction, 14*, 1-43.

Morrow, D.G. (1985). Prominent characters and events organize narrative understanding. *Journal of Memory and Language, 24*, 304-319.

Morrow, D.G., Greenspan, S.L. & Bower, G.H. (1987). Accessibility and situation models in narrative comprehension. *Journal of Memory and Language, 26*, 165-187.

Murray, J.D., Klin, C.M. & Myers, J.L. (1993). Forward inferences in narrative text. *Journal of Memory and Language, 32*, 464-473.

Myers, J.L. & O'Brien, E.J. (in press). Accessing the discourse representation during reading.

Myers, J.L., O'Brien, E.J., Albrecht, J.E. & Mason, R.A. (1994). Maintaining global coherence. *Journal of Experimental Psychology: Learning, Memory and Cognition, 20*, 876-886.

Myers, J.L., Shinjo, M. & Duffy, S.A. (1987). Degree of causal relatedness and memory. *Journal of Memory and Language, 26*, 453-465.

Noordman, L.G.M. (1979). *Inferring from language.* Berlin: Springer.

Noordman, L.G.M. & Vonk, W. (1992). Readers' knowledge and the control of inferences in reading. *Language and Cognitive Processes, 7*, 373-391.

Noordman, L.G.M., Vonk, W. & Kempff, H.J. (1992). Causal inferences during the reading of expository texts. *Journal of Memory and Language, 13*, 573-590.

O'Brien, E.J. & Albrecht, J.E. (1992). Comprehension strategies in the development of a mental model. *Journal of Experimental Psychology: Learning, Memory and Cognition, 18*, 777-784.

O'Brien, E.J., Plewes, P.S. & Albrecht, J.E. (1990). Antecedent retrieval processes. *Journal of Experimental Psychology: Learning, Memory and Cognition, 16*, 241-249.

Potts, G.R. (1972). Information processing strategies in the encoding of linear orderings. *Journal of Verbal Learning and Verbal Behavior, 11*, 727-740.

Potts, C.R., Keenan, J.M. & Golding, J.M. (1988). Assessing the occurrence of elaborative inferences: Lexical decision versus naming. *Journal of Memory and Language, 27,* 399-415.

Prince, E.F. (1981). Towards a taxonomy of given-new information. In P. Cole (ed.), *Radical pragmatics.* New York: Academic Press.

Ratcliff, R. & McKoon, G. (1978). Priming in item recognition: Evidence for the propositional structure of sentences. *Journal of Verbal Learning and Verbal Behavior, 17,* 403-417.

Rumelhart, D.E. (1977). Understanding and summarizing brief stories. In D. LaBerge & S.J. Samuels (eds.), *Basic processes in reading: Perception and comprehension.* Hillsdale, N.J.: Erlbaum.

Sachs, J.S. (1967). Recognition memory for syntactic and semantic aspects of connected discourse. *Perception and Psychophysics, 2,* 437-442.

Sanders, T.J.M., Spooren, W.P.M. & Noordman, L.G.M. (1992). Toward a taxonomy of coherence relations. *Discourse Processes, 15,* 1-35.

Sanford, A.J. & Garrod, S. C. (1981). *Understanding written language: Explorations in comprehension beyond the sentence.* Chichester: Wiley.

Sanford, A.J., Moar, K. & Garrod, S. C. (1988). Proper names as controllers of discourse focus. *Language and Speech, 31,* 43-56.

Schmalhofer, F. & Glavanov, D. (1986). Three components of understanding a programmer's manual: Verbatim, propositional and situational representations. *Journal of Memory and Language, 25,* 279-294.

Schustack, M.W., Ehrlich, S.F. & Rayner, K. (1987). Local and global sources of contextual facilitation in reading. *Journal of Memory and Language, 26,* 322-340.

Seuren, P.A.M. (1985). *Discourse semantics.* Oxford: Blackwell.

Sheldon, A. (1974). The role of parallel function in the acquisition of relative clauses in English. *Journal of Verbal Learning and Verbal Behavior, 13,* 272-281.

Simons, W.H.G. (1993). *De regulering van inferenties door de kennis van de lezer.* [The control of inferences by the knowledge of the reader.] Unpublished doctoral dissertation, Nijmegen University, Nijmegen.

Singer, M. (1994). Discourse inference processes. In M.A. Gernsbacher (ed.), *Handbook of psycholinguistics.* San Diego: Academic Press.

Singer, M. & Ferreira, F. (1983). Inferring consequences in story comprehension. *Journal of Verbal Learning and Verbal Behavior, 22,* 437-448.

Singer, M., Halldorson, M., Lear, J.C. & Andrusiak, P. (1992). Validation of causal bridging inferences in discourse understanding. *Journal of Memory and Language, 31,* 507-524.

Sweetser, E. (1990). *From etymology to pragmatics: Metaphorical and cultural aspects of semantic structure.* Cambridge: Cambridge University Press.

Swinney, D.A. (1979). Lexical access during sentence comprehension: (Re)Consideration of context effects. *Journal of Verbal Learning and Verbal Behavior, 18,* 645-659.

Trabasso, T. & van den Broek, P. (1985). Causal thinking and the representation of narrative events. *Journal of Memory and Language, 24,* 612-630.

van den Broek, P.W. (1990). The causal inference maker: Towards a process model of inference generation in text comprehension. In D.A. Balota, G.B. Flores d'Arcais & K. Rayner (eds.), *Comprehension processes in reading.* Hillsdale, NJ: Erlbaum.

van den Broek, P.W. (1994). Comprehension and memory of narrative texts: Inference and coherence. In M.A. Gernsbacher (ed.), *Handbook of psycholinguistics.* San Diego: Academic Press.

van Dijk, T.A. & Kintsch, W. (1983). *Strategies of discourse comprehension.* New York: Academic Press.

Vonk, W. (1984). Eye movements during comprehension of pronouns. In A.G. Gale & F. Johnson (eds.), *Theoretical and applied aspects of eye movement research.* Amsterdam: Elsevier.

Vonk, W. (1985). The immediacy of inferences in the understanding of pronouns. In G. Rickheit & H. Strohner (eds.), *Inferences in text processing.* Amsterdam: Elsevier.

Vonk, W., Hustinx, L.G.M.M. & Simons, W.H.G. (1992). The use of referential expressions in structuring discourse. *Language and Cognitive Processes, 7,* 301-333.

Vonk, W. & Noordman, L.G.M. (1990). On the control of inferences in text understanding. In D.A. Balota, G.B. Flores d'Arcais & K. Rayner (eds.), *Comprehension processes in reading.* Hillsdale, NJ: Erlbaum.

Vonk, W. & Noordman, L.G.M. (1992). Kennis en inferenties bij het lezen van tekst. [Knowledge and inferences in reading text.] *Toegepaste Taalwetenschap in Artikelen, 43,* 39-54.

Zwaan, R.A., Magliano, J.P. & Graesser, A.C. (1995). Dimensions of situation model construction in narrative comprehension. *Journal of Experimental Psychology: Learning, Memory and Cognition, 21,* 386-397.

Chapter 9

The Neurobiology of Language Comprehension

Angela D. Friederici

9.1 Introduction

The process of language comprehension consists of a number of distinct subprocesses which operate on different knowledge sources. The process from the input to the neutral representation of the meaning that has been conveyed may be described as follows: as a first step peripheral *input systems* will have to process the auditory or visual language input, the *phonological processing level* will analyze the input and build up a phonological representation which allows access to the lexicon and identification of given lexical entries. At the *lexical level* morphological aspects and semantic aspects become evident. When processing lexical elements in sentential context syntactic aspects such as the word's syntactic category comes into play. Moreover, during sentence processing the system not only has access to those words that refer to the outside world, i.e. the content words, but access to function words also. These latter words indicate the grammatical relations holding between the content words and are therefore of major importance for a sentence's interpretation. Grammatical relations may, depending on the language, also be marked by inflectional morphology. Function words and inflectional elements constitute the class of minor category items, the so-called closed class, whereas content words constitute the class of major category items, the so-called open class. The former class plus the information about a word's syntactic category allow the building of a syntactic structure at the *sentence level*. The further integration of such sentence representations into world knowledge may be viewed as the process of 'understanding' in the most general use of this term. To achieve this the processing system furthermore identifies relations between different sentences in order to construct a propositional representation at a *text or discourse level*. All these processes must be completed with extreme speed in order to guarantee normal comprehension.

Models of language comprehension agree that these different subprocesses are part of the comprehension process. They disagree, however, with respect to the issue, if and to what extent those subprocesses interact in time (see Frauenfelder & Tyler, 1987 for a review). Two extreme positions can be identified with the current models: the so-called serial or syntax-first models (e.g., Frazier, 1978, 1987a,b; Gorrell, 1995) and the so-called interactive models (e.g., Marslen-Wilson & Tyler, 1980; McClelland, St.John & Taraban, 1989). Serial or syntax-first models claim that the parser initially builds up a syntactic structure independent of lexical-semantic or sentential-semantic information and that semantic aspects only come into play during a second processing stage. Interactive models, in contrast, assume that structural and semantic information interact at any time during parsing. The serial approach is related to the view that the language processing system consists of modular subsystems. Modularity as defined by Fodor (1983) holds that a subsystem is domain specific, that it is informationally encapsulated, based on a fixed neural substrate and that it can be selectively affected by brain lesions. A subsystem's modularity can thus not only be tested behaviorally, but can also be validated by neuroscientific data.[1] Interactive approaches are either neutral with respect to the assumption of subsystems, as for example (MacDonald et al., 1992) who assumes such subsystems but allows them to interact directly or they deny separate subsystems for syntactic and semantic processes (Marslen-Wilson & Tyler, 1980).

The following Section 9.2 will describe those brain systems that are involved in language processing. Section 9.3 will specify the temporal structure of language comprehension on the basis of neurophysiological evidence. In Section 9.4 I will present a model of language processing that incorporates the neurotopological/neuroanatomical and the temporal parameters characterizing the different subsystems.

9.2   Neuronal Subsystems of Language Processing

The neuroscientific evidence suggesting different subsystems which will be discussed in this paper is mainly based on findings from behavioral studies with patients with circumscribed brain lesions and results from brain imaging studies with normal subjects. The latter studies mostly used positron emission tomography (PET) as a measure of brain activity and in some cases functional magnetic resonance tomography (fMRT).

PET measures the regional cerebral bloodflow in the brain. The spatial resolution of the method is relatively good, its temporal resolution, however, does not support any conclusions about cognitive processes in real time. For this reason I will use the results gained by this method to identify different subsystems only and refrain from interpreting the dynamics of the interplay between the subsystems. All PET studies use the so-called subtraction paradigm (Friston et al., 1996). It is based on the assumption that cognitive functions as well as the neuronal activity underlying these functions are additive. The simplest version of this paradigm investigates subjects in two tasks (a critical task and a baseline task) which often involve a number of common operations or processes. The goal is to isolate these subprocesses by substracting

---

[1]   Further criteria for modularity of a subsystem are that it works obligatorily, fast and automatically.

the brain activity registered during the baseline task from the critical task. This paradigm, however, has a weakness as it assumes that the two tasks only differ with respect to one subprocess. This assumption is often difficult to maintain; the assumption of the additivity of cognitive processes may not always hold as there might be interactions between processes and the specific tasks involved (Friederici et al., 1996; Jennings et al., 1977). Thus it is not clear that the subtraction isolates the particular subprocesses under investigation.

A relatively new method measuring the regional bloodflow of the metabolic brain activity is functional magnetic resonance imaging which allows a higher spatial resolution than PET. As there are only few studies on language processing using this new method I will only refer to them selectively.

The relevant neurolinguistic evidence provided by aphasia research can be specified in the following way. Ideally the evidence comes from studies involving patients with circumscribed brain lesions and whose language break down is specific and not caused by general degenerative processes (e.g., Alzheimer's disease) or by non-language deficits (e.g., memory deficit). The term aphasia as used here will only cover language processing deficits that occur in the adult speaker / hearer not including language deficits during development (Friederici, 1984; Goodglass, 1993).

Unfortunately, many papers published in the field of aphasia do not provide clear neuroanatomical data and, therefore, do not allow direct conclusions about the language - brain relationship. These studies follow an approach which may be labeled 'Neuropsychology of Cognition'. This approach beginning in the seventies but still in vogue, investigates cognitive deficits independent of a specification of its neural basis (Ellis & Young, 1988). The availability of neuroanatomical data provided by computed tomography, structural magnetic resonance imaging and more recent functional imaging techniques, however, gave rise to a new type of neuropsychology investigating cognitive functions in relation to its neural basis. The approach is covered by the term 'Cognitive Neuroscience' (Kosslyn, 1994).

The present chapter follows the 'Cognitive Neuroscience' approach. Nonetheless, patient studies without clear neuroanatomical data will be used to illustrate specific language break down whenever these may help to specify the functional aspects of the language processing system. In some, but not in all cases these findings be complemented by studies using functional imaging.

9.2.1   Phonological Subsystem and Auditory Word Recognition

9.2.1.1   Evidence from Aphasia
The first phase of lexical processing, i.e. from the analysis of the acoustic-phonetic input to the phonological representation was described by many models as a purely perceptive process, either based on phoneme identification (Eimas et al., 1971) or on spectral information (Klatt, 1979, 1986). Liberman and colleagues (Liberman et al.,

1967; Liberman & Mattingly, 1985), in contrast, proposed the so-called 'motor theory of speech perception'. This theory holds that the acoustic input is analyzed into units that correspond to articulatory gestures. According to this theory processes of language perception are closely related to processes of language production. This aspect appears to be relevant with respect to recent findings from PET studies which found word perception to be correlated not only with activity in the left superior temporal gyrus, but also with activity in the premotor and motor cortex (Brodmann area (BA) 4, 6, 44, see Figure 1) (Zatorre et al., 1996). Studies with aphasics who suffer from deficits of the acoustic-phonetic aspects of speech processing, indicate that the ability to discriminate phonemes can be selectively impaired (Auerbach et al., 1982; Shankweiler & Studdert-Kennedy, 1967; Blumstein et al., 1977b). Blumstein et al. (1977b) report that the ability to identify 'voice-onset-time' (i.e. the difference between a voiced and a voiceless consonant) is more likely to be disrupted in Wernicke patients than in Broca patients. Basso, Casati and Vignolo (1977), in contrast, found Broca aphasics to perform worse than Wernicke aphasics in a phoneme discrimination task. Both studies classify their patients according to aphasia type without providing detailed information about lesion site. Broca's aphasia, however, is known to correlate with lesions in the anterior language cortex, whereas Wernicke's aphasia is mostly caused by lesions in the posterior language cortex. The finding that both aphasia types show deficits in phoneme discrimination may be taken to indicate that parts of the posterior language cortex as well as parts of the premotor or motor cortex are involved in phoneme discrimination.

Impaired perception of segmental contrasts during phoneme discrimination may in principle affect the representation of the abstract phonemic features as well as the acoustic parameters associated with these abstract features. To clarify this issue Blumstein et al. (1977a) conducted a study investigating categorial perception of phonemes varying in their locus of articulation and their voicedness. Aphasics and controls demonstrated a similar discrimination performance. However, aphasics, in contrast to normal controls, had more difficulty with these stimuli in a production task compared to a discrimination task. This suggests that a deficit in phoneme discrimination is not based on an inability to extract the spectral pattern, but rather on the inability to activate the phonetic and/or phonological representation. It appears that this aspect of language processing requires the anterior brain structures to be intact.

A case report by Berndt and Mitchum (1990) seems to suggest a possible distinction between acoustic-phonetic processes on the one hand and access to the auditory lexicon on the other. They present a patient whose acoustic-phonetic processes are intact, but who is unable to access the mental lexicon. Her phoneme discrimination was good, but her ability to discriminate between words and non-words was poor. However, as this patient was able to understand single words quite well, her word discrimination deficit may be due to a memory deficit. Thus the assumed distinction between acoustic-phonetic processes and lexical access must await further validation.

The numerous studies investigating processing abilities at the phoneme level and at the level of auditory comprehension do not provide firm evidence for a direct relation between these abilities. On the one hand there are studies reporting patients with minimal deficits at the phoneme level who are nonetheless severely impaired in auditory language comprehension, on the other hand there are reports on patients with a maximal deficit at the phoneme level whose auditory comprehension is relatively intact (Blumstein et al., 1977b; Miceli et al., 1980; Caplan & Aydelott-Utman, 1994). These findings suggest, that auditory word recognition may not necessarily be based on phoneme discrimination, but that it may also be possible on the basis of sublexical units (e.g., syllables). An other explanation for the observed data would be the assumption of a direct mapping between acoustic and lexical information (Klatt, 1979, 1989).

9.2.1.2   Evidence from Functional Brain Imaging
The phonological subsystem of the auditory language processing system has been investigated in a number of PET studies (Dèmonet, Wise & Frackowiak, 1993; Zatorre, Evans, Meyer & Gjedde, 1992). The ability to identify phonemes has generally been localized in the left temporal cortex, the so-called Wernicke area (Kertesz, 1979, 1983). In terms of the Brodmann scheme these are the Brodmann areas (BA) 42, 22 and 40 in the left hemisphere (see Figure 1).

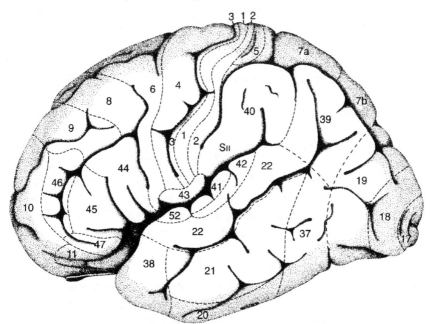

Figure 1. Brodmann's cytoarchitectonically defined areas of the human cortex

PET studies focusing on auditory perception and auditory word recognition show that the superior temporal gyrus of the left and the right hemisphere are responsible for the perceptual analysis of speech signals. These areas are active when subjects listen to language stimuli passively (Petersen et al., 1988; Wise et al., 1991; Zatorre et al., 1992). This finding is supported by a recent fMRI study (Binder et al., 1994). The posterior region of the left superior temporal gyrus and the adjacent temporal operculum support the auditory language comprehension (Petersen et al., 1989; Zatorre et al., 1996). This region is not active during the processing of simple tones (Lauter et al., 1985; Zatorre et al., 1992) or during the discrimination of tones (Dèmonet et al., 1992, 1994). Price et al. (1992) observed a linear increase of the regional bloodflow with the presentation rate of words in the left and the right primary auditory cortex, but no increase in the left posterior superior temporal gyrus (Wernicke's area). This again provides evidence for the view that these two areas serve different functions.

Interestingly, PET studies also indicate activation in the left anterior regions of the left hemisphere or in the vicinity of the Broca's area as a function of phonetic processing. This is most evident when the task requires a detailed analysis of phonetic units or of phonetic sequences (Dèmonet et al., 1992; Zatorre et al., 1996). The foci of this activation are located in the upper, posterior part of BA 44 adjacent to BA 6, but not in the lower part of BA 44 (i.e., lower part of the frontal operculum), classically called Broca's area. This suggests a functional distinction between a superior posterior region of BA 44 and an inferior region of BA 44. While the former region may primarily support the processing of phonetic details and sequences, the inferior region may mainly be responsible for the processing of syntactic elements (i.e. elements of the closed class) and syntactic sequences. These PET results, moreover, might provide a possible explanation for the apparently controversial findings in the aphasia literature concerning phoneme discrimination. Blumstein et al. (1977b) reported Wernicke patients to be particularly impaired in their ability to discriminate phonemes, whereas Basso et al. (1977) found Broca patients to be particularly impaired in a phoneme discrimination test. Although it is problematic to compare the two studies directly, a possible assumption is that the Broca patients in the two studies did not suffer from comparable lesions. Based on the PET findings Broca patients with impaired phoneme discrimination abilities should have lesions which include the superior posterior part of BA 44, whereas this should not be the case for Broca patients with intact phoneme discrimination. Future research will have to show whether is assumption is valid.

9.2.2 Visual Word Recognition

The differences in processing spoken and written words is discussed in detail by Engelkamp & Rummer (in this volume). This discussion includes evidence from aphasia research for separate access systems for acoustically and visually presented words in the lexicon. These findings will not repeated here.

The different models of visual word processing agree that the processing of visually presented words activates a number of abstract codes in the brain (a) a visual code active during perceptual analysis, (b) an orthographic-lexical code representing the visual word form and (c) a semantic code representing the meaning. However, the discussion is still ongoing with respect to the question of whether the semantic code can be activated directly via the orthographic code or whether this is only possible by phonological meditation (e.g., Humphreys & Evett, 1985; Coltheart, 1978; Rubenstein, Lewis & Rubenstein, 1971; Shallice, Warrington & McCarthy, 1983). Although there are multiple studies addressing this question, their findings do not allow to draw a final conclusion. From the available data, however, the assumption of a dual-route system of word reading emerges. Thus visual word input may in principle be processed via two routes: (1) a lexical route, i.e. from the orthographic word form directly to the semantic representation and (2) a nonlexical route, i.e. from the orthographic representation via grapheme-to-phoneme correspondence to the phonological word form and the semantic representation (Morton & Patterson, 1980; Ellis, 1982). Seidenberg et al. (1984) proposed that high frequency words are likely to be processed directly via route 1, whereas low frequency words are processed via route 2.

9.2.2.1 Aphasiological Evidence

Different types of reading impairments have been used to model the process of visual word recognition.

Patients with a so-called *deep dyslexia* are characterized by a difficulty to read nonwords, and by semantically related reading errors (e.g., *liberty* instead of *freedom*) as well as visually related reading errors (e.g., *perfume* instead of *perform)* (Coltheart, Patterson & Marshall, 1980). These data suggest the existence of a lexical route from orthographic input to the semantic representation (Morton & Patterson, 1980).

Patients with the syndrome of *phonological dyslexia* are characterized by an inability to read nonwords, but a spared ability to read words (Beauvois & Derousnè, 1979; Shallice & Warrington, 1980; Patterson, 1980). Reading errors can be classified as visual, but not as semantic. The interpretation of this deficit assumes that these patients have lost the ability to use the phoneme-to-grapheme conversion rules. Suggesting an impairment of the nonlexical route and a relatively intact lexical route.

Patients with a so-called *surface dyslexia* display a reverse pattern of behavior. These patients are able to read nonwords aloud, but their word reading is poor (Marshall & Newcombe, 1973; Shallice & Warrington, 1980). Reading of regular words is better than reading of exception words. It appears as if these patients' reading is reliant on the application of grapheme-to-phoneme correspondence rules suggesting an intact nonlexical route, but an impaired lexical route.

Patients with the syndrome of *letter-by-letter reading* (Patterson & Kay, 1982) appear unable to either generate or use an adequate orthographic description of the visual input. When reading they have to pronounce letter-by-letter in order to generate a phonological form on the basis of what the word is identified. Dèjerne (1891, 1892) was the first to report such a case. He interpreted this behavioral pattern neuroanatomically as a disconnection between the two occipital cortices responsible for primary visual processes and the system of the visual word form representation located in the left hemisphere. This neuroanatomical interpretation was rejected by Kinsbourne and Warrington (1962) in favor of a functional description. They claimed that the phenomenon of letter-by-letter reading is the reflection of a more general deficit, namely the disability to perceive several forms (here letters) simultaneously.

Functionally the four syndroms suggest a system of visual word recognition allowing for a lexical as well as a nonlexical access to the lexicon. When reading aloud the semantic representation can, in principle, be by-passed completely. This route, normally probably only used for reading new words, can be selectively spared in brain-lesioned subjects. The functional description provided in the literature does not allow a description of the neuroanatomical basis for word reading and its impairment. In the following we will discuss the possible neuroanatomical basis of visual word processing taken PET studies into account.

9.2.2.2 Evidence from Functional Brain Imaging

Visual processing of words (silent reading) and reading aloud has been investigated in a number of PET studies. In their pioneering studies Petersen, Posner and colleagues (Petersen et al., 1988, 1989, 1990; Posner et al., 1988) measured the regional bloodflow during silent reading and reading aloud. Their studies suggest that visual word forms are represented in the left extrastriate visual cortex. silent reading of words was compared to the visual processing of simple visual stimuli (flashing plus sign). A substraction of the activation evoked by the latter condition from the former revealed a selective activation in the left extrastriate visual cortex, not in the temporal lobe (Posner et al., 1988; Petersen et al., 1989, 1990). In an other study investigating the process of visually presented words (Petersen et al., 1989) activation in the extrastriate cortex was found bilaterally. In yet an other study (Petersen et al., 1990) words and nonwords evoked activation in the left medial extrastriate cortex (gyrus lingualis and cuneus). Words, but not nonwords, additionally caused activation in the left inferior frontal cortex (possibly BA 45). The latter two studies were taken to indicate that orthographic encoding is located in the left medial extrastriate cortex. The finding of additional activation in the left inferior frontal cortex for words, but not for nonwords seemed to suggest that this region in the frontal cortex supports semantic processes.

Howard et al. (1992) also evaluating the processes underlying reading word aloud found activation in the posterior part of the left middle temporal gyrus, but no activation in the extrastriate cortex. In a follow-up study, Price et al. (1992) similarly deserved activation in the posterior part of the left middle temporal gyrus and additional activation in the occipital cortex bilaterally. These apparent contradictory results may find their explanation when considering the following study.

Chertkow et al. (in press) used four different conditions in a PET study to investigate the process of word reading: concrete words, abstract words, xx-letter strings and + - signs. The visual processing of concrete and abstract words (by substracting the activation for + - sign) was correlated with an activation in the left occipital region. When substracting the activation for xx-letter strings from word processing no activation was found in the region, but in the left temporal lobe. These data suggest that the processing of letters, in contrast to other signs, evokes an activation in the left extrastriate cortex. It appears that this region of the left hemisphere is specialized for the processing of letters, whereas processing of lexical aspects is supported by the superior and middle temporal gyrus of the left hemisphere (BA 22, 21) (Price et al., 1994; Bookheimer et al., 1995; Chertkow et al., in press).

9.2.3 Semantic Subsystems
The description of the neuronal basis of the semantic system is a difficult enterprise. As evident from chapter 9 any model of the semantic subsystem must distinguish between conceptual-semantic aspects and lexical-semantic aspects. Bierwisch and Schreuder (1992) formulate a theoretical basis for such a distinction. In their approach they distinguish between a level of semantic form (SF) representing the lexical-semantic aspects, i.e. meaning, and a level of conceptual structure (CS) representing factual knowledge and assumptions not represented in (SF). The relation between these two levels of representation is described as follow it "requires SF to be embedded into representations of CS, where embedding is to be conceived as the relation of a partial model to a more complete model the partial model is compatible with" (p. 33). Due to this kind of relation SF can be subject to principles that do not hold for CS, and vice versa. According to Bierwisch and Schreuder (1992) "this seems to be a natural consequence of the modular organization of the mind / brain, according to which the computational structure of language might be partially autonomous with respect to the organization of general world knowledge". An empirical test of this model is hard to achieve as SF and CS are only partly autonomous. Nonetheless, I will discuss the neuropsychological literature on semantic processing, in two separate Sections one focusing on lexical-semantic aspects (9.2.3.1.) and the other focusing on conceptual-semantic aspects (9.2.3.2). The issue of the interface between the lexical-semantic subsystem and the conceptual-semantic subsystem will be taken up in Section 9.2.3.3.

9.2.3.1 Lexical-Semantic Subsystem
Since the beginning of the seventies the lexical-semantic subsystem has been located in the Wernicke area. Early psycholinguistic studies demonstrated a selective impairment of lexical-semantic processing in Wernicke's aphasics. These patients not only showed problems in understanding and generating words either in picture naming or object naming tasks, they were also unable to judge words according to

their semantic category (Goodglass & Baker, 1976; Whitehouse, Caramazza & Zurif, 1978; Zurif, Caramazza, Myerson & Galvin, 1974). These studies were taken as evidence for a selective semantic deficit in Wernicke's aphasics. Zurif et al. (1974) used a paradigm in which subjects were asked to select two semantically related words from a word triple. These words varied in semantic dimensions such as human - nonhuman, wild - harmless etc. In contrast to Broca patients and to normal controls, Wernicke patients were not able to categorize the words according to their semantic features. Paradigms used by Goodglass and Baker (1976) and by Whitehouse et al. (1978) required explicit semantic judgments. Wernicke aphasics again demonstrated a clear lexical-semantic deficit. This behavior was explained either by a loss of semantic information in the lexicon or as an impairment of the organization in the mental lexicon.

Blumstein and colleagues (Blumstein et al., 1982; Milberg & Blumstein, 1981) conducted a series of experiments using semantic priming. In this paradigm subjects are not required to explicitly judge semantic aspects, but they are only asked to judge whether a sequence of letters or sounds are a word of their language or not. Normally reaction times are faster when the target word is preceded by a semantically related word than when preceded by a non-related word. This reaction time difference, called semantic priming effect, is taken to reflect semantic processing. Wernicke patients, similar to normal healthy subjects, show a semantic priming effect in such tasks.

On the basis of the finding that Wernicke patients show deficits when asked for explicit judgments (Goodglass & Baker, 1976; Whitehouse et al., 1978; Zurif et al., 1974), but not in tasks requiring lexical-semantic processing implicitly Milberg et al. (1987) formulated the following hypothesis. They postulated that controlled lexical-semantic processes are impaired in Wernicke patients, although automatic lexical-semantic processes are relatively intact.

Hagoort (1993) investigated this hypothesis in a number of priming experiments. In these experiments subjects were presented with triplets of words, e.g., *river - bank - money* versus *coin - bank - money* in which the second word had two meanings, each of which was primed by the first word. In these experiments which were conducted with different interstimulus intervals (ISI) between the words of the triplet no deficit was found for Wernicke patients when the ISI was short (100 ms, 500 ms). Wernicke patients as well as Broca patients displayed normal priming effects. At an ISI of 1250 ms both patient groups, in contrast to normals, showed no priming effects. Hagoort (1993) presented two explanations for the results observed for the patients: (1) semantic information decays early, (2) controlled processes which normally might come into play at long ISI may be disrupted.

The combined data indicate that patients with lesions in the posterior language region (Wernicke patients) as well as patients with lesions in the anterior language region are able to process lexical-semantic information automatically, as revealed by priming experiments. Wernicke patients, however, demonstrate problems in processing lexical-semantic information when explicit judgments are required. Thus it appears that declarative lexical-semantic knowledge is represented in the posterior parts of the left hemisphere.

9.2.3.2 Conceptual-Semantic System

It is interesting to note that the majority of the semantic deficits discussed in the literature are modality specific. A central conceptual-semantic deficit, however, would require a concept to not be accessed by either verbal or non-verbal routes. This still would not be a sufficient proof of a central deficit concerning the representation of the concept as there would always be the possibility that the observable deficit could be due to a deficit in each of the access routes. What is clear, however, is that if the concept is accessible through at least one route, deficits in all the other domains have to be defined as access problems.

For a description of a large number of semantic deficits which are due to general or modality specific word recognition problems or due to problems in object recognition the reader is referred to Caplan (1992).

For the discussion concerning the organization of the semantic-conceptual system reports describing category specific semantic deficits may be most relevant. Warrington and Shallice (1984) report that patients with bilateral temporal lesions (due to herpes simplex encephalitis) show a selective impairment in object recognition for living things and food items with a relatively intact performance for non-living things. Similar cases were reported by Sartori & Job (1988) and Silveri & Gainotti (1987) (for a review, see Saffran & Schwartz, 1994). In contrast, patients who had more problems in processing words labeling non-living things had lesions in the left temporal lobe and the basal ganglia (due to cerebral vascular diseases). These latter patients were all classified aphasic (see Saffran & Schwartz, 1994). Warrington and Shallice (1984) take the difference in processing living things and non-living things to be due to the fact that the semantic description of living things usually contain perceptual features whereas the semantic description of non-living, man-made objects contains functional attributes. Therefore, a valid distinction relevant for a specification of possible subsystems in the brain may rely on perceptual versus functional attributes rather than on living versus non-living things.

Jackendoff (1987) raises difficulties for theories assuming a single representational format for the encoding of object concepts. He postulates two levels of conceptual structures, one geometric (perceptual) and one algebraic (propositional or functional). Both levels are necessary parts of the conceptual representation. Reaction time experiments support the distinction between perceptual and functional aspects in the representation of word meaning. Schreuder and Flores d'Arcais (1989) investigated this issue in a lexical decision task and a word naming task. In these tasks the target item (e.g., *cherry*) was either preceded by a prime bearing a perceptual relationship (e.g., *ball*) or a functional relationship (e.g., *banana*) to the target. Functional primes were more effective in lexical decision while perceptual primes were more effective in word naming. On the basis of the fact that word naming is generally faster than lexical decision the authors take it that perceptual information can be accessed faster than functional information. They conclude that both types of information are differentiated in semantic memory.

Such a model enables us to explain selective deficits in processing living and non-living things. The combined data seem to suggest that the semantic features of concepts determine how they are organized in the mental representation and possibly also their neuronal representation. As different brain diseases from encephalitis to vascular lesions can cause category specific deficits, a description of the underlying neuronal system is not yet available.

In a first PET study investigating the neuronal aspects of the distinction between living and non-living things subjects were required to read words labeling these objects and to judge the objects with respect to animacy (Kapur et al., 1994). This task evoked a selective activation of Brodmann Area BA 46/47 with extension to BA 10. As these regions are also active during other semantic tasks as for example judging the relation between objects and certain colors (Martin et al., 1995, 1996), they appear to be relevant for semantic processing in general.

PET studies investigating semantic memory which did not involve language production but only perception usually show activation in the left inferior prefrontal cortex (Kapur et al., 1994). This also holds for those studies in which both the experimental condition and the (to be subtracted) control condition involve language production (Martin et al., 1995; Frith et al., 1991). However, those studies which involve language production in the experimental but not the control condition additionally display activation in BA 45/46 and in BA 44 (Buckner et al., 1995; Wise et al., 1991). These findings indicate that left inferior prefrontal areas support semantic processes during word perception whenever the task requires accessing semantic aspects from the memory system. Based on PET studies Fiez (1997) specifies the involvement of the inferior prefrontal cortex during phonological and semantic processing as follows: inferior prefrontal areas are active whenever strategic processes come into play. BA 47 supports strategic semantic processes whereas BA 44 guarantees the strategic control of phonological processes. When only passive listening or silent reading is required only BA 22/42 are active (Petersen et al., 1989, 1990; Frith et al., 1991; Howard et al., 1992), to some degree bilaterally.

9.2.3.3 Lexical-Semantic vs Conceptual-Semantic Processing

Schreuder and Bierwisch (1992) differentiate lexical-semantic from conceptual-semantic processing. If there are separate processing systems for these two different aspects, the question of how lexical-semantic information is mapped onto lexical-conceptual information arises. A rather direct and simple answer to this question is given by Herrmann (1985). He denies a representation of lexical-semantics altogether and assumes direct mapping from word form (phonological or visual) onto the concept. According to Schreuder and Bierwisch (1992), however, a lexical entry must contain more information than just the word form. As in order to be able to use words correctly in a sentence, syntactic information such as word category information, verb-argument information, or syntactic gender information is necessary in addition to information about a word's form. Schreuder and Bierwisch (1992) assume that mapping between the lexical-semantic and the conceptual-semantic representation is achieved by specifying a set of relevant semantic features in the lexical-semantic representation. This set of features is not as complete as those included in the conceptual representation, but the set must provide sufficient information to fulfill language internal requirements (such as selectional restriction requirements of a given verb) and to guarantee mapping from the lexical entry onto the corresponding concept.

Functional neuroanatomical studies investigating a possible distinction between lexical-semantic and conceptual-semantic knowledge are not available. This issue is not easily reconciled empirically, as it is likely that brain activation correlated with word processing (verbal input) and brain activation correlated with picture processing (nonverbal input) partly overlap. Martin et al. (1996) report results from a PET study concerning category specific processes in which subjects were asked to name pictures of living objects (animals) and non-living objects (tools). Compared to viewing non-real objects distinct activation patterns were observed for the two types of objects. Both types of objects evoked activation in the inferior temporal gyrus bilaterally, in the Broca's area and adjacent cortical areas. Selective activation was found for animal naming in the medial occipital lobe (gyrus lingualis and cuneus). Naming of tools was associated with selective activation in the premotor and the motor cortex similar to the activity pattern observed during imaging motor movements (Decety et al., 1994). Moreover, naming of tools was correlated with activation in the region of the left medial temporal gyrus, similar to an activation pattern usually seen during the production of action verbs (Wise et al., 1991; Raichle et al., 1994; Martin et al., 1995). Although patients with category specific deficits usually suffer from large lesions, deficits in naming non-living, man-made objects have been connected with anterior and dorsal lesions. The PET study by Martin et al. (1996) agrees with the neuropsychological patients data in general; it allows, however, a more fine grained specification of the particular brain regions involved in processing living and man-made objects. The data suggest that the semantic representation of nameable objects involves a neural network including the ventral region of the temporal lobe and additional areas which are activated as a function of the intrinsic properties of objects.

In addition to the studies discussed here there are a number of PET studies investigating semantic and episodic memory (Cabeza & Nyberg, 1997). The combined data lead to a model in which the left anterior prefrontal cortex is taken to support the processing of semantic memory and the right anterior or prefrontal cortex to subserve processing of episodic memory (Tulving et al., 1994). As this distinction is primarily relevant for the discussion of how memory is represented in the brain but only indirectly relates to the issue of how language is processed, the various studies underlying this model will not discussed here any further.

9.2.4 Syntactic Subsystem

The understanding of sentences requires more than the activation of phonological and semantic information. In addition to these information types the use of syntactic information is a necessary condition as this information determines the grammatical relations in a sentence. For example, a sentence such as *The boy was kissed by the girl* can only be interpreted correctly if the auxiliary *was* and the preposition *by* are recognized as markers of the passive. In languages such as German which mark case overtly it is the article that carries relevant grammatical information. A sentence such as *Den Jungen küßt das Mädchen / The (ACC) boy kisses the (NOM) girl* can only be interpreted if case information encoded in the first article is correctly analyzed as accusative. These examples may help to exemplify the importance of syntactic information for the interpretation of sentences. An introduction into the theory and processing of syntax can not be given here. The reader is referred to Caplan (1992) for this matter.

As discussed at the beginning of this chapter, some language processing models view the syntactic component to be primary and independent from the semantic processing component, whereas other models assume a permanent on-line interaction between semantic and syntactic aspects.

The description of the neuronal basis of the syntactic processes presented here follows a syntax-first model of language comprehension. This model (Frazier, 1978, 1987a,b) not only received multiple support from behavioral studies (which, however, is also true for interactive models), but it is also more compatible with the high temporal resolution data from event-related brain potential measures. The model (Frazier, 1978, 1987a,b) assumes two serial processing phases. In a first phase the parser builds up an initial structure on the basis of word category information, independent of semantic information. In case the language input allows more than one structure as in temporarily syntactically ambiguous sentences (*The horse raced past the barn fell*) the parser initially computes the simplest structure compatible with the input. In the above example the parser initially constructs a structure in which *raced* is the main verb of the sentence. However, when confronted with the verb *fell* it is clear that the word *raced* must be read as introducing a reduced relative clause, meaning *The horse that raced past the barn and fell*. Thus with the appearance of the word *fell* a structural reanalysis is triggered in order to revise the initial structure. The model assumes a syntactic subsystem for the initial parse which is modular, i.e. informationally encapsulated (Fodor, 1983). If the first-pass parsing phase is modular in the Fodorian sense it should, moreover, be associated with a fixed neural architecture and exhibit a characteristic and specific breakdown pattern.

Selective deficits in syntactic processing are reported classically for language production. In particular the aphasic syndrome of agrammatism in language production suggest a selective impairment in this processing domain (Pick, 1913; Goldstein, 1913). At the beginning of the seventies this classical output oriented view was abandoned in favor of a central syntactic deficit hypothesis (Zurif et al., 1972; Caramazza & Zurif, 1976). The view is based on studies showing that Broca aphasics not only demonstrate problems in processing syntactic information during language production, but also during language comprehension (Berndt & Caramazza, 1980). As deficient syntactic processes during language production *and* comprehension were correlated primarily with lesions in the left frontal cortex and the syndrome of Broca's aphasia, syntax was localized in the Broca's area. There are, however, some case studies of patients with agrammatic production and relatively intact comprehension (Miceli et al., 1983; Sasanuma et al., 1990), yet these studies do not provide specified information about the patient's lesion site and therefore only provide quite indirect evidence for the brain-language relationship. In contrast to these case studies, there is a large number of studies reporting the correlation of lesions in the anterior part of the left hemisphere including Broca's area with a selective deficit both in language production and comprehension.

Studies published in the seventies mostly investigated the syntactic impairment using so-called off-line paradigms (Friederici, 1984). They usually used sentence-picture matching tasks. In these tasks Broca patients were particularly impaired whenever a correct interpretation necessarily relied on a correct syntactic analysis of the sentence, as in the sentence *The girl the boy is chasing is tall.* This sentence can only be interpreted correctly on the basis of syntactic information whereas a sentence such as *The boy the dog is patting is tall* can be interpreted on the basis of lexical pragmatic information alone (Caramazza & Zurif, 1976; Heilman & Scholes, 1976; von Stockert & Bader, 1976).

In the eighties more and more studies in aphasia research used so-called on-line paradigms (Bradley, Garrett & Zurif, 1980; Swinney, Zurif & Cutler, 1980; Friederici, 1983). Whether the observable deficit was due to a loss of the representation of syntactic knowledge or to an impairment in accessing or processing syntactic knowledge (Berndt & Caramazza, 1980) became a central issue (Bradley, Garrett & Zurif, 1980; Linebarger, Schwartz & Saffran, 1983; Kolk & van Grunsven, 1985).

Bradley, Garrett and Zurif (1980) hypothesized a loss of a specialized lexical retrieval mechanism as the basis of the observed syntactic deficit in Broca's aphasics. These elements which carry most of the syntactic information in a sentence constitute the closed class (articles, conjunctions, prepositions and pronouns). These elements are to be contrasted to the content words (i.e. nouns, verbs, adjectives) which are labeled the open class as this class can be extended by new members generated by word formation rules. The closed class, in contrast, consists of a fixed set of few elements. As the latter elements are selectively impaired during language production the obvious next step was to investigate these elements during language comprehension.

In a lexical decision task Bradley, Garrett and Zurif (1980) found normal subjects' recognition times for open class elements to be a function of the word's frequency (high frequency words were recognized faster than low frequency words) but this was not the case for closed class elements. Agrammatic subjects, in contrast, recognized both open and closed class words as a function of their frequency. On the basis of these data the authors proposed a special mechanism for the retrieval of closed class elements active during normal language perception which was supposed to be selectively impairment in Broca patients. This result which provided the basis of an interesting explanation for the syntactic comprehension deficit in Broca's aphasia, however, was not replicated (Gordon & Caramazza, 1982; Segui et al., 1982; Kolk & Bloomert, 1985). The latter studies found frequency dependent lexical decision times for both word classes in normals and thus no specialized retrieval mechanism for the closed class elements.

Friederici (1985) argued that the hypothesis of a special retrieval mechanism for closed class elements might still be found to be valid if these elements are presented in sentential context and not as isolated items in a lexical decision task. It is only in the former experimental situation that closed class elements serve their function. Friederici (1985), therefore, investigated the processing of open and closed class elements in a sentential monitoring paradigm. In this paradigm a target word is specified prior to each sentence and subjects are required to indicate the detection by a button press. The material varied word class (open/closed) and semantic context (related/unrelated). The monitoring latency revealed clear differences between normal subjects and Broca patients. Normal subjects recognized closed class elements faster than open class elements. Recognition of open class elements was faster in semantically related contexts than in unrelated context whereas closed class elements were recognized equally fast in both context conditions. This difference in the dependency on semantic context was also observed for Broca patients. However, in contrast to normal subjects, Broca patients' recognition of closed class elements was dramatically slowed down compared to elements of the open class. A group of left hemisphere control patients, i.e. Wernicke patients, showed a reaction time pattern similar to that of normal controls (Friederici, 1983). It was, therefore, concluded that the selective delay in recognizing closed class elements might be viewed as the underlying deficit of the comprehension impairment seen in Broca patients. In this study it was shown, furthermore, that the delay in recognizing particular lexical elements is not a function of the word class per se, but a function of the amount of syntactic versus semantic information a given element carries. This was demonstrated by investigating Broca aphasics ability to recognize different types of prepositions either clearly carrying semantic information (locative preposition: *Er steht auf dem Stuhl / He stands on the chair*) or not (obligatory preposition: *Er hofft auf den Sommer / He hopes for the summer*).

Based on these and similar findings it was hypothesized that Broca aphasics suffer from a selective impairment of a specialized fast access to syntactic information, whereas the representation of this information is intact (Friederici, 1985, 1988; Haarmann & Kolk, 1991, 1994). In studies using the syntactic priming paradigm it was shown that Broca aphasics are able to process syntactic information although with a considerable delay. Either processing time as such was slowed (Friederici & Kilborn, 1989) or the presentation of prime sentence and target word had to be slowed down (Haarmann & Kolk, 1991). These results suggest that those brain areas which are lesioned in Broca patients support the fast and automatic processing of syntactic information. The slowing down of syntactic processes in patients with lesions in the anterior part of the left hemisphere suggests that this part of the brain represents syntactic knowledge in a procedural format. This knowledge concerning syntactic procedures which must be activated during language production also appears to support the syntactic analysis of incoming language input. The representation of syntactic knowledge in a declarative format is rather represented in the posterior language region as it was shown that Broca patients are able to judge a sentence's grammaticality (Linebarger, Schwartz & Saffran, 1983; Wulfeck, 1988). Parts of the left temporal lobe seem to be responsible for the recognition of words in general. While closed class words (at least when presented in isolation) activate the perisylvian region of the left hemisphere, open class words also seem to activate parts of the right hemisphere as well (Pulvermüller et al., 1995). These findings lead to the idea that content words which allow for more associations activate a larger neuronal network including the right hemisphere whereas function words are processes in the left hemisphere only (Braitenberg & Pulvermüller, 1992; Eulitz et al., 1996). In general, more right hemisphere activation is observed for concrete words than for abstract words. This suggests that the right hemisphere involvement rather reflects associative aspects than aspect of word class per se (open versus closed). A study by Kounios and Holcomb (1994) comparing the processing of concrete and abstract words supports this view as concrete words were shown to evoke a larger N400 than abstract words in particular over the right hemisphere.

Here we assume that the superior and middle temporal gyrus of the left hemisphere represent the lexicon in a modality independent form. This representation is conceived of as an abstract representation which not only includes information about the form of the word but also syntactic information (e.g., word category and semantic information). According to the processing model of Frazier (1987) first-pass parsing is primarily based on word category information. Whether a lexical entry is organized hierarchically with word category information being high on the list, or whether this information is just processed prior to other information can not be decided empirically. In the next Section we will see, however, that word category information is available prior to lexical-semantic information.

9.3 Neuronal Dynamics of Language Processing

A central question for an adequate description of the language comprehension system is how the different language related subsystems interact. Such a description necessarily focuses on the temporal parameters of the processes underlying language comprehension. To define these on-line measures are needed. Behavioral on-line measures use different paradigms (see Zwitserlood, this volume) which register reaction times to different types of stimuli. These measures have so far been unable to unambiguously differentiate between different models of language processing. Depending on the specific paradigm used they provide support either for interactive or for serial syntax-first models (see Ferstl & Flores d'Arcais, this volume and Kempen, this volume).

9.3.1 Event-Related Brain Potentials

Neurophysiological on-line measures may provide additional information concerning the temporal pattern of language processes. The two techniques available are electroencephalography (EEG) and magnetoencephalography (MEG). EEG measures the electrical activity at the scalp, MEG its magnetic field. While EEG signals can be affected by different structures through which the electrical potential must travel (brain tissue, bone, skin) the magnetic field is unaffected by these intervening structures. Because of the major financial investment required for the MEG, however, most of the neurophysiological studies in language processing have used and are continuing to use the EEG method. Both types of measure allow a registration of the brain's activity in the millisecond domain. The event-related brain potential (ERP) represents the electrical activity of the brain correlated with a particular stimulus event. To achieve a better signal to noise ratio for a given event in the brain's general activity the brain's activity is averaged over a number of similar stimuli. The potentials registered at the surface of the scalp are the summation of simultaneous post synaptic activities of a larger number of neurons. The distribution of the activity measured at the surface of the scalp does not allow direct conclusions concerning the locus of the generator. However, techniques have been developed which allow one to draw indirect conclusions regarding the generators of particular event-related components (Scherg, 1990; Scherg & von Cramon, 1986). The event-related brain potential has been used quite extensively during the last years to investigate temporal aspects of language processes. In contrast to behavioral measures such as reaction times which only vary in one dimension, the ERP varies along four dimensions and does not require the conscious reaction of the subject. The ERP can vary as a function of a particular cognitive process in its latency, its polarity, its amplitude and in its topological distribution. These characteristics make the ERP an instrument which has the potential to contribute to the specification of language processing models.

Early processes of acoustic visual processes are reflected in early ERP components, the so-called N1-P2 complex. The label, N1-P2 stands for a negativity around 100 ms which is followed by a positivity around 200 ms post onset of an acoustic or a visual stimulus. The magnetic counterpart of the N1 in the auditory domain was localized in the auditory cortex (Pantev et al., 1989). Source analyses of the visual N1 indicate activity in the visual cortex (Mangun et al., 1993). N1 and P2 vary in amplitude and latency as a function of stimulus intensity, presentation rate and attention (Näätänen & Picton, 1987). These components reflecting early modality-specific input analyses will not be discussed here any further.

In the following Sections we will focus on those ERP components which reflect central processes of language comprehension. Before we turn to semantic and syntactic processes some studies investigating the processing of phonemes will be described. A number of EEG and MEG studies explored the phonological processes at the level of consonant-vowel-syllables (Kaukoranta et al., 1987; Kuriki & Murase, 1989; Poeppel et al., 1996). Kuriki and Murase (1989) compared the processing of the vowel /a/ and the syllable /ka/ in a MEG experiment. They found a magnetic response around 100 ms post onset localized in the posterior part of the auditory cortex. PET and fMRI studies often found bilateral activity in the superior temporal cortices for language stimuli in a passive listening condition, whereas the active processing of language stimuli mostly showed the activation to be lateralized to the left. These findings lead Poeppel et al. (1996) to further investigate the specific relation between phoneme processing and its neuronal bases in an MEG study. They compared passive perception of the syllables /bæ/ and /dæ/ versus /pæ/ and /tæ/ with the perception of these items during a discrimination task. In the passive listening condition they found symmetrical activation (M100) in the upper part of the temporal lobe of both hemispheres, in the discrimination task asymmetrical activation with a dominance in the left hemisphere. The latency of the M100 component was larger in the left and in the right hemisphere. These findings suggest that primary auditory language processes are represented bilaterally, but that language specific processes become active quite early during auditory language processing.

9.3.2   Semantic Processes

Semantic processes were shown to be reflected in the ERP in 1980. Kutas and Hillyard (1980, 1983) observed a negativity 400 ms post onset of a word which did not match the preceding context semantically. This component, called the N400 is normally present between 300 and 600 ms after the onset of the critical stimulus and is broadly distributed over the posterior part of both hemispheres. Its amplitude varies as a function of the semantic expectation built up by the preceding context for a given word. The amplitude is high when the cloze probability of the target is low, and low when the cloze probability is high (Kutas, Lindamood & Hillyard, 1984; Holcomb & Neville, 1991). The N400 component was observed in different languages including English, French, Dutch and German for visual and in auditory language processing (for a review, see Van Petten, 1995). This component correlates with semantic-pragmatic violations (i.e. plausibility: Kutas & Hillyard, 1983) and with semantic-lexical violations (e.g., selectional registration of verbs: Friederici, Pfeifer & Hahne, 1993). The study by Kutas, Lindamood and Hillyard (1984) had shown that the amplitude of the N400 component varies as a function of semantic expectations of a word in a sentence context. The modulation of the N400 component was also demonstrated in simple word context (Bentin, McCarthy & Wood, 1985; Holcomb & Neville, 1990) in which the amplitude is larger when the target word is proceeded by a word which is semantically related than when it is unrelated. Similar effects are reported for the processing of pictures of objects, although the topography of these is somewhat different (Barrett & Rugg, 1990; Mecklinger & Meinshausen, in press). The question of which phase of lexical-semantic processes the N400 might reflect was only addressed recently.

Whether the N400 reflects processes of lexical access and/or processes of lexical integration is an issue for psycholinguistic modeling. Three phases are assumed during lexical-semantic processing: lexical access, selection and integration (Frauenfelder & Tyler, 1987). Starting from the assumption that lexical access is automatic whereas lexical integration requires controlled processes, Chwilla, Brown and Hagoort (1995) investigated which phase of lexical processing the N400 might represent. In a lexical decision task subjects had to decide whether a letter sequence (a) was a word or not, or (b) was written in small or capital letters. Each target was preceded by a word which in the case of word targets was either semantically related or not. A semantic priming effect evidenced by a reduction of the N400 for a target preceded by semantically related words was found in the lexical decision condition (a) but not in the physical judgment condition (b). These findings were taken to suggest that the N400 functionally reflects lexical integration processes. With respect to the neuroanatomical basis of the N400 component intracranial ERPs provide suggestive evidence. They specify the location of the N400 generators within the anterior medial part of the temporal lobe adjacent to the anterior lateral sulcus (Nobre, Allison & McCarthy, 1994).

Besides representing aspects of lexical integration, the N400 also varies with a number of parameters usually taken to reflect aspects of lexical access. The amplitude of the N400 is smaller for low frequency words than for high frequency words (Van Petten & Kutas, 1990). The distribution of the N400 varies as a function of word class (Neville, Mills & Lawson, 1992; Nobre & McCarthy, 1994, 1995). While content words (elements of the open class evoke a large N400 between 200 and 500 ms at central and posterior electrodes, function words (elements of the closed class elicit a negativity between 400 and 700 ms over frontal areas. In addition to this late negativity, function words show a left anterior negativity between 200 and 300 ms (N280). This differential pattern for open and closed class words was taken as evidence for anatomically distinct systems supporting the different word classes (Neville, Mills & Lawson, 1992). Left anterior areas, in particular, are viewed to support the processing of function words. These ERP findings are compatible with results from aphasia research showing that patients with lesions in the anterior part of the left hemisphere, in particular Broca's area, display a selective impairment in processing function words in language production as well as in language comprehension.

Taken together, the combined data from aphasia research, PET research and ERP research suggest that the left temporal lobe support lexical semantic processes. Lexical access and integration appear to be completed 400 ms after the presentation of the stimulus. ERP results indicate a processing difference between those lexical elements that mainly carry semantic information and those that mainly carry syntactic information.

9.3.3 Syntactic Processes

Syntactic processes are investigated more and more often using the ERP method. Two ERP components have been identified to vary as a function of syntactic processes: (a) a left anterior negativity either present between 100 and 200 ms or between 300 and 500 ms, and (b) a late positivity observable around 600 ms and later. Late positivities have been found for the processing of infrequent sentence structures (Osterhout & Holcomb, 1992, 1993; Osterhout, Holcomb & Swinney, 1994; Mecklinger et al., 1995; Hagoort, Brown & Groothusen, 1993) as well as for the processing of syntactically incorrect structures (Neville et al., 1991; Friederici et al., 1993; Osterhout & Mobley, 1995). In the following we will try to specify the functional relevance of the early negativity and the late positivity. The discussion of which processes are reflected in these different ERP components determines the studies in this research area. When considering the different studies we should keep in mind that most studies presented the sentence stimuli visually in a word-by-word presentation mode with relatively long pauses between each word (300 ms, 500 ms, or even 700 ms). It is not unlikely that the presentation mode affects the normally highly, automatic language procedures active when listening to connected speech.

Early Negativities

An early study by Neville et al. (1991) investigated a number of different sentence structures in a sentence reading ERP experiment. For almost all of the different structures and the violations of them they found specific ERP patterns but also some common components. They interpreted this finding as a support of the theoretically defined functional distinction between the different types of syntactic structures. Violations for most of these structures were correlated with a late positivity. The violation of phrase structure, in particular, also elicited a left anterior negativity (around 125 ms) which was followed by a left temporo-parietal negativity between 350 and 500 ms. This early left anterior negativity was evoked by a word category error (e.g., *Max's of proof the theorem*). Other types of syntactic violations did not evoke a similar negativity. Note that in this study the stimulus material was presented visually, but in a rapid serial visual presentation mode with an interstimulus interval of only 200 ms. The only studies which found an early left anterior negativity between 100 and 200 ms besides the one by Neville et al. (1991) are studies which have used auditory presentation.

Friederici and colleagues (Friederici et al., 1993; Friederici et al., 1996) presented syntactically correct and incorrect sentences as connected speech. Syntactic incorrectness was realized as a word category violation (e.g., *Der Freund wurde im besucht / The friend was in the visited*). Note that German is a verb final language and that the case marked preposition necessarily requires a noun or an adjective-noun combination to follow. In this study an early left anterior negativity (ELAN) present around 180 ms was followed by a second negativity between 300 and 500 ms. Münte and colleagues (1993) also investigated word category violations (e.g., your write), however, again used a visualpresentation technique with interstimulus intervals of 800 ms. They did not find an early negativity but only a negativity between 300 and 700 ms. A possible explanation for the absence of the early negativity is that automatic processes of initial structure building are not triggered with drastically delayed stimulus input. Two studies seem to support this explanation. Firstly, the assumption that the early negativity reflects highly automatic processes was supported by a study in which the influence of attentional factors on the early left anterior negativity was investigated (Hahne & Friederici, 1997). The ELAN component was found to be independent of attentional factors. The study varied the proportion of the number of correct and incorrect sentences in two experimental conditions (20% incorrect versus 80% incorrect). The ELAN was present with a similar latency and amplitude in both conditions, not, however, the P600. The latter component was only present when 20% of the sentences in the experiment were incorrect. These findings indicate that those processes that are reflected by the early negativity are highly automatic and independent of attentional aspects whereas those processes that are reflected by the late positivity rather are controlled in nature. Secondly, a recent study investigating the observed variation in the latency of the left anterior negativity found that the latency varies as a function of the input parameters (Gunter, Friederici & Hahne, in preparation). In this study the sentence material was presented visually (300 ms stimulus presentation, 200 ms interstimulus interval), however, under different contrast conditions (high versus low). Under the high contrast condition an early left anterior negativity (ELAN) was found, under the low contrast condition a left anterior negativity was present between 300 and 500 ms. Thus good input conditions seem to trigger fast syntactic processes.

Other ERP studies have investigated the processing of other syntactic violations in particular the subject-verb disagreement. All these studies used a word-by-word visual presentation paradigm. This violation type was investigated in English (Kutas & Hillyard, 1983; Coulson et al., 1995; Osterhout & Mobley, 1995), in Dutch (Hagoort et al., 1993; Gunter, Stowe & Mulder, in press) and in German (Penke et al., 1997). With the exception of one study (Hagoort et al., 1993) all found a negativity between 300 and 500 ms which was followed by a late positivity. Most of these negativities displayed a centro-frontal or frontal maximum often with a left dominance. This left anterior negativity has been labeled LAN (Coulson et al., 1995). A similar pattern was also found by Friederici et al. (1993) for inflectional errors during auditory sentence presentation. In this study the violation was not realized a a subject-verb-incongruency but as a violtion of tense and mode. The combined data seem to suggest that morphosyntactic violations realized as incongruency of the inflection elicit a frontal negativity around 400 ms followed by a late positivity independent of the input modality. Why should there be different ERP patterns for the processing of phrase structure violations and morphosyntactic violations? A possible explanation is provided by the model of Frazier (1987) which holds that initial structure building is based on word category information alone. At this level of processing it is irrelevant whether a verb is carrying the correct verb inflection or not as long as the inflection allows the identification of the word category. Agreement information only becomes relevant when thematic role assignment is applied. In Frazier's model this is supposed to take place at a second processing phase.

Violations of the verb-argument-structure are correlated with a negativity around 400 ms with a left maximum as well (Rösler, Friederici, Pütz & Hahne, 1993). Rösler and colleagues (1993) interpret the left anterior negativity as a correlate for processes associated with information about a verb's argument structure.

The left anterior negativity (LAN) between 300 and 500 ms was also observed in sentences whose processing require working memory. Kluender and Kutas (1993) investigated the processing of so-called 'filler-gap' constructions in which a constituent is moved from its original position in the sentence to an other position, e.g., to the beginning of the sentence or clause. A left anterior negativity was found for the moved element as well as at its original position. This result was taken to indicate that the moved constituent was identified as a moved element and held in memory up to the identification of its original position. The working memory load associated with this operation was assumed to be reflected in the left anterior negativity. A left anterior negativity observed with the processing of object relative versus subject relative sentences was interpreted in the same sense (King & Kutas, 1995).

Rösler et al. (in press) found a left anterior negativity for the processing of correct but non-canonical sentences. They also interpret their findings within a working memory framework. Since the negativity is observed at the case marked article of the non-canonical noun phrase they interpret the left anterior negativity as a manifestation of 'preparatory processes' to allow the 'storage' of the following noun.

From a linguistic point of view the latter two phenomena may tap similar underlying processes. As soon as a constituent is identified as a moved one the initial structure is built accordingly. The moved constituent must be held in memory until its original position is identified. From the available studies it is not clear whether the left anterior negativity observed is a function of working memory or of early structuring processes or both. Further research must reveal whether (a) the ELAN observed for phrase structure violations, (b) the left anterior negativity found for violations of verb-agreement (sometimes called LAN), and (c) the LAN observed in processing conditions requiring working memory are members of the same component.

Given the PET findings that the left frontal Brodmann areas BA 46/45 which appear to be relevant for working memory, and BA 44, which seems to be involved in phonological and syntactic sequencing, are adjacent it is likely that the activation of these regions elicit a left anterior negativity in the ERP. Additional ERP research including dipole modeling might be able to pull these aspects apart.

Late Positivities

In addition to the discussed negativities late positivities were found for the processing of syntactic anomalies. Osterhout and colleagues (Osterhout & Holcomb, 1992, 1993; Osterhout, Holcomb & Swinney, 1994) observed late positivities for temporarily ambiguous structures. Theyview the late positivity (P600) as a marker of the garden-path effect and hold that this effect is found whenever the parser has to revise a structure. This interpretation receives support from those studies which investigated the processing of complex non-preferred, but correct sentence strctures.

Mecklinger et al. (1995) presented subjects visually with subject and object relative sentences in German (e.g., *Das ist die Managerin, die die Arbeiterinnen gesehen HAT/HABEN / This is the manager that the workers seen HAS/HAVE*). Note that in this correct sentence the sentence final auxiliary indiates which noun phrase is the subject in the sentence (by subject verb agreement). The disambiguating auxiliary elicited a positivity with a peak at 345 ms. According to the model by Frazier (1987) the reader when reading such a sentence initially builds up the simplest structure compatible with the input (i.e. subject relative structure) which then has to be revised when the disambiguating auxiliary signals an object relative structure.

In a similar fashion, a reanalysis is also necessary in the so-called garden-path sentences used by Osterhout and Holcomb (1992) (e.g., *The broker persuaded to sell the stock...*). At the disambiguating element *to* it is clear that the underlying structure of the sentence is not a simple subject-verb-object structure (e.g., *The broker persuaded the man*). While the positivity observed for these types of sentences appeared around 600 ms and later, the positivity in the sentences investigated by Mecklinger et al. (1995) was present earlier. This difference in latency was interpreted as a function of the difficulty of reanalysis necessary to recover from the garden-path, with less difficult reanalyses showing shorter latencies. For the details of this argument see Friederici and Mecklinger (1996).

To end the Section on syntactic processes we will briefly discuss the few imaging studies available for this processing domain. These are partly compatible with the assumption made above and are able to specify the topographic aspect of syntactic processes to some degree. In a PET study Stromswold et al. (1996) registered subject's brain activation while reading English subject and object relative sentences. They found a selective activation as the function of syntactic complexity of the pars opercularis in the left third frontal gyrus (i.e., the Broca area, BA 44).[2] The study by Stromswold et al. (1996) in comparison to the PET studies on phonological process-ing suggests that syntactic processes are supported by the inferior part of BA 44 whereas phonological processes are suppored by the upper, posterior part of BA 44. In a fMRI study Just et al. (1996) also investigated the processing of subject and object relative sentences and found maximal activation in the third frontal gyrus, BA 44 and BA 45, as well as in the left Wernicke region. Homologue areas in the right hemisphere were also active though to a lesser degree.

9.4 A Neurocognitive Model of Language Processes

How can we integrate the combined findings into a model of the functional neu-roanatomy of language processes? A difficulty for providing an adequate description of these processes is caused by the heterogeneity of the paradigms underlying the different results. The paradigms included lesion studies and studies with healthy subjects, using behavioral off-line and on-line paradigms, as well as imaging tech-niques of different kinds (PET, fMRT, EEG and MEG). Being aware of the difficulty the following model should be viewed as a first approach to an integration of results coming from the different studies (Figure 2).

Language comprehension is a process that unrolls intime.It is lso a prcess during which the different assumed subprocesses such as phonological, syntactic and lexi-cal-semantic must be coordinated in time. Given the functional distinction between these processes it is likely that they are supported by different neural systems. Friederici (1995) proposed a model focusing on the temporal parameters of lan-guage processing. The present model will consider temporal as well as neuroana-tomical aspects.[3]

The data available on auditory language processing indicate that the auditory lan-guage input is analyzed around 100 ms post stimulus onset (see EEG and MEG findings: N100 and M100) by auditory cortices in the left and the right hemisphere.

---

[2] See, however, Mazoyer et al. (1993) for a different result.
[3] The following description will focus on auditory language processing.

The identification of the phonological word form is supported by left planum temporal (see PET and fMRI evidence). The segmental phonetic extraction as well as phonological sequencing of auditory language information appears to involve the upper and posterior part of BA 44 (see PET studies).

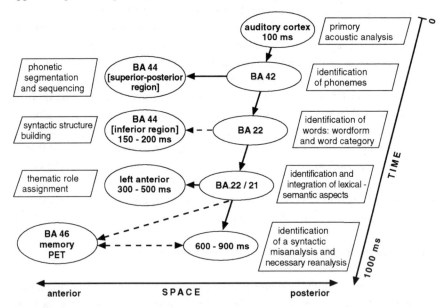

Figure 2. Neurocognitive model of language comprehension

The model assumes that word category identification takes place early during processing and that this is accomplished by the involvement of BA 22. This information appears to be transmitted to left anterior parts, possible BA 44 (inferior part) (see PET evidence) which subserve initial syntactic parsing processes active around 150 ms to 200 ms post stimulus onset (see ERP result: ELAN).

Lexical-semantic processes are assumed to be active in parallel. Automatic lexical-semantic processes appear to involve the temporal language region and mediobasal temporal structures in the left hemisphere (see lesion studies), cotrolled semantic processes involving aspects of semantic memory seem to be supported by the inferior prefrontal cortex (see PET studies). Lexical-semantic integration requires a check between prior contextual information and a given lexical element. This checking mechanism completed around 400 ms and later may involve the activation of extra-linguistic, conceptual-semantic subsystems in addition to a primary linguistic subsystem (see ERP component: N400). The activation of the association cortices in the left and the right hemisphere seems likely (see PET data). Thematic role assignment on the basis of verb-argument-structure information and inflectional information are assumed to take place at the same time as lexical-semantic processes though in different neural networks (see ERP result: LAN). While the processing of structural information encoded in the verb involves left anterior regions, semantic aspects appear to primarily involve posterior regions (see ERP result: LAN versus N400).

If the initially constructed syntactic structure and the representation based on the lexical-semantic information can be mapped onto each other, understanding has taken place. If such a mapping is not possible, processes f reanalysi or repair must take place to achieve understanding. These processes are active at 600 ms and beyond (see ERP result: P600). Which brain systems support this latter process can not be specified on the basis of the data at hand. The wide distribution of the P600 component suggest that processes of reanalysis and repair may be based on a network involving dfferent subsystems.

A fundamental distinction between the traditional view of the neural basis of language comprehension and the present model is the clear involvement of left anterior brain regions during the comprehension process. If one would have to characterize the involvement of these, the left frontal areas might be viewed as representing procedural language knowledge, whereas the left posterior areas may rather represent declarative language knowledge.

Acknowledgments

I thank Yves von Cramon for the time he took to discuss with me the neuroanatomical details of the activation studies referred to in this chapter. I would like to thank Doug Saddy for his help in stylistic matters .

References

Auerbach, S.H., Allard, T., Naeser, M., Alexander, M.P. & Albert, M.L. (1982). Pure word deafness: Analysis of a case with bilateral lesions and a defect at the pre-phonemic level. *Brain, 105,* 271-300.

Barrett, S.E. & Rugg, M.D. (1990). Event-related potentials and the semantic matching of pictures. *Brain and Cognition, 14,* 201-212.

Basso, A., Casati, G. & Vignolo, L.A. (1977). Phonemic identification defect in aphasia. *Cortex, 13,* 85-95.

Beauvois, M.F. & Derousné, J. (1979). Phonological alexia: Three dissociations. *Journal of Neurology, Neurosurgery and Psychiatry, 42,* 1115-1124.

Berndt, R. & Caramazza, A. (1980). A redefinition of the syndrom of Broca's aphasia. *Applied Psycholinguistics, 1,* 225-278.

Berndt, R.S. & Mitchum, C.C. (1990). Auditory and lexical information sources in immediate recall: Evidence from a patient with a deficit to the phonological short-term store. In: G. Vallar & T. Shallice (eds.), *Neuropsychological impairments of short-term memory,* Cambridge: Cambridge University Press.

Bierwisch, M. & Schreuder, R. (1992). From concepts to lexical items. *Cognition, 42,* 23-60.

Binder, J.R., Rao, S.M. & Tammeke, T.A. (1994). Functional MRI of human auditory cortex. *Annales of Neurology, 35,* 662-672.

Blumstein, S.E., Baker, E. & Goodglass, H. (1977a). Phonological factors in auditory comprehension in aphasia. *Neuropsychologia, 15,* 19-30.

Blumstein, S., Cooper, W.E., Zurif, E.B. & Caramazza, A. (1977b). The perception and production of voice-onset time in aphasia. *Neuropsychologia, 15,* 371-383.

Blumstein, S.E., Milberg, W. & Schrier, R. (1982). Semantic processing in aphasia: Evidence from an auditory lexical decision task. *Brain and Language, 17,* 301-315.

Bookheimer, S.Y., Zeffiro, T.A., Blaxton, T., Gaillard, W. & Theodore, W. (1995). Regional cerebral blood flow during object naming and word reading. *Human Brain Mapping, 3,* 93-106.

Bradley, D.C., Garrett, M.F. & Zurif, E.B. (1980). Syntactic deficits in Broca's aphasia. In D. Caplan (ed.), *Biological studies of mental processes,* Cambridge, MA: MIT-Press.

Braitenberg, V. & Pulvermüller, F. (1992). Entwurf einer neurologischen Theorie der Sprache. *Naturwissenschaft, 79,* 103-117.

Buckner, R.L., Petersen, S.E., Ojemann, J.G., Miezin, F.M., Squire, L.R. & Raichle, M.E. (1995). Functional anatomical studies of explicit and implicit memory retrieval tasks. *The Journal of Neuroscience, 15,* 12-29.

Cabeza, R. & Nyberg, L. (1997). Imaging Cognition: An empirical review of PET studies with normal subjects. *Journal of Cognitive Neuroscience, 9,* 1-26.

Caplan, D. (1992). *Language: Structure, processing, and disorders.* Cambridge, MA: MIT Press.

Caplan, D. & Aydelott-Utman, J. (1994). Selective acoustic phonetic impairment and lexical access in an aphasic patient. *Journal of the Acoustic Society of America, 95,* 512-517.

Caramazza, A. & Zurif, E. (1976). Dissociation of algorithmic and heuristic processes in language comprehension: Evidence from aphasia. *Brain and Language, 3,* 572-582.

Chertkow, H., Bub, D. & Caplan, D. (in press). Stages of semantic memory: Evidence from dementia. *Cognitive Neuropsychology.*

Chwilla, D.J., Brown, C. & Hagoort, P. (1995). The N400 as a function of the level of processing. *Psychophysiology, 32,* 274-285.

Coltheart, M. (1978). Lexical access in simple reading tasks. In B. Underwood (ed.), *Strategies of Information processing.* London: Academic Press.

Coltheart, M., Patterson, J. & Marshall, J.C. (1980). *Deep dyslexia.* London: Routledge.

Coulson, S., King, J. & Kutas, M. (1995). The late show: The syntactic positive shift meets the late positive component. *Paper presented at the Eight Annual CUNY conference on human sentence processing.* Tucson, Arizona .

Decety, J., Perani, D., Jeannerod, M., Bettinardi, V., Tadary, B., Woods, R., Mazziotta, J.C. & Fazio, F. (1994). Mapping motor representations with positron emission tomography. *Nature, 371,* 600-602.

Dejerne, J. (1891). Sur un cas de cecité verbale avec agraphie, suivi d'autopsie. *Compte rendu des séances de la société de biologie, 3,* 197-201.

Dejerne, J. (1892). Contribution à l'étude anatomoclinique et clinique des differentes variétés de cecité verbale. *Memories de la Société de Biologie, 4,* 61-90.

Démonet, J.F., Chollet, F., Ramsay, S., Cardebat, D., Nespoulous, J.L., Wise, R., Rascol, A. & Frackowiak, R.S.J. (1992). The anatomy of phonological and semantic processing in normal subjects. *Brain, 115,* 1753-1768.

Démonet, J-F., Wise, R. & Frackowiak, R.S.J. (1993). Language functions explored in normal subjects by positron emission tomography: A critical review. *Human Brain Mapping, 1,* 39-47.

Démonet, J.-F., Price, C., Wise, R. & Frackowiak, R. (1994). Differential activation of right and left posterior sylvian regions by semantic and phonological tasks: A positron-emission tomography study in normal human subjects. *Neuroscience Letters, 182,* 25-28.

Eimas, P.D., Siqueland, E.R., Juszyk, P. & Vigorito, J. (1971). Speech perception in infants. *Science, 171,* 303-306.

Ellis, A.W. (1982). Spelling and writing (and reading and speaking). In A.W. Ellis (ed.), *Normality and pathology in cognitive function,* London: Academic Press.

Ellis, A.W. & Young, A.W. (1988). *Human Cognitive Neuropsychology.* Hove: Lawrence Erlbaum .

Eulitz, C., Maeß, B., Pantev, Chr., Friederici, A.D., Feige, B. & Elbert, T. (1996). Oscillatory neuromagnetic activity induced by language and non-language stimuli. *Cognitive Brain Research, 4,* 2748-2755.

Fiez, J.A. (1997). Phonology, semantics, and the role of the left inferior prefrontal cortex. *Human Brain Mapping, 5,* 79-83.

Fodor, J.A. (1983). *The modularity of mind.* Cambridge, MA: MIT Press.

Frauenfelder, U.H. & Tyler, L.K. (1987). The process of spoken word recognition: An introduction. *Cognition, 25,* 1-20.

Frazier, L. (1978). *On Comprehending Sentences: Syntactic Parsing Strategies.* Doctoral Dissertation, University of Connecticut.

Frazier, L. (1987a). Sentence processing: A tutorial review. In M. Coltheart (ed.), *Attention and performance XII: The psychology of reading.* London: Lawrence Erlbaum.

Frazier, L. (1987b). Theories of sentence processing. In J. Garfield (ed.), *Modularity in knowledge representation and natural-language processing.* Cambridge, MA: MIT Press.

Friederici, A.D. (1983). Aphasics' perception of words in sentential context: Some real-time processing evidence. *Neuropsychologia, 21,* 351-358.

Friederici, A.D. (1984). *Neuropsychologie der Sprache.* Stuttgart: Kohlhammer.

Friederici, A.D. (1985). Levels of processing and vocabulary types: Evidence from on-line comprehension in normals and agrammatics. *Cognition, 19,* 133-166.

Friederici, A.D. (1988). Agrammatic comprehension: Picture of a computational mismatch. *Aphasiology, 2 (3/4),* 279-284.

Friederici, A.D. (1995). The time course of syntactic activation during language processing: A model based on neuropsychological and neurophysiological data. *Brain and Language, 50,* 259-281.

Friederici, A.D., Hahne, A. & Mecklinger, A. (1996). The temporal structure of syntactic parsing: Early and late effects elicited by syntactic anomalies. *Journal of Experimental Psychology: Learning, Memory and Cognition, 5,* 1-31.

Friederici, A.D. & Kilborn, K. (1989). Temporal constraints on language processing: Syntactic priming in Broca's aphasia. *Journal of Cognitive Neuroscience, 1,* 262-272.

Friederici, A.D. & Mecklinger, A. (1996). Syntactic parsing as revealed by brain responses: First-pass and second-pass parsing processes. *Journal of Psycholinguistic Research, 25, 1,* 157-176.

Friederici, A.D., Pfeifer, E. & Hahne, A. (1993). Event-related brain potentials during natural speech processing: Effects of semantic morphological and syntactic violations. *Cognitive Brain Research, 1,* 183-192.

Friston, K.J., Price, C.J., Pletcher, P., Moore, C., Frackowiak, R.S. & Dolan, R. (1996). The trouble with cognitive substraction. *NeuroImage, 4,* 97-104.

Frith, C.D., Friston, K.J., Liddle, P.F. & Frackowiak, R.S.J. (1991). A PET study of word finding. *Neuropsychologia, 29 ,* 1137-1148.

Goldstein, K. (1913). Über die Störungen der Grammatik bei Hirnkrankheiten. *Monatsschrift für Psychiatrie und Neurologie, 34 ,* 540-568.

Goodglass, H. & Baker, E. (1976). Semantic field, naming, and auditory comprehension in aphasia. *Brain and Language, 3,* 359-374.

Goodglass, H. (1993). *Understanding aphasia.* San Diego: Academic Press.

Gordon, B. & Caramazza, A. (1982). Lexical decision for open- and closed-class words: Failure to replicate differential frequency sensitivity. *Brain and Language, 15,* 143-160.

Gorrell, P. (1995). *Syntax and parsing.* Cambridge, Engl.: Cambridge University Press.

Gunter, T.C., Stowe, L.A. & Mulder, G. (in press). When syntax meets semantics. *Psychophysiology.*

Haarmann, H.J. & Kolk, H.H.J. (1991). Syntactic priming in Broca's aphasics: Evidence for slow activation. *Aphasiology, 5,* 247-263.

Haarmann, H.J. & Kolk, H.H.J. (1994). On-line sensitivity to subject-verb agreement violations in Broca's aphasics: The role of syntactic complexity and time. *Brain and Language, 46,* 493-516.

Hagoort, P., Brown, C. & Groothusen, J. (1993). The syntactic positive shift as an ERP measure of syntactic processing. *Language and Cognitive Processes, 8,* 439-483.

Hagoort, P. (1993). Impairments of lexical-semantic processing in aphasia: Evidence from the processing of lexical ambiguities. *Brain and Language, 45,* 189-232.

Hahne, A. & Friederici, A.D. (1997). Language comprehension: The brain dissociates early automatic and late controlled processes. *Journal of Cognitive Neuroscience.*

Heilman, K.M. & Scholes, R.J. (1976). The nature of comprehension errors in Brocas conduction, and Wernickes aphasics. *Cortex, 12,* 258-265.

Herrmann, T. (1985). *Allgemeine Sprachpsychologie.* München: Urban & Schwarzenberg.

Holcomb, P.J. & Neville, H.J. (1990). Semantic priming in visual and auditory lexical decision: A between modality comparison. *Language and Cognitive Processes, 5,* 281-312.

Holcomb, P.J. & Neville, H.J. (1991). Natural speech processing: An analysis using event-related brain potentials. *Psychobiology, 19,* 286-300.

Howard, D., Patterson, K., Wise, R., Brown, W.D., Friston, K., Weiller, D. & Frackowiak, R. (1992). The cortical localization of the lexicons. Positron emission tomography evidence. *Brain, 115,* 1769-1782.

Humphreys, G.W. & Evett, L.J. (1985). Are there independent lexical and nonlexical routes in word processing? An evaluation of the dual-route theory of reading. *Behavioral and Brain Sciences, 8,* 689-740.

Jackendoff, R. (1987). On beyond zebra: The relation of linguistic and visual information. *Cognition, 26,* 89-114.

Jennings, J.M., McIntosh, A.R., Kapur, S., Tulving, E. & Houle, S. (1977). Cognitive substraction may not add up: The interaction between semantic processing and response mode. *NeuroImage, 5,* 229-239.

Just, M.A., Carpenter, P.A., Keller, T.A., Eddy, W.F. & Thulborn, K.R. (1996). Brain Activation modulated by sentence comprehension. *Science, 274,* 114-116.

Kapur, S., Craik, F.I.M., Tulving, E., Wilson, A.A., Houle, S. & Brown, G. (1994). Neuroanatomical correlates of encoding in episodic memory: Levels of processing effect. *Proceedings of the National Academy of Sciences of the USA, 91,* 2008-2011.

Kaukoranta, E., Hari, R. & Lounasma, O.V. (1987). Responses of the human auditory cortex to vowel onset after fricative consonants. *Experimental Brain Research, 69,* 19-23.

Kertesz, A. (1979). *Aphasia and associated disorders: Taxonomy, localization and recovery.* New York: Grune & Stratton.

Kertesz, A. (1983). Localization of lesions in Wernicke's aphasia. In A. Kertesz (ed.), *Localization in neuropsychology.* Orlando, Fl.: Academic Press.

King, J. & Kutas, M. (1995). Who did what and when? Using word and clause related ERPs to monitor working memory usage in reading. *Journal of Cognitive Neuroscience, 7,* 378-397.

Kinsbourne, M. & Warrington, E.K. (1962). A variety of reading disability associated with right hemisphere lesions. *Journal of Neurology, Neurosurgery and Psychiatry, 25,* 339-344.

Klatt, D.H. (1979). Speech perception: A model of acoustic-phonetic analysis and lexical access. In R.A. Cole (ed.), *Perception and production of fluent speech.* Hillsdale, NJ: Lawrence Erlbaum.

Klatt, D.H. (1986). The problem of variability in speech recognition and in models of speech perception. In J. Perkell & D. Klatt (eds.), *Invariance and variability in speech processes* Hillsdale, NJ: Lawrence Erlbaum.

Klatt, D.H. (1989). Review of selected models of speech perception. In W. Marslen-Wilson (ed.), *Lexical representation and process.* Cambridge, MA: MIT Press.

Kluender, R. & Kutas, M. (1993). Subjacency as a processing phenomenon. *Language and Cognitive Processes, 8,* 573-633.

Kolk, H.H.J. & Blomert, L. (1985). On the Bradley-hypothesis concerning agrammatism: The non-word interference effect. *Brain and Language, 21,* 47-67.

Kolk, H.H. & van Grunsven, J.J.F. (1985). Agrammatism as a variable phenomenon. *Cognitive Neuropsychology, 2,* 347-384.

Kosslyn, S.M. (1994). On cognitive neuroscience. *Journal of Cognitive Neuroscience, 6,* 297-303.

Kounios, J. & Holcomb, P.J. (1994). Concreteness effects in semantic processing: ERP evidence supporting dual-coding theory. *Journal of Experimental Psychology: Learning, Memory and Cognition, 20,* 804-823.

Kuriki, S. & Murase, M. (1989). Neuromagnetic study of the auditory responses in right and left hemispheres of the human brain evoked by pure tones and speech sounds. *Experimental Brain Research, 77,* 127-134.

Kutas, M. & Hillyard, S.A. (1980). Reading senseless sentences: Brain potentials reflect semantic incongruity. *Science, 207,* 203-205.

Kutas, M. & Hillyard, S.A.(1983). Event-related potentials to grammatical errors and semantic anomalies. *Memory and Cognition, 11,* 539-550.

Kutas, M., Lindamood, T. & Hillyard, S.A. (1984). Word expectancy and event-related brain potentials during sentence processing. In S. Kornblum & J. Requin (eds.), *Preparatory states and processes.* Hillsdale, NJ: Lawrence Erlbaum.

Lauter, J.L., Herscovitch, P., Formby, C. & Raichle, M.E. (1985). Tonotopic organization in human auditory cortex revealed by positron emission tomography. *Hearing Research, 20,* 199-205.

Liberman, A.M., Cooper, F.S., Shankweiler, D.P. & Studdert-Kennedy, M. (1967). Perception of the speech code. *Psychological Review, 74,* 431-461.

Liberman, A.M. & Mattingly, I.G. (1985). The motor theory of speech perception revised. *Cognition, 21,* 1-36.

Linebarger, M.C., Schwartz, M.F. & Saffran, E.M. (1983). Sensitivity to grammatical structure in so-called agrammatic aphasics. *Cognition, 13,* 361-392.

MacDonald, M.C., Just, M.A. & Carpenter, P.A. (1992). Working memory constraints on the processing of syntactic ambiguity. *Cognitive Psychology, 24,* 56-98.

Mangun, G.R., Hillyard, S.A. & Luck, S.J. (1993). Electrocortical substrates of visual selective attention. In D. Meyer & S. Kornblum (eds.), *Attention and Performance,* Cambridge, Mass.: MIT Press.

Marslen-Wilson, W.D. & Tyler, L.K. (1980). The temporal structure of spoken language understanding. *Cognition, 8,* 1-71.

Marshall, J.C. & Newcombe, F. (1973). Patterns of paralexia: A psycholinguistic approach. *Journal of Psycholinguistic Research, 2 (3),* 175-199.

Martin, A., Haxby, J.V., Lalonde, F.M., Wiggs, C.L. & Ungerleider, L.G. (1995). Discrete cortical regions associated with knowledge of colour and knowledge of action. *Science, 270,* 102-105.

Martin, A., Wiggs, C.L., Ungerleider, L.G. & Haxby, J.V. (1996). Neural correlates of category-specific knowledge. *Nature, 379,* 649-652.

McCarthy, G. & Wood, C.C. (1985). Scalp distributions of event-related potentials: An ambiguity associated with analysis of variance models. *Electroencephalography and Clinical Neurophysiology, 62,* 203-208.

McClelland, J.L., St. John, M. & Taraban, R. (1989). An interaction model of context effects in letter perception: Part I. An account of basic findings. *Language and Cognitive Processes, 4,* 287-336.

Mecklinger, A. & Meinshausen, R.-M. (in press). Recognition memory for object form and location: An event-related potential study. *Memory & Cognition.*

Mecklinger, A., Schriefers, H., Steinhauer, K. & Friederici, A.D. (1995). Processing relative clauses varying on syntactic and semantic dimensions: An analysis with event-related potentials. *Memory and Cognition, 23,* 477-494.

Miceli, G., Gainotti, G., Caltagirone, C. & Masullo, C. (1980). Some aspects of phonological impairment in aphasia. *Brain and Language, 11,* 159-169.

Miceli, G., Mazzucchi, A., Menn, L. & Goodglass, H. (1983). Contrasting cases of Italian agrammatic aphasia without comprehension disorder. *Brain and Language, 19,* 65-97.

Milberg, W. & Blumstein, S.E.(1981). Lexical decision and aphasia: Evidence for semantic processing. *Brain and Language, 14,* 371-385.

Milberg, W., Blumstein, S.E. & Dworetzky, B. (1987). Processing lexical ambiguities. *Brain and Language, 31,* 138-150.

Morton, J. & Patterson, K.E. (1980). A new attempt at an interpretation, or, an attempt at a new interpretation. In M. Coltheart, K.E. Patterson & J.C. Marshall (eds.), *Deep dyslexia* London: Routledge.

Münte, T.F., Heinze, H.J. & Mangun, G.R. (1993). Dissociation of brain activity related to syntactic and semantic aspects of language. *Journal of Cognitive Neuroscience, 5,* 335-344.

Näätänen, R. & Picton, T.W. (1987). The N1 ware of the human electric and magnetic response to sound: A review and an analysis of the component structure. *Psychophysiology, 24,* 375-425.

Neville, H.J., Nicol, J., Barss, A., Forster, K.I. & Garrett, M.F. (1991). Syntactically based sentence processing classes: Evidence from event-related brain potentials. *Journal of Cognitive Neuroscience, 3,* 151-165.

Neville, H.J., Mills, D.L. & Lawson, D.S. (1992). Fractionating language: Different neural subsystems with different sensitive periods. *Cerebral Cortex, 2,* 244-258.

Nobre, A.C., Allison, T. & McCarthy, G. (1994). Word recognition in the human inferior temporal lobe. *Nature, 372,* 260-263.

Nobre, A.C. & McCarthy, G. (1994). Language-related ERPs: Scalp distribution and modulation by word type and semantic priming. *Journal of Cognitive Neuroscience, 6,* 233-255.

Nobre, A.C. & McCarthy, G. (1995). Language-related field potentials in the anterior-medial temporal lobe: II. Effects of the word type and semantic priming. *The Journal of Neuroscience, 15 (2)*, 1090-1098.

Osterhout, L. & Holcomb, P.J. (1992). Event-related potentials and syntactic anomaly. *Journal of Memory and Language, 31*, 785-804.

Osterhout, L. & Holcomb, P.J. (1993). Event-related potentials and syntactic anomaly: Evidence of anomaly detection during the perception of continuous speech. *Language and Cognitive Processes, 8*, 413-437.

Osterhout, L., Holcomb, P.J. & Swinney, D. (1994). Brain potentials elicited by garden-path sentences: Evidence of the application of verb information during parsing. *Journal of Experimental Psychology: Learning, Memory, and Cognition, 20*, 786-803.

Osterhout, L. & Mobley, L.A. (1995). Event-related brain potentials elicited by failure to agree. *Journal of Memory and Language, 34*, 739-773.

Pantev, C., Hoke, K., Lehnertz, K. & Lütkenhöner, B. (1989). Neuromagnetic evidence of an amplitopic organization of the human auditory cortex. *Electroencephalography and Clinical Neurophysiology, 72*, 225-231.

Patterson, K.E. (1980). Derivational errors. In M. Coltheart, K.E. Patterson & J.C. Marshall (eds.), *Deep dyslexia*. London: Routledge.

Patterson, K.E. & Kay, J. (1982). Letter-by-letter reading: Psychological descriptions of a neurological syndrome. *Quarterly Journal of Experimental Psychology, 34A*, 411-441.

Penke, M., Weyerts, H., Gross, M., Zander, E., Münte, T.F. & Clahsen, H. (1997). How the brain processes complex words: An ERP-study of German verb inflections. *Cognitive Brain Research, 6*, 37-52.

Petersen, S.E., Fox, P.T., Posner, M.I., Mintum, M. & Raichle, M.E. (1988). Positron emission tomographic studies of the cortical anatomy of single-word processing. *Nature, 331*, 585-589.

Petersen, S.E., Fox, P.T., Posner, M.I., Mintum, M. & Raichle, M.E. (1989). Positron emission tomographic studies of the processing of single words. *Journal of Cognitive Neuroscience, 1*, 153-170.

Petersen, S.E., Fox, P.T., Snyder, A.Z. & Raichle, M.E. (1990). Activation of extrastriate and frontal cortical areas by visual words and word-like stimuli. *Science, 249*, 1041-1044.

Pick, A. (1913). *Die agrammatischen Sprachstörungen*. Berlin: Springer.

Poeppel, D., Yellin, E., Phillips, C., Roberts, T.P.L., Rowley, H.A., Wexler, K. & Marantz, A. (1996). Task-induced asymmetry of the auditory evoked M 100 neuromagnetic field elicited by speech sounds. *Cognitive Brain Research, 4,* 231-242.

Posner, M.I., Peterson, S.E., Fox, P.T. & Raichle, M.E. (1988). Localization of cognitive operations in the human brain. *Science, 240,* 1627-1632.

Price, C., Wise, R., Ransay, S., Friston, K., Howard, D., Patterson, K. & Frackowiak, R. (1992). Regional response within the human auditory cortex when listening to words. *Neuroscience Letters, 146,* 179-182.

Price, C.J., Wise, R.J.S., Watson, J.D.G., Patterson, K., Howard, D. & Frackowiak, R.S.J. (1994). Brain activity during reading: The effects of exposure duration and task. *Brain, 117,* 1255-1269.

Pulvermüller, F., Lutzenberger, W. & Birbaumer, N. (1995). Electrocortical distinction of vocabulary types. *Electroencephalography and Clinical Neurophysiology, 94,* 357-370.

Raichle, M.E., Fiez, J.A., Videen, T.O., MacLeod, A.M., Pardo, J.V., Fox, P.T. & Petersen, S.E. (1994). Practice-related changes in human brain functional anatomy during nonmotor learning. *Cerebral Cortex, 4 (1),* 8-26.

Rösler, F., Friederici, A.D., Pütz, P. & Hahne, A. (1993). Event-related brain potentials while encountering semantic and syntactic constraint violations. *Journal of Cognitive Neuroscience, 5,* 345-362.

Rubenstein, H., Lewis, S.S. & Rubenstein, M.A. (1971). Evidence for phonemic recoding in visual word recognition. *Journal of Verbal Learning and Verbal Behavior, 19,* 645-657.

Saffran, E.M. & Schwartz, M.F. (1994). Of cabbages and things: Semantic memory from a neuropsychological perspective - A tutorial view. In C. Umilta & M. Moscovitch (eds.), *Attention and performance XV.* Cambridge, MA: MIT Press.

Sartori, G. & Job, R. (1988). The oyster with four legs: A neuropsychological study on the interaction of visual and semantic information. *Cognitive Neuropsychology, 5,* 105-132.

Sasanuma, S., Akio, K. & Kubota, M. (1990). Agrammatism in Japanese: Two case studies. In L. Menn & L. Obler (eds.), *Agrammatic Aphasia.* Amsterdam: Benjamins.

Scherg, M. & von Cramon, D. (1986). Evoked dipole source potentials in the human auditory cortex. *Electroencephalography and Clinical Neurophysiology, 65,* 344-360.

Scherg, M. (1990). Fundamentals of dipole source potential analysis. In F. Grandori, M. Hoke & G.L. Romani (eds.), *Auditory evoked magnetic fields and electric potentials*. Basel: Karger.

Schreuder, R. & Flores d'Arcais, G.B. (1989). Psycholinguistic issues in the lexical representation of meaning. In W.D. Marslen-Wilson (ed.), *Lexical representation and process*. Cambridge, MA: MIT-Press.

Segui, J., Mehler, J., Frauenfelder, U. & Morton, J. (1982). Word frequency effect and lexical access. *Neuropsychologia, 20,* 615-627.

Seidenberg, M.S., Waters, G.S., Barnes, M.A. & Tanenhaus, M.K. (1984). When does irregular spelling or pronunciation influence word recognition? *Journal of Verbal Learning and Verbal Behavior, 23,* 383-404.

Shallice, T. & Warrington, E.K. (1980). Single and multiple component central dyslexic syndromes. In M. Coltheart, K.E. Patterson & J.C. Marshall (eds.), *Deep dyslexia*. London: Routledge & Kegan Paul.

Shallice, T., Warrington, E.K. & McCarthy, R. (1983). Reading without semantics. *The Quarterly Journal of Experimental Psychology, 35A,* 111-138.

Shankweiler, D. & Studdert-Kennedy, M. (1967). Identification of consonants and vowels presented to left and right ears. *The Quarterly Journal of Experimental Psychology, 19,* 59-63.

Silveri, M.C. & Gainotti, G.B. (1987). Interaction between vision and language in category specific semantic impairment for living things. *Cognitive Neuropsychology, 5,* 677-907.

Stromswold, K., Caplan, D., Alpert, N. & Rauch, S. (1996). Localization of syntactic comprehension by positron emission tomography. *Brain and Language, 52,* 452-473.

Swinney, D.A., Zurif, E.B. & Cutler, A. (1980). Effects of sentential stress and word class upon comprehension in Broca's aphasics. *Brain and Language, 10,* 132-144.

Tulving, E., Markowitsch, H.J., Kapur, S., Habib, R. & Houle, S. (1994). Novelty encoding networks in the human brain: Positron emission tomography data. *NeuroReport, 5,* 2525-2528.

Van Petten, C. (1995). Words and Sentences: Event-related brain potential measures. *Psychophysiology, 32,* 511-525.

Van Petten, C. & Kutas, M. (1990). Interactions between sentence context and word frequency in event-related brain potentials. *Memory and Cognition, 18 (4),* 380-393.

von Stockert, T.R. & Bader, L. (1976). Some relations of grammar and lexicon in aphasia. *Cortex, 12,* 49-60.

Warrington, E.K. & Shallice, T. (1984). Category specific semantic impairments. *Brain, 107,* 829-853.

Whitehouse, P., Caramazza, A. & Zurif, E.B. (1978). Naming in aphasia: Interacting effects of form and function. *Brain and Language, 6,* 63-74.

Wise, R., Chollet, F., Hadar, U., Friston, K., Hoffner, E. & Frackowiak, R. (1991). Distribution of cortical neural networks involved in word comprehension and word retrieval. *Brain, 114,* 1803-1817.

Wulfeck, B. (1988). Grammatically judgement and sentence comprehension in agrammatic aphasia. *Journal of Speech and Hearing Research, 31,* 72-81.

Zatorre, R.J., Meyer, E., Gjedde, A. & Evans, A.C. (1996). PET studies of phonetic processing of speech: Review, replication, and reanalysis. In M. Raichle & P.S. Goldman-Rakic (eds.), Special Issue: Cortical imaging - microscope of the mind, *Cerebral Cortex, 6,* 21-30.

Zatorre, R.J., Evans, A.C., Meyer, E. & Gjedde, A. (1992). Lateralization of phonetic and pitch discrimination in speech processing. *Science, 256,* 846-849.

Zurif, E.B., Caramazza, A. & Myerson, R. (1972). Grammatical judgements of agrammatic aphasics. *Neuropsychologia, 10,* 405-417.

Zurif, E.B., Caramazza, A., Myerson, R. & Galvin, J. (1974). Semantic feature representation for normal and aphasic language. *Brain and Language, 1,* 167-187.

Index

Abney 189, 202, 223, 225
Aitchison 71, 90
Albrecht 234, 242, 251, 257, 260
Allison 282, 297
Altmann 27, 33, 35, 37, 39, 56, 62,
  83, 90f, 98, 185, 190ff, 220, 225f
Ambiguities 186
ambiguities 181, 184, 186
ambiguity 2, 49, 58, 85f, 183ff, 192,
  196, 198, 255
ambiguous 186f, 194f
Anderson 101, 126, 140, 143, 163, 180,
  201, 234, 257
Andrews 106, 126
Andrusiak 247, 262
Aslin 28, 33
Attapaiboon 53, 63
Auerbach 266, 290
Aydelott-Utman 267, 291

Baars 80, 90
Baayen 44, 69, 105ff, 111, 115ff, 122ff,
  126, 130
Bach 217, 225
Bäckman 152, 163
Bacri 31, 33
Badecker 116, 129
Bader 223, 225, 277, 301
Bagley 77, 90
Baillet 246f, 259
Baker 221f, 225, 272, 290, 293
Balota 76, 90, 177ff, 197, 201, 208f
Banel 31, 33
Barattelli 142, 161, 169f
Barclay 159, 163, 233, 257

Bard 27, 33, 83, 90
Bari 119
Barrett 282, 290
Barsalou 159, 163
Bartram 146, 163
Basili 164
Bassili 150, 163
Basso 266, 268, 290
Bastiani 151, 173
Bates 185, 198, 201, 206
Beach 43, 62
Beardsley 240, 258
Beauvillain 118, 121, 126f
Beauvois 269, 290
Becker 109, 130
Béland 45, 68
Bentin 77, 91, 112, 126, 282
Bergman 109f, 120, 126
Bern 246, 257
Bernard 50, 65
Berndt 150, 164, 266, 277, 290
Bertelson 21, 39
Bertoncini 28, 30, 33, 40
Besner 144, 169
Bestgen 234, 257
Bever 183, 201, 215, 219, 225f
Biederman 146, 163
Biegelmann 154, 162, 166, 175
Bienkowski 85, 97
Bierwisch 139, 163, 271, 274f, 290
Bijeljac-Babic 28, 33
Birch 51f, 62
Black 246, 257
Blank 82, 90, 92
Blasko 22, 34, 78, 91
Bleasdale 178, 201

Bloom 84, 92, 234, 258
Bloomert 278
Blumstein 266ff, 272, 290, 297
Blutner 51, 62
Bock 52, 57, 62, 66
Boles 145, 163
Bölte 44, 61
Bond 57, 60, 62, 78, 90, 93
Booj 119, 126, 128
Bookheimer 271, 291
Boves 52, 68
Bower 234, 260
Bowers 144f, 164
Boyce 84, 94
Boysson-Bardies 28, 33, 36
Bradley 8, 14, 33, 46, 62, 73, 90, 118,
    127, 277f, 291, 295
Braitenberg 279, 291
Branigan 220, 225
Bransford 163, 183, 201, 233, 257
Brems 147, 174
Brent 29, 33
Bresnan 184, 187, 201f, 204
Briand 144, 165
Britt 191f, 194, 202
Broca and Wernicke aphasia 82
Broca aphasics 266, 277ff
Broca patients 266, 268, 272, 277ff
Brodbeck 145, 164
Brokx 43, 68
Brooks 147, 171
Browman 60, 62
Brown 26, 33, 82, 87, 89, 93f, 142,
    164, 199, 205f, 217, 225, 246f,
    259, 282f, 291, 294f
Bruce 139, 168
Brysbaert 224f
Bub 151, 164
Buckner 274, 291
Bühler 164
Burani 106, 111, 114, 116ff, 124,
    126f, 129
Burnham 53f, 63
Butterfield 9, 34, 44, 57, 64f, 65
Butterworth 105f, 123, 127
Buxton 48, 51, 63
Byrne 146, 164

Cabeza 275, 291
Cairns 82, 90
Calvanio 151, 170
Caplan 198, 202, 221, 225, 267,
    273, 276, 291, 300
Caramazza 106f, 110, 116, 118, 121,
    127, 129, 150, 155f, 164, 240,
    258, 272, 277f, 290f, 293, 301
Carlson 51, 64, 69, 72f, 98, 181,
    184, 190, 204, 206, 208, 210f
Caroll 146, 164
Carpenter 189, 197f, 202, 205ff, 216f,
    222, 226f
Carter 29, 34, 44, 56, 62, 64
Cartwright 29, 33
Cary 16, 38
Casati 266, 290
Cassidy 57, 63
Cattell 179
Cermele 111, 129
Chaffin 135, 169
Challis 145, 164
Chambers 178, 204
Chater 224f
Chen 53ff, 63f, 69, 145, 164
Cherry 79, 90
Chertkow 271, 291
Cheung 145, 164
Chialant 107, 127
Ching 53, 63
Chomsky 183f, 202
Christiansen 224f
Christophe 30, 33, 45, 49, 63, 68
Chrysler 231, 234, 258
Chumbley 76, 90, 178, 201
Church 5, 9, 33, 149f, 173
Chwilla 282, 291
Cirilo 82, 92
Clark 183f, 202, 237f, 240, 246, 257f
Clifton 52, 57, 62ff, 99, 189, 191,
    202ff, 207, 209, 211, 214, 220,
    225f, 240, 242, 257
Cluytens 14, 17, 36, 45, 66
cognitive categories in 246
Cohen 152, 154, 164, 198, 202
Cole 9, 34, 36, 50, 60, 62f,
    80, 90f, 106, 113, 118,
    127, 129, 295

Collier 43, 63
Collins 135, 143, 158, 164
Colombo 85, 98
Coltheart 169, 170ff, 257f, 269,
      291f, 297f, 300
conceptual interpretation 214
conceptual structure 248, 271, 273
connectionist 74, 142, 179f, 224
Connine 22, 34, 57, 63, 71,
      78f, 91, 178, 202
Conrad 85, 91
Content 6, 16, 23, 34f, 38
contextual information 230
Coolen 113, 128
Cooper 50, 63, 91f, 146, 163, 173
Corbett 250, 257
Corley 192, 207
Cortese 115, 130
Cotton 83, 91
Coulson 285, 291
Cowart 81f, 90f, 95
Cox 30, 38
Coyote 145, 175
Craik 144, 164f, 171
Crain 190, 193, 202f, 208, 220, 225
Crocker 224, 226
Crystal 26, 34, 101, 103, 127
Cuetos 18, 34, 223, 226
Curtis 242, 259
Cutler 5ff, 9, 13ff, 24, 26, 29,
      34, 36, 38f, 41f, 44f, 50f,
      53ff, 57ff, 60f, 63ff, 73, 75,
      82, 91, 111, 116, 118, 122, 124,
      127, 130, 214, 277, 300

Dahan 41, 47, 50, 61, 64f
Daneman 189, 197, 202
Danneburg 145, 165
Dannenbring 144, 165
Davis 157, 167
Davy 26, 34
de Gelder 25, 40, 44, 46, 70, 91
de Groot 145, 158, 165
de Jong 183, 212
de Pijper 43, 68
de Renzi 155, 165
de Rooij 43, 68, 69
de Smedt 224, 226f

de Vega 18, 34
Decety 275, 291
Deese 135, 165
Dehaut 221f, 225
Dèjerne 270
Delany 145f, 173
Dell 72, 82, 91, 98, 106, 127, 181,
      211, 242, 257
Delphine Dahan 61
Dèmonet 267, 268, 292
Den Heyer 144, 165
Denis 154, 165f
Derousnè 269
Deutsch 77, 91, 161, 168
Dhawan 148, 165, 172
Dijkstra 21, 34, 35, 107, 115ff, 119,
      123, 126, 224, 226f
Dimmendaal 119, 127
disambiguation 178, 181f, 186
discourse 41, 42, 52, 184f, 190ff, 199,
      214, 217ff, 220, 229ff, 231,
      236ff, 263
discourse interpretation 229
discourse processing 258
discourse referents 239
Dominguez 18, 34
Dommergues 14, 38, 45, 67
Donnenwerth-Nolan 85, 98, 154, 173
Dopkins 234, 257
Dosher 250, 257
Dovetto 118, 127
Downie 122, 128
Drews 113, 128
Duffy 182, 202, 208, 246f, 260
Dumay 17, 34
Dunn 144, 148f, 169
Dupoux 7, 14, 30, 33, 39,
      45, 49, 60, 63, 65
Durso 144, 148, 165

Eberhard 51, 69
Eefting 50, 65
Ehrlich 181, 203, 220, 226, 240,
      242, 257, 261
Eimas 82, 84, 92, 97, 265, 292
Eling 109, 126
Ellis 137, 139, 141, 150f, 160,
      165, 169, 265, 269, 292

Elman 9ff, 38, 74, 92, 95, 157,
    171, 224, 226
Emmeroy 121f, 128
Engelkamp 133ff, 137ff, 144f, 149, 151ff,
    159, 165f, 171, 175, 214, 268
Eulitz 279, 292
Evans 267, 301
Evett 144, 169, 180, 203, 269, 294

Farmer 87, 95
Farrar 186, 203
Faulconer 140, 172
Faulkner 198, 202
Faust 198, 205
Fear 57, 65
Feldman 105f, 110, 112ff, 122, 126ff,
    129f, 140, 172
Felguera 45, 68
Ferreira 188f, 191, 197, 203, 226, 240,
    242, 252, 257, 261
Ferstl 177, 187, 195f, 203, 209, 214, 280
Fiez 274, 292, 299
Fischler 84, 92, 198, 203
Fletcher 231, 234, 258
Floccia 1, 18, 28, 33, 35, 214
Flores d'Arcais 113, 128, 131, 155f,
    167, 177, 201, 208f, 214, 227,
    273, 280, 300
Fodor 51, 64, 72, 76, 92, 177,
    183f, 197, 199, 203f, 215, 219f,
    226, 264, 276, 292
Ford 184, 188, 204
Forster 8, 33f, 73, 84, 90, 92, 105,
    108, 110, 123, 132, 157, 167,
    174, 177, 178, 204, 208, 297
Foss 50, 64, 82f, 90, 92, 181, 204
Fowler 105f, 112ff, 122, 128, 130
Fox 53f, 65, 143, 172
Frackowiak 267, 292ff, 299, 301
Francis 53, 63, 91f
Franks 163, 183, 201, 233, 257
Frauenfelder 1, 6, 8, 14, 16, 18, 21ff, 34ff,
    38, 40, 45, 52, 67, 69, 72ff, 92, 93,
    106f, 128, 214, 263, 82, 292, 300
Frazier 5, 9, 35, 73, 92, 99, 113,
    128, 182, 184, 186f, 190, 196f,
    204, 207ff, 211, 214, 219f, 225f,
    230, 258, 264, 276, 279, 285f, 292

Freeman 109, 130
Friederici 29, 35f, 76, 82, 84, 87, 93,
    106, 131, 141, 195, 198, 203f,
    207, 209, 221, 226, 263, 265,
    277ff, 282ff, 287, 292ff, 297, 299
Friston 264, 293f, 299, 301
Frith 274, 293
Frost 110, 128
Funnell 172

Gainotti 273, 297, 300
Galvin 272, 301
Garcia-Albea 14, 46
garden-path 187, 188, 189, 214, 220,
    222, 287
garden-path model 185, 188
garden-path sentences 216, 219, 286
Gardiner 149, 167
Garnes 60, 62, 78, 90, 93
Garnham 192, 201, 207, 233, 258
Garnsey 51, 62, 76, 93, 188, 189, 199,
    205, 211
Garrett 183, 204, 208, 215, 226, 277,
    278, 291, 297
Garrod 192, 202, 209, 215, 226, 230,
    234, 237, 239, 242, 257, 258, 261
Gee 7, 9, 36
general knowledge 250
Gernsbacher 82, 92, 94, 95, 97, 115,
    128, 178, 198, 201, 205, 207,
    210, 213, 226, 227
Gibbs 181, 205
Gibson 197, 205, 217ff, 226
Gilligan 122, 127
Givón 238ff, 258
Gjedde 267, 301
Glaser 140, 167
Glass 136, 167
Glavanov 234, 261
Glazenborg 155, 167
Glenberg 233f, 258
Glucksberg 85, 93
Golding 234, 252, 259, 261
Goldinger 24f, 35, 37
Goldman 6, 35, 301
Goldstein 84, 94, 277, 293
Goodglass 265, 272, 290, 293, 297
Goodman 149, 170, 181, 205

Goodsitt 29, 35
Gordon 24, 35, 278, 293
Goring 144, 165
Gorman 149, 167
Gormican 161, 174
Gorrell 217, 220f, 226, 264, 293
Gow 24, 35
Grabowski 142, 152, 166, 168
Graesser 234, 246, 250, 258f, 262
Graetz 106, 131
Graf 142, 144, 167f
Grainger 106, 113, 118, 128f
Grant 141, 168
Green 78f, 93, 95
Greenspan 234, 260
Gregg 149, 167
Griffith 197, 207
Grober 240, 258
Grondelaers 224f
Groothusen 87, 93, 199, 283, 294
Grosjean 7, 9, 21, 27, 35f, 40, 75f,
    83, 91, 93
Grosser 160, 167
Gunter 199, 205, 284f, 293
Günther 105, 129

Haarmann 222, 226, 279, 294
Hagman 44, 58, 66
Hagoort 87, 93, 199, 205, 272, 282f,
    285, 291, 294
Hahne 87, 93, 282, 284f, 293, 294, 299
Hakes 85, 97
Hall 112, 131
Halldorson 247, 262
Halle 101, 129
Hallé 28, 36
Hambley 105
Hamburger 17, 39, 40
Hampton 149, 167
Hankamer 124, 129
Hanney 121, 132
Harley 150, 167
Harras 168
Hart 43, 63
Hatano 45, 68
Haviland 237f, 258
Hawkins 122, 127
Healy 143, 171, 179, 205

Hebb 142, 167
Hebrew 77
Heilman 153, 173, 277, 294
Heinze 199, 207
Heise 77, 95
Helstrup 152, 167
Hemforth 223, 227
Hemphill 151, 167
Henderson 108ff, 112f, 120, 129, 188,
    197, 203
Hernon 112, 131
Herrmann 135f, 142, 152, 160f,
    167ff, 275, 294
Heuer 152, 168
Hier 151, 168
Hildebrandt 222, 225
Hilliard 87, 94
Hillis 164
Hillyard 181, 206, 281, 282, 285, 296
Hines 145, 168
Hirshkowitz 85, 97
Hobbs 245, 258
Hoffmann 137, 160, 168
Höhle 46, 66
Holcomb 76, 87, 88, 94, 96, 188,
    199, 208, 279, 282, 283,
    286, 294, 295, 298
Holmes 118, 129
Holyoak 136, 167
Homa 146, 153, 168
Hoosain 54, 70
Hörmann 134f, 168
Howard 270, 274, 294, 299
Howe 141, 168
Hudson 109, 126
Huggins 14, 36
Humphreys 139, 144, 146f, 168f, 172,
    180, 203, 269, 294
Hustinx 244, 252, 262

Imhoff 48, 67
inferences 249
Inhoff 178, 205
interactive 179f, 181, 184f, 189, 198
interactive activation 11ff
Isaak 155, 170
Isard 77, 95, 183, 207, 216, 227

Jablon 82, 90
Jackendoff 273, 294
Jackson 150, 169
Jacobs 118, 128
Jakimik 50, 60, 63, 80, 91, 94
Jarvella 231, 259
Jennings 265, 294
Jensen 143, 170
Job 85, 98, 143, 173, 273, 299
Johns-Lewis 26, 36
Johnson 135, 144, 148, 165, 169
Johnson-Laird 135, 169, 233, 259
Johnston 179, 205
Jongenburger 58f, 66
Jongman 116, 131
Juliano 224, 228
Jurafsky 217, 226
Jusczyk 29, 33, 36
Just 183, 189, 197f, 205ff, 216f, 222,
    22f6, 253, 259, 287, 294, 296

Kaan 218, 227
Kakehi 45, 66
Kamp 236, 259
Kaplan 184, 187, 202, 204
Kapur 274, 294f, 300
Kashino 45, 66
Kato 45, 66
Katz 84, 94, 116, 129
Kaukoranta 281, 295
Kawamoto 186, 203
Kay 151, 169, 269, 298
Kearns 14, 16, 35, 38, 46, 66
Keefe 180, 208, 252f, 259
Keenan 246f, 252, 259, 261
Kellas 182, 205
Keller 53, 63
Kellows 188, 211
Kelly 57, 63, 66
Kelter 134, 169
Kempen 213, 215, 222, 227f, 280
Kempff 246, 260
Kempley 120, 122, 129
Kertesz 151, 164, 267, 295
Kiefer 142, 161f, 169f
Kilborn 84, 93
Kimball 184, 206, 219, 227
King 197, 199, 202, 206, 285, 291, 295

Kinoshita 105, 132
Kinsbourne 270, 295
Kintsch 135, 169, 181f, 185, 196, 206,
    211, 231ff, 244, 253f, 256,
    259f, 262
Kirkwood 54, 63
Kirsner 122, 128, 144, 146, 148f,
    164, 169
Klatt 6, 7, 36, 50, 66, 265, 267, 295
Kleiman 84, 94
Klin 252, 260
Klix 137, 169
Kluender 285, 295
Knight 109, 113, 129
Koelbing 142, 170
Kolinsky 14, 16ff, 36, 38, 45, 66
Kolk 277ff, 294, 295
Konieczny 223, 227
Koopmans-van Beinum 50
Kornadt 166
Kosslyn 140, 169, 265, 295
Koster 58f, 65, 67, 70
Kostic 105, 129, 130
Kounios 279, 295
Kraak 52, 68
Kreuz 85, 93
Kroll 158, 170
Krumnacker 152, 166
Kuhl 28f, 35f
Kurbjuweit 149, 166
Kuriki 281, 296
Kutas 76, 87, 94, 99, 181f, 199,
    202, 206, 211, 282f, 285,
    291, 295f, 300

Labov 26, 37
Lacerda 28, 36, 53, 63
Lagerquist 57, 67
Lahiri 6f, 11, 14, 19, 37, 40, 46, 70
Langer 76, 97
Lasser 223, 225
Lau 145, 164
Laudanna 106, 111, 116ff, 127, 129
Lauter 268, 296
Lawson 282f, 297
Lear 247, 262
Lee 53, 67
Leek 164

Lehiste 43, 67
Leiman 85, 97f, 181, 210f
Lentz 50, 65
Lesgold 242, 259
Levelt 7, 37, 68, 75, 94, 209, 215, 227
Levin 26, 37
Levine 151, 170
Lewis 269, 299
lexical elements 229
lexical access 36f, 9f, 14, 31, 52, 73f,
    79f, 83f, 86ff, 104, 111, 122ff,
    179ff, 197, 199, 267, 282f
Libben 120, 129
Liberman 265f, 296
Lichten 77, 95
Lieber 101, 117f, 126, 130
Lieberman 59, 67
Liepmann 170, 173
Lin 54, 68
Lindamood 282, 296
Lindblom 28, 36
Lindem 233f, 258
Lindsay 135, 173
Linebarger 198, 206, 277, 279, 296
linguistic representation 236
Liversedge 192, 207, 220, 225
Lockhart 144, 164
Loftus 143, 158, 164
Logie 148, 166, 170
Long 82, 95, 234, 258, 259
Lorch 143, 170
Lucas 72, 85, 94, 98
Lucchelli 155, 165
Luce 7, 24f, 35, 37, 39, 44, 73, 96
Lukatela 84, 94, 105f, 116, 129, 130
Luksaneeyanawin 53f, 63
Lupker 143, 170
Lussier 45, 68
Lyons 137, 170

MacDonald 185, 187, 195f, 197, 206,
    208, 216, 219, 227
Mackay 80
MacLeod 150, 163
MacWhinney 123, 131, 185, 201, 206
Madigan 146, 153, 170
Magee 140, 174
Magliano 234, 262

Mandler 144, 149, 167, 170
Manelis 110, 130
Mangold-Allwinn 142, 156, 160ff,
    166f, 169f
Mangun 199, 207, 281, 296f
Mani 233, 259
Mann 245, 259
Marantz 101, 129
Marcario 24, 35
Marcus 217, 227
Marin 143, 174
Marks 155, 170
Marr 139, 170
Marshall 171, 174, 269, 291, 296ff, 300
Marslen-Wilson 2, 5ff, 18, 21f, 25, 37,
    40, 73ff, 79, 81ff, 91f, 94f,
    98, 114, 120ff, 127, 129f, 132,
    185f, 206, 211, 215, 217, 225,
    227, 264, 295, 296, 300
Martin 48, 67, 69, 143, 170,
    274f, 296
Mason 234, 251, 260
Massaro 12, 14, 37f, 72f, 95
Masterson 143, 173
Mattingly 266, 296
Mattys 57, 67
Mazzella 52, 62
McAllister 60, 67, 83, 95
McCallum 87, 95
McCarrell 163
McCarthy 141, 155, 170, 174, 269,
    282, 296ff, 300
McClelland 9ff, 38, 74, 95f, 157, 1
    70f, 179ff, 185, 189, 205f,
    210f, 219, 227, 264, 297
McDaniel 252f, 259
McElree 197, 207
McHugh 48, 69
McKoon 72, 96, 232, 242, 250,
    252f, 257, 259ff
McNamara 143, 171, 235, 260
McNeill 142, 164
McQueen 13, 24, 30, 38f, 46, 59f, 67,
    69, 73, 91, 111, 116, 118, 122,
    124, 130
McRae 219f, 227
Mecklenbräucker 175
Mecklinger 87, 93, 190, 198, 204, 207,
    282f, 286f, 293, 297

Mehler 7, 14, 16f, 28, 30, 33f,
    38ff, 45f, 49, 60, 63ff, 67ff, 300
Mehta 48, 50, 60, 67
Meinshausen 282, 297
Meltzer 48, 51, 67
Mens 48, 51, 68
Merikle 145, 173
Metha 26, 38
Metsala 80, 99
Meunier 16, 38
Meyer 72, 95, 143, 159, 171, 180,
    204, 207, 233f, 258, 267, 296, 301
Miceli 267, 277, 297
Milberg 272, 290, 297
Milech 122, 128, 149, 169
Miller 77f, 95, 183, 201, 207, 209,
    211, 216, 227, 228
Mills 48, 67, 282f, 297
Milroy 26, 38
Mintun 143, 172
Miozzo 164
Mitchell 177, 184, 192, 197, 207,
    215, 220f, 223ff
Mitchum 266, 290
Miyake 198, 207
Moar 239, 261
Mobley 283, 285, 298
Mohr 151ff, 165f, 168, 171
Morais 14, 16ff, 21, 36, 38f, 45, 66
Morgan 29, 35
Morris 182, 202, 209, 230, 258
Morrow 234, 240, 260
Morton 8, 33, 38, 82, 95, 120, 122,
    129, 136, 150, 157, 169, 171,
    174, 178, 207, 269, 297, 300
Moskolievic 113, 128
Moss 22, 37, 85, 95
Motley 80, 90
Mousty 21, 39
Mross 181, 206, 211
Mulder 199, 205, 285, 293
Münte 199, 207, 284, 297, 298
Murase 281, 296
Murray 192, 207, 252, 260
Myers 234, 245ff, 251ff, 256, 260
Myerson 272, 301

Näätänen 281, 297
Nakamura 18, 38

Nakatani 5, 39, 49, 68
Napps 106, 113, 128, 130
Navon 161, 171
Nazzi 28, 33
Neely 143, 159, 171, 180, 208
Neisser 111f, 131
Nelson 136, 147f, 171f
Neville 87f, 94, 199, 208, 282ff,
    294, 297
Newcombe 269, 296
Newman 82, 91
Ni 193f, 203, 208
Nilsson 152, 163
Nitsch 163
Nobre 282, 297f
Noordman 229, 245f, 248f, 260ff
Nooteboom 43, 52, 63, 68, 70
Norman 135, 173
Norris 5, 6, 9f, 13, 14, 16, 24f, 34,
    38f, 44ff, 59, 64f, 67, 75, 82, 84,
    91, 95, 122, 130
Nothdurft 161, 172
Nyberg 275, 291
Nygaard 82, 92

O'Brien 230, 234, 242, 245, 251,
    253, 256ff, 260
Oden 14, 38, 86, 96
Older 120, 130
Olive 43, 50, 67, 69
Onifer 85, 96f, 182, 208
O'Reagan 118, 129
O'Seaghdha 72, 96
Ostendorf 43, 70
Osterhout 76, 87, 96, 188, 199, 208,
    283, 285f, 298
Otake 7, 15, 34, 38, 45f, 55, 65f, 68
Ottevanger 80, 96

Painton 112, 131
Paivio 135ff, 172
Pallier 45, 60, 65, 68
Pansottee 54, 63
Pantev 281, 292, 298
parsing principles 220, 223
Patterson 137, 171, 174, 269, 291,
    294, 297ff

Pearlmutter 197, 205f, 208, 219, 227
Peeters 8, 22f, 35
Pellegrino 148, 165, 172
Penke 285, 298
Peretz 45, 68
Perfetti 80, 91, 187, 192, 195,
    202, 208f
Petersen 268, 270, 274, 291, 298f
Peterson 143, 150, 172
Peynircioglu 147, 174
Pfeifer 87, 93, 282, 293
phonetic representations 229
phonological processes 3, 274, 281, 287
Pick 277, 298
Pickering 220, 225
Picton 281, 297
Pinker 123, 130
Pisoni 7, 24f, 35, 37, 39, 73, 83, 96
Pitt 48f, 68
Plewes 242, 260
Pnini 110, 128
Pobel 160f, 167, 172
Pocock 87, 95
Poeppel 281, 299
Pollack 115, 130, 185, 196, 211
Popovics 151, 170
Posner 141, 143, 172, 180, 208,
    270, 298f
Potter 140, 172
Potts 233, 252, 260f
Povel 48, 51, 68
Prather 85, 97
Price 43, 70, 268, 270f, 292f, 299
priming 232
Prince 239, 261
Prinz 137, 172
Pritchett 221, 223, 227f
propositional 232, 234
propositional representation 231, 235
psychological representation 236
Pulvermüller 279, 291, 299
Pütz 285, 299
Pylyshyn 140, 172

Quené 49, 68
Quillian 135, 164
Quinlan 144, 169

Rabinowitz 141, 168
Radeau 17, 21, 34, 39
Raichle 141, 143, 172, 275, 291, 296,
    298f, 301
Ratcliff 72, 96, 232, 242, 250, 252f,
    257, 259ff
Rayner 178, 181f, 184, 186f, 190, 192,
    197, 201ff, 207, 208f, 211, 220,
    225f, 230, 240, 242, 257f, 261f
Read 52, 68
reading 248
Redanz 29, 36
Reed 148, 171f
referential ambiguity 220
referential coherence 237ff, 241f, 244f,
    248
referential expressions 237ff, 243
referential information 192
referential processes 214
referential support 190f
referential theory 190
Reicher 179, 209
Reichert 175
relational coherence 245
Rentoul 121, 132
Repp 54, 68
representation 235
Rexer 116, 129
Reyle 236, 259
Rho 85, 93
Riddoch 137f, 146f, 168, 172
Riegler 144, 173
Riesbeck 183, 209
Rietveld 49, 69
Roediger 144, 147f, 172f
Roelofs 106, 121, 131
Roeper 220, 226
Romani 106, 127
Rosati 151, 173
Rosenbaum 152, 173
Rösler 199, 209, 285, 299
Ross 83, 92, 180, 208

Roth 242, 259
Rothi 153, 173
Rubenstein 115, 130, 269, 299
Rubin 109, 130

Ruddy 180, 207
Rugg 282, 290
Rumelhart 74, 95f, 135, 157, 171,
    173, 179, 206, 246, 261
Rummer 133, 268

Sachs 232, 261
Saffran 143, 174, 273, 277, 279,
    296, 299
Salasmo 116, 127
Salasoo 83, 96
Salomon 197, 205
Saltz 154, 173
Samuel 7, 39, 48f, 57, 67f,
    78, 80, 88, 96f
Sanchez-Casas 14, 16, 34, 46
Sandeman 43
Sanders 76, 97, 245f, 248, 261
Sandra 120, 130
Sanford 215, 226, 234, 237, 239, 242,
    257f, 261
Sansavini 28, 40
Santa 136, 167
Sartori 143, 173, 273, 299
Sasanuma 277, 299
Scarborough 115, 130
Schacter 144ff, 149f, 164, 173
Schaffer 5, 26, 37, 39, 49, 68
Schank 135, 173, 183, 209
Scheepers 223, 227
Scherg 280, 299f
Schermer 78, 95
Schmalhofer 234, 259, 261
Schmidt 152, 174
Scholes 277, 294
Scholten 23, 34
Schreuder 44, 69, 105ff, 111, 113,
    115ff, 123f, 126, 128, 130f, 139,
    155, 163, 167, 271, 273ff, 290,
    300
Schriefers 46, 66, 70, 86, 99, 101,
    106, 114, 121f, 131, 297
Schustack 242, 261
Schütze 197, 205
Schvaneveldt 72, 95, 171, 180, 207
Schwanenflugel 72, 97, 178, 180f, 209
Schwartz 143, 174, 273, 277, 279,
    296, 299

Schwarz 139, 169, 174
Schweizer 142, 168
Scott 43, 69
Sebastiàn-Gallés 14ff, 39, 45, 59, 65
Sedivy 51, 69, 194, 210
segmentation 229
Segui 7, 14, 16f, 21, 34f, 38f,
    45, 64, 67, 69, 106, 113,
    118, 127ff, 278, 300
Seidenberg 73, 76, 85, 97f, 104, 123,
    131, 177, 180ff, 206, 209ff,
    219, 227, 269, 300
Sellen 153, 166
semantic analysis 229ff
Sengul 240, 257
Sereno 116, 131, 180, 209f
Seuren 236, 261
Shallice 269, 273, 290, 300f
Shankweiler 193, 203, 208, 266, 296, 300
Shanon 145, 174
Shattuck-Hufnagel 43, 70
Sheldon 240, 261
Shields 48, 51, 69
Shillcock 24, 27, 33, 39, 83, 90
Shinjo 246f, 260
Shoben 181, 209
Shubert 84, 97
Siegel 148, 172
Sieloff 154, 175
Silveri 273, 300
Simons 244, 246, 252, 261f
Simpson 85f, 97, 99, 177, 205, 209f
Singer 235, 247f, 250, 252, 258, 261f
Skinner 134, 174
Slobin 135, 174
Slowiaczek 17, 39f, 57f
Small 57, 62
Smith 140, 150, 163, 174
Smolensky 180, 210
Snodgrass 136, 174
Snow 26, 37
Snyder 180, 208
So 140, 172
Solso 145, 174
Sommer 51, 62
Soto 59, 69
spatial information 234
Speer 189, 202
Spira 86, 96

Spitzer 133, 141, 155f, 174
Spivey-Knowlton 51, 69, 193f, 197,
    210, 220, 227
Spooren 245, 248, 261
St.John 264
Stadler 144, 173
Standen 144, 148f, 169
Stanners 111ff, 131
Stanovich 84, 97, 181, 210, 212
Steedman 185, 190ff, 201f, 220, 225
Steele 101, 131
Stemberger 123, 131
Stengel 151, 167
Stevens 28, 36
Stewart 158, 170, 220, 225
Stolz 217, 228
Stowe 189, 205, 209f, 285, 293
Strange 54, 69
Streeter 43, 67, 69
Stromswold 287, 300
Strube 135, 174, 223, 227
Studdert-Kennedy 266, 296, 300
Stunpfel 149, 169
Suomi 46f, 60, 69
surface 234
surface level 241
surface representation 231, 235
Svenkerud 29, 36
Sweetser 248, 262
Swets 79, 93
Swinney 20, 40, 85, 96f, 182, 188,
    208, 210, 249, 262, 277, 283,
    286, 298, 300
syllable 4, 6f, 9, 13ff, 24ff, 44ff,
    53, 55ff, 62, 79, 149, 281
syntactic analysis
    183f, 213, 229f, 277, 279
syntactic processes
    183, 276f, 279, 281, 283f, 287

Tabor 224, 228
Tabossi 20, 40, 72, 85, 87, 97f,
    182, 199, 210f
Taft 54, 69, 105, 108ff, 116, 118, 123,
    131f, 157, 174, 220, 226
Tanenhaus 51, 69, 72f, 85, 97f, 177,
    181, 185, 188f, 193, 195, 204ff,
    210f, 215, 219f, 224, 227f

Taraban 189, 211, 264, 297
Tees 28, 40
temporal information 234
Terken 52, 70
text comprehension 253
text representation 237, 262
Tharp 110, 130
thematic fit 220
thematic grid 188
thematic roles 188, 195
thematic structure 243f
Thompson 245, 259
Thornton 118, 127
Till 181, 211
Titone 22, 34
Trabasso 234, 246, 250, 258, 262
Treisman 161, 174
Trueswell 177, 185, 188f, 193,
    195f, 210f, 215, 219f, 228
Tsang 54, 70
Tulving 144, 165, 169, 173, 276,
    294f, 300
Tyler 21, 40, 49, 70, 72ff, 81ff, 9f1,
    94f, 98, 120f, 127, 130, 132, 186,
    206, 211, 263f, 282, 292, 296

Unkefer 53, 65
Urbach 220, 225

Vakoch 53, 67
van Bergem 50, 67
van den Broek 234, 246, 248, 262
van der Lugt 55, 68
van Dijk 231ff, 245, 253f, 262
van Donselaar 14, 40f, 46, 50,
    61, 64f, 70
van Grunsven 277, 295
van Halen 22, 37
van Hell 145, 165
van Heuven 44, 58f, 66f
van Leyden 58, 67
van Ooijen 16, 28, 34, 40
van Petten 76, 87, 94, 98f, 182,
    282, 300
van Santen 50, 69
van Zon 44, 70
Varner 198, 205

Viera 146, 153, 168
Vignolo 266, 290
von Cramon 280, 289, 299
von Eckart 172
von Stockert 277, 301
Vonk 229, 234, 240f, 244, 246,
    249, 252, 257, 260, 262
Vos 199
Vosse 222, 228
Vroomen 25, 40, 44, 46, 70

Waksler 120, 127, 130
Walley 80, 99
Walling 148, 172
Wallis 109, 113, 129
Walsh Dickey 55, 70
Waltz 185, 196, 211
Wang 78, 91
Warren 5, 7, 37, 49, 70, 77, 84,
    99, 136f, 148, 157, 174
Warrington
    141, 155, 170, 174, 269, 270,
    273, 295, 300f
Waters 76, 97
Watkins 147, 174
Webster 53, 63
Weidmann 175
Weldon 144f, 147f, 172f, 175
Wells 148, 175
Welsch 234, 259
Welsh 7ff, 37, 74, 79, 81, 95
Werker 28, 40
Wernicke aphasia 82
Wernicke area 267, 271
Wernicke patients 266, 268, 272f, 278

Wessels 21, 29, 35, 36, 40, 83f, 98
West 84, 97, 181, 210, 212
Wheeldon 7, 37
Wheeler 179, 212
Whitehouse 272, 301
Wightman 43, 70
Wilkes-Gibbs 149, 170
Williams 28, 36, 46, 65, 181, 212
Wippich 145, 166, 175
Wise 267f, 274f, 292, 294, 299, 301
Wood 282, 296
working memory 189, 197, 215f, 222,
    254, 285f
Wulfeck 198, 201
Wurm 53, 67

Yoneyama 45, 55, 68
Young 137, 139, 141, 150f, 160,
    165, 265, 292

Zardon 85, 87, 98, 182, 210
Zatorre 266ff, 301
Zhou 18, 40
Zimmer 133f, 137, 139, 145, 149,
    152ff, 156, 159ff, 166, 175
Zimny 234, 259
Zohar 48, 67
Zurif 272, 277f, 290f, 300f
Zwaan 234, 262
Zwitserlood 14f, 20ff, 37, 40, 46, 70f,
    73, 83, 86ff, 99, 106, 113,
    120f, 128, 131f, 280

Printing: Mercedesdruck, Berlin
Binding: Buchbinderei Lüderitz & Bauer, Berlin